FUTURE PEOPLE

Future People

A Moderate Consequentialist Account of our Obligations to Future Generations

TIM MULGAN

CLARENDON PRESS · OXFORD

OXFORD

UNIVERSITY PRESS

Great Clarendon Street, Oxford OX2 6DP

Oxford University Press is a department of the University of Oxford.
It furthers the University's objective of excellence in research, scholarship,
and education by publishing worldwide in

Oxford New York

Auckland Cape Town Dar es Salaam Hong Kong Karachi
Kuala Lumpur Madrid Melbourne Mexico City Nairobi
New Delhi Shanghai Taipei Toronto

With offices in

Argentina Austria Brazil Chile Czech Republic France Greece
Guatemala Hungary Italy Japan Poland Portugal Singapore
South Korea Switzerland Thailand Turkey Ukraine Vietnam

Oxford is a registered trade mark of Oxford University Press
in the UK and in certain other countries

Published in the United States
by Oxford University Press Inc., New York

First published 2006

British Library Cataloguing in Publication Data

Data available

Library of Congress Cataloging in Publication Data

Mulgan, Tim.
Future people : a moderate consequentialist account of our obligations to
future generations / Tim Mulgan.
p. cm.
Includes bibliographical references (p.   ) and index.
1. Duty. 2. Consequentialism (Ethics) I. Title.
BJ1451.M78 2006   171'.5—dc22   2005023340

Typeset by Newgen Imaging Systems (P) Ltd., Chennai, India
Printed in Great Britain
on acid-free paper by
Biddles Ltd., King's Lynn, Norfolk

ISBN 0–19–928220–X   978–0–19–928220–3

1 3 5 7 9 10 8 6 4 2

For Janet

Contents

Acknowledgements

I began serious work on this project while visiting the Social and Political Theory programme at the Australian National University in 2001. I am very grateful to the programme for providing such a stimulating working environment. I am also grateful to the University of Auckland for generous financial support during the completion of this book, in the form of an Early Career Research Excellence Award.

Many conversations over the years have improved this book. While I cannot hope to remember them all, I particularly wish to thank Elizabeth Ashford, John Broome, Tim Chappell, Roger Crisp, James Griffin, Robert Goodin, Brad Hooker, Rahul Kumar, Gerry Mackie, Janet McLean, Andrew Moore, Derek Parfit, Philip Pettit, Thomas Pogge, and Peter Vallentyne.

For detailed comments on previous drafts, I am especially grateful to Brad Hooker, Andrew Moore, Derek Parfit, and several anonymous readers. For turning my disk into a book, I am grateful for the editorial assistance of Rebecca Bryant, Rupert Cousens, Peter Momtchiloff, and Veronica Ions.

Several sections of this book draw on material presented in *The Demands of Consequentialism* (OUP Oxford 2001). In addition, Chapter 3 draws on other material I have previously published elsewhere. I am grateful to Oxford University Press, Calgary University Press, and Kluwer Publishers for permission to reproduce material from the following articles: 'The Reverse Repugnant Conclusion' (2002) 14 Utilitas, 360–4; 'Critical Notice of Jeff McMahan, *The Ethics of Killing*' (2004) 34 Canadian Journal of Philosophy, 443–60; and 'Two Parfit Puzzles', in J. Ryberg and R. Tannsjo (eds), *The Repugnant Conclusion: Essays on Population Ethics* (Kluwer Academic Publishers Dordrecht 2004), 23–45.

I am also grateful to Andrew Moore for permission to draw on our jointly authored unpublished manuscript 'Growing Up in the Original Position'.

1

Introduction

Unless something goes drastically wrong in the next few centuries, most of those who will ever live are yet to be born. Our actions have little impact on those who are dead, considerable impact on those currently alive, and potentially enormous impact on those who will live in the future. Perhaps the most significant impact is that our decisions affect who those future people will be, and even if there will be any future people at all. If we measure the moral significance of an action by the number of people it affects and the impact is has on them, then our obligations to future generations deserve to be the central topic of moral philosophy. Potential environmental crises give a new urgency to this discussion, as we now have some inkling of the magnitude of our impact on future generations.

Despite its obvious importance, intergenerational ethics has not loomed large in traditional moral philosophy. Only in the last few decades have philosophers really begun to grapple with the complexities involved. Much of the discussion has been highly technical, focusing on logical puzzles regarding the value of existence, and the possibility of comparing the lives of different possible individuals, or the value of different possible futures for humanity. But underlying these abstruse technicalities are some of the deepest moral questions. What makes life worth living? What do we owe to our descendants? How do we balance their needs against our own?

This book is not a comprehensive treatment of the philosophy of our obligations to future generations. Moral philosophy is an essentially comparative exercise. No theory is perfect, so our principal reason for adopting a theory is that it does a better job than its rivals. A full treatment would thus include a detailed evaluation of the leading alternatives. This would be too large a task for a single book. Accordingly, I focus on developing my account, and defending it against direct objections. While the first two chapters sketch some of the difficulties facing competing accounts, I do not pretend to offer any sustained critique of those alternatives. My aim is modest. I claim that a particular kind of moderate Consequentialism does a surprisingly good job of making sense of an independently plausible picture of the moral terrain in this area. I do not claim to show that it is the only theory that does so, nor that the underlying picture is the only possible one. As this area of morality is still at the exploratory stage, such self-contained projects are a necessary preliminary task.

The book is limited in another way, as it focuses primarily on rules governing individual morality. The accompanying theories of value and justice are merely sketched. Once again, this is partly for reasons of space. However, there are also more principled reasons. The construction of an adequate Consequentialist theory of the morality of individual reproduction requires a value theory with certain general features. These general requirements rule out some popular accounts of value, but leave many questions undecided. While a complete Consequentialist theory would have to answer these further questions, we can leave them to one side for our present purposes. (My own attempt at a full theory of value is presented in 'Valuing the Future'.) At the other end, I argue that any Consequentialist theory of justice must be built on our theory of individual morality. While we can draw some general lessons about justice from that account of individual morality, many of the details of the former depend on empirical factors not strictly relevant to the evaluation of the latter. Such details can also be put to one side for the moment.

1.1. Two Kinds of Intuition

One primary purpose of a moral theory is to unify and makes sense of our considered moral judgements or intuitions. Such intuitions fall into two general categories. A *decisive* intuition represents a judgement any acceptable moral theory must accommodate. Most thought experiments are designed to generate decisive intuitions. The usual aim is to construct a story where the recommendations of a particular theory conflict with a decisive intuition. Once we accept that the intuition is decisive, we must abandon the theory.

If we all always agreed in our considered moral judgements, then all our intuitions would be decisive. However, such agreement is not to be found. Sometimes intuitions are used, not to refute theories, but to *distinguish* them. This role of intuitions is particularly useful in teaching moral philosophy, especially as students are often more divided in their intuitive reactions than professional philosophers. For instance, many philosophers treat Nozick's experience machine as a decisive blow against hedonism.[1] My second-year undergraduate classes consistently divide in half over this thought experiment. At least half the class hold that a passive life in the

---

[1] Nozick, *Anarchy, State, and Utopia*, 42–5.

experience machine would be just as valuable as a real life filled with struggle and achievement. Unsurprisingly, this group does not make it through the rigours of graduate school, and thus their view is under-represented in professional philosophy.

There is no definite line between decisive and distinguishing intuitions. No intuition is uncontroversially decisive, if only because there is always a niche in the philosophical marketplace for the first person who rejects it. Partisans of particular moral theories often present an intuition as decisive, when their opponents would see it as distinctive of that particular theory.

In this book I present a theory designed to make sense of a set of intuitions concerning the comparative value of possible futures and our obligations to future generations. Some of these intuitions I take to be decisive: any acceptable theory must accommodate them. I believe, however, that there are very few decisive intuitions in this complex and underexplored moral terrain. I certainly do not claim that my account is the only one capable of accommodating these decisive intuitions. However, my theory also accommodates a number of secondary intuitions. My claim is that this total set of intuitions represents a reasonable and coherent picture of morality, and that the theory I construct around them is the best way to make sense of that picture. This is enough to render the theory worthy of further exploration.

Much contemporary debate over our obligations to future generations centres on stark choices or comparisons, where we are told that a given theory offers one verdict, and that 'our moral intuitions' deliver the opposite. Both claims should always be treated with suspicion. We must ask whether the theory really does yield that particular conclusion. We must also look behind our intuitive reactions or judgements, to see what implicit theoretical or practical assumptions they presuppose. Intuitions are often as theory-laden as our moral theories themselves. We must always be wary of deploying our intuitions too far from home. In particular, I argue that many of our strongest intuitions relate, not to the values of outcomes, but to the rightness or wrongness of actions. The solution to common puzzles in value theory may lie in a new theory of right action.

On the other hand, we cannot develop our theory of right action in isolation. Both our theory of value and our theory of right action must respond to morally significant features of human well-being, especially human agency. Consequentialists often treat well-being as a 'black box'. Our theory of value aggregates 'whatever makes life worth living', and then our theory of right action responds to 'whatever makes outcomes valuable'. If this were a feasible strategy, then much of the present book would be redundant. Unfortunately, this eudaimonic agnosticism is untenable. Any given moral intuition reflects a total picture of morality, with implicit accounts of individual well-being, of the aggregation of well-being, and of right action. In particular, I shall argue that the intuitions behind the Demandingness Objection, along with some compelling intuitions presented in this chapter, show that our moral theory must reflect two key features of human beings: our physiological needs and our rational agency. We shall see these two features play many roles throughout this book.

I am aware that the use of intuitions and examples in ethics is not uncontroversial. We need to be wary of placing too much weight on intuitions, especially those relating to fantastical examples. However, it is hard to see how ethics could be pursued at all without some reference to intuitions or examples. It is also worth noting that most of the examples discussed in this book are not too fantastical, at least not by the standards of contemporary analytic philosophy.

Two topics dominate the literature on future generations. Consequentialists study an array of puzzles in value theory. They seek Parfit's Theory X: a complete, consistent, intuitively plausible account of the comparative values of different possible histories of the world.[2] For non-Consequentialists, debate focuses on the Non-Identity Problem presented in Section 1.3, and on related problems in political philosophy.

My approach is different. I argue that the real difficulty for the Consequentialist approach lies not in value theory, but in its account of rightness—the bridge from value to action. I begin with three basic intuitions that any adequate account of our obligations to future generations should accommodate. I then show that non-Consequentialist moral theories struggle with the first two intuitions (I extend this to cover non-Consequentialist political theories in Chapter 2), while extant Consequentialist theories struggle with the last. This is why a Consequentialist theory that accommodates all three intuitions is worth seeking.

1.2. Three Basic Intuitions

Consider the following tale.

The Selfish Parents. Jane and Jim are a new age couple, keen to explore their own capacity for self-awareness and compassion. Although they could conceive a perfectly healthy child, they choose to have a child with a very severe disability, as this will provide them with a range of new emotional

---

[2] Parfit, *Reasons and Persons*, 378.

experiences. Suppose their child will suffer from Tay-Sachs disease, whose usual course is as follows.[3]

The child appears well at birth and develops normally for six to eight months when progressive psychomotor degeneration slowly begins. By eighteen months the child is likely to be paralysed and blind, unable to take food by mouth, suffering from constipation and decubitus ulcers. There are increasingly frequent convulsions which cannot be controlled by medication. The last few years of the child's life are usually spent in a vegetative state.

If we find Jane and Jim's behaviour morally unacceptable, then we endorse the following decisive intuition.

The Basic Wrongness Intuition. It is wrong gratuitously to create a child whose life contains nothing but suffering.

This is a minimal intuition.[4] Commonsense morality places more stringent constraints on parents. If you opt to have children, then there are many things you are obliged to do for them. For instance, it is wrong to reproduce if one cannot ensure that one's child's basic needs will be provided for, or to create a child merely in order to sell her into slavery or keep her in a cage.[5]

Many people also believe it is wrong gratuitously to create a child with (even mild) disabilities, when one could have just as easily (i.e. at no greater cost to oneself) created a perfectly healthy child. This intuition is not universal, but it represents a distinctive commitment of any broadly Consequentialist approach to our obligations to future generations, as we shall see.

The Basic Wrongness Intuition also has a collective analogue. Consider the following tale.

The Selfish Policy. The present generation in a particular community frivolously adopt a leisure activity that releases radiation that will cause great suffering to those alive in three centuries' time.

---

[3] This description is from Steinbock, 'Wrongful Life', 17; quoted in Feinberg, 'Wrongful Life and the Counterfactual Element in Harming', 156.

[4] I am not aware of any serious attempt to deny the Basic Wrongness Intuition. Susan Moller Okin argues that Robert Nozick's libertarianism entails the conclusion that mothers own their children, in the strong libertarian sense that mothers can do *anything* they like to their children. (Okin, *Justice, Gender and the Family*, 74–88.) However, (1) even Okin's argument establishes only a political right of non-interference, not a moral right; and (2) no defender of libertarianism has embraced Okin's conclusion. (For discussion of libertarian replies to Okin's argument, see Cohen, 'Okin on Justice, Gender, and Family'; and Perrett, 'Libertarianism, Feminism, and Relative Identity'.) Similarly, while David Heyd's Generocentrism implies that we owe nothing directly to those we create, Heyd does not deny that the selfish parents do wrong (Heyd, *Genethics*, 106–11).

[5] The last two examples are taken from Kavka, 'The Paradox of Future Individuals', and Okin, *Justice, Gender and the Family*, 74–88 respectively.

If we find this behaviour morally unacceptable, then we endorse the following decisive intuition.

The Basic Collective Intuition. The present generation cannot gratuitously cause great suffering to future generations.

A striking feature of commonsense moral thought is a widespread commitment to reproductive freedom. People should be able to decide for themselves whether or not, and in what way, to reproduce. This is partly a belief that no outside agency, especially the state, should interfere with such choices. Yet we also believe that reproductive choice is morally open. There is no obligation to have children, nor an obligation not to. This commitment to reproductive autonomy is a basic value in modern liberal societies.[6] (Call this the *Basic Liberty Intuition*.)

To illustrate this third basic intuition, we focus on a simple case. Suppose an affluent person in the developed world (call her 'Affluent') must choose between the following three projects.

The Reproduction Project. Affluent has a child of her own, and then allocates a substantial amount of her income to the project of raising that child.

The Adoption Project. Affluent adopts an already existing child, and then allocates a substantial amount of her income to the project of raising that child.

The Oxfam Project. Affluent has no children, and donates a substantial amount of her income to charity.

Other things equal, most people believe that Affluent is morally permitted to pursue any of the three projects.

Of course, almost no one would think that our obligations and permissions regarding future generations were exhausted by these three intuitions. We all think parents have many more obligations to their children, and that the obligation to ensure that children's lives are worth living is not limited to their parents. And almost everyone agrees that we have much stronger obligations to future people in general. We ought not to harm them, unnecessarily deplete resources they might need, etc. Perhaps we also have obligations to benefit them, or at least to pass on the cultural wealth bequeathed us by previous generations. And, while we may not agree on the precise scope of reproductive freedom, we all agree that there is more to it than the basic liberty intuition suggests.

---

[6] As we shall see in Section 6.6, there is strong evidence that the basic liberty intuition is also widely shared outside Western liberal democracies.

Much of this book is taken up with the exploration of more specific obligations and permissions. The significance of the basic intuitions is that many contemporary moral and political theories have surprising difficulty accommodating them. Simple Consequentialism cannot accommodate reproductive freedom, while prominent non-Consequentialist views have trouble generating any obligations to future people.

1.3. The Non-Identity Problem

The problems facing non-Consequentialists owe their prominence to the work of Derek Parfit.[7] Parfit distinguishes two kinds of moral choice: Same People Choices and Different People Choices.[8] A *Same People Choice* occurs whenever our actions affect what will happen to people in the future, but not which people will come to exist. If our actions do affect who will get to exist in the future, then we are making a *Different People Choice*. (Parfit also further distinguishes two kinds of Different People Choices: Same Number—where our choice affects who exists, but not how many people exist—and Different Number—where we decide how many people ever exist.)

Parfit makes three central claims.

1. Different People Choices occur very frequently, and in situations where we might not expect them.
2. It is often difficult to tell, in practice, whether we are dealing with a Same People Choice or a Different People Choice.
3. Many traditional moral theories cope much better with Same People Choices than with Different People Choices.

These three claims constitute the *Non-Identity Problem*, so called because, in a Different People Choice, those who will exist in one possible outcome are not (numerically) identical to those who will exist in an alternative possible outcome. Parfit's third claim is well illustrated by the following tale.[9]

The Summer or Winter Child.   Mary is deciding when to have a child. She could have one in summer or in winter. Mary suffers from a rare condition which means that, if she has her child in winter, it will suffer serious ailments which will reduce the quality of its life. However, a child born in winter would still have a life worth living, and, if Mary decides to have a child in summer, then an altogether different child will be born. It is mildly

---

[7] Parfit, *Reasons and Persons*, 351–79.   [8] Ibid. 355–6.
[9] This tale is adapted from one given by Parfit, ibid. 358.

inconvenient for Mary to have a child in summer. (Perhaps she doesn't fancy being heavily pregnant during hot weather.) Therefore, she opts for a winter birth.

Mary's behaviour seems morally wrong. However, several common moral principles imply that she does nothing wrong. Suppose we think that an act is wrong only if it wrongs some particular person, that people are wronged only if they are harmed, and that x is harmed if and only if x is left worse off than x would otherwise have been. We now apply these principles to Mary's case. The Winter Child has a life worth living, and would not have existed at all if Mary had acted otherwise.[10] It would thus be odd to say that this child has been harmed. It would be even odder to argue that Mary harms the Summer Child. How can someone who never exists be harmed?

To illustrate Parfit's first claim, that Different People Choices are more common than we ordinarily think, consider the following tale, also due to Parfit.[11]

The Risky Policy. As a community, we must choose between two energy policies. Both would be completely safe for at least three centuries, but one would have certain risks in the further future. This policy involves the burial of nuclear waste in areas where, in the next few centuries, there is no risk of an earthquake. But since this waste will remain radioactive for thousands of years, there will be risks in the distant future. If we choose this Risky Policy, the standard of living will be somewhat higher over the next century. We do choose this policy. As a result, there is a catastrophe many centuries later. An earthquake releases radiation, which kills thousands of people. Though they are killed by this catastrophe, these people will have had lives that are worth living. (The radiation gives people an incurable disease that will kill them at about the age of 40, but has no effects before it kills.)

Knowing the effects of the different policies, it seems clearly wrong to choose the Risky Policy. Yet, if we do so, we cannot be said to have harmed the people who will be killed by the catastrophe, as they would not otherwise have existed at all. If we had embarked on the alternative policy, patterns of migration would have been very different in the intervening

---

[10] The claim that the Winter Child would not have existed at all if Mary had chosen to have a child in summer is based on Parfit's 'Time-Dependence Claim': If any particular person had not been conceived within a month of the time when he [or she] was in fact conceived, he [or she] would in fact never have existed. (Parfit, *Reasons and Persons*, 352.) This in turn is based on a more general claim that, if any particular person had not been created from (at least some of) the particular genetic material from which he or she was in fact created, he or she would in fact never have existed. Parfit argues that these claims come out true under all philosophically respectable accounts of the nature of personal identity (ibid. 351–5).   [11] Ibid. 371–2.

years. For any particular individual killed by the catastrophe, it is almost certain that her parents would never even have met if we hadn't embarked on the Risky Policy. So she herself would never have existed.

This example thus brings out the ubiquity of Different People Choices, as those who adopt the Risky Policy are not making a directly reproductive choice. It also illustrates Parfit's second claim. In early generations, it will be very hard to determine, for any particular individual, whether she would have existed at all if we'd chosen the alternative policy. It is thus hard to tell whether we face a Same People Choice or a Different People Choice.

1.4. Person-Affecting Principles

The Non-Identity Problem is a significant threat to non-Consequentialist accounts of our obligations to future generations. This is because they tend to be 'person-affecting'—endorsing something like the following principle.[12]

The Person-Affecting Principle. An action can be wrong only if there exists some particular person who is worse off after that action than they would have been if some other action had been performed instead.

The Person-Affecting Principle presents only a necessary condition for an action to be wrong, not a sufficient condition. In some cases, for every option, there is someone who will be worse off than they would otherwise have been if that option is taken. The Person-Affecting Principle does not imply that all such options are wrong. A full moral theory thus needs to supplement this principle with other moral principles to adjudicate such cases. We will focus on the key claim that a person-affecting element is necessary for wrongful action.

Person-affecting views are common outside philosophy. For instance, much economic analysis is built on the paretian family of concepts. One outcome is pareto superior to another if at least one person is better off in the former than in the latter, and no one is worse off. An outcome is pareto optimal if no alternative is pareto superior. These are explicitly person-affecting notions. Pareto concepts are often used in moral philosophy. For instance, it is often thought that an action cannot be wrong if it is pareto superior to all available alternatives. (Perhaps because every pareto optimal

---

[12] For discussions of this, and related principles, see esp. Feinberg, 'Wrongful Life and the Counterfactual Element in Harming'; Heyd, *Genethics*; Kumar, 'Who can be Wronged?'; Roberts, *Child versus Childmaker*; Roberts, 'A New Way of Doing the Best we Can'; Roberts, 'Is the Person-Affecting Intuition Paradoxical?'; Roberts, 'Present Duties and Future Persons: When Are Existence-Inducing Acts Wrong?'; Robertson, 'Liberty, Identity, and Human Cloning'; Temkin, *Inequality*, ch. 9; Woodward, ' The Non-Identity Problem'.

principle will pass the Categorical Imperative test, or some other test of universalizability.) Yet this is merely a restatement of the Person-Affecting Principle.

Even in Same People Choices, pareto notions are often criticized for their limited applicability. In a Different People Choice, these notions may be even less useful. In particular, a rule instructing me to bring about only pareto-optimal outcomes will hardly restrict me at all in Different People Choices. (Section 1.5.)[13]

Another common source of person-affecting principles is the law of torts, which deals with civil wrongs arising when one person harms another. Legal notions of harm are often explicitly person-affecting, as harm is usually defined in terms of a worsening of the victim's condition. If Mary's choice does not leave anyone worse off than they would otherwise have been, then she has committed no wrong. Judges faced with 'wrongful life suits' struggle to apply this familiar reasoning in Different People Choices.[14]

In all these cases, the relevant comparison is between how someone fares in the actual situation and how they *would have* fared under some alternative, not between their situation before and after a particular action or decision. If a patient's condition is deteriorating, then surgery may leave her worse off than she was initially, even though every alternative would have left her even worse off. This does not violate the person-affecting principle. Alternatively, someone may be better off after a particular action, but only because their condition was improving anyway. If their improvement would have been greater without the intervention, then they have been harmed for the purposes of the Person-Affecting Principle.

Some opponents of the Person-Affecting Principle argue that it cannot even endorse the Basic Wrongness Intuition. If our selfish parents had acted differently, then their particular child would never have existed. We can make no sense of the claim that x is worse off than x would have been if x had never existed, as we cannot compare existence with non-existence. No person-affecting theory can ever condemn any creation choice, however horrific the resulting life.[15]

This argument is too swift. For instance, we could (at least in principle) compile a list of positive features which make a life better and a list of negative features which make a life worse. Our own lives contain a mix of

---

[13] In addition, I argue elsewhere that pareto optimality must be rejected altogether in some possible cases concerning infinite utilities, as it conflicts with universalizability (Mulgan, 'Valuing the Future').

[14] For extended discussion, see Feinberg, 'Wrongful Life and the Counterfactual Element in Harming', and Roberts, *Child versus Childmaker*.

[15] For discussion of the arguments for and against this claim, see McMahan, 'Wrongful Life: Paradoxes in the Morality of Causing People to Exist'. (See also Section 1.5.)

features from both lists. We could then imagine possible lives which contain only features from the negative list. Such a life would be worse than a life which contained no features from either list. It seems perfectly natural to conclude that a Tay-Sachs child has such a life. It is then plausible to say that she is worse off than she would have been if she had never existed.

In practice, it makes little difference whether or not we say that such lives are literally worse than non-existence. Instead, we might speak of a life being 'non-comparatively bad' or 'worth not living'.[16] We can then say that it is wrong to create such a life, not because it is worse than no life at all, but because it is a bad life.[17]

These non-comparative idioms are inconsistent with our original comparative formulation of the Person-Affecting Principle. However, we could adopt the following non-comparative formulation.

The Revised Person-Affecting Principle.   An action can only be wrong if there exists some particular person for whom it is either (*a*) worse than some relevant alternative (if the alternative is a situation where that agent exists); or (*b*) non-comparatively bad (if the alternative is a situation where that agent does not exist).

It is obviously very difficult to specify the precise point below which lives are no longer worth living. However, any form of Consequentialism also faces such problems. They thus constitute no particular objection to the Person-Affecting Principle, and will return to preoccupy us at some length in later chapters.

A person-affecting approach can consistently accommodate the basic wrongness intuition. Unfortunately, the non-identity problem generates a whole spectrum of problematic cases. At the opposite end of that spectrum we find the following tale.

The Gratuitously Satisficing Mother.   Betty has decided to have a child. She could have one in summer (Sonny) or in winter (Winnie). Winnie will not suffer any serious ailments or disabilities. However, if Betty opts to have a child in winter, this will force her to forgo a job offer. Betty herself is completely indifferent between taking the job and not taking it, but it is located in a city where her child would enjoy a better quality of life. Winnie will thus have a lower quality of life than Sonny. On a whim, Betty decides to have her child in winter.

---

[16] These alternative turns of phrase are borrowed from McMahan, 'Wrongful Life'.

[17] We could also utilize the notion of the 'zero level', a crucial feature of many Utilitarian theories (Section 3.3). A good life is one whose value is above zero, while a bad life falls below the zero level. A life exactly equal to zero is no more or less valuable than no life at all.

As Winnie has a very worthwhile life, it is hard to imagine how any person-affecting theory could fault Betty's choice.

We are examining an instance of blatant moral satisficing, where an agent deliberately produces a sub-optimal outcome on the grounds that it is 'good enough', even though she could have produced a significantly better outcome at absolutely no cost to herself. The rationality and morality of satisficing behaviour have been much discussed. I and others have argued elsewhere that blatant satisficing is clearly unjustified in Same People Choices.[18] Why should we permit it in Different People Choices? If other things are completely equal, what possible justification is there for Betty's failure to produce a person with a better life?

This tale thus generates intuitions that a person-affecting theory will find much harder to avoid than the basic wrongness intuition. On the other hand, these new intuitions are much less forceful than the basic wrongness intuition. Proponents of the person-affecting approach may simply deny that it is wrong to opt for the less valuable life in this case. Indeed, they might conclude that the fact that it condemns this choice is yet another strike against Consequentialism.

I agree that this thought experiment generates no decisive intuitions. However, it does bring out a cluster of intuitions incompatible with the person-affecting approach. It is at least plausible to believe (a) that Betty has good reason to opt to create the more valuable life over the less valuable one, (b) that she ought to do so if other things are equal, and (c) that the source of these reasons lies in the fact that the former option leads to a more valuable outcome, even if that outcome is better for no one. Not everyone shares these intuitions. For those who do, however, they provide one motivation for exploring alternatives to the person-affecting approach.

Between these two extremes lie a broad range of non-identity intuitions. We can imagine someone creating a life almost, but not quite, worth living; a life barely worth living; or a life well worth living but marred by some serious disability. In each case, the objection to the Person-Affecting Principle consists of the two claims:

1. that such an act of creation is wrong, and
2. that the Person-Affecting Principle cannot fault it.

---

[18] Mulgan, *The Demands of Consequentialism* (2001), ch 5; Mulgan, 'Slote's Satisficing Consequentialism' (1993); and Mulgan, 'How Satisficers Get Away with Murder' (2001). The classic contemporary presentations of Satisficing Consequentialism are Slote, 'Satisficing Consequentialism'; Slote, *Commonsense Morality and Consequentialism*; and Slote, *Beyond Optimizing*. Slote himself has since abandoned Satisficing Consequentialism, in favour of a form of virtue ethics. (See esp. Slote, *From Morality to Virtue*.)

For instance, even our revised Person-Affecting Principle cannot fault Mary's choice, as her Winter Child has a life that is worth living overall. Defenders of the person-affecting approach typically deny (2) for cases near the start of the spectrum (where the new life is bad) and then switch to denying (1) before we reach the gratuitous sub-optimization end of the spectrum.

In Mary's case, defenders of the person-affecting approach might argue that Mary's action is wrong because the Winter Child has been harmed even though he is no worse off than he would have been; or because he has been wronged even though he has not been harmed (perhaps because some of his vital interests are left unmet, or some of his basic rights violated); or because Mary's obligation was to 'her child', and 'her child' is worse off than 'her child' would have been (even if the definite description picks out different individuals in the two possible outcomes); or because of some obligation owed to a third party or to society as a whole.[19] All these moves are controversial. One way to side-step such controversy is to abandon the person-affecting approach and adopt a Consequentialist perspective.

1.5. Kant and Non-Identity

In moral philosophy, the most prominent person-affecting theory is that of Immanuel Kant.[20] It is therefore worth pausing to explore five general problems for Kantian ethics flowing from the Non-Identity Problem. (As we shall see several times, these problems are not confined to Kant's original moral theory.)

Our first two problems relate to the key Kantian notion of universalizability. Under Kant's Categorical Imperative, agents are permitted to act only on universalizable maxims: those they can consistently will as universal laws for all rational beings. In other words, if I want to do something, I must first ask if I could consistently will that everyone did it.

1. Universalizability may be too lenient

On many formulations of the Universalizability Test, any rule that permits only actions that are pareto improvements can be univerzalised. (This is because many universalizability tests are explicitly person-affecting, and thus a moral rule can fail the test only if someone would be harmed by its

---

[19] For critical discussion of these (and other) defences of the person-affecting approach, see the works cited in n. 12 of this chapter.

[20] For Kant's most accessible account of moral philosophy, see his *Groundwork of the Metaphysics of Morals*. An excellent historical introduction to contemporary themes in Kantian ethics is Schneewind, 'Autonomy, Obligation, and Virtue: An Overview of Kant's Moral Philosophy'. See also Korsgaard, 'Kant', and O'Neill, 'Kantian Ethics'.

universal application.) We saw in Section 1.4 that, in many Different People Choices, almost all options are pareto optimal. Therefore, a universalizability test cannot constrain our treatment of future generations. So long as everyone we create has a life worth living, nothing we do can be wrong. (This is especially significant for Rawls and Scanlon, who both operate with explicitly person-affecting Kantian universalizability tests. Sections 2.2.3 and 11.3 respectively.)

2. Universalizability cannot critique the status quo
Kant's comments on suicide suggest that you cannot consistently will a maxim as a universal law if a world where that maxim was always followed would be a world where you do not exist. For instance, suppose you exist only because your father tricked your mother into having sex by pretending to be a millionaire. Can you consistently will, as a universal law, 'do not lie'? If not, the universalizability test cannot find fault with any type of action that was necessary for your existence. For any imaginable maxim, the prehistory of your conception may include violations of that maxim. Therefore, you may be unable to consistently will *any* maxim as a universal law. (Even if you can universalize a maxim, this will be for purely fortuitous historical reasons.) So the universalizability test becomes either completely restrictive or hopelessly arbitrary. (This is especially true if past generations are explicitly included in the scope of universalization, as they are in Rawls's recent account of intergenerational justice (see Section 2.2.3).[21]

Our next three problems relate to a second key Kantian notion: respect for persons. For Kant, being moral requires respect for personhood (or rational agency), both in oneself and in others. One general puzzle is how (if at all) an act of creation can be respectful of the person created. This general question gives rise to two further puzzles.

3. Is creation a violation of autonomy?
In many other contexts, the appropriate way to respect a person is to act in accordance with (or at least not contrary to) their wishes or intentions, and never to do anything to them without their prior consent. As the act of creation cannot either fulfil any pre-existing desire or be the object of prior consent, some philosophers argue that creation cannot be respectful of the person created, and thus that the creation of persons is always wrong.[22]

---

[21] Universalizability encounters other problems on some interpretations, especially those that rule out any reference to the agent's empirical desires, or any other empirical circumstances, in the formulation of moral rules. (See Ch. 6 n. 21 below and the accompanying text.)

[22] For related discussion, see Shiffrin, 'Wrongful Life, Procreative Responsibility, and the Significance of Harm'.

4. *Does creation treat the created person as a means?*

Kant's dictum that rational agents always be treated as ends in themselves is often used in popular discussions of the morality of reproduction. It is sometimes suggested that, if one has children as means to some end (such as economic security, social status, affection, satisfaction, achievement, etc.) then one thereby fails to show them adequate respect.[23] (A classic example in popular debate is when parents deliberately have a child to provide a suitable donor for a transfusion to an existing sibling. This type of creation is often criticized as illegitimately using the new child as a means.)

This is a misreading of Kant's principle. He explicitly says that it is perfectly acceptable to treat other people as means to one's own ends, so long as one does not treat them *merely* as a means, 'but also at the same time as an end'.[24] The classic example is my dealings with a shopkeeper. My motivation for entering this particular shop probably has nothing to do with respect. I am simply pursuing my own interests. If I could gain the same goods at the same price by putting money into a vending machine, then that would serve me just as well. However, having chosen to use shopkeepers rather than vending machines as the means to my own ends, I must interact with them in a way that recognizes that they, unlike the machine, are rational agent's valuable in themselves. I should thus bargain honestly and courteously, rather than seeking to steal, threaten, or cheat to acquire the goods. If I cannot use shopkeepers as means without violating respect, then I should not use them at all.

Analogously, Kant would not object to the creation of children as a means. The crucial question is whether, in using my child as a means to my own ends, I *also* treat her as an end in herself. In this particular case, this would seem to require my assisting her in the development of her rational agency, and then respecting her autonomy just as I would respect the autonomy of any other adult. The search for a pure Kantian motivation for having children is thus misplaced. This is just as well, as it is not clear that it would be possible to create someone solely in order to respect them as an end. Even if one's end is to create a new rational agent, it still seems natural to say that one is using the child herself as a means to this end. It is not possible to treat someone solely as an end before they even exist.

5. *Human beings who are not (yet) persons*

If respect is owed only to (adult) rational agents, then human babies who never develop the capacity for rational agency need never be treated as ends-in-themselves. There would thus be nothing wrong with creating a

---

[23] For a critique of this line of argument, see Moore and Mulgan, 'Open Letter: The Ethics of Non-Commercial IVF Surrogacy'.   [24] Kant, *Groundwork of the Metaphysics of Morals*, 79.

child and deliberately preventing her from becoming a rational agent. If the child never becomes a person, then nothing her creator does to her can count as wrong. That creator would be morally free to sell such a child as a slave, keep her in a cage, or eat her.[25]

Many other person-affecting views are subject to a related objection. If an act is wrong only if it harms a *person*, then a human child who never becomes a person cannot be wronged.[26] One advantage of the Consequentialist account defended in this book is that it provides a clear account of why such behaviour would be wrong.

1.6. The Compulsory Reproduction Objection

Despite all these problems, the person-affecting approach has many strengths. It easily accommodates the basic liberty intuition. If a couple opt not to have another child, then this decision cannot be wrong, as there exists no one who is worse off than they would otherwise have been. Furthermore, commonsense morality contains a host of obligations to particular others that are most naturally construed as person-affecting. The obligations of parents to their own children are a paradigm example. Much of the most interesting contemporary work in this area comes from non-Consequentialists who seek to dissolve the Non-Identity Problem, explain the moral significance and limits of reproductive freedom, and accommodate a wide range of intuitively compelling special obligations to children and general obligations to future people.

These developments challenge Consequentialists to provide a Consequentialist underpinning for the three basic intuitions, as well as all the other freedoms and obligations of commonsense morality. This book is a response to this challenge. Along the way, we will borrow many elements from various person-affecting theories, but our foundation remains Consequentialist.

[25] These examples are from Susan Okin, who uses this feature of the Kantian notion of personhood as the basis for her attack on Robert Nozick's libertarianism. (Okin, *Justice, Gender and the Family*, 74–88.)

[26] For a general account of the difficulties facing Kantian theories in this area, see McMahan, *The Ethics of Killing*, 203–32; 464–93. For attempts to defend one particular Kantian theory, see Scanlon, *What We Owe to Each Other*, 177–87; and Kumar, 'Who can be Wronged?' We return to Scanlon in Section 11.3. There is a connection here with the inability of Kantian theories to account for direct obligations regarding the welfare of animals. (For the case against Kantian theories, see Hooker, *Ideal Code, Real World* (2000), 66–70; and Hooker, 'Rule-Consequentialism, Incoherence, Fairness' (1994), 23. For defences of one particular Kant-inspired theory, see Singer, 'An Extension of Rawls's Theory of Justice to Environmental Ethics'; Elliot, 'Rawlsian Justice and Non-human Animals'; and VanDeveer, 'Of Beasts, Persons and the Original Position'.)

I begin with a theory I call Simple Consequentialism, also known as direct maximizing individual act Consequentialism. (Or simply as 'Act Consequentialism', or 'Direct Consequentialism'.) Simple Consequentialism says that the right action in any situation is the one that, of all the actions available to that agent at that time, produces the best possible outcome. The addition of a life containing nothing but excruciating suffering make things worse overall. By creating such a child we make the world a worse place then it would have been had we created no one. Similarly, Betty's decision is wrong, as the world is a worse place than it would have been if she had chosen otherwise.

Simple Consequentialism is thus largely untroubled by the Non-Identity Problem: it accommodates the basic intuition about wrongness, forbids gratuitous sub-maximization, and easily generates obligations to future generations with whom we cannot interact. This is a major plus.

Unfortunately, Consequentialism faces problems of its own. Consider two conscientious parents who strongly do not want another child, yet know that any new child would have a life worth living. Suppose the value of the extra child's life would exceed the combined loss of welfare suffered by those parents and their existing children. Simple Consequentialism requires them to have another child. It thus violates the Basic Liberty Intuition. (Call this the *Compulsory Reproduction Objection*.[27])

I agree that people are not generally obliged to have children, and that any theory generating such an obligation is unacceptable. However, I believe that sophisticated Consequentialists can avoid this result, and accommodate the basic liberty intuition. The first step is to notice that this objection has nothing to do with future generations or reproduction—it is merely an instance of a much broader problem.

There are very many very needy people in the world.[28] A variety of charitable agencies can alleviate these needs. No doubt governments,

---

[27] Analogous objections are raised by David Heyd, Partha Dasgupta, and Melinda Roberts, among others. (See Heyd, *Genethics*; Dasgupta, 'Savings and Fertility'; and Roberts, 'A New Way of Doing the Best we Can'.)

[28] An estimated 1.2 billion people live below the World Bank's minimum international poverty line. On average, these people have an annual purchasing power equivalent to what US$326 would buy in the developed world. 2.8 billion people live below the World Bank's slightly more generous poverty line. On average, these people have an annual purchasing power equivalent to what US$522 would buy in the developed world (World Bank, *World Development Report 2000/2001*, 17, 23); 790 million people lack adequate nutrition, 1 billion lack access to safe drinking water, 2.4 billion lack basic sanitation, 880 million have no access to basic medical care, 1 billion have no adequate shelter, 2 billion have no electricicty. (For the first three figures, see United Nations Development Programme, *Human Development Report 2000*, 30. The figure on basic medical care comes from United Nations Development Programme, *Human Development Report 1999*, 22. The last two figures are from United Nations Development Programme, *Human Development Report 1998*, 49.) About 20 million people a year starve to death. (This figure is drawn from *The Economist Pocket World in Figures*, 86–7; quoted in Hooker, *Ideal Code, Real World*, 147.)

multinationals, and others could do far more than they do. But the question still remains: faced with such urgent needs, at least some of which I could meet at comparatively little cost to myself, how should I as an individual act?

Simple Consequentialism tells me to put my next dollar wherever it will do the most good. In the hands of a reputable aid agency, my dollar could save a child from a crippling illness. A few more dollars might make a substantial contribution towards a clean water supply for an entire village. Could I do anything nearly as valuable with my dollar if I kept it for myself? It is highly unlikely. Dollars don't go very far in the developed West any more.

So I should give my next dollar to charity. How should I then spend my next remaining dollar? Well, in the hands of a reputable aid agency . . . It looks as if I must keep donating till I reach the point where my own basic needs, or my ability to keep earning dollars, are in jeopardy. Most of my current activities will have to go. Nor will my sacrifice be only financial. According to Simple Consequentialism, I should also spend my time where it will do most good. I should devote all my energies to charity work, as well as all my money.

Perhaps we would admire someone who behaved in this way. But is it plausible to claim that those of us who do not are guilty of wrongdoing; or that we have a moral obligation to devote all our resources to charity? Some advocates of Simple Consequentialism have even suggested that our failure to do so is morally no different from murder. (On the grounds that there is no morally significant difference between killing someone and allowing them to die when one could have saved them.[29])

Such conclusions strike many people as absurd. This leads to the common objection that Consequentialism is unreasonably demanding, as it leaves the agent too little room (time, resources, energy) for her own projects or interests. I call this the Demandingness Objection.[30] A seldom noted

---

[29] Consider Peter Singer's famous example where I pass a drowning person on my way to work (Singer, 'Famine, Affluence and Morality', 231). For critique of Singer's particular example, see Cullity, 'International Aid and the Scope of Kindness', esp. p. 5; and Mulgan, *The Demands of Consequentialism* (2001), 26–31. For discussion of a related example, see Unger, *Living High and Letting Die*, especially the elaborate tale introduced at pp. 88–90; Haslett, 'Values, Obligations, and Saving Lives'; Hooker, 'Sacrificing for the Good of Strangers—Repeatedly' (1999); and Mulgan, review of *Living High and Letting Die* (2000). The debate between Consequentialists and their opponents here turns on the existence of a general Reason to Promote the Good. For a classic presentation of the case against such a reason, see Foot, 'Utilitarianism and the Virtues', 227. See also Dancy, 'Non-Consequentialist Reasons', and Scheffler, 'Agent-Centred Restrictions, Rationality and the Virtues', 409–13.

[30] The Demandingness Objection is often linked to the 'integrity' objection, made famous by Bernard Williams (Smart and Williams, *Utilitarianism: For and Against*, 116. For an overview of the debate surrounding this objection, see Crisp, *Mill: On Utilitarianism*, 135–53.) Peter Railton expresses a similar

fact is that this objection arises most starkly in relation to reproduction.[31] Recall Affluent's choice between the three projects of reproduction, adoption, or charity.

The Oxfam project is almost certain to yield the best consequences.[32] Simple Consequentialism thus tells Affluent to donate all her money to Oxfam rather than reproducing. This result will strike many as unreasonably harsh.

Our initial objection to Simple Consequentialism was that we would all be obliged to have as many children as possible. We have just seen that, for affluent citizens of the developed world, the reverse is the case. Simple Consequentialism obliges such people not to have any children. (Our Compulsory Reproduction Objection has been replaced by a Compulsory Non-Reproduction Objection.) This radical change hardly improves the intuitive plausibility of Simple Consequentialism. However, it transforms a novel problem in intergenerational ethics into a familiar problem in contemporary Consequentialist theory. Our account of our obligations to future generations must be based on a solution to the Demandingness Objection.

Obviously, none of this helps if we cannot solve the Demandingness Objection. Following the solution presented in *The Demands of Consequentialism*, I focus on two key departures from Simple Consequentialism: Samuel Scheffler's Hybrid View (combining the impersonal perspective of Simple Consequentialism with elements derived from the agent's own personal perspective) and Rule Consequentialism (judging acts against the set of rules whose internalization by everyone would produce the best consequences).[33] (My own solution to the Demandingness Objection was a 'Combined Consequentialism' that mixes Scheffler's Hybrid View and Rule Consequentialism. In Chapter 11, I argue that such an approach also provides the best account of our obligations to future generations.)

Simple Consequentialism violates the basic liberty intuition because it cannot accommodate moral freedom at all. Agents are always required to maximize the good. Either this general feature of Consequentialism bothers us or it does not. If not, then we will reject not only the basic liberty

---

objection in terms of *alienation*, which 'can be characterised as a kind of estrangement resulting in some sort of loss' (Railton, 'Alienation, Consequentialism and Morality', 134.) For an account of the relations between these three objections, see Mulgan, *The Demands of Consequentialism* (2001), 15–16.

[31] Two recent exceptions are Young, 'Overconsumption and Procreation'; and Munthe, 'The Argument from Transfer', 26–31.   [32] See chapter endnote A, p. 22.

[33] See Scheffler, *The Rejection of Consequentialism* (1982), and Ch. 4 n. 1 below. For Rule Consequentialism, see e.g. Hooker, *Ideal Code, Real World* (2000), and the various works cited in Ch. 5 n. 1 below. Other departures from, and defences of, Simple Consequentialism are examined, and found wanting, in Mulgan, *The Demands of Consequentialism* (2001), chs. 2, 4, and 5.

intuition, but also the intuitions behind the Demandingness Objection. It will thus not surprise or bother us that Consequentialism produces highly counterintuitive results in most areas of morality. Alternatively, if the Simple Consequentialist violation of the basic liberty intuition does bother us, then we will also be worried by the Demandingness Objection.

Two things follow from this:

1. Any version of Consequentialism that cannot resolve the Demandingness Objection is of no use to us, even if it does accommodate the basic liberty intuition or other particular obligations regarding future people.
2. As the Compulsory Reproduction Objection is an instance of the Demandingness Objection, we should expect a version of Consequentialism that resolves the latter to provide the best account of our obligations to future generations.

Consequentialists face two options:

1. A hard-nosed Simple Consequentialism that embraces extreme demands across the board and thus obliterates reproductive freedom.
2. A moderate Consequentialism that avoids the Demandingness Objection and accommodates reproductive freedom together with a range of obligations to future generations in general and to specific future people in particular.

The rest of this book develops the second option.

1.7. The No Difference Intuitions

This section explores a cluster of reasonable intuitions which, I will argue, further motivate the development of moderate Consequentialism as opposed to either Simple Consequentialism or a person-affecting approach. Consider the following tale.

The Two Mothers. Debbie and Sally have each decided to have a child. Both must choose between having a child in summer or in winter, where the child born in winter will have a lower quality of life than the child born in summer. On a whim, both decide to have their children in winter. However, owing to differences in their respective fertility treatments, Debbie faces a Different People Choice while Sally is making a Same People Choice.

The literature contains two extreme responses to these cases.[34]

---

[34] Parfit, *Reasons and Persons*, 366–71, defends the No Difference View. The full person-affecting view is adopted by Heyd, *Genethics*, and is implicit in many defences of the person-affecting approach.

1. There is no difference between the two cases.
2. There is a very significant difference between the two cases: while Sally's choice may well be wrong, Debbie's cannot be.

The first response is most naturally combined with a Consequentialist theory, while the second is obviously suited to a person-affecting theory. There is something to be said for both extremes. My aim is to develop and defend a middle road: while there are good reasons for Debbie to opt for a summer birth, perhaps Sally has additional reasons.

Of course, not everyone will share these intuitions. But then, no intuition in this area is shared by everyone. By seeking to accommodate the intuitive appeal of both the No Difference View and the person-affecting approach, I am building my value theory on a foundation not everyone accepts. On the other hand, one common motivation for rejecting my preferred package of intuitions is the belief that no coherent moral theory can accommodate them. One main purpose of this book is to undermine that motivation by constructing such a theory.

1.8. Morality and Politics

An additional motivation for the Consequentialist approach comes from political philosophy. Consequentialists insist on combining moral and political philosophy: building the latter on the foundation of the former. This goes against the prevailing ethos in contemporary political philosophy, especially liberal political philosophy, where political philosophy is constructed largely in isolation from (or independently of) moral philosophy. One key plank of the Consequentialist case is the claim that, once we introduce an intergenerational dimension, such independence is impossible.

Much traditional non-Consequentialist political theory is foundationally person-affecting. In Different People Choices, it thus inherits all the problems of the person-affecting approach. In contemporary discussions of intergenerational justice, the Non-Identity Problem is reinforced by the following thesis.

The Unequal Circumstances Thesis. The quality of life of future generations depends to a very large extent on the decisions of the present generation. By contrast, our quality of life is not affected at all by their decisions. We can do a great deal to (or for) posterity but posterity cannot do anything to (or for) us. This power imbalance is often characterized in terms of the absence of Hume's 'circumstances of justice'.[35]

---

[35] The phrase is borrowed from Rawls, *A Theory of Justice* (1971), 126–30.

This thesis is significant because Western political philosophy has often treated justice as an arrangement of reciprocity for mutual advantage, either in the actual world or in some hypothetical choice situation. Combined with the Non-Identity Problem, the Unequal Circumstances Thesis demonstrates the futility of applying any such approach to justice between generations, as it is a mistake to speak of 'the people of the future' as if this phrase designated some definite group of individuals who will exist independently of our present decisions and with whom we might interact. Chapter 2 explores at length the failings of such contract-based approaches to political philosophy. The fact that it offers an alternative foundation for political philosophy is a thus a major plus for Consequentialist moral theory.

Endnote

A. This note defends the claim that the Oxfam project leads to a better outcome than either the Adoption or Reproduction projects. We begin by comparing the Adoption project to the Oxfam project. This is the easiest comparison, as it concerns a Same People Choice. (In fact, this may not be the case, as our decisions regarding famine relief almost certainly have some impact on other people's reproductive behaviour, if not on our own. For the sake of simplicity, let us at least assume that we are dealing with a Same Number Choice, though even this assumption is also likely to be false.) A central theme of contemporary Consequentialism is that, for affluent people in the developed world, charitable donation is a much more efficient way of promoting the good than devoting one's resources to those particular individuals closest to oneself. Adoption saves one child from poverty and gives them a very good life. Many of the resources Affluent allocates to her adopted child will produce only small marginal improvements in that child's well-being. The allocation of those resources to Oxfam could save many children from poverty. The Oxfam project will produce a better outcome than the Adoption project. (I use 'the Oxfam project' as a generic name for the project of devoting all one's energies to an efficient charity. I thus assume merely that there are some charities which do, on balance, considerably more harm than good.) We now compare the Oxfam project with the Reproduction project. This is a slightly trickier comparison, as it involves a Different Number Choice. Reproduction brings a new person into the world, whereas charitable donation does not. We need to examine the different theories of value designed for Different Number Choices. For simplicity, we focus on the Total View and the Average View. (See Section 3.2 and endnote A to Ch 3 respectively for expositions of these views.) Under the Total View, reproduction is better than charity if and only if the value of the new life Affluent creates outweighs the value she could otherwise have added to existing lives. This seems unlikely. Affluent's child has a very good life. However, as with adoption, diminishing marginal returns suggest that the resources she devotes to her child would have produced greater marginal improvements elsewhere. (What if Affluent were to give her own child a life barely worth living, and then donate her remaining resources to charity? This would still be unlikely to produce as much good as the Oxfam project, given the greater cost of providing even the necessities of life in the Western world. (We will explore other objections to this option in Chs. 3 and 4.) If reproduction leads to a lower (or equivalent) total well-being than charity, then it must also produce a lower average level of well-being, as the lower total will be divided among a larger population. The Total and Average Views thus agree that the Oxfam project is better than the Reproduction project. Most other contemporary Utilitarian value theories blend elements of these two theories. They will thus share this common verdict. (For discussion of these alternatives, see the references in endnote A to Ch 3.)

Another alternative is a person-affecting theory of value, where each state of affairs is evaluated relative to those who exist in it. (Dasgupta, 'Savings and Fertility'; and Roberts, 'A New Way of Doing the Best we Can' both develop sophisticated accounts along these lines.) Any such theory coincides with one of the standard views in Same People Choices. A person-affecting theory of value is thus not sufficient to enable Simple Consequentialism to avoid the Demandingness Objection in general. Furthermore, any person-affecting value theory must hold either the Oxfam project or the Reproduction project to be superior in Affluent's situation. If combined with Simple Consequentialism, the person-affecting value theory must therefore succumb to either the Compulsory Reproduction Objection or the Compulsory Non-Reproduction Objection. (It is more likely to be the latter. As it gives special weight to those who already exist, a person-affecting value theory is even more likely than other theories to find the Oxfam project superior to the Reproduction Project.) Accordingly, value theory alone cannot dissolve our present objection. Of course, a person-affecting value theory could be combined with some other solution to the Demandingness Objection, to produce a complete moral theory. (Indeed, both Roberts and Dasgupta sketch such solutions.) A full exploration of the morality of reproduction would then compare the resulting theory to the one developed in this book.

2

The Contract Theory

In this book, I develop a Consequentialist account of our moral and political obligations to future generations. While Consequentialist moral theory has continued to be popular, Consequentialist approaches to political theory have fallen out of favour in recent times. One subsidiary aim of this book is to motivate a return to Consequentialism, by highlighting its comparative advantage over its dominant contemporary rival in the area of intergenerational justice: the Contract Theory. I do not pretend to offer a comprehensive critique of alternative theories, but merely to establish the modest claim that Consequentialist political theory is worthy of further scrutiny. A further justification for focusing on the Contract Theory is that it is the leading *liberal* political theory. As one aim of this book is to establish the liberal credentials of Consequentialism, we focus on its claim to replace the Contract Theory.

The literature on all forms of the contract theory is vast. Our focus here is on obligations to future generations. I discuss two prominent contemporary contract theories: the Contractarianism of David Gauthier and the liberal egalitarianism of John Rawls. These illustrate the two primary forms of Contract Theory: a contract based on agents' actual inclinations and information (Gauthier) and a more hypothetical or idealized contract (Rawls). Gauthier and Rawls also represent two general alternatives to my Consequentialist strategy of building political morality on individual morality. Gauthier derives political morality directly from individual rationality, while Rawls attempts to make political philosophy independent of controversies in moral philosophy. The failure of both these alternatives clears the way for the messier, but ultimately more satisfactory, approach of Consequentialism.

2.1. Gauthier and Contractarianism

2.1.1. *The Contractarian Approach*

The basic Contractarian idea is simple.[1] Justice consists in an agreement agents would reach if they were self-interested and sought a mutually

---

[1] The classic contemporary text is Gauthier, *Morals by Agreement*. See also Arhennius, 'Mutual Advantage Contractarianism and Future Generations'; Barry, *Theories of Justice*; Gosseries, 'What do we

advantageous bargain. David Gauthier, the theory's most prominent modern exponent, himself reads self-interest as 'non-tuism': agents take no interest in the interests of those with whom they are interacting in a particular context, although they may take an interest in the interests of third parties. (For instance, I may bargain with you, to whose interests I am indifferent, in order to obtain some benefit for my children.) As Gustave Arhennius notes, 'the main advantage of Contractarianism is that it would answer the moral sceptic's question: Why be moral? The answer: for your own good.'[2]

For any group of individuals, there are many possible mutually advantageous arrangements. The Contractarian must choose among these. This choice has two stages. The first is the specification of the State of Nature: a non-cooperative baseline against which all potential systems of cooperation are compared. If justice is to be mutually advantageous, then we need only consider *feasible* systems: those where all agents fare better than in the baseline.

Many different Contractarian baselines have been proposed. One crucial issue is whether *strategic* moves (such as threats, violence, and fraud) are permitted in the state of nature. There are two basic answers, drawn from two Contractarian pioneers. Thomas Hobbes permits strategic moves. His state of nature is a war of all against all. John Locke, by contrast, rules them out. His state of nature is a far more orderly place, where people respect one another's 'natural rights'.[3] Some cooperative alternatives are feasible compared to a Hobbesian baseline but infeasible under a Lockean theory, and vice versa.

Gauthier himself defends a strongly Lockean baseline. Non-cooperation is equated with non-interference, where everyone respects everyone else's natural property rights. This prevents my 'taking advantage' of others: worsening their situation to improve my own. Gauthier employs a revised version of the Proviso developed by Locke and Robert Nozick.[4] To simplify his account, I take advantage of you if and only if two conditions are met:

(a) I leave you worse off than you would have been in my absence; and

(b) I leave myself better off than I would have been in your absence.

To illustrate Condition (a), if you are drowning in the lake (through no fault of mine), I do not take advantage if I leave you to drown. If I hadn't come

---

Owe the Next Generation(s)?'; Heath, 'Intergenerational Cooperation and Distributive Justice'; Kavka, *Hobbesian Moral and Political Philosophy*, 443–6; Mulgan, 'Reproducing the Contractarian State' (2002); and Sauve, 'Gauthier, Property Rights and Future Generations'.

[2] Arhennius, 'Mutual Advantage Contractarianism and Future Generations', 25.

[3] Hobbes, *Leviathan*; and Locke,*Two Treatises of Government* (Second Treatise, ch. 5, and First Treatise, ch. 9).   [4] Nozick, *Anarchy, State, and Utopia*, 175–82.

along, you would have drowned anyway. By contrast, if you are sitting by the lake and I shoot you to steal your lunch, I do take advantage.

To illustrate Condition (b), suppose I discharge waste into a stream. Sadly, you live downstream, and your crops are destroyed. You are worse off than if I'd never existed. However, I do not take advantage, as I gain no benefit from having destroyed your crops. I would have reaped the same benefits even if no one were living downstream. I might not even be aware of your existence. By contrast, suppose we are competitors. My waste kills you, and I then steal your crops. This would constitute taking advantage, as I gain benefits which I would not have gained if no one lived downstream (as your crops would not have existed). My actions would have been different if I'd been unaware of your existence.

In Gauthier's Lockean baseline, individuals will enter into pareto improving exchanges. The overall result of such exchanges is a pure market economy, where everyone pursues their own interests, subject only to the Lockean proviso. One option for Gauthier's bargainers is to introduce no additional moral constraints. The central moral question is whether any feasible social arrangement is pareto superior to the Initial Bargaining Position.

Gauthier argues that, as the market can fail in certain circumstances, everyone is better off if the market is appropriately regulated or constrained. For Gauthier, morality constrains the pursuit of individual self-interest in the marketplace. Morality is thus only appropriate as a response to market failure. A just society cannot offer anyone any less than they would have received in a completely free market, as the market is the baseline.

As an account of the state of nature, this Lockean picture may seem bizarre. The state of nature is meant to exemplify the behaviour of rational utility maximizers unconstrained by any moral obligations. Is Gauthier thus claiming that it is never rational to make threats or breach the rules of the free market? This seems implausible. To better understand the role of the Lockean proviso in Gauthier's theory, it is helpful to distinguish three scenarios.

The State of Nature. The Hobbesian world of unconstrained non-cooperation.

The Initial Bargaining Position. The Lockean world of constrained non-cooperation, where everyone obeys the revised Lockean proviso.

Civil Society. A world of social cooperation, where people's pursuit of their own interests is constrained by principles of justice agreed to in the Initial Bargaining Position.

Gauthier's aim is to justify civil society as against the State of Nature, demonstrating that it is rational for everyone to prefer the former to the latter. The move to civil society will be rational only if (*a*) every agent prefers life in civil society to life in the state of nature. Gauthier also adds the additional criterion that the move to civil society will be rational only if (*b*) every agent prefers life in civil society to life in the Initial Bargaining Position.

In Gauthier's theory we are trying to escape the State of Nature, but the default position for our bargaining is the Initial Bargaining Position. We are bargaining our way *out of* the State of Nature, but we bargain *from* the Initial Bargaining Position. We negotiate, compromise, make claims, etc., *as if* the Initial Bargaining Position were the starting point, the status quo ante, the default position. The Initial Bargaining Position is an appropriate starting point because it eliminates the 'taking of advantage'. It thus represents those of our advantages which we are permitted to bring to the bargaining table. In the State of Nature, agents can better their own positions by worsening the positions of others. If agents could bring such advantages to the bargaining table, then this would encourage them to improve their own bargaining position by means of predation. Gauthier argues that, as it is irrational to encourage others to predate, agents will not agree to bargain from any position where predation is permitted. Consequently, they will bargain from the Initial Bargaining Position.

Assume we have agreed on a baseline, and compiled a list of the feasible alternatives: those systems of cooperation where everyone fares better than in the baseline. The second stage of our Contractarian theory is to choose between them. One assumption common to all mutual advantage theorists is that the result must take us to the 'Pareto frontier'. Rational agents will not agree to a non-pareto optimal bargain. This condition alone does not determine the outcome of bargaining, as there may be many possible Pareto optimal points. Most Contractarians argue that the move to the Pareto frontier is determined by the relative bargaining power of the parties. Different theorists defend different bargaining solutions, each offered as an account of a division of the benefits of cooperation reflecting initial bargaining power. Gauthier's own bargaining solution is eccentric.[5] Agents begin by calculating the level of utility they would enjoy under the system of cooperation which would be best for them. They then subtract from this the utility they would enjoy in the Initial Bargaining Position. The result is the agent's maximum possible utility gain from cooperation. Agents then

---

[5] For general discussion of many aspects of Gauthier's bargaining solution, see the articles collected in *Social Philosophy and Policy*, 5/2 (1988); and in Vallentyne (ed.), *Contractarianism and Rational Choice*.

bargain in order to secure the highest possible percentage of that maximum possible benefit. They will agree on an equilibrium where every agent receives an equal proportion of her maximum possible benefit. This solution is sometimes known as 'splitting the difference' or as 'minimax relative complaint'.

2.1.2. *The Zipper Argument*

Our relations with future generations are significant for any Contractarian theory, as they provide a striking example of the absence of reciprocal power relations. Those alive today cannot be affected by the actions of those who will live in two centuries. No 'pattern of cooperation' between distant generations can offer present people more than they would receive in the State of Nature, no matter how our baseline is specified.[6]

Gauthier's proviso forbids the taking of advantage. In his terminology, I cannot take advantage of someone who lives two hundred years in the future. While I may benefit from an action which harms them, I do not benefit *because* my action harms them. I am no better off than I would have been if they never existed. Consequently, nothing we could possibly do to future generations would violate Gauthier's Lockean Proviso. For instance, the present generation are free to do with natural resources as they please. Distant generations might find themselves inheriting resources which were insufficient to meet their needs. However, any such harm is merely a side effect of the benefit to the present generation, not a means to it. Therefore the present generation have no obligations of justice with respect to future generations.

Contractarians seeking to avoid this conclusion have three options:

1. to derive obligations to future generations from their original bargain;
2. to change the motivations of the parties to the bargain;
3. to change the other parameters of the bargain.

Gauthier offers variants of the last two responses.[7] We begin, however, with the first, as it is the purest Contractarian response.

As successive generations overlap, there are opportunities for them to interact for mutual advantage. This raises the possibility of a bargain

---

[6] This argument might not go through, of course, if we exist after our death in a form that permits beneficial mutual interaction with the living. Modern Contractarians such as Gauthier would not be happy to rely upon this possibility. (For general discussion of the tendency of contemporary political theorists to ignore the possibility of life after death, and its implications for current debates, see Mulgan, 'The Place of the Dead in Liberal Political Philosophy' (1999); and Mulgan, 'Neutrality, Rebirth and Intergenerational Justice' (2002).)   [7] Gauthier, *Morals by Agreement*, 299 ff.

between them. Such a bargain must assume non-tuism between generations. The present generation cannot be constrained by the possible existence of future generations with whom they won't overlap. However, the next generation, if there is one, *will* constrain the actions of the present generation, as the overlap between them gives rise to the possibility of taking advantage.

The present generation have good reason to avoid being constrained by the Lockean Proviso. It may seem that they cannot avoid such constraints, as they need a next generation to look after them in their old age. However, there are two possible ways to obtain such assistance without bringing the proviso into play. The first would be to avoid creating a next generation of rational agents at all. One can only take advantage of rational agents, not of animals, inanimate objects, or machines. If the present generation can find a way of providing for their own needs without creating new rational agents, then it will make sense for them to do so. For instance, they might seek to create robots, or breed a generation of automatons, or raise a generation of human children to be 'natural slaves', unable to think for themselves. None of these alternatives could violate the Lockean Proviso (Section 1.5). Of course, the resulting society may not be able to persist once the present generation are dead. But this need not bother them.

The second option for the present generation begins with the observation that, if the present generation had never existed, then the next generation would not exist either. Unless the next generation are worse off than if they themselves had never existed, they cannot be worse off than they would have been in the absence of the present generation. So long as the present generation give the next generation lives worth living, they cannot violate the Lockean Proviso.

This argument is too swift. In another context, Gauthier explicitly says that, if you interact with someone on an ongoing basis, you cannot justify actions which harm them by pointing out that the overall pattern of interaction leaves them better off than they would have been in your absence. Each interaction must be judged separately. One can take advantage even within the context of a generally beneficial relationship.[8] Therefore, the present generation will be constrained by the proviso, even if their children have worthwhile lives.

In response, the present generation might aim for negative effects on the next generation that were inseparable from the act of creating them. For instance, the current generation might find it convenient to modify their children genetically, to produce humans who were stronger and more

---

[8] Ibid. 212.

resilient, but also doomed to die young. The resulting children would be unable to complain that they had been harmed by such modification, as they cannot compare their actual existence with some alternative possible world where they exist without those genetic modifications. Any child lacking such modifications would have been someone else (Section 1.3). Owing to the person-affecting foundations of his theory, the Non-Identity Problem is potentially fatal for Gauthier.

It is thus not clear that a Contractarian bargain can even generate obligations between overlapping generations. However, the real problem for this approach is the time bomb example, where an action beneficial to the present generation has a devastating effect on some distant future generation, but no direct impact on intervening generations.[9] Almost everyone would agree that planting a time bomb is wrong, especially if the benefit involved for the present generation is negligible. Planting a time bomb purely on a whim, with no benefit to oneself at all, is clearly wrong. (It violates the Basic Collective Intuition, one of our three decisive intuitions.) Any theory based on relations between overlapping generations must accommodate this decisive intuition.

One common response is as follows. Suppose we have only three generations: G1, G2, and G3. G1 leave a bomb to explode during the lifetime of G3. G1 and G3 do not interact, but G2 and G3 do. G3 will expect G2 either to disconnect the bomb's mechanism, or to compensate G3 for their failure to do so. The existence of the bomb thus weakens G2's bargaining position with respect to G3. G2 will be aware of this in advance, and will thus bargain with G1 not to plant the bomb. As a rule against planting a time bomb is included in the contract between any two adjacent generations, the planting of time bombs is wrong. (Axel Gosseries, whose presentation I follow, dubs this 'the zipper argument'.[10])

Variants of the zipper argument can be used by theories not built on mutual advantage. The general idea is that the existence of the bomb worsens the position of G2, by placing them under a (potentially very costly) obligation to G3. If we care about the next generation, then we will wish to ensure that they are able to meet their own moral obligations in as congenial a way as possible. (Our concern for the next generation might be based on self-interest, as in a mutual advantage theory, or it might be direct genuine concern.) Accordingly, we will not construct a time bomb.

If the zipper argument succeeded, this would seriously reduce the comparative advantage of Consequentialism, as any theory built on relations

---

[9] Gosseries, 'What do we Owe the Next Generation(s)?', 296–7, provides an overview of both the issues and the literature.   [10] Ibid. 296.

between contemporaries could be extended, via overlapping generations, to include obligations to all distant future generations. Fortunately for my project, there are several problems with the zipper argument.

1. It is inconsistent with Gauthier's own theoretical framework. In particular, instead of ceding ground to G2, it seems natural for G1 to use the *threat* of constructing a time bomb to extract concessions from G2. Gauthier could reject this move only if such a threat constituted 'taking advantage', in his technical sense of that phrase. However, given that the threat of a bomb imposes no direct harm on G2, it is not clear how it could ever satisfy Gauthier's own criteria for taking advantage. Either G2 will be able to disarm the time bomb, or they will not. If not, then the existence of a time bomb has no effect on G2's bargain with G3. If G2 can disarm the bomb, then its existence seems to strengthen G2's bargaining position with respect to G3, as G2 could threaten not to disarm it. By not disarming the bomb, G2 would clearly not be taking advantage of G3 in Gauthier's sense, as they would leave G3 no worse off than they would have been in *G2's* absence. As there is no bargain between G1 and G3, it does not matter whether G3 are worse off than they would have been in *G1's* absence. Therefore, G2 are free to threaten not to disarm the bomb, and to use this threat to extract concessions from G3.

The creation of the bomb by G1 thus advantages G2 in the long run. In the bargain between G1 and G2, the former are *offering* to create a time bomb, not threatening. If there is a threat, it is that G1 will not create a time bomb. But this threat is also clearly legitimate, as it would leave G2 no worse off than they would have been in the absence of G1.[11] So Gauthier's bargain leaves G1 entirely free to plant a time bomb.

2. If either the creating of a time bomb, or the act of disarming such a bomb, affects the identity of the members of G3, then neither creating a bomb (for G1) nor opting not to disarm it (for G2) could constitute taking advantage for Gauthier's purposes, so long as G3's lives are worth living overall. This is significant, as many real-world candidate time bombs will be identity-affecting. (For instance, consider a use of radioactive material by G1 that leaves G2 unscathed but changes the genetic make-up of G3.)

3. Even if the zipper argument generates the right result, it does so for the wrong reasons. Is it really plausible to say that the reason G1 ought not to construct a time bomb is because this will harm G2? The implausibility

---

[11] Of course, if G2 embark on the strategy of (*a*) encouraging G1 to create a time bomb, and then (*b*) using the threat not to disarm that bomb to force concessions out of G3, then one could argue that this entire strategy constitutes a taking advantage of G3 by G2. However, G1 and G2 could no doubt find some way around this accusation. Besides, this looks a rather flimsy basis on which to condemn G1's action in planting the bomb.

of this explanation is best seen in imaginary cases where the connections between the three generations are severed.[12] However, for those suspicious of bizarre thought experiments, a more mundane example should suffice. Suppose G1 has the power to create an undetectable threat to G3, such that G2 will never know of the existence of this threat. Any moral theory adopting the principle that 'ought implies can' will say that G2 have no obligations with respect to this threat, either to disarm it or to compensate G3 for its effects. Accordingly, the construction of the bomb has no impact on the obligations of G2. Nor could it affect the bargain between G2 and G3, as G3 are unaware of the threat also. (Indeed, the bomb has no real impact on G2, under Gauthier's theory, even if G2 are aware of the threat, so long as they can conceal it from G3.) As it has no other impact on G2, the bomb does not affect them at all. If we are relying on the zipper argument, G1 cannot have any moral reason not to construct such a bomb.

The possibility of a hidden time bomb is obscured because proponents of the zipper argument focus on the obligations of each generation, taken as a whole, to the next. It might be very difficult for an entire generation successfully to conceal its time bomb activities from everyone in the next generation. However, it would certainly be possible for an individual or group to construct an undetected bomb. No zipper argument can find any fault with such behaviour.

2.1.3. Sentimental Contractarians

As a matter of fact, people care about their descendants. When rational agents come to design political institutions, they will take account of the interests of their descendants. Future generations might thus be represented at the bargaining table, not in their own right, but because of their ancestors' concern for them.

Gauthier's defence of inheritance fits this model. He argues that his contractors will seek the system of property rights which best promotes productivity. As people are concerned for their descendants, they will work harder if they know that the fruits of their labours, if unconsumed at their death, will benefit their children. Accordingly, productivity will be greater under a system of property which permits inheritance than

---

[12] For instance, I have elsewhere tested both Gauthier and Rawls (among other theories) against an imaginary case where adjacent generations do not overlap. (Mulgan, 'A Minimal Test for Political Theories' (2001).)

under one which prohibits it. Rational egoists will thus agree to rules of inheritance.[13]

I argue in an endnote that Gauthier's own bargain will not yield his own principles of inheritance, as it cannot yield any definite result at all.[14] His approach also faces two more general difficulties. The first is that, even if it succeeds on its own terms, sentiment cannot generate obligations to distant future generations. People's concern for their own descendants definitely does *not* extend indefinitely into the future. It is quite strong for a generation or two, and then it peters out very sharply.[15]

A second problem is that the introduction of parental sentiment exacerbates a limitation of Gauthier's theory. In common with other Contractarian theories, Gauthier makes a crucial simplification, which is especially significant in regard to future generations. Unless her basic needs are met, a human being cannot survive. As Partha Dasgupta points out, needs are often ignored in the traditional economic theory of resource allocation. 'The standard theory . . . does not accommodate the notion of basic physiological needs.'[16] Different methods of resource allocation are compared with a baseline where all agents can survive without interaction. 'The theory in its textbook guise assumes that each household is capable of surviving in good health even were it to be autarkic . . . exchange in the theory allows households to improve their lot; it is not necessary for survival.'[17] Dasgupta also notes that 'much contemporary ethics assumes . . . that basic needs have been met.'[18] I shall refer to this claim as the Optimistic Assumption. Gauthier carries this assumption across into his own theory: 'in exercising one's powers one need not interact with others'.[19] In particular, Gauthier assumes that the basic needs of every person are met both in the Initial Bargaining Position and in civil society. This is a common move.

The Optimistic Assumption is unwarranted. A central question for any theory of justice is whether it ensures that all citizens will have their basic needs met. By assuming this question away, Gauthier simplifies his task enormously. Once we admit basic needs into Gauthier's framework, we see that his mode of argument yields very different conclusions. (If, indeed, it yields any conclusions at all.)

[13] Gauthier, *Morals by Agreement*, 300–1. For critical discussion, see Sauve, 'Gauthier, Property Rights and Future Generations', 167.   [14] See chapter endnote A, p. 50.

[15] For relevant empirical evidence regarding people's concern for their own descendants, see Dasgupta, 'Savings and Fertility: Ethical Issues', 103; and Dasgupta, *An Inquiry into Well-being and Destitution*, ch. 12.   [16] Dasgupta, *Well-being and Destitution*, 11.

[17] Ibid. 169–70.

[18] Ibid. 45. See also, Dasgupta, *Human Well-being and the Natural Environment*, 37; and Sen, *Development as Freedom*, 162 ff.   [19] Gauthier, *Morals by Agreement*, 209.

If the Initial Bargaining Position corresponds to anything in the real world, then it is a place where some basic needs may go unmet. If my basic needs will not be met in civil society, then I still have no reason to agree to move from the Initial Bargaining Position, even if my basic needs would go unmet there also. Gauthier thus needs to ensure that all potential cooperators know (*a*) that their basic needs are at least as likely to be met in civil society as in the Initial Bargaining Position, and (*b*) that there is some chance they will be better off in civil society.

Abandoning the Optimistic Assumption radically alters the bargaining situation. Those who know that their basic needs are met in the Initial Bargaining Position have a much stronger bargaining position, as they do not need to reach agreement on a point beyond that initial position.[20] They can hold out for the bargain which best suits them. Gauthier's bargaining solution takes no account at all of a key component of individuals' bargaining power: the comparative urgency of their desire to reach agreement. If I can survive without agreement, while you cannot, then I will get a better deal than you. (For instance, I may survive in the Initial Bargaining Position simply because my nutritional requirements are smaller than yours. Yet this has little bearing on my productivity as a worker in a capitalist society.) Nothing in Gauthier's formula allows for this, whether the non-agreement point is the Initial Bargaining Position or the State of Nature.[21]

Although Gauthier's bargain proceeds from the Initial Bargaining Position, the State of Nature underlies his contract. Relaxing the Optimistic Assumption increases the significance of that state. One of the principal evils of the State of Nature, especially for Hobbes, is that it is a place where one continually fears for one's survival. The social contract presents itself as a way of ensuring one's survival. If one's survival is not assured in civil society, then one might rather take one's chances in the State of Nature. For instance, suppose I am a hopeless agriculturalist with few marketable talents. These two facts combine to place me at a distinct disadvantage in Gauthier's bargain. I can thus expect not to fare terribly well in civil society. However, I may be a very good fighter. In the Initial Bargaining Position, I would fail to cultivate enough to feed myself. In the State of Nature, I would be well placed to prey on my neighbours. So I will not find Gauthier's bargaining table congenial.[22]

[20] The fact that an individual's 'breakdown position' affects her bargaining power is well known in bargaining theory. (See e.g. Sen, 'Gender and Cooperative Conflicts', 135.) Dasgupta notes, in a similar context, that 'Nash (1950) showed that those who enjoy better outside options would enjoy a greater share of the benefits of cooperation.' Dasgupta, *Human Well-being and the Natural Environment*, 112. The reference is to Nash, 'The Bargaining Problem'.   [21] See chapter endnote B, p. 51.

[22] Defenders of the market may reply that the talents which make me a good fighter will be highly prized in the market society. For instance, in our own society, boxers, rugby league players, and

The introduction of future generations renders the Optimistic Assumption even less plausible. In the Initial Bargaining Position, some people will be unable to meet the basic needs of their children, even if they can meet their own needs. This additional complication has several implications.

1. Bargaining Strength.   The introduction of chidren exacerbates existing differences in bargaining strength. Suppose I have children while you do not. If my children will starve if we do not agree, then I will be desperate to reach agreement. Being well-informed, you will be aware of my comparative weakness. Being rational, you will exploit it. The result will be a bargain which serves your interests far better than mine.[23]

2. Risk and Motivation.   Gauthier implicitly assumes that my concern for my children's welfare is analogous to my concern for my own welfare. In particular, my attitudes to risk are the same in both cases. As an account of any plausibly human psychology, this seems too simple. I may feel comfortable taking risks on my own account, while desiring to play it safe when my children's survival is at stake. I may also have more confidence in my ability to predict how a course of action will impact on me than in my ability to make analogous predictions regarding my children.

3. Ignorance.   Gauthier explicitly permits agents to be aware of their own talents and abilities, and to opt for social structures which reward those talents. (This distinguishes his bargaining table from that of John Rawls, considered in Section 2.2.) Yet one cannot be aware, in advance, of the talents and abilities of one's children. One may hope that they will inherit one's own abilities (or that they will be more talented); one may endeavour to instil in them one's own sober work habits; one may invest in the most expensive available education and training, and the most sought-after old school tie; but one simply cannot know how well they will be able to survive in the market society, if they can survive there at all.

In a market society, according to Gauthier, each person's reward is proportional to her contribution. (I leave aside the question of whether a market society actually would emerge from Gauthier's own bargaining solution, even if children are excluded.) If you and I are bargaining, perhaps it is reasonable for us to strike such a bargain. However, why should we strike it

mercenaries all make a good living. However, in a developed capitalist society, such jobs may be comparatively few. In the marketplace of thuggery, supply may outstrip demand. I may be unlucky: perhaps I'm just not a marketable sort of thug.

[23] Family dynamics might further enhance the differences between state of nature and civil society. For instance, perhaps I belong to a large family of poor farmers who fight well. In the state of nature, our familial bonds may make us a potent threat to our disorganized peaceful neighbours.

also on behalf of our respective children? I am not interested in how much my children contribute, nor is there any obvious sense in which, when signing up to the bargain, I am offering their contributions. I am interested in how well they will fare.

Instead, it seems more likely that I will aim to use my ability to contribute to the cooperative surplus to ensure that my children's needs are met, regardless of what happens to me. The result might well be a welfare state for future generations. Because we are ignorant of our children's talents and motivations, our interest in them brings Gauthier's bargaining situation much closer to Rawls's original position (Section 2.2). After all, do any rational persons really want a meritocracy for their own children? (I have yet to hear of any parent who behaved as if they did.) As you will obviously not agree to any system that would favour my children over yours, perhaps some form of egalitarianism would be the most appropriate compromise.

Accommodating both basic needs and future generations greatly increases the complexity of Gauthier's bargaining situation. It is doubtful that any definite bargain will emerge from such a situation. It is even more doubtful that we could predict, in advance, the content of that bargain. Finally, even if a definite bargain did emerge and even if we could predict it, it would not extend further than the next generation or two. If our Contract Theory is to cover obligations to distant future generations, then we must look elsewhere.

2.1.4. A New Bargain

To accommodate longer-term obligations, Gauthier provides a principle of just savings. He argues that 'the rational rate of investment is determined by applying minimax relative concession to claims based on the rate of possible accumulation'.[24] In other words, we imagine an intergenerational analogue of the Initial Bargaining Position, where the parties are generations rather than individuals. The result is that 'members of each generation receive the same proportion of their claim as did their predecessors and as will their successors, but the productivity of investment guarantees continuing enrichment'.[25] Each generation thus makes the same sacrifice, even though each is better off than the last.

Gauthier argues that, in the Initial Bargaining Position, there will be a zero rate of savings. Any system of capitalist accumulation will thus be a superior alternative. He argues that his bargainers will chose a system

---

[24] Gauthier, *Morals by Agreement*, 304.   [25] Ibid. 304.

whereby each generation makes the same contribution to intergenerational savings. There are several problems with Gauthier's argument.

Let us grant Gauthier's assumption that there are feasible alternatives, pareto superior to the Initial Bargaining Position. (See below for a critique of this assumption.[26]) We must now ask which would be chosen by rational agents. Gauthier argues that his bargainers choose the option which minimizes every generation's maximum possible complaint. Each generation's complaint is found by dividing what it actually receives from cooperation by the difference between what it would have received under the system which best served its interests and what it would have received in the Initial Bargaining Position.

For any given rate of savings, later generations benefit more than earlier ones. The maximum possible benefit of a later generation is thus much greater than the maximum possible benefit of an earlier generation. If all generations fare equally well in the baseline situation, then relative complaints will be equalized when each generation is better off than the last.

This looks like an appealing result. (It is the result Gauthier arrives at, and he praises his theory for reaching it.) We return to the appeal of the result in Section 7.6. Whatever its appeal, however, this result cannot possibly follow from any bargaining solution. In the intergenerational case, the size of one's maximum possible benefit varies inversely with one's bargaining power. Concentrate on a single generation (G). G are in a very strong bargaining position in relation to later generations, especially those with whom they can never interact. Gauthier argues that, despite this advantage, the rational thing for G to do is to endorse a system of cooperation which will provide greater benefit to later generations than to G. Yet elsewhere in Gauthier's theory, as in any mutual advantage theory, those with stronger bargaining positions expect to gain more from cooperation than those who are weaker.

Gauthier generates a plausible result only because his 'bargaining solution' is a highly implausible account of bargaining. In general, the more credible a theorist's bargaining solution, the less his chances of producing principles of justice which do not implausibly favour the present generation.

Gauthier's intergenerational bargain is also at odds with the rest of his theory. Throughout his discussion of the just savings problem, Gauthier speaks as if he were imagining a cooperative venture where the parties are different generations. This is a classic example of a theorist exploiting the conventional implications of a term, in a manner inconsistent with his own theory. Given the sense which 'cooperation' has within a mutual advantage theory, the notion of a cooperative venture involving many different

---

[26] See chapter endnote C, p. 52.

generations is incoherent. Cooperation is interaction for mutual advantage. Generations who do not overlap cannot interact. Therefore, they cannot cooperate. Whatever its rhetoric, any Contractualist account must be founded solely on relations between overlapping generations. Gauthier's multigenerational cooperative agreement is a fiction. The real cooperative agreements are a series of concrete bargains between overlapping individuals. This obviously complicates our task. We must ask how billions of individuals, spread across many different generations, might bargain about social institutions. Once again, there is no reason to suppose we can hope to answer this question.

2.1.5. Beyond Gauthier

Some of our particular criticisms apply only to Gauthier's own peculiar bargaining solution. However, other traditional bargaining solutions face similar problems, as they all tie rationality to orthodox utility functions: rationality consists in the maximization of expected utility, where utility is measured in terms of the satisfaction of preferences. This is to be expected, as standard specifications of the bargaining problem ensure that richer information regarding the structure of agents' needs and goals is not available.[27] Unfortunately, this simplification seems less plausible when (a) some agents face death in some possible social systems; and (b) some agents are motivated by concern for their descendants. We need accounts of rationality and bargaining when death is a possibility, when dependants are involved as well as the agent herself, and especially when non-cooperation will bring death to some and not to others.

Bargaining solutions are presented as short-cuts, designed to avoid the need to simulate or observe the actual course of bargaining. Such short-cuts may be appropriate in the simplified world of the orthodox bargaining problem. However, they are not plausible in any situation remotely approximating real life. There is no way to predict in advance how agents would bargain in a state of nature. As no one is ever actually in the state of nature, this is a serious problem for Contractarian political philosophy.

Gauthier cannot provide a plausible account of our obligations to future generations. Furthermore, the revisions he needs to introduce once basic needs and future generations enter the picture bring his bargaining situation ever closer to Rawls's hypothetical social contract, to which we now turn.

---

[27] For a full critique of the use of bargaining theory in political philosophy, see Roemer, 'The Mismarriage of Bargaining Theory and Distributive Justice'.

2.2. Rawls and Liberal Egalitarianism

John Rawls's *A Theory of Justice* was the most influential work in political philosophy in the twentieth century. Rawls's theory is superficially similar to Contractarianism, with the crucial difference that Rawls is not interested in a contract which actual people might enter into. Rather, he asks what contract people *would* agree to under certain idealized circumstances. Rawls christens his approach 'justice as fairness', as the underlying motivation is to find principles of justice that everyone will recognize as a fair basis for mutual interaction.

The basic device Rawls uses to establish the fairness of his principles of justice is the Original Position, where people choose principles to govern their society. This choice is made from behind a veil of ignorance. The choosers know *what* their society will look like if any given principle is adopted, but they do not know *who* they will be in that society.[28] To take a simplified example, suppose that, in a very simple society, there are two groups: the Rich and the Poor. To discover what justice requires in such a society, we ask the following question: Which principles of justice would rational people choose, if they did not know whether they themselves would be one of the Rich or one of the Poor?

In the Original Position, the parties do not know their 'conception of the good'. So they cannot calculate their welfare under alternative policies. Instead, they focus on their access to 'primary goods': the general goods all people need in order to pursue their conception of the good life, whatever that conception might be. These goods include 'liberty and opportunity, income and wealth, and the bases of self-respect'.[29]

Rawls stipulates that the participants in the Original Position are *maximiners*. When choosing under conditions of uncertainty, they choose a course of action where the worst possible outcome is at least as good as the worst possible outcome under any alternative course of action. (This stipulation ensures that the original position models the anti-utilitarian intuition that fair principles of justice should not allow a worse-off minority to be sacrificed for a better-off majority.) Rawls also assumes that everyone in the Original Position belongs to the same generation.

Like Gauthier, Rawls looks set to have trouble generating obligations to future generations. Suppose we place the present generation in the Original Position. As rational egoists, they will choose the general principle that the present generation can do whatever they like to future generations. After all, they know they will not be on the receiving end of that

---

[28] Rawls, *A Theory of Justice* (1971), 17–22.   [29] Ibid. 303.

principle themselves. (By contrast, they would not choose a principle permitting the rich to do whatever they like to the poor, as they would not know whether or not they would end up on the receiving end of such a principle.)

Given his strong egalitarian commitments, the inference from the defencelessness of future generations to their lack of enforceable rights is not palatable to Rawls. He attempts to accommodate obligations to future generations within the framework of the Original Position. Furthermore, Rawls wants to solve the following particular problem.

The Accumulation Problem. (Also known as the 'Just Savings Problem'.) Suppose a society begins in a very primitive state, with minimal technology and low life expectancy. Each generation needs to balance investment against consumption. If the first generation consume everything, then subsequent generations will be left with nothing and will starve. If the first generation consume exactly as much as they produce, then subsequent generations will face the same situation as the first generation. Each generation will survive, but society will never progress. If the first generation produce more than they consume, then subsequent generations will be better off. What does justice require of each generation?

This tale brings two very powerful arguments into conflict. The first is that accumulation must be permissible, as otherwise every human society is necessarily built on injustice. What could be more natural than the thought that each generation should strive to leave later generations better off? The second argument turns on the observation that, under many plausible scenarios, future generations will be better off than the present generation. Accumulation thus involves sacrificing the interests of those who are worse-off in order to provide benefits to the better-off. This is especially striking if the 'consumption' alternative to accumulation is in fact a policy of redistributing resources in favour of the worst-off in the current generation. Viewed in this light, accumulation seems impermissible.

The two challenges for any political theory are to show that it neither permits too much accumulation (at the expense of present people), nor forbids accumulation entirely. These two goals are obviously in tension. The accumulation problem is especially acute for Rawls. As the Original Position gives absolute priority to the worse-off individuals, it looks as if he must forbid accumulation.

Rawls does not welcome this conclusion. In his long philosophical career, he offers two distinct accounts of how, in spite of its maximin orientation, justice as fairness can permit accumulation.

2.2.1. Rawls's Original Solution

Rawls's original solution was to add a motivational assumption, whereby those in the Original Position are assumed to care about the fate of their descendants, at least for the next generation or two.[30] This solution faces problems similar to those facing sentimental Contractarians (Section 2.1.3). First of all, it seems ad hoc. Why are we allowing some altruistic concern for descendants into the Original Position, when we do not allow concern for one's contemporaries? Furthermore, as we saw in Section 2.1.3, any plausible motivational assumption only works for two generations or so. This might be sufficient for relations between one generation and the next, but it doesn't cover relations between this generation and far distant ones. For instance, it would permit the present generation to pursue a policy with disastrous effects on those who will be alive in three centuries time, so long as it would not harm the next few generations. (At this point, Rawls could appeal to the zipper argument, if only it were valid.)

In his original discussion, Rawls focuses on the just rate of savings between one generation and the next, not on longer term issues such as environmental pollution. This focus seemed much more reasonable in 1971 than it does today. (For more on the significance of Rawls's optimism, see Section 7.5.) To account for longer-term issues, Rawls must stipulate that those in the Original Position are concerned for all their descendants, indefinitely far into the future. (We could see this stipulation as enabling the Original Position to model the intuition that fair principles of justice should give equal weight to the interests of all generations.)

I follow Rawls himself in regarding his original solution as unsatisfactory. His stipulation faces two key objections. The first is that the Original Position now looks unbalanced. The parties to it are concerned for their own descendants for hundreds and hundreds of years, but they are not at all concerned about the people who live next door. This seems a very odd way to generate principles of justice.

A related problem is that Rawls's stipulation does not provide sufficient information to derive definite conclusions from the Original Position. We need to know how the parties balance the competing interests of their many descendants. In the case of contemporaries, this detail is provided by the veil of ignorance together with the assumption that the parties are self-interested maximiners. The challenge for Rawls is to provide something analogous for the intergenerational case. He takes up this challenge in his second book.

---

[30] Rawls, *A Theory of Justice* (1971), 284–93.

2.2.2. Rawls's Recent Solution

In *Political Liberalism*, Rawls abandons his original motivational solution. Instead, he prefers 'a better approach . . . based on an idea given to me by Thomas Nagel and Derek Parfit. [In *A Theory of Justice*] I simply missed this better solution which leaves the motivational assumption unchanged.'[31] We stipulate that, when determining their behaviour towards future generations, those in the Original Position must behave in a way that they would want previous generations to have behaved.[32]

More specifically, Rawls proposes the following method for choosing a schedule of savings. ('A schedule is a rule stating a fraction of social product to be saved at any given level of wealth.'[33])

> We say the parties are to agree to a savings principle subject to the condition that they must want all previous generations to have followed it. They ask themselves how much they are prepared to save should all previous generations have followed the same schedule. . . . The correct principle is one the members of any generation (and so all generations) would adopt as the principle they would want preceding generations to have followed, no matter how far back in time.[34]

Using this idea, we could then rank possible schedules by deducting the cost to us of following a given schedule from the total benefit we would have received if previous generations had followed it. A policy of total self-sacrifice fails this new Rawlsian test, as the cost to us of implementing it outweighs the benefit we gain from the sacrifices of previous generations. A policy of total selfishness also fails, as the cost to us of previous generations being completely selfish outweighs the benefit of behaving that way ourselves. Therefore, we need something in between. Unfortunately for Rawls, it is very hard to say what that something will be.[35]

I focus on two sets of problems, arising from the Non-Identity Problem and from Rawls's assumption of favourable conditions.

---

[31] Rawls, *Political Liberalism* (1993), 20, n. 22

[32] For Rawls's more recent views, see ibid. 273–4; Rawls, *Justice as Fairness: A Restatement* (2001), 159–60; and Rawls, *The Law of Peoples* (1999), 107. Some good discussions are Gosseries, 'What do we Owe the Next Generation(s)?'; Paden, 'Reciprocity and Intergenerational Justice'; and Paden, 'Rawls's Just Saving Principle and the Sense of Justice'.   [33] Rawls, *Justice as Fairness: A Restatement*, 160.
[34] Ibid.

[35] Rawls's new solution is also in tension with his claim that saving is optional once liberal institutions are established. Rawls argues that intergenerational savings is merely a *transitional* requirement of justice (Rawls, *Justice as Fairness: A Restatement*, 159). Human history begins with an accumulation phase when saving is compulsory, until the necessary conditions for a just society are reached. After that point, saving is optional and society may remain in a steady state. As the discussion in the text makes clear, this picture is obviously sharply at odds with any schedule likely to emerge from Rawls's own method for choosing a schedule of saving. We return to these issues in Chs. 7 and 9.

2.2.3. Rawls and Non-Identity

Rawls offers an explicitly Kantian account of the choice of a schedule of savings. (Before we can act on any maxim for saving, we ask if we could will it as a universal law for all generations.) His procedure is analogous to applying the Categorical Imperative to the procreative choices of one's own parents. The size and identity of the present generation depend on the behaviour of previous generations, including their attitude to saving. How could this procedure find fault with the schedule actually followed? Could we prefer a different rate of savings that would have produced a present situation that was more just, but where we would not have existed at all? (See Section 1.5.)

Rawls's proposed method for selecting a schedule of saving is akin to an intergenerational original position.[36] Therefore, our present question is analogous to the problem of incorporating the Non-Identity Problem into the Original Position itself. That earlier problem admits of two solutions.

One solution is to extend the veil of ignorance, so that we do not even know whether we will ever exist at all. It is a very contingent matter which particular people get to exist. As the number of possible combinations of genetic material in any generation is enormous, the number of possible people is vastly greater than the number of people who will ever actually exist. This new original position is thus very hard to imagine.[37] Furthermore, it seems likely to generate some uncomfortable results. It will lead either to policies favouring universal non-existence, or to those favouring a situation where a vast number of people each have a bare minimum of primary goods over a situation where a slightly smaller number of people have an ample share each of primary goods.[38]

The alternative solution is to assume that, despite the Non-Identity Problem, those in the Original Position know that they will exist, no matter what policies they choose. However, this will lead them to prefer a situation where a very small number of people each have a very large share of primary goods over a situation in which a much larger number of people each have a very slightly smaller share of primary goods. This preference will remain even if the former population will be so small that it lacks the resources to produce a new generation. If I know that I will exist, then I am

---

[36] Rawls denies that his method of choice involves an intergenerational original position, as 'we must not imagine a direct agreement between all generations'. (Rawls, *Justice as Fairness: A Restatement*, 160.) However, the argument in the text relies only on a similarity between the Original Position and Rawls's method of choosing a schedule.

[37] Also, as Brian Barry notes, 'we are bound to worry about the good sense of choosing principles to advance the interests of potential people most of whom will never exist' (Barry, *Theories of Justice*, 195).

[38] See chapter endnote D, p. 52.

concerned only to maximize the opportunities open to those who will exist. This seems a very unattractive result.[39]

In the analogous case of choosing a schedule of savings, the dilemma is the same. If we know that we exist, then we will want previous generations to have focused on producing a small present generation with high per capita wealth. If we do not know whether we exist, then we want previous generations to have produced a present generation as large as possible.

These are serious problems, especially as Consequentialism copes much better with Different People Choices. Rawls himself notes, in another context, that there is no way of knowing what we might have been if things had been different.[40] Yet his theory of just savings rests on a comparison between the actual situation and the situation that would have resulted if previous generations had followed a different schedule. It is thus not clear that this procedure can offer Rawls any definite result.

However, I propose to put these problems aside. Rawls himself never explicitly discusses Different People Choices, and the issues they raise for his theory are familiar from our previous discussions and from the literature. I shall argue that his solution does not work even when it is confined (somewhat artificially) to Same People Choices.

2.2.4. Favourable Conditions

Rawls does not endorse Gauthier's Optimistic Assumption. He does not assume that everyone's basic needs are met. However, he does make a related assumption. Throughout his theory of justice, Rawls assumes that 'favourable conditions' apply: that we are dealing with a society capable of establishing just institutions, where all basic needs can be met without any threat to liberty.[41]

A cornerstone of Rawls's theory of justice is the priority of liberty. Liberty cannot be sacrificed for any gain in economic productivity. Yet Rawls explicitly denies that liberty always has priority over efficiency. In some circumstances, liberty could come into conflict with the meeting of basic needs—and then basic needs would take priority.[42] The priority of liberty arises only under favourable conditions.

The assumption of favourable conditions is thus vital to Rawls. He defends it on the grounds that he is developing a theory of justice for a modern liberal democratic society, and such societies enjoy favourable

---

[39] This argument is analogous to one of Parfit's objections to Average Utilitarianism. (*Reasons and Persons*, 421–2.) But the problem is even worse for Rawls, owing to his commitment to giving priority to the worst-off. [40] Rawls, *Political Liberalism* (1993), 270.

[41] Ibid. 297. [42] See chapter endnote E, p. 53.

conditions. Unfortunately, even if it is reasonable in itself, Rawls's assumption of favourable conditions leads him to ignore basic needs, just as Gauthier did. This renders his theory vulnerable at the boundaries of favourable conditions, when basic needs come into play. These boundaries are exposed by intergenerational and international justice. We briefly return to the latter in endnote A to Chapter 9 in the context of a comparison with my own Rule Consequentialist account. To illustrate the former, we now look at two boundaries: childhood and disability.

2.2.4.1. Childhood

For Rawls, political justice is owed to moral persons, who have the two moral powers: the capacity for a conception of the good, and the capacity for a sense of justice.[43] Moral persons also have higher-order interests in the development and exercise of their two moral powers, and thus also in whatever is necessary for their development of these moral powers.[44]

Parties to the Original Position know that they represent human beings. They also know 'the basic facts of social life and the conditions of human growth and nurture'.[45] These presumably include the following facts: that each human life begins with a childhood; that no child is born with realized moral powers, or spontaneously develops such powers; that whether any given child does develop those powers depends upon the quality of the social conditions of early childhood; that many actual and possible social arrangements provide inadequate social conditions of early childhood for many children; and, finally, that these inadequate conditions ensure, or make it highly likely, that those children never develop the moral powers to *any* significant degree.

The parties know that those whom they represent might be children who are thus disadvantaged. They have good reason to select principles of justice that ensure their society has few such children, if any. So the following principle of justice will be selected in the Original Position.

> *The Development Principle.* Each person has an equal claim to a fully adequate scheme of equal conditions of early care, which is compatible with a similar scheme of such conditions for all.

This principle is modelled on Rawls's own Liberty Principle.[46] The Liberty Principle is pointless unless the persons to whom it applies already have minimally developed moral powers. The Development Principle aims to

---

[43] Rawls, *A Theory of Justice* (1971), 505. Rawls, *Political Liberalism* (1993), 34. Rawls, *Political Liberalism*, p. xlvi. The argument of this section is drawn from Mulgan and Moore, 'Growing Up in the Original Position'.   [44] Rawls, *Political Liberalism*, 74.

[45] Ibid. 178.   [46] As formulated ibid. 291.

secure at least that minimum level of development of those powers. So the Development Principle has *lexical* priority over the Liberty Principle. Social conditions of nurture cannot be sacrificed for the sake of *any amount of* basic liberty. Given Rawls's maximin orientation, we should aim to prevent *any* children from failing to develop their moral powers. This aim will have lexical priority over all other social policy goals.[47] A society governed by the Development Principle would be very different from both the traditional picture of the Rawlsian liberal state and from any actual society.

2.2.4.2. Disability and Intergenerational Justice

It can be extremely expensive to meet the basic needs of someone with severe disabilities. The technology and wealth needed to meet such needs require economic development. Liberty does not trump basic needs. If some basic needs can only be met through economic development, then it is no longer plausible to say that liberty is lexically prior to economic efficiency or development. If the severely disabled fell within the scope of a theory of justice, this would threaten to destabilize the simple Rawlsian priorities.

If we wish to avoid this extreme result without rejecting Rawls's commitment to the idea of fairness embodied in the maximin stipulation, and if we admit that there are some people whose basic needs can only be met by the development of new and very expensive technologies, then we must find some principled motivation for excluding the severely disabled from the Original Position. Unfortunately, whatever its merits in the case of a single generation, this strategy falls apart in the intergenerational context. To illustrate this failure, we consider one strategy for excluding the severely disabled, based on Rawls's own discussion.[48]

---

[47] One obvious complication for Rawls here is that some children are physically unable to develop their moral powers at all, no matter how they are raised. Others would be able to develop those powers, but only if vast resources were devoted to them. Should a Rawlsian state devote all its resources to the care of the severely disabled? As we shall see in the next section, Rawls can only avoid this conclusion by excluding the severely disabled from the scope of the Original Position. The need to include children within the scope of the theory complicates this move, as the vulnerability of children is in many ways analogous to the vulnerability of the severely disabled. (Neither group can contribute to the cooperative surplus without considerable assistance.)

[48] Rawls states his own position in Rawls, 'Social Unity and Primary Goods' (1999), 368–9, responding to Arrow, 'Some Ordinalist-Utilitarian Notes on Rawls's Theory of Justice', 253–4. (For subsequent debate, see Daniels, Preface in *Reading Rawls*, p. xxvi; and Daniels, 'Democratic Equality: Rawls's Complex Egalitarianism'.) Rawls's own actual position is more subtle. While the severely disabled are put to one side when the basic principles of justice are derived in the Original Position, they do re-enter the theory of justice at a later stage, where their needs are taken into account by public debate and legislation in the liberal society. However, this total package only makes methodological sense if (a) the disabled are a distinct class who can be put to one side; and (b) the principles of justice allow sufficient leeway to accommodate the interests of those left out of the original constitutional framework. The discussion in the text suggests that, in the intergenerational context, these two conditions are not met.

Our aim is to put to one side any obligations society might have to the severely disabled. Like Gauthier, we regard justice as ultimately a scheme of cooperation for mutual benefit. Those who cannot contribute to the cooperative surplus are not parties to the agreement that underlies justice as fairness. It does not follow that we have no obligations to such people, but these would not be essential requirements of justice.

This approach treats 'the severely disabled' as a phrase referring to a fixed group of people, who can be put to one side for the purposes of developing a theory of justice. It thus falls apart in the intergenerational case. We have defined the notion of a serious disability with reference to a person's ability to contribute to the cooperative surplus. A serious disability *is* one that places individuals beyond the scope of the original position *because* it prevents them from contributing to the cooperative surplus. However, whether someone can contribute to the cooperative surplus depends, not only on the person's natural abilities or disabilities, but also on the cost and availability of treatments for those disabilities, and on the economic or social value of the person's abilities. If a person's disability can be cheaply alleviated, and if his or her other abilities are highly marketable, then they may be easily able to contribute. These other factors are affected by a society's level of development. Many severe physical disabilities loom much larger in a pre-industrial society than in the modern world. We can easily imagine a person who would have been 'severely disabled' in an earlier generation, but who is perfectly able to contribute to the cooperative surplus in the present generation.

As we know that *we* are a later generation in favourable conditions, we know that some of us will be such people. Behind the veil of ignorance, I know that I might be someone who, without the saving undertaken by previous generations, would have been severely disabled, and thus would not have been a party to the choice about justice taking place in the Original Position. Indeed, even if I am not severely disabled, I know that, in a liberal society, both the quality of my life and the probability that I will live a worthwhile life at all depend upon the level of medical technology available. That level in turn depends upon the savings of previous generations. Behind the veil of ignorance, I know that I may be someone who enjoys a worthwhile life in a liberal society, but who would have died from an untreatable disease if that saving had not occurred. (There is an obvious parallel here with the difficulties exposed in section 2.2.3. Instead of a Different People Choice, we now face a different parties choice. Even if they know that they exist, how can those in the Original Position know whether or not they will be contributors to the cooperative surplus (and, hence, whether they will be parties to the Original Position at all) when the answer depends upon the choice they must make?) Two things follow.

1. The present generation must choose a schedule of saving that ensures that medical progress continues at (at least) its present rate. They must save at least as much as their ancestors, even if the latter were fanatical savers.

2. It is very likely that the worst-off people in the present generation (among those who are not 'severely disabled') will be those whose opportunities are limited by medical conditions that could have been alleviated if medical technology had been slightly more advanced. The risk that they will be one of those people will lead parties behind the veil of ignorance to prefer a higher rate of saving than their ancestors. This argument looks likely to lead to a rate of saving designed to maximize technological advancement.[49]

Rawls's method for selecting a schedule of saving thus generates powerful arguments for an obligation to save at a higher rate than previous generations. Unfortunately, these arguments all privilege the status quo to an unacceptable degree. We cannot rule out a priori the possibility that previous generations have saved at an unjustly *high* rate. Perhaps they were not liberal egalitarians, and thus neglected their worse-off contemporaries in order to over-save. If consistency requires that we save at (at least) the same rate as our predecessors, then the just schedule of savings will clash with our obligations to our contemporaries.

One obvious solution is to subordinate the just savings principle to the principles of contemporary justice. If previous generations have over-saved, then we should save at the highest rate consistent with the implementation of liberal egalitarian principles in the present generation. There are two

---

[49] Rawls himself seems to offer a response to this objection. In another context, he appeals to Amartya Sen and Partha Dasgupta in support of the claim that the priority of liberty does not presuppose a high level of wealth, as poor nations can do an equally good job of meeting basic health needs. (Rawls, *Justice as Fairness: A Restatement* (2001), 47.) Rawls's comment is not a response to the present objection, but rather to the general suggestion of a link between economic development and health. This is significant because, for our present purposes, Rawls's comment would only be true if we put the severly disabled to one side. Yet this would beg the question, as the whole point of the arqument in the text is to challenge that move. Unfortunately, if we are considering an original position that includes the severly disabled, then Rawls's comment will be false. To see this, we need to distinguish two claims. (1) A relatively poor country can meet all the basic needs of its citizens to a high level in a world where the necessary technologies have been already developed by people in rich developed nations. (2) A relatively poor country can meet those needs to a high level in complete isolation. The empirical evidence that Rawls cites may support the first claim, but not the second. (Extrapolation from recent history suggests that further advances in technology to meet basic needs would not be achieved without continued economic development in the most advanced nations.) Yet it is the second claim that is relevant for a theory of domestic justice. Improved health care does require saving *by someone*. (One further complication is that, in the international context, developments in other societies may alter the definition of basic needs within the poor country, so that some new technology becomes essential to meet a new threshold of basic needs. See Section 9.2, and Ch. 9 endnote A.)

problems for this solution. We saw in Section 2.2.4.1 that obligations of justice between contemporaries are much more onerous than Rawls himself admits. Accordingly, a theory that accords such obligations priority over intergenerational justice may leave no room at all for the latter.

Secondly, even if it balances the various demands of justice, this solution leaves the present generation no room to move. All available resources will be commandeered either by the contemporary principles of justice or by the just savings principle. Obligations other than those of justice will not enter the picture. This is a problem for our present Rawls-inspired solution for two reasons. The first is that solution explicitly places some very significant moral obligations (such as obligations to the severely handicapped) outside the scope of the initial principles of justice. So, if those obligations are all-encompassing, then no resources whatever will be available for the severely disabled in the present generation. Secondly, the whole point of a *liberal* political theory is to provide a protected private sphere where agents enjoy some moral freedom.

This illustrates a general problem. Rawls offers only a theory of justice. He admits that there are other obligations. However, what we urgently need in the intergenerational context is some way to balance the competing obligations of justice: both against one another, and against other kinds of obligation. Justice as fairness provides no principled way to accomplish this balancing, as the just savings principle and the other principles of justice do not flow from a single original position. Justice between contemporaries is governed by a commitment to maximin, and the resulting priority to the worst-off. If we were to imagine each generation choosing its savings principle behind the (intra-generational) veil of ignorance, then the result would be extremely demanding. Yet Rawls's theory offers no alternative way for a generation to balance its principle of justice.

Rawls balances liberty and basic needs by assuming they do not conflict. He balances obligations to future generations and obligations to our contemporaries in the same way. These are optimistic assumptions. If we reject them, then Rawls, like Gauthier, cannot offer a coherent way to balance these competing demands.[50]

Like Gauthier's simple bargain, Rawls's simple lexical hierarchy comes apart under the pressure of future generations. The Original Position cannot deliver a definite defensible account of intergenerational justice, any more than could the state of nature.

We have focused thus far on a simple case, where the present generation both know that they can leave future generations better off than themselves,

---

[50] See chapter endnote F, p. 53.

and know how to do so. The introduction of uncertainty, and of the possibility of a severe intergenerational decline in well-being or access to primary goods, would create even more serious problems for Rawls's justice as fairness.

We return to Rawls's theory several times in the following chapters, when I compare it explicitly to my preferred version of Consequentialism. In the final chapter, I also offer an explanation of Rawls's inability to accommodate intergenerational justice. In the meantime, however, we leave the contract theory behind and begin our evaluation of the Consequentialist alternative.[51]

The challenge that Rawls sets for any political theory is to justify accumulation while giving adequate weight to the interests of the worst-off. In Chapter 7 we return to this challenge, to see if Consequentialism can meet it. Before we reach that stage, we must outline a Consequentialist account of value.

Endnotes

A. Recall that in Gauthier's baseline people already participate in pareto superior exchanges of goods, and respect one another's property rights. In a world where people die at different times, individuals' property rights must be distributed on their death. The possibilities are numerous. Let us consider five simple alternatives: (a) people dispose of their property as they see fit; (b) the property of the dead is redistributed to a specified individual (the next of kin); (c) the property of the dead is divided among all living persons; (d) the property of the dead becomes common property; and (e) the property of the dead is classified as unowned, and becomes the property of whoever first acquires it.

The Initial Bargaining Position represents a possible ongoing social arrangement, against which ongoing life under alternative social arrangements can be measured. As people will die in the Initial Bargaining Position, something must be done with their belongings. One of our five scenarios must prevail. If it is (a), then Gauthier's inheritance scheme is no improvement over the Initial Bargaining Position. Indeed, there may be no feasible alternatives to the Initial Bargaining Position. This would be a serious problem for Gauthier, for the following reason. In contrast to intuitive libertarians such as Robert Nozick, Gauthier claims to offer a Contractarian *foundation* for his political theory. The justification for his principles of justice is that agents in the Initial Bargaining

---

[51] As Axel Gosseries notes, once maximin is rejected, it is comparatively easy to construct a Consequentialist defence of accumulation, even for those committed to the priority of egalitarian values (Gosseries, 'What do we Owe the Next Generation(s)?', 320). The violation of egalitarian principles could then be justified as necessary to promote the greater realization of egalitarian values in the long run.

Position would agree to them. If there are no feasible alternatives to the Initial Bargaining Position, then the Lockean proviso does all the work in Gauthier's theory. Gauthier's proviso would then be a substantive moral principle, rather than a feature of the Contractarian bargaining situation. Morals by agreement will have collapsed into a doctrine of natural rights.

If (b) is the correct description of the Initial Bargaining Position, then a shift to inheritance would presumably disadvantage those who, in the Initial Bargaining Position, stand to gain more from redistribution than from inheritance. Gauthier argues that economic productivity overall is greater under a system of property rights which incorporates inheritance, but it does not follow that *everyone* will be better off under a system of inheritance than in the Initial Bargaining Position. Similar remarks apply to the other three possibilities. Gauthier's inheritance scheme is unlikely to be pareto superior to any of them.

B. Contractarians might reply that, in fact, everyone's survival is assured in the Initial Bargaining Position. In a pure market, we reach an equilibrium where supply equals demand. Suppliers of labour power will always find employment, so long as they are willing to meet the market price.

Unfortunately, this is insufficient. Even if we grant that, in a pure free market, everyone will have something they are able to sell, the market price of that commodity may be less than the market price of meeting the person's basic needs. If so, the person will die. Nothing in Gauthier's derivation, or in any other a priori discussion of the market, can rule out this empirical possibility. If civil society leads to a process of industrialization, as many of its defenders claim that it will, then the demand for unskilled labour may drop below the level at which the price of labour equals the cost of survival. Those without desired skills may be unable to earn a living in such a society. They may find little comfort in the fact that they die without ever having been 'unemployed'. As Amartya Sen has argued, 'even gigantic famines can result without any one's libertarian rights (including property rights) being violated' (Sen, *Development as Freedom*, 66. The comment is based on work presented in Sen, *Poverty and Famines*; and Drèze and Sen, *Hunger and Public Action*.) Contractarians might reply that, if my land holdings in the Initial Bargaining Position are sufficient to meet my needs, then, if I wish to ensure my continued survival, I need only retain those holdings. If things go badly for me in the marketplace, I can return to my farm and survive. Unfortunately, nothing in the structure of Gauthier's market-based economy ensures that I will be able to retain this option. Certainly, people in real-world societies who move from rural subsistence to the city in search of wealth often find that, when things turn bad, their previous sources of subsistence are unavailable to them. Farms and/or common property reserves may have been degraded, repossessed, sold off to meet expenses associated with earning a living in the marketplace, etc.

This last point is crucial. The claim that I will be better off in civil society than in the Initial Bargaining Position does not entail that my options in the former always include a return to the latter. By moving from the Initial Bargaining

Position to civil society, I may forfeit my ability to survive non-cooperatively. I may no longer have access to sufficient resources (or skills) to meet my basic needs without entering into market transactions with others. If my survival in the civil society is assured, then this loss may be of merely sentimental signifi-cance. However, if my survival is not assured, then the loss of a non-market backstop will loom large in my calculations. While the expected utility of civil society may be much higher than that of the Initial Bargaining Position, my chances of meeting my maintenance requirement may be reduced.

C. Gauthier assumes that the development of a capitalist economy is beneficial. In the case of distant future generations, this assumption is questionable. If every generation adopts a zero rate of savings, then resources will not accumulate and traditions of scientific and technological inquiry will never develop. This suggests that the human population would remain at a comparatively low level. Throughout human history, a few people would eke out a subsistence living. The renewable natural resources of the planet would thus never be strained. nor would human pollution upset the ecosystem. The standard of living enjoyed by distant future generations in such a scenario would be far below our own. However, it might be higher than the standard of living which distant future generations would enjoy if their predecessors practised unconstrained capitalism. The accumulation of capital which Gauthier applauds is, to a large extent, the accumulation of power to affect the world. Given the tendencies of human beings, we can hardly take it for granted that such power will always be used to the benefit of those who will follow. Gauthier follows Rawls in assum-ing that the accumulation of capital is bound to leave future generations better off than ourselves. As the debates between economic growth optimists and ecological pessimists shows, this assumption is at least highly questionable (Section 7.8).

An economic system such as that favoured by Gauthier is thus not necessarily superior to the Initial Bargaining Position. His own principles may not be feasi-ble. This raises a stark question: Are there *any* feasible systems of cooperation? It is by no means clear that there are. To be feasible, a system of cooperation must both accumulate resources *and* ensure that such accumulated resources will not be used to bring net harm to future generations, without leaving any individual in any generation any worse off than they would have been in the Initial Bargaining Position.

D. This endnote explains why the intergenerational original position must lead to one of these two extreme results. A rational person will prefer non-existence to a life that is not worth living. According to Rawls, those in the Original Position are exceptionally risk-averse. Therefore, they will prefer an empty world to a world with millions of extremely happy people and one person whose life is not worth living. (In the Original Position, no one would know whether they would be the one who ends up with the life not worth living.) Any population policy which brings into existence a new generation will produce some people whose lives are not worth living. Therefore, in the new Original Position, the only just population policy will be one which leads to universal non-existence.

We could only avoid this result by denying that any life is ever not worth living. Those in the Original Position would then want to maximize the number of people who exist, irrespective of the quality of their lives, as they will want to minimize their chances of failing to exist. They would thus favour a situation where a vast number of people each have a bare minimum of primary goods over a situation where a slightly smaller number of people each have an ample share of primary goods. It seems bizarre to say that justice requires such a result! (This puzzle is analogous to Parfit's Repugnant Conclusion (Section 3.2). (The discussion in this endnote owes much to Barry, *Theories of Justice*, 179–203.)

E. 'The first [liberty] principle may be preceded by a lexically prior principle requiring that basic needs be met, at least insofar as their being met is a necessary condition for citizens to understand and to be able fruitfully to exercise the basic rights and liberties' (Rawls, *Justice as Fairness: A Restatement* (2001). 44 n. 7.) Rawls makes similar concessions in *Political Liberalism*: 'The priority of liberty is not required under all conditions. I assume that it is required under what I shall call "reasonably favourable conditions", that is, under social circumstances which, provided the political will exists, permit the effective establishment and of full exercise of these liberties' (Rawls, *Political Liberalism* (1993), 297). See also ibid. 325: 'It will rightly be objected that I have not considered the provisions made for the material means required for persons to advance their good. Whether principles for the basic liberties and their priority are acceptable depends upon the complementing of such principles by others that can provide a fair share of these means.' Finally, in *The Law of Peoples*, we find the following: 'I agree [with Henry Shue], since the sensible and rational exercise of all liberties, of whatever kind, as well as the intelligent use of property, always implies having general all-purpose economic means.' (Rawls, *The Law of Peoples* (1999), 65).

F. Given his Kantian roots, it is not surprising that Rawls faces a problem here that also troubled Kant. For Kant, the establishment of a liberal society is the purpose of human history. However, this history can give rise to a liberal society only by trampling over the rights and needs of earlier generations. The liberal society can be established only through a series of actions that no rational agent would be permitted to perform. It would be wrong for any rational agent to treat human beings as means to the end of the creation of the liberal state, even though this is the way human history is designed to work. Kant is able to avoid this problem, to some extent, because he ascribes to nature a kind of teleology distinct from the purposiveness of a rational agent. The moral categories used to evaluate human actions are simply not applicable to the workings of nature through human history. (For Kant's original views, see Kant, *Religion within the Boundaries of Mere Reason*; Kant, *Idea for a Universal History with a Cosmopolitan Purpose*; Kant, *Reviews of Herder's Ideas*; and Kant, *Conjectures on the Beginning of Human History*. See also Wood, *Kant's Ethical Theory*, chs. 6 and 7.)

Rawls could try an analogous response. Because the accumulation phase occurs prior to the emergence of favourable conditions, the moral notions employed in a theory of justice cannot be applied to that phase of human history. While this might place Rawls at a disadvantage compared to moral theories (such as Consequentialism) that can apply during the accumulation phase, this need not be a decisive blow, especially if his theory offers a better account of justice for societies (such as our own) in favourable conditions.

While tempting, this Kantian response would sit very uneasily with Rawls's overall methodology, which is explicitly individualistic.

3

Value Theory

Both Simple and Moderate Consequentialists base morality on the promotion of value. Until we know what makes one outcome better than another, we cannot know what to do. Accordingly, Consequentialists focus on value theory, seeking a complete account of what makes different possible futures valuable, and of how to compare them. The literature abounds with puzzles—situations where common theories of value yield strange or paradoxical results. The debate has been organized around a challenge thrown down by Derek Parfit in 1984.[1] Through a series of puzzle cases, Parfit suggests that no current theory of value is adequate. As he puts it, Theory X has yet to be found.

Most Consequentialists employ one of two strategies. The *foundationalist* strategy begins by seeking to construct a complete value theory—assigning a cardinal value to each possible history of the world. Only once this task is completed can we turn our attention to the theory of right action. As Consequentialism is an account of the proper response to value, we cannot begin until we know (exactly) what value is. The *independence* strategy, by contrast, proceeds on the assumption that we can pursue the two inquiries independently of one another, and then bring the two completed theories (of value and of right action) together into a complete Consequentialist moral theory.

Both approaches assume we can construct a theory of value in isolation from our theory of right action. I believe this is a mistake. Our strongest moral convictions concern the morality of actions, not the values of possible worlds. Asked to compare two possible outcomes, we instinctively imagine an agent choosing between them. It is this choice that we evaluate, unconsciously appealing to our own preferred theory of right action. Our intuitive objection is typically to the combination of a particular value theory and a particular theory of right action, rather than to the value theory on its own. Attempts to construct an intuitive value theory thus operate (often implicitly) with a theory of right action. For most participants in the contemporary debate, this is Simple Consequentialism, where

---

[1] Parfit, *Reasons and Persons*, 351–441.

the right action in any situation is whatever produces the best consequences. Because it involves such a straightforward link between judgements of value and judgements of right action, Simple Consequentialism blurs the boundary between the two, enabling its proponents to overlook their commitment to it.

Unfortunately, as we saw in Chapter 1, Simple Consequentialism places unrelenting demands on all moral agents. We can only avoid an obligation to choose A over B if A is not better than B. Yet we often feel that there is no obligation to choose A over B because we value moral freedom, or because choosing A would violate an intuitively compelling deontological principle. Simple Consequentialism cannot accommodate these explanations. It thus places too much weight on value theory.

A much better strategy is to abandon our implicit commitment to Simple Consequentialism. Simple Consequentialism is implausible, both as a general moral theory and as an account of our obligations to future generations. A plausible Consequentialist theory of right action will not always oblige us to produce the best available outcome. Once we have a more moderate theory, we can avoid an obligation to choose A over B without denying that A is better than B. This flexibility enables us to dissolve the most troubling puzzles without abandoning standard Consequentialist value theory.

I aim to remain as agnostic as possible regarding value theory. I begin with the simplest, most mainstream theory of value, and introduce only those changes that are strictly necessary for the purposes of the moderate Consequentialist theory developed in this book

Any complete theory of value must answer three questions:

1. What makes an individual human life worth living?
2. How is the value of an outcome related to the values of the individual lives it contains?
3. What else (if anything) affects the value of an outcome?

I do not offer a complete theory of value.[2] Our focus in this chapter is on theories of aggregation: answers to the second question. We begin, however, with a sketch of the theory of well-being required by moderate Consequentialism.

---

[2] My attempt at a complete theory of value is presented in Mulgan, 'Valuing the Future' (draft MS). Several components are discussed in Mulgan, 'The Reverse Repugnant Conclusion'; Mulgan, 'What's Really Wrong with the Limited Quantity View?' (2001); Mulgan, 'Dissolving the Mere Addition Paradox' (2000); Mulgan, 'Transcending the Infinite Utility Debate' (2002); Mulgan, 'Two Parfit Puzzles' (2004); and Mulgan, 'Critical Notice of McMahan' (2004).

3.1. A Skeletal Account of Well-being

I argued in *The Demands of Consequentialism* that there is no one specific account of human well-being that must be adopted by proponents of the best forms of moderate Consequentialism. However, moderate Consequentialism does need a distinction between two components of well-being. Following Joseph Raz, I call these needs and goals.[3] Roughly speaking, needs are the biologically determined necessities of life, such as food, oxygen, or shelter. Goals, by contrast, are our chosen pursuits, projects, and endeavours, which give life much of its meaning and purpose. This distinction is not peculiar to some specific theory of value. On any plausible theory of the human good, one can generate something like the contrast between needs and goals. Furthermore, the Demandingness Objection itself presupposes the distinction between needs and goals.[4] In utilizing the distinction, therefore, we are simply exploring the implications of taking that objection seriously.

It seems obvious that there are some basic needs, determined by human physiology, such that any valuable human life is all but impossible if they are not met. (We saw in Chapter 2 that Gauthier and Rawls both underestimate the moral significance of needs. But neither denies their existence.) The more significant question is whether any viable theory of well-being can avoid recognizing the value and distinctness of goals. Goals are valuable in many different ways. The first is the value of what is produced, generated, or created by pursuit of a given goal. This may be a work of art, a public utility such as a dam, or a valuable relationship such as a friendship. A second way goals might contribute to the value of a life is through the value of the realization of the good of achievement within the agent's life. As a result of a valuable achievement, the agent's well-being may be increased, at least on many contemporary accounts of the human good.[5] A third value produced by goals is the satisfaction or pleasure the agent herself takes in her achievement. An agent who believes that her achievements are valuable may derive pleasure from those achievements, even if they are not actually valuable. Therefore, even those who seek to reduce well-being to pleasure can admit that different goals have different values for the agent herself, because of the diverse pleasures involved.[6]

---

[3] Raz, *The Morality of Freedom*, 290–1. For a full discussion of the physiological and environmental basis of basic needs, see Dasgupta, *Well-being and Destitution*, esp. ch 1. For more on their moral significance, see Braybrooke, *Meeting Needs*, ch. 4; Griffin, *Well-being*, 41–5; Mulgan, *The Demands of Consequentialism (2001)*, 173–9.   [4] Mulgan, *The Demands of Consequentialism* (2001), section 9.3.

[5] For defences of the claim that achievement is a distinct good, see Griffin, *Well-being*, 64–8; Hurka, *Perfectionism*, 39–51; and Raz, *The Morality of Freedom*, 288–307.

[6] For a full discussion of the issues involved here, see Hurka, *Perfectionism*, 84–98.

Many contemporary accounts of the human good accord intrinsic value to achievement and to the development of rational capacities. Any such account must make room for the value of goals. Furthermore, in a modern, liberal society such as ours, not even the most blinkered hedonist could avoid recognizing goals. In such societies, people gain most of their pleasure from goals they have chosen to pursue, rather than from the meeting of basic needs, or from tasks arbitrarily assigned to them. The pleasure of pursuing goals is very different from the pleasure produced when basic needs are met. As we are seeking a moral theory to guide our own delibera-tions and actions, we need not ask whether this is a contingent feature of modern societies, or a necessary feature of valuable human lives.[7] Only on a very limited view of the human good would no goals be valuable, especially in a society such as ours where the pursuit of goals plays such a central role in most of our individual lives and social institutions.[8]

One further distinguishing feature of goals is their intimate connection to human communities. No human agent can successfully pursue any valuable goals without some background social framework. Furthermore, most valu-able goals cannot even be imagined outside the context of some particular social framework. For instance, one cannot aim to become a lawyer outside of a certain type of legal framework. While many needs can only actually be met by social interaction, basic needs are not essentially tied in this way either to community in general or to particular human communities.[9]

The moral significance of this distinction is that the value of a goal depends upon how it is pursued, whereas the value of a need is not directly affected by the way it is met. The best way to promote the good with respect to needs is to directly meet those needs. One meets the needs of others much as one meets one's own needs. By contrast, promoting the pursuit of goals depends upon whose goals they are. The best way to promote the successful pursuit of one's own goals is to pursue them. One cannot pursue another person's goals for them. Until they choose their goals, there may be no way (even in principle) to determine which goals it would be best for

[7] For an argument that the commitment to freedom is not peculiarly Western, see Section 6.6.

[8] Raz provides several striking examples of what a life solely devoted to meeting one's own basic needs might be like: Raz, *The Morality of Freedom*, 373–4.

[9] This point is often obscured by a focus on derived needs rather than basic needs. Consider the controversy regarding the 'need' for literacy or access to television. Opponents of these needs point out that in previous centuries, not to mention prehistoric times, no one was literate or owned a television. Therefore, they conclude, there is no basic human need for such things. The most plausible response points to some more general, underlying need. Everyone needs the ability to participate in the culture around them. In a predominantly literate culture, this need can only be met if one is literate. In a televisual culture, it requires television. Because we cannot predict the future course of technology or other social changes, we cannot accurately predict the *derived needs* of those in the far future. (Mulgan, *The Demands of Consequentialism*, 198–9.)

them to have. Furthermore, a person's goals, once chosen, are often activities they seek to perform, rather than impersonal results which they seek to bring about.[10] Accordingly, the best ways to promote the successful pursuit of goals by others are: meet their needs, remove obstacles in their path, and then join their pursuit by adopting those goals for oneself. (We can treat the existence of an adequate social framework as something every agent needs, as it is a necessary precondition for agents to pursue any goals, and as every agent needs to pursue some goals.[11] Once we have made this assumption, an agent can only promote the successful pursuit of goals by others by meeting their needs, and perhaps by joining with them in pursuing those goals.)

The distinction between needs and goals will play a number of roles in this book. The first is that it provides a natural way to cash out the lexical level—a device needed to avoid the Repugnant Conclusion, to which we now turn.

3.2. The Repugnant Conclusion

Moderate Consequentialism requires a morally significant distinction between needs and goals. Armed with this minimal commitment, we now address our second question. How does the value of an outcome relate to the values of the lives within it? We thus turn to the question of aggregation, the site of much contemporary controversy.

The simplest theory of aggregation is the Total View, where one outcome is better than another if and only if it contains more happiness. (I use 'happiness' as a placeholder, as it is more elegant than Parfit's more accurate 'whatever makes life worth living'.) The basic argument for the Total View is simple. For any x, if x is valuable, then more x is better than less. This starting point also makes historical sense, as the Total View has been the most popular account of value in the utilitarian tradition.[12]

Unfortunately, the Total View produces some intuitively problematic results, especially in Different Number Choices. I focus on the most famous of these results. Under the Total View one possible outcome is better than another if and only if it contains more happiness. If the best way to increase total happiness is to greatly increase the number of people while greatly reducing their average happiness, then the Total View must advocate population growth. Derek Parfit uses this feature of the Total View to generate the following conclusion.[13]

---

[10] See Raz, *The Morality of Freedom*, 306–7; and Hurka, *Perfectionism*, 59.

[11] See also Raz, *The Morality of Freedom*, 199–206; and Scheffler, *Human Morality* (1992), 138–43.

[12] At least among philosophers. Economists often favour the Average View discussed in endnote A of this chapter.   [13] Parfit, *Reasons and Persons*, 388.

The Repugnant Conclusion.   Under the Total View, for any possible population of at least ten billion people, all with a very high quality of life, there must be some much larger imaginable population whose existence, if other things are equal, would be better, even though its members have lives that are barely worth living.

Begin with a world where ten billion people all have extremely good lives. Call it A. Imagine a second world, with twice as many people each of whom is more than half as happy as the people in A. Call this new world B. Total happiness in B exceeds that in A. Now repeat this process until we reach a world where in a vast population each has a life that is barely worth living. Call this world Z. As each step increases total happiness, Z must be better than A.

Parfit finds this conclusion 'intrinsically repugnant'.[14] If this is a consequence of the Total View, then the Total View is an unacceptable moral theory. The Repugnant Conclusion is one of the organizing problem of contemporary Consequentialist value theory.[15]

Two broad strategies emerge from the vast literature on the Repugnant Conclusion.

1. Restructure our value theory so that A is no longer worse then Z. (Typically, we seek a value theory where A is better than Z.)
2. Undermine Parfit's intuition that the conclusion, as originally presented, is repugnant.

I explore both options. My focus in this book is on the second, as I present my views on value theory at length elsewhere. The two options are most powerful if taken together, as the shift from Simple Consequentialism to moderate Consequentialism both opens up new options for dissolving Parfit's intuition and also complicates the relationship between value theory and the theory of right action.

Many Consequentialists argue that we should embrace the Repugnant Conclusion. Parfit's intuition is thus not decisive. However, it is widely shared. Furthermore, I shall argue that Parfit's intuition has strong affinities with a general picture of morality we must adopt if we are to resolve the Demandingness Objection—or indeed to practise moral philosophy at all.

[14] Parfit, *Reasons and Persons*, 390.

[15] For critical discussions of Parfit's Repugnant Conclusion, see: Cowen, 'What do we Learn from the Repugnant Conclusion?'; Dasgupta, 'Savings and Fertility: Ethical Issues'; Feldman, 'Justice, Desert and the Repugnant Conclusion' (2002); Locke, 'The Parfit Population Problem'; Mulgan, 'The Reverse Repugnant Conclusion' (2002); Ng, 'What should we do about Future Generations?'; Portmore, 'Does the Total Principle Have Any Repugnant Implications?'; Ryberg, 'Is the Repugnant Conclusion Repugnant?'; Ryberg, 'Parfit's Repugnant Conclusion'; and Sikora, 'Classical Utilitarianism and Parfit's Repugnant Conclusion: A Reply to McMahan'; Ryberg and Tannsjo (eds.), *The Repugnant Conclusion: Essays on Population Ethics*.

On the other hand, we must be careful not to mislocate the intuitive force of the Repugnant Conclusion. In particular, it is not obvious that what is really troubling us is the judgement that Z is better than A.

One striking feature of the literature on future generations is the widely divergent intuitions people report in relation to puzzle cases, especially the Repugnant Conclusion. One plausible explanation is that people are focusing, perhaps unconsciously, on different questions. A common defence of the Total View argues that Parfit's intuition confuses a comparison of the impersonal value of A and Z with a range of other questions, such as the following: Would we rather live in A or Z? If we were choosing between A and Z, which would we choose? If we were in A, would we be obliged to turn A into Z? For instance, Yew-Kwan Ng objects that, when we consider the Repugnant Conclusion, we privilege our own perspective and are guilty of 'misplaced partiality'.[16] We picture the A lives as similar to our own, and imagine the A people choosing between A and Z. If we were more impartial, we might see that Z contains more total value than A, and is thus preferable. Ng concludes that the Repugnant Conclusion is not repugnant. Conversely, if we are focusing on intuitions concerning right action, and if our account of right action permits partiality, then our tendency to privilege A over Z may be legitimate. Moderate Consequentialism puts Ng's argument on its head. The decisive intuition is that it is repugnant to force agents to choose Z over A.

The truly decisive intuition behind the Repugnant Conclusion concerns a separate conclusion, resulting from the combination of the Total View with Simple Consequentialism.

The Repugnant Obligation Conclusion. If any agent faces a choice between two actions whose outcomes correspond to Parfit's A-world and Z-world, then she is obliged to opt for Z over A. This remains true even if the result is a Z-life rather than an A-life both for herself and for all her nearest and dearest. For instance, if an agent can transform an A-world into a Z-world by a process that creates a new species of Z-creature while greatly reducing the well-being of everyone who already exists, then she ought to do so.

In the Repugnant Obligation Conclusion all existing people are sacrificed to further the interests of people who otherwise would not have existed at all. This is much more counterintuitive than the original Demandingness Objection, where Simple Consequentialism tells us to sacrifice ourselves to meet urgent needs that would otherwise go unmet.

---

[16] Ng, 'What should we do about Future Generations?'

The Repugnant Obligation Conclusion arises from the combination of the Total View and Simple Consequentialism. There are thus two (possibly complementary) responses.

1. Abandon the Total View and reject the original Repugnant Conclusion. I explore the most promising option (the adoption of a lexical level), and outline the problems it encounters.
2. Abandon Simple Consequentialism. Even if the Total View is the correct account of impersonal value to place at the foundation of our Consequentialist moral theory, individual agents are still permitted to act *as if* some alternative account of value were correct. This does not mean that agents must consciously adopt some particular value theory other than the the Total View. However, it does mean that the best theory of right action will include something analogous to the adoption of an alternative value theory. Once again, I explore this option using the most plausible alternative to the Total View: the Lexical View.

In any moderate Consequentialist theory there are various places where a judgement favouring A over Z might feature:

1. in the foundational value theory—the account of the impersonal value of outcomes;
2. as a judgement that agents are permitted to opt for A over Z;
3. somewhere in between.

Option (3) will prove to be crucial. The two forms of moderate Consequentialism we will examine in subsequent chapters both encourage agents to adopt a certain perspective and certain values. The theory of value a Consequentialist theory tells agents to adopt may not be that same Consequentialism's foundational theory. To adopt the terminology made famous by Sidgwick, our foundational value theory is an attempt to see value from 'the point of view of the universe'. Under moderate Consequentialism, the agent may be encouraged to adopt an account of value that also takes account of her point of view as an individual moral agent. The crucial point for our present purposes is that a lexical level might feature either in the foundational theory only, or in the agent's value theory, or both.

The Repugnant Conclusion has a structure common to many objections to Consequentialism. We are presented with a conflict between a particular theory of value, telling us that one outcome is better than another, and a strong intuition to the contrary. The intuition itself is often simply taken as a datum. This is a mistake. We have seen one mistake: assuming that the intuition deals with value when it may deal with permission or obligation.

However, even within the realm of value, intuitions rest on unstated theoretical presuppositions, especially theories of well-being. To take the intuition seriously is to take those views seriously. I shall argue that, in the Repugnant Conclusion, our intuitions presuppose a certain difference in kind between life in A and life in Z. To take the conclusion seriously is thus to take that underlying assumption seriously.

3.3. The Zero Level

By definition, the Z-lives are just worth living. If we are to evaluate the Z-world, then we need to know what such lives are like. This brings us to the notion of the 'zero level'. Roughly speaking, the Total View tells us to create extra people who will be happy. Whenever an agent considers adding an extra life, we need to know whether this would raise or lower the total amount of happiness. If the net effect on already existing people will be zero, then a given act of creation will raise total happiness if and only if the extra life itself will be better than zero. Compare two possible outcomes: both contain Amy, whose life is worth x. The second outcome also contains Bob, whose life is worth y. The second outcome will contain more total happiness if and only if y is greater than zero.

Some have argued that we can use the location of the zero level to avoid the Repugnant Conclusion.[17] If the zero level is higher than Parfit's discussion suggests, then the Z-lives may be comparatively good, and thus it is no longer repugnant to suggest that Z is better than A.

Sadly, this simple solution does not work. We can see this by beginning with the most pessimistic view of human life: that all possible human lives are below the zero level.[18] This would dissolve the Repugnant Conclusion altogether, as Parfit's A and Z worlds become impossible. But now consider the following claim.

The Reverse Repugnant Conclusion. Let A-minus be a world where ten billion people live long lives of unalloyed excruciating agony. There will be some other world (Z-minus) where a vast number of people have lives

---

[17] For such arguments, see Dasgupta, 'Savings and Fertility: Ethical Issues'; Ng, 'What should we do about Future Generations?'; and Ryberg, 'Is the Repugnant Conclusion Repugnant?' For critical discussion, see Mulgan, 'The Reverse Repugnant Conclusion' (2002).

[18] For instance, Cristoph Fehige argues that, while the satisfaction of a desire cannot leave the agent any better off than she would have been if she had never had the desire in the first place, the frustration of desires always moves one further below the zero level. As every actual human life includes frustrated desires, every life is worse than no life at all. No human life could possibly be as worthwhile as the lives in Parfit's Z-world, as no life could rise above the zero level. (Fehige, 'A Pareto Principle for Possible People'.)

which are almost but not quite worth living, and *Z-minus will be worse than A-minus*.

The Total View implies the Reverse Repugnant Conclusion, just as it implies the original Repugnant Conclusion. A Total View incorporating the extreme pessimistic view implies that a world where ten billion people suffer dreadfully is *better* than a world where a vast number of people are better off than any human being has ever been. Even by the standards of Consequentialist moral philosophy, this is a strange result.[19]

The Reverse Repugnant Conclusion is easily avoided. For instance, we could set the zero level so low that any possible human life is worth living, no matter how much pain and suffering it contains. Unfortunately, this would make the Repugnant Conclusion especially repugnant. If all possible human lives are above zero, and the Z-lives are just above zero, then the Z-lives are among the worst imaginable human lives.

We can escape the Repugnant Conclusion by raising the zero level, and the Reverse Repugnant Conclusion by lowering it, but these two strategies are obviously mutually exclusive.[20] Any credible theory must allow that there are some actual human lives below the zero level, and some above. The precise location of the zero level is a central task for any complete value theory, and we will return to it several times in subsequent chapters. However, moderate Consequentialism as such does not require any particular specification of the zero level.

3.4. The Lexical View

In this section, I explore the most plausible attempt to restructure value theory.[21] I begin by asking when and why the Repugnant Conclusion might be repugnant. The Repugnant Conclusion is under-described. Some possible instances of the conclusion are not repugnant at all. For instance, suppose that A and Z are both inhabited by the same simple creature. This creature has no memory, and experiences a set quantity of pleasure in each time period. The only difference is that the creatures in A live much longer than those in Z. Each A-life lasts a hundred years, while each life in Z lasts a few minutes. The A-lives and Z-lives thus differ only by degree. An A-life is only

---

[19] Fehige's own overall moral theory does not quite yield the result in the text, as he replaces the Total View with a set of pareto principles. These merely imply that the two worlds (A-minus and Z-minus) cannot be ranked. This seems implausible enough.

[20] I argue elsewhere that the Reverse Repugnant Conclusion also undermines a number of rivals to the Total View, notably the Critical Level View and the Valueless Level View. (Mulgan, 'The Reverse Repugnant Conclusion'.) (For references to these alternatives, see endnote A to this chapter.)

[21] See chapter endnote A, p. 80.

better than a Z-life because it contains more of the same. Each A-life can be partitioned into segments, such that each segment lasts ten years and contains 10 per cent of the total value of the A-life. We can then compare a single A-life with a world containing ten lives each equivalent in value to a segment of A-life. *Ex hypothesi*, the A-life and the set of segment lives are equivalent in value. We can then repeat this process, by partitioning each of the segment lives. Eventually we reach a comparison between a single A-life and a very large set of Z-lives, where each Z-life is very short. If each A-life is equivalent to a set of n Z-lives, and Z itself contains more than n Z-lives for each A-life, then Z is better than A. Therefore, the Repugnant Conclusion is dissolved.

This partition argument plays down the significance of differences between lives. Its crucial premise is that each individual life is (only) as valuable as a series of lives of lesser duration.[22] This premise may seem to embody an implausible account of well-being. However, while certainly controversial, this central premise is merely a necessary result of taking seriously our initial assumption that the A- and Z-lives differ only in degree. If we reject the premise, then we should reject the assumption. The assumption that the A- and Z-lives differ only in degree is thus much more restrictive than it might initially appear.

If the lives in A and Z differed only by degree, the Repugnant Conclusion would be unobjectionable. Our intuitive reaction to the contrary thus strongly suggests that different human lives can, and do, differ in kind. A single long life might contain valuable connections which, as a matter of fact, cannot arise between members of a set of shorter lives. If A-lives and Z-lives differ in kind, then A may be better than Z.

Yet a simple difference in kind also seems unproblematic. Suppose A contains ten billion angels while Z contains a vast number of slugs. In this case, most would conclude that A is better than Z. The obvious solution is to posit a lexical priority between the lives of angels and those of slugs, so that the value of a sufficient number of angelic lives trumps any number of slug lives. When the two types of creature differ so starkly, the Repugnant Conclusion easily dissolves.

To illustrate this notion of lexicality, suppose you believe that both Mozart and Muzak are valuable. Listening to either type of music is better than nothing. Someone offers you the following choice: you can either live for one day listening to Mozart's music or live as long as you like listening to Muzak. You opt for the former. This might be because you believe you

[22] In Mulgan, 'Two Parfit Puzzles' (2004), I explore the parallel between this premise and Parfit's Reductionist account of personal identity (Parfit, *Reasons and Persons*, Pt. 3). I raise the possibility that, for a consistent Reductionist, the Repugnant Conclusion is not repugnant.

would reach Muzak saturation at a certain point, so that further Muzak would have no value. Alternatively, you might believe that every additional Muzak experience is positive, but that *no amount* of that kind of pleasure could match the value of the smallest amount of Mozart. If so, you believe that the value of Mozart is lexically prior to that of Muzak. Lexicality is a very popular notion among philosophers. We now ask whether it can help us resolve the Repugnant Conclusion.[23]

We need to distinguish lexicality within a life from lexicality between lives. The former holds that a certain kind of experience or achievement has lexical priority over a lower pleasure or accomplishment. A stock philosopher's example is that no amount of successful grass blade counting adds as much to the value of an individual's life as proving an important mathematical theorem. The latter view is that one sort of life has lexical priority over another: the life of a single human being is more valuable than the lives of any number of contented slugs.

If the components of the Z-lives are the same as the components of the A-lives, and the only difference is that the latter contain more of the same good things (or fewer of the same bad things), then the idea of a lexical priority among lives begins to seem rather odd. Even if the value of a life is not simply the sum of the values of its parts, it is hard to see how different combinations of the same elements could yield a lexical hierarchy.

The two kinds of lexicality are thus linked. Lexicality between lives is hard to motivate unless the better lives contain some positive component of a kind not found in the lesser lives, or the lesser lives contain a distinctive negative component. If both Z-lives and A-lives contain both Muzak and Mozart, and differ only in the quantities of each, then why can't any given number of A-lives be outweighed by a suitably large group of Z-lives? A lexical gap between lives requires additional values in the superior lives. These additional values might be emergent, in the sense that a century of listening to Mozart might give rise to a level of appreciation unavailable in a life containing only a few isolated Mozart moments.

A lexical gap is plausible only if we are dealing with lives of different kinds. It thus provides a solution to only some versions of the Repugnant Conclusion. Yet, as we have just seen, these are precisely the situations where the Repugnant Conclusion is most repugnant. Suppose, for instance, that the creatures in A and Z belong to entirely different species. Perhaps the former are flourishing human beings while the latter are slugs. Lexicality seems plausible in such a case, and the Repugnant Conclusion does seem

---

[23] For an introduction to lexical accounts of well-being in general, Griffin, *Well-being*, 85–9. On lexical solutions to the Repugnant Conclusion, see Crisp, 'Utilitarianism and the Life of Virtue'; Griffin, *Well-being*, 338–40 n. 27; Parfit, 'Overpopulation and the Quality of Life'.

repugnant. Suppose each slug in Z experiences only a minimal level of the most basic positive sensation, while each human being lives a life full of achievement, and experiences a wide range of sophisticated pleasures. Ten billion of the latter lives are worth more than any number of the former.

Embracing a lexical gap requires some departure from the Total View. There are many ways to depart, and thus many different alternatives to the Total View. We begin with a general claim.[24]

The Lexical Claim.   If x is lexically more valuable than y, then, once we have a *sufficient* amount of x, no amount of y can compensate for a *significant* reduction in x.

The Lexical Claim is sufficient to avoid the Repugnant Conclusion, so long as the lives in A are lexically more valuable than those in Z, and so long as ten billion lives gives us a sufficient amount of the value contained in those lives.

I shall use 'the Lexical View' as a generic name for any position that departs from the Total View by endorsing the Lexical Claim. At this stage, we leave open the possibility of further departures from the Total View. (In particular, we may need to add an explicit egalitarian element to our value theory, to compensate for the introduction of lexicality. See Section 3.6.)

The Repugnant Conclusion seems entirely dissolved. Either the creatures in A and those in Z differ merely by degree, or they differ in kind. If the difference is one of degree, then Z is better than A. It is thus no objection to the Total View that it yields this conclusion. Once we replace the Total View with a Lexical View, the Repugnant Conclusion disappears.

Unfortunately, things are not so simple. In the original Repugnant Conclusion, both A and Z contain human beings. The contrast between flourishing and destitute humans is unlike either of our simple cases. On the one hand, flourishing human lives are significantly different from deprived human lives, so that we may feel that the former are lexically more valuable than the latter. On the other hand, we can picture a continuum between the two kinds of human lives. The Repugnant Conclusion is problematic when the creatures in A and Z appear to differ *both* in degree *and* in kind.

3.5. Two Objections

We now address the two most prominent objections to the Lexical View. Parfit agrees that the Lexical View offers the best solution to the

---

[24] I owe the main ideas behind this formulation to conversations with John Broome and James Griffin. (See also Griffin, *Well-being*, 85–9.)

Repugnant Conclusion. However, he then raises a serious problem for any such view:

The Continuuum Objection.

The good things in life do not come in quite different categories. . . . Mozart and Muzak . . . seem to be in quite different categories. But there is a fairly smooth continuum between these two. Though Haydn is not as good as Mozart, he is very good. And there is other music which is not far below Haydn's, other music not far below this, and so on. Similar claims apply to the other best experiences, activities, and personal relationships, and to the other things which give most to the value of life. Most of these things are on fairly smooth continua, ranging from the best to the least good. Since this is so, it may be hard to defend the view that what is best has more value than any amount of what is nearly as good.[25]

The fact that the most valuable possible experiences seem to shade indistinguishably into the least valuable experiences undermines the claim that lives containing the former might be lexically superior to lives containing the latter.

The Elitist Objection.   The Lexical View also seems to imply a particularly unpleasant form of anti-egalitarianism.[26] Consider the following two possible outcomes.

> *A+ world.*   Twenty billion people exist. Ten billion have an extremely high level of well-being, while the other ten billion are considerably less well-off, though their lives are worth living.

> *B world.*   Twenty billion people exist. Everyone has the same level of well-being, between the two levels represented in A+. Average and total happiness are both higher than in A+.

If the better-off people in A+ are above the lexical level, and those in B are below it, then the Lexical View implies that A+ is better than B. Yet this seems outrageous. B contains greater total happiness, greater average happiness, much more equality, and a much higher standard of living for the worst-off. Surely B is much better than A+, rather than worse.

These two objections are related. The first argues that there is nowhere to put a lexical divide in a world where value supervenes on continuous natural properties. The second argues that, wherever we do put the lexical level, it cannot bear the weight placed upon it. Until we have addressed the

---

[25] Parfit, 'Overpopulation and the Quality of Life', 164.

[26] This objection is based on one presented in Parfit, 'Overpopulation and the Quality of Life'. It leads to one component of Parfit's Mere Addition Paradox (Parfit, *Reasons and Persons*, 419 ff.). I discuss this paradox in Mulgan 'Valuing the Future' (draft MS), and Mulgan, 'Dissolving the Mere Addition Paradox' (2000).

Continuum Objection, we cannot hope to solve the Elitist Objection. On the other hand, we might hope that a solution to the Continuum Objection will itself provide a solution to the Elitist Objection.

To illustrate this connection, consider a case involving angels and ants. Here we have no continuum between the lives of the two kinds of beings. The Elitist Objection also dissolves, as it is no longer objectionable to claim that a world containing equal numbers of angels and (sad) ants is preferable to a world with twice as many (happier) ants.

The Consequentialist literature on future generations contains many proofs of 'impossibility theorems'. These purport to show that no value theory can possibly meet a set of intuitively plausible criteria.[27] In effect, these proofs all formalize the intuitions behind the Repugnant Conclusion and the Elitist Objection, exploiting an irreconcilable clash between a desire to avoid the Repugnant Conclusion and a commitment to some principle of egalitarianism. These results are unsurprising, as the best solution to the Repugnant Conclusion is the introduction of a lexical level, which is by definition anti-egalitarian.

The impossibility theorems show that, under their most natural initial formulations, two common intuitions are incompatible. However, it does not follow that an intuitively satisfactory value theory cannot be constructed. We need to distinguish between our initial intuitions, however strong, and the intuitions that would survive a process of reflective equilibrium. In any particular case, either the lexical level can be adequately justified or it cannot. If it can, then the Elitist Objection will also dissolve, and the appeal of egalitarianism is diminished. If it cannot, then the Repugnant Conclusion is no longer repugnant. Either way, we will have moved from a pair of irreconcilable intuitions to an intuitively coherent total picture. Or, at least, so I shall argue.

3.6. An Egalitarian Lexical View

We naturally think that, in some very important sense, all human beings are equal. We object to giving *priority* to the interests of the well-off, the powerful, or the elite. We are likely to be suspicious of the Lexical View on these grounds. In practice, however, the Lexical View may actually have extremely *egalitarian* implications. Parfit's brief discussion suggests that a life falls below the lexical level as soon as the best things in life disappear, where the best things are very narrowly defined (the loss of Mozart's music

---

[27] Two classic discussions are Cowen, 'What do we Learn from the Repugnant Conclusion?'; and Ng, 'What should we do about Future Generations? Impossibility of Parfit's Theory X'.

is his stock example). The lexical level need not be so high. Our first step is to flesh out the Lexical View. Our account of well-being suggests that the lexical level will be defined in terms of the successful autonomous pursuit of independently valuable projects. We could identify the lexical level, not with the best possible particular experiences or accomplishments, but with certain central human capacities, such as autonomy, the ability to pursue valuable goals, etc. A human life is above the lexical level if and only if it is a reasonably successful autonomous life. While the boundaries of the concept are vague, and while some aspects of autonomy and success clearly do admit of degrees, our primary notion of an autonomous life is not easily divisible. A person either is autonomous or she is not. We cannot draw sharp boundaries, but our use of the concept suggests that a morally significant divide exists.

A lower lexical level means that, in practice, the lexical level is most likely to come into play in situations where a few people fall below the lexical level in a society where most people live above it. A Lexical View may then give priority to the worst-off people, as it is better to raise everyone above the lexical level than to confer additional benefits on those already above it. The Lexical View thus supports the intuitions that drive people to favour egalitarianism over the Total View.

This may seem too quick. Nothing we have said so far rules out the possibility that an additional benefit to someone already above the lexical level might outweigh the step that crosses the lexical threshold. For instance, suppose we have the option of doubling the value of the life of someone currently above the lexical level. This seems to add much more value than taking someone whose life is barely worth living and raising him above the lexical level. In this case, the Lexical View will be anti-egalitarian.

In response, we must note that a commitment to the lexical level does not completely determine our theory of value. We could combine a lexical level with an explicit commitment to egalitarianism: even if it is possible to provide a greater benefit to those above the lexical level than to those below it, we might decide that the best outcome results from conferring the lesser benefit to those who are worse off. Many Consequentialists depart from the Total View by adding explicit distribution-sensitive elements. The adoption of a lexical level is no barrier to this.

If we define our lexical level in terms of the successful pursuit of valuable goals, then certain connections between goals, agency, and community will reinforce the egalitarian implications of the Lexical View.

It is not clear whether a perfectly isolated agent is possible even in theory. Many philosophers argue that the very possibility of thought is conceptually dependent upon interaction with others.[28] What is clear is that, in practice, no human being could develop or exercise the capacity for autonomous choice in complete isolation. A human being can only have a worthwhile life if she belongs, as an agent, to a community.[29]

If an adequate social framework is not available, then no one is above the lexical level, and we would do best to create a suitable framework if at all possible. Conversely, if some people are above the lexical level, then an adequate social framework exists. The best thing we can do is to extend it, enabling those currently below the lexical level to rise above it. (This style of argument plays a key role in subsequent chapters.)

Suppose our universe contains two inhabited planets, one like Parfit's A-world and the other like his Z-world. If all creatures on both planets are ordinary human beings, then it is almost certainly better to transform Z by raising the Z-lives above the lexical level than by assisting the inhabitants of A.

3.7. Beyond Value Theory

The Elitist Objection thus does not show that there cannot be a plausible Lexical View. However, problems still remain. Unless we can dissolve the Continuum Objection, any precise location of the lexical level will seem arbitrary. Furthermore, even if we dissolve some versions of the Elitist Objection, others still remain. For instance, the Lexical View must say that it is better to raise a single person above the lexical level than to benefit any number of worse-off people, if one is unable to raise them above that level also. Combined with Simple Consequentialism, this judgement may be unpalatable. Moderate Consequentialism offers an alternative way to dissolve the impossibility results: by reconstructing one (or both) of the intuitions in terms of right action rather than outcome value. We could then retain the full force of both intuitions.

Consequentialists seeking a value theory have two options:

1. Retain the Total View: no lexical level, embrace the Repugnant Conclusion. If we are escape the Repugnant Obligation Conclusion, this value theory must be combined with a moderate Consequentialism

---

[28] See e.g. Pettit, *The Common Mind*, pt. 3; and Mulgan, *The Demands of Consequentialism* (2001), 254–5.

[29] These connections between goals and community explain why the claim that Z is better than A often seems less repugnant when A contains a tiny number of people instead of 10 billion. We cannot have a single life above the lexical level. We must have a human community where at least a significant number of lives are above that level. As we imagine progressively smaller populations for the A-world, at some point those populations become too small to support a broad range of goals, or to permit the development of autonomous agency. We have then ceased to imagine a world where people live above the lexical level.

giving strong permissions to favour one's own interests and perspective over impersonal value. Z is better than A, but agents can opt for A over Z in some circumstances. Just as only the lexical level avoids the Repugnant Conclusion, only a moderate Consequentialism allowing agents to act *as if* they adopted the Lexical View will suffice to avoid the Repugnant Obligation Conclusion.

2. Embrace the lexical level: reject the Repugnant Conclusion, and accept some anti-egalitarian value judgements. To yield a plausible overall moral theory, the value theory must be combined with a strongly egalitarian moderate Consequentialist account of right action, limiting the ability of agents to favour those above the lexical level at the expense of those below. We might admit that A+ is better than B, but argue that we are not obliged (and perhaps not even permitted) to produce the better outcome in this case.

The Total View and the Lexical View tell us what makes one outcome better than another. Neither directly tells us what to do. Furthermore, neither value theory combines plausibly with Simple Consequentialism. Accordingly, in either case a concern for fairness or equality might trump a concern for goodness, even in a theory ultimately founded on Consequentialist principles.

Here is my overall plan:

1. I aim to leave open the possibility that the Lexical View can be defended as our foundational value theory.
2. I aim to show that the best form of moderate Consequentialism will instruct agents to adopt a lexical level, whether or not it is included in our foundational value theory.

Moderate Consequentialists come to consideration of future generations already committed to the general proposition that agents are not always required to attempt to view the world from the perspective of impersonal value. So the present strategy represents no radical new departures for them.

Moderate Consequentialism allows agents to privilege their own projects, values, and perspectives. If a judgement in favour of A over Z reflects such bias, then it may permit, and even encourage, such judgements. If the lexical level is implicit in these judgements, then Moderate Consequentialism will encourage agents to use the lexical level.

The basic argument for the lexical level is simple. Unless agents operate (albeit unconsciously) with the notion of a lexical divide between A-lives and Z-lives, their permission to opt for an A-life for themselves, their nearest and dearest, or their society, can always be over-ruled if a sufficiently large number of Z-lives are at stake.

3.7.1. A Kantian Defence

Our general defence of the lexical level could be cashed out in several different ways. The most ambitious is to claim that moral agents must adopt a lexical level. This argument might draw on the Kantian notion that deliberation (or, 'the adoption of the standpoint of practical reason') carries commitments that theoretical speculation can avoid. A good example of this style of argument is Christine Korsgaard's claim, in response to Parfit's account of the link between Reductionism and Utilitarianism, that the fact that we can do metaphysics without supposing deep further facts about the identity of persons does not mean that ethics can be equally parsimonious. To deliberate, one must see oneself as a unified conscious agent whose projects and identity endure through time.[30]

I argue elsewhere that certain concepts are especially salient for any agent adopting the practical perspective: agency, autonomy, and community. These generate a cluster of beliefs that underpins our intuitive reactions to the Repugnant Conclusion, the Compulsory Reproduction Objection, and the Demandingness Objection. It reflects a set of intuitions that, while not decisive, are certainly very powerful.

The transcendental version of this argument holds that the very adoption of the practical standpoint requires one to accord one's own agency, and the agency of other similar agents, a different order of value from lives lacking agency. One cannot see oneself as an autonomous agent and, at the same time, see the value of one's life as falling on a continuum containing lives lacking agency or inanimate matter. We thus have both a natural account of the lexical level and a new reason to adopt such a level in the first place.

The practical standpoint may also give priority to some intuitions over others. The practical standpoint is primarily concerned with action. If our intuitions are driven by that standpoint, then we should expect them to deal principally with the rightness and wrongness of actions, and only derivatively with the value of outcomes. I have already suggested that this is precisely what we do find.

---

[30] Korsgaard, 'Personal Identity and the Unity of Agency'. Parfit presents his Reductionism in Parfit, *Reasons and Persons*, 199–347. For a fuller presentation of the arguments in the text, see Mulgan, 'Two Parfit Puzzles'(2004).

3.7.2. A Demandingness Defence

Many philosophers are unconvinced by any Kantian transcendental argument. So I shall place no weight on such arguments here. Instead, I focus on two more modest Consequentialist alternatives. The first claims that the successful pursuit of valuable projects requires the adoption of a lexical level. One cannot pursue such projects and place their value on a continuum with the value of inanimate matter. This flows from the more general point that one cannot meaningfully pursue projects and adopt the point of view of the universe. As a worthwhile life requires the successful pursuit of independently valuable goals, human beings are unlikely to successfully lead valuable lives unless they adopt a lexical level based on agency and autonomy.

Perhaps Simple Consequentialists, and others who embrace an extremely demanding morality, can avoid the lexical level altogether. However, moderate moral theorists must allow agents to live worthwhile lives. If such lives require the adoption of a lexical level, then moderate Consequentialism must permit (indeed, encourage) that adoption.

If moderate Consequentialism encourages agents to act in ways that privilege their own interests, then it may also encourage them to privilege their own perspective in their evaluations, at least in some contexts. In particular, agents may be permitted to adopt different interpretations of the lexical level for different purposes. An agent consulting her own interests may find a lexical level helpful: as a threshold below which she does not wish the value of her life to drop, or a threshold to which she aspires.

3.7.3. A Practical Defence

Even if the decisive intuition behind the Repugnant Obligation Conclusion does not support these strong arguments, it does suggest that it is very psychologically difficult for human beings to deliberate without a lexical level. If we want either to obtain the best consequences from the deliberations of human beings and/or to encourage human beings to deliberate in a psychologically healthy manner, then we should advise them to adopt such a lexical level.

The rest of this book explores various arguments along these lines, focusing on the significance of the lexical level for the morality of reproduction and for broader social issues regarding future generations. Our ultimate preference for Rule Consequentialism over the Hybrid View reflects a judgement that a collective version of this final argument (based on the consequences of the general adoption of a lexical level) is the most secure.

If we seek a coherent account of the comparative values of possible outcomes, then we need a single lexical level. Even if we grant that the practical standpoint requires that we view the moral world through a lexical lens, it does not follow that there is any *particular* lexical lens through with which we must view the moral world. (Analogously, one might accept that any perceiver must impose *some* spatio-temporal structure on her experiences, without accepting that all perceivers must impose the same structure.) The same goes for Consequentialist arguments encouraging agents to adopt a lexical level in their deliberations, or to privilege their own perspectives. There is no guarantee that everyone will adopt the same lexical level. Indeed, the perspectives of different rational agents may be irreconcilable.[31] Those whose lives resemble the lives in the A world might prefer A to B, while those whose lives resemble B regard B as superior to either A or C, and those with Z-like lives prefer Z over all less populous alternatives.

There are two solutions. Our Consequentialist moral theory might be built on a foundational value theory that itself reflects the value of agency and autonomy, and includes a lexical level that applies to all rational agents, or at least to everyone in a particular community, if we decide it is reasonable to limit the scope of Consequentialist concern in this way.[32]

The second solution is simply to accept that the lexical level has no place in a foundational value theory. Our Consequentialist moral theory would then include a foundational value theory without a lexical level, that is prior to the adoption of the practical perspective. This foundation could be purely naturalistic, if a naturalistic account of value turns out to be possible. Consequentialism would then provide a bridge from a world of continuous natural properties to the realm of practical deliberation, via the necessary features of the deliberations of embodied moral agents.

After all, we should not expect all agents to adopt exactly the same lexical level for personal deliberation. A different role for the lexical level might be in collective deliberation, where we set ground rules for our life together, and to coordinate common goals and projects. A lexical level plays a role here, analogous to its role in purely prudential deliberation.[33] I argue in subsequent chapters that a just society aims to raise everyone above the

---

[31] Thomas Nagel raises an analogous worry for T. M. Scanlon's Contractualist attempt to find rules that no one can reasonably reject (Nagel, *Equality and Partiality*; and Nagel, 'One-to-One'). We return to this debate in Ch. 9 and, with particular reference to Scanlon, in endnote D to Ch. 11.

[32] See chapter endnote B, pp. 80–1.

[33] This suggests a new interpretation of Kant's view that one goal of morality is to aim at a universal kingdom of ends. We should aim for a world where every person's adoption of the deliberative perspective drives them to adopt the same perspective of the world, and the same picture of the lexical priority between rational agency and inanimate matter.

lexical level. If the lexical level is determined in part by the perspective of the community in question, then this challenge is ever present, as the advancement of society raises the lexical level.

Consider our own judgements regarding life in the contemporary Third World, life in the Middle Ages, or life in prehistoric times. We can always ask whether anyone there has a life which we would regard as adequate for ourselves. We can also ask whether a particular life is adequate or acceptable in that particular social context. For instance, no one in prehistoric times was literate. For us, literacy is a necessary requirement of an acceptable quality of life. It does not follow that every life in prehistoric times was below the lexical level, when judged from the perspective of that situation.

Increases in life expectancy provide a striking example of an evolving lexical level. In the developed world today, many people would interpret the lexical level so that someone dying at 30 would not reach that level. Yet 200 years ago, it would have been thought possible to live a full life in thirty years, as this was the average life expectancy. Medical treatment to cure conditions that cause people to die in their thirties might thus be regarded as a necessity in the developed world, while it was a luxury in the same countries 200 years ago. A context-dependent lexical level is needed to make sense of this disparity.

Both individual and collective deliberation thus require context-dependent lexical levels. We shall see in later chapters that this relativized interpretation of the lexical level explains many intuitions and paradoxes in our obligations to future generations.

This explains both the strength and the divergence of intuitions regarding the Repugnant Conclusion. When asked to compare two or more outcomes in the abstract, we naturally supply a deliberative context. If different comparisons yield different contexts, then our intuitions support incompatible lexical levels. This does not show that we cannot construct a coherent account of comparative value, although it does suggest that any such account must rest on an interpretation of the lexical level that will not be suitable for all deliberative tasks. Therefore, we should not attempt a full account of the lexical level in the abstract. Many details can be explored only in the context of a particular theory of moral deliberation.

3.7.4. Equality and Patterns

The combination of Simple Consequentialism and the Total View yields a number of other controversial results. The most striking of these is the following.

The Monstrous Creation. By creating a child whose life will contain nothing but a very significant quantity of uncompensated suffering, we can provide a small pleasure to each of a large number of well-off people. If the number of beneficiaries is sufficiently large, then their combined additional pleasure outweighs the child's suffering. According to the Total View, this act of creation will produce the more valuable outcome. According to Simple Consequentialism, we should perform it.

There are two ways to avoid this result:

1. Revise our theory of value, so that the monstrous creation no longer produces the better outcome.
2. Abandon Simple Consequentialism, so that we are no longer obliged to choose the better outcome.

A common move is to introduce an egalitarian, or prioritarian, element. (An egalitarian attaches intrinsic value to an equal distribution, while a prioritarian attaches extra weight to the well-being of those who are worse off, without valuing equality as such.[34]) We could avoid the monstrous creation, for instance, by introducing a negative lexical level, so that the creation of a life below that level outweighs any number of less significant benefits.

While some of our egalitarian concerns can be accommodated in this way, it is unlikely that they all can.[35] Furthermore, we saw earlier that, while the lexical level alleviates some anti-egalitarian implications of the Total View, it exacerbates others. (Perhaps a judicious combination of prioritarianism and lexicality can accommodate all our considered intuitions, but it would be unwise to assume that it will.)

As we have already decided to abandon Simple Consequentialism, this need not trouble us. Moderate Consequentialism has two ways to avoid any particular counterintuitive result:

1. It may include deontological constraints or restrictions, forbidding agents from torturing or harming innocent people, especially those

---

[34] The *locus classicus* for prioritarianism is Parfit, 'Equality and Priority'. See also Jensen, 'What is the Difference between (Moderate) Egalitarianism and Prioritarianism?'; Mason, 'Egalitarianism and the Levelling Down Objection'; Persson, 'Equality, Priority and Person-Affecting Value'.

[35] Brad Hooker has argued that the Total View is more impartial than prioritarianism. (Hooker, *Ideal Code, Real World* (2000), 59–65.) His argument is as follows. Suppose x is better off than y. The Total View gives the same weight to 'the same benefit', whether it is given to x or to y, whereas prioritarianism gives y priority over x. If y is below the lexical level, and the benefit in question would raise her above that level, then the Lexical View also seems to violate impartiality. Prioritarians who adopt a lexical level can blunt the force of this objection. If the benefit in question raised y above the lexical level, while it would not result in a similar change in x's well-being, then we are not talking about giving 'the same benefit' to the two individuals.

who are worse off, merely in order to provide benefits to those who are already well off.

2. Moderate Consequentialism permits agents to privilege their own perspectives. This permission may extend, not only to individuals, but also to groups or communities. A given human society might choose to evaluate different possible futures for itself without direct reference to the impersonal value theory. Both individuals and groups might thus introduce distributive elements into their evaluations.[36]

This last point can be particularly helpful with regard to future generations. Consider two possible histories for a given community. In both, history is divided into two periods, the same number of human lives are spread over the same time, and the number of lives of each quality is the same.

Improvement.   In the first period, the quality of life is quite low, as people are forgoing present consumption to contribute to the development of new technology. In the second period that technology significantly improves the quality of life.

Decline.   In the first period, everyone lives well by consuming non-renewable resources and polluting the environment. In the second period, the quality of life falls.

Many people prefer Improvement to Decline. Yet the two histories contain the same number of lives, of exactly the same quality. So they are equally valuable, according to either the Total View or the Lexical View.

There are two solutions. We could build historical patterns into our foundational value theory. However, it will be very difficult to find a principled and consistent way to do this. Alternatively, we might build our concern for historical patterns into moderate Consequentialism, as an indirect strategy for maximizing value, or as a recognition of the natural and justified perspectives of particular generations.

Suppose one necessary requirement of agency is the ability to participate in the social and political life of one's community on a basis of approximate equality. This requirement clearly involves different things in different communities. A given level of education or literacy might be sufficient to place an agent above the lexical level in one context, but come to be inadequate at a later more sophisticated stage. Even though the earlier lives in Improvement are, in one sense, just as good as the later lives in Decline, the former may be above the relevant lexical level (or, at least, not far below it), while the latter fall well below the lexical level set by the earlier level of

---

[36] See chapter endnote C, p. 81.

accomplishment in Decline. This reinforces the suggestion that the lexical level could be context-dependent.

3.8. Conclusion

I conclude that the Lexical View can provides a coherent resolution to the Repugnant Conclusion, embedded in a plausible theory of rational deliberation. The connection between the lexical level and an agent's moral permission to favour herself is explored in the next chapter, in the context of Scheffler's Hybrid View.

Our examination of value theory has been very incomplete. We have barely touched on the crucial question of where the lexical level is to be located. We have also avoided a number of pressing issues concerning the aggregation of value above and below the lexical level. We will return to some of these issues as we proceed. The basic outlines presented in this chapter are sufficient to begin the search for a moderate Consequentialist account of the morality of reproduction and of our obligations to future generations.

We have also assumed that human well-being is the only relevant source of value. Other values, such as environmental values and the well-being of animals, and various possible holistic evaluations of human communities have been put to one side.

At several points in our subsequent argument, these (and other) additional departures from the Total View would assist us. However, it is worth asking how far moderate Consequentialism can proceed without altering its underlying values. My main aim is to argue that moderate Consequentialism can be plausible, even when based on the comparatively uncompromising value theory sketched in this chapter. Those favouring a more pluralistic view can attach the qualification 'so far as the value of human well-being is concerned' to the view presented in this chapter.

A crucial question for any Consequentialism is where it places its lexical level. In Simple Consequentialism, the lexical level must be purely foundational. If a lexical level is unavoidable at some level, and if the foundational lexical level cannot be rendered coherent, then Simple Consequentialism must fail. I leave open the possibility that the impossibility theorems (perhaps together with the Kantian argument for the necessity of the lexical level) will prove fatal for Simple Consequentialism. By contrast, moderate Consequentialism offers an escape route, as it allows the agent's value theory to depart from the theorist's foundational value theory. The two forms of moderate Consequentialism explored in the rest of this book (the Hybrid View and Rule Consequentialism) offer different accounts of this departure. We shall see that one crucial question is whether the Hybrid View relies more heavily on foundational elements than does Rule Consequentialism.

Endnotes

A. Historically, the most popular alternative to the Total View has been the Average View, which claims that extra lives improve the value of an outcome if and only if they are above the average level of happiness. (For good recent discussion, see Hurka, 'Average Utilitarianisms'; and Hurka, 'More Average Utilitarianisms'). In Same Number Choices, the Average View and the Total View coincide, as the best way to maximize the average is by maximizing the total. In Different Number Choices, however, we can often maximize the average without maximizing the total. This is how the Average View avoids the Repugnant Conclusion. Under the Average View, the A-world is much better than the Z-world.

Unfortunately, the Average View is unacceptable, as it implies that the addition of a set of perfectly isolated, extremely worthwhile lives may make things worse (if average happiness is already high), while the addition of a set of perfectly isolated lives far below the zero level may constitute an improvement (if average happiness is sufficiently low). (These objections are from Parfit, *Reasons and Persons*, 421–2.)

The literature contains many other theories of aggregation. (For a taste of these alternatives, see the following: Arrhenius, 'Future Generations'; Blackorby, Bossert, and Donaldson, 'Intertemporal Population Ethics'; Blackorby, Bossert, and Donaldson, 'Critical-Level Utilitarianism and the Population-Ethics Dilemma'; Feldman, 'Justice, Desert and the Repugnant Conclusion'; Hudson, 'The Diminishing Marginal Value of Happy People'; Hurka, 'Value and Population Size'; and Sider, 'Might Theory X be a Theory of Diminishing Marginal Value?'.) However, I argue elsewhere that these all either share the fate of the Average View (Mulgan, 'What's Really Wrong with the Limited Quantity View', 2001) or fall foul of the Reverse Repugnant Conclusion (Mulgan, 'The Reverse Repugnant Conclusion', 2002).

B. From a Kantian point of view, we might distinguish the standpoint of practical reason from the perspective of any individual agent. Kant himself offers some materials to guide our thinking here. If we seek a lexical level reflecting the essence of the practical standpoint, rather than the individual perspective of particular agents, then we might focus on the necessary preconditions of a life of human dignity. In some respects, this will point to a lexical level closer to that endorsed by a destitute person than by an affluent person, as the latter would be more likely to recognize what is truly essential. On the other hand, the lexical level might include several elements beyond those posited by many destitute people, especially if they live in illiberal societies. If a life of human dignity requires the successful pursuit of valuable goals, autonomously chosen from a diverse range of genuinely valuable options, made available within a liberal society, then the lexical level may be fairly high. (For Kant's views, see the works cited in endnote E of Ch. 2 above. For a defence of the claim that a life of human dignity does require all these things, see Mulgan, *The Demands of Consequentialism* (2001), ch. 7.)

C. I argue elsewhere that the notorious infinite utility problem can be satisfactorily resolved only by allowing individuals and communities such evaluative licence (Mulgan, 'Transcending the Infinite Utility Debate' (2002); and 'Valuing the Future', draft MS.) The problem of infinite utility arises as follows. Simple Consequentialism tells us to perform the act that would produce the best outcome. If there is no best outcome, then Consequentialism offers no advice at all. Many familiar theories of aggregation fail to yield a definite ordering of possible worlds if the future is infinitely long. For instance, the Total View implies that, if humanity continues forever, all possible infinite futures have the same value. (For other discussions of the infinite utility problem, see Vallentyne and Kagan, 'Infinite Value and Finitely Additive Value Theory'; Nelson, 'Utilitarian Eschatology'; and Vallentyne, 'Utilitarianism and Infinite Utility'.) For the sake of simplicity, I put the infinite utility problem aside in the text. If it cannot be solved, then it is a problem for all moral theories instructing us to take account of future welfare. If Simple Consequentialists can solve the problem, then there is no reason to suppose that the moderate Consequentialism developed in this book cannot help itself to their solution.

4

Hybrid Moral Theories

Simple Consequentialism is impartial, with no special place for the costs incurred by the agent. The Demandingness and Compulsion Objections show that, if we are to construct an intuitively plausible moral theory, we must make room for such costs in our moral theory. We must supplement the Reason to Promote the Good with other moral ideals. One prominent recent attempt to construct such a theory is that of Samuel Scheffler, who seeks to make room for moral agents by building Agent Centred Prerogatives into a Consequentialist moral theory, without also embracing Agent Centred Restrictions.[1] (Prerogatives permit agents to refrain from maximizing the good, while restrictions require agents to sometimes refrain from maximizing the good.)

In this chapter, I outline Scheffler's 'Hybrid View' and apply it to the special case of reproduction. I conclude that the Hybrid View does not provide a satisfactory account of our obligations regarding reproduction and future generations. (However, I argue in Chapter 11 that it can provide the overarching framework within which those obligations are situated.) This chapter concludes with a suggestion that the primary failing of the Hybrid View is that it cannot appreciate the collective moral significance of reproduction. Our discussion of the Hybrid View also sheds light on the general limits of all forms of Individual Consequentialism: theories that retain the individualist focus of Simple Consequentialism. This helps motivate the exploration of collective forms of Consequentialism, which begins in Chapter 5.

4.1. Scheffler's Hybrid View

In *The Rejection of Consequentialism*, Samuel Scheffler outlines a 'Hybrid View' of ethics. Under Simple Consequentialism, the weight an agent is allowed to give to her own personal projects is in strict proportion to their impersonal value. For instance, I should only pursue a particular hobby or

---

[1] Scheffler's original presentation of the Hybrid View is in his *The Rejection of Consequentialism* (1982). For further literature, see chapter endote A, p. 128.

interest of my own to the extent that the well-being I receive from so doing is at least as great as the total well-being I could generate for others by acting differently. The basis of the Hybrid View is the Agent Centred Prerogative, which 'has the effect of denying that one is always required to produce the best overall states of affairs'.[2] Scheffler goes on to say that 'a plausible Agent Centred Prerogative would allow each agent to assign certain proportionately greater weight to his own interests than to the interests of other people'.[3] The justification for such a prerogative is that it 'constitutes a structural feature whose incorporation into a moral conception embodies a rational strategy for taking account of personal independence, given one construal of the importance of that aspect of persons'.[4]

As Scheffler initially presents it, the notion of the Agent Centred Prerogative is somewhat vague. In a later article he provides the following explication.[5]

Suppose, in other words, that each agent were allowed to give M times more weight to his own interests than to the interests of anyone else. This would mean that an agent was permitted to perform his preferred act (call it P), provided that there was no alternative A open to him, such that (1) A would produce a better overall outcome than P, as judged from an impersonal standpoint which gives equal weight to everyone's interests, and (2) the total net loss to others of his doing P rather than A was more than M times as great as the net loss to him of doing A rather than P.

To illustrate this prerogative, consider the following simple tale.[6]

Affluent's Tale. Affluent is a well-off member of a contemporary first world society, sitting at her desk with her cheque book. In front of her are two pamphlets: one from a reputable international aid organization, the other from her local theatre company. Affluent has three options: donate all her money to charity, donate most of her money to charity (and buy one or two tickets), or donate nothing (and buy several tickets).

The more Affluent gives away, the greater the cost to her of making a further donation, as she will be required to give up progressively more central elements of her lifestyle. The values and costs of her options are represented in the table.

	Impersonal value	*Cost to Affluent*
Donate All	10,000	10
Donate Most	9,900	1
Donate Nothing	5,000	0

[2] Scheffler, *The Rejection of Consequentialism* (1982), 5.   [3] Ibid. 20.   [4] Ibid. 67.
[5] Scheffler, 'Prerogatives without Restrictions' (1992), 378.
[6] This tale is from Mulgan, *The Demands of Consequentialism* (2001), 146.

Let us assume that each agent is allowed to give 600 times more weight to her own interests than to the interests of distant strangers. Affluent is thus not permitted to donate nothing, as the extra impersonal value of donating most of her income rather than nothing is 4,900 times as great as the extra cost to Affluent of donating most of her income rather than nothing. As 4,900 is greater than 600, Affluent is not permitted to donate nothing rather than donating most of her income. Affluent has no Agent Centred Prerogative to donate nothing.

However, this does not mean that Affluent is required to donate all of her income. The extra value of donating all her income rather than most of it is less than the extra cost to Affluent multiplied by the extra weighting she is allowed to give to her own interests. Affluent can donate most of her income rather than donating all of it. Yet donating all is the only option with better consequences than donating most. So Affluent does have an Agent Centred Prerogative to donate (only) most of her income.

The weighting of 600 may seem implausibly high. However, a much lower weighting would lead to almost all inhabitants of developed countries being overwhelmed by their obligations to distant strangers in the developing world. As one aim of the Hybrid View is to provide a less demanding theory than Simple Consequentialism, this would largely defeat its purpose. We should note, however, that this very high weighting means that, in everyday life, agents will always be allowed to actively sacrifice others in pursuit of their own ends.[7] (This is the basis of the objections explored in Section 4.1.3.)

4.1.1. The Demands of the Hybrid View

Simple Consequentialism leaves the agent too little room (time, resources, energy) for her own projects or interests. It must condemn any agent who deliberately fails to maximize the good. This seems unreasonably harsh. One benefit of Scheffler's Hybrid View is that its demands seem much more intuitively plausible. To see this, let us first make a number of simplifying assumptions. Assume that Affluent has available a set number of dollars (call it n), and that she can give Oxfam any number of dollars from zero to n. Under the Hybrid View, we can then prove that, unless Affluent is required to donate all her money to charity, there is some number of dollars between zero and n (call it x), such that (a) Affluent is permitted to donate x dollars to charity rather than donating more, (b) Affluent is required to

---

[7] See Myers, 'Prerogatives and Restrictions from the Cooperative Point of View', 136; and Brink, 'Self-love and Altruism', 618.

donate at least x dollars to charity, and (c) the additional amount of good which would be produced by a donation of x + 1 dollars rather than one of x dollars is equal to the cost to Affluent of donating her (x + 1)th dollar multiplied by the extra weight Affluent is permitted to give to her own interests over the interests of anyone else (Scheffler's M).[8]

The Hybrid Theorist's reply to the Demandingness Objection is now obvious. By altering the value of M (the weighting the agent is allowed to give to her own interests), we can change the value of x (the amount of money she is required to donate). By choosing an appropriate weighting we can thus ensure that the maximum donation required of Affluent is not unduly demanding.

The Hybrid Theorist has a similar reply to the two compulsion objections introduced in Chapter 1. Both abandoning the chance to have any children if one strongly wanted to, and having children if one really did not want to, represent very significant costs for the agent. So long as we choose a sufficiently high value for M, the additional good available will be outweighed by the weighted costs to the agent. Unless some great tragedy would thereby be averted, agents will not be required to act against their considered preferences.

4.1.2. The Autonomy Objection

Unfortunately, the Hybrid View is open to two complementary objections: that it is not sufficiently permissive, and that it is too permissive. The first objection is that the Hybrid View does not leave sufficient room for the agent's autonomy. Consider the following tale.

The Forced Choice.   Mary is choosing between life as a parent and life as a charity worker in Africa. The latter option is not the obsessive nightmare sometimes associated with Simple Consequentialism. Mary would have time out for herself, her friends, her other projects. But she cannot both take the job in Africa and have a child. Mary is unsure which option is better for her. Her friend Sam counsels her as follows. 'Life as a charity worker produces the better outcome impersonally considered. So you must do that, unless you have a prerogative to do otherwise. A prerogative is justified in terms of the cost to you of opting for one life *rather than another*. You yourself agree that, so far as you can tell, life as a charity worker would not be worse for you than life as a parent. There is thus no cost in opting for life as a charity worker. Therefore, you have no prerogative. You must take the job.'

---

[8] For the proof, see Mulgan, *The Demands of Consequentialism*, 295–6.

Sam's conclusion can be generalized. Whenever an agent faces a choice between two options (A and B) where A produces better impersonal results than B, the agent is only permitted to opt for B if she would be significantly better off under that option than under the alternative. If the agent cannot really judge one outcome to be clearly better than the other, then she must opt for A.

At first sight, this result seems fair enough. If A and B are (more or less) equally valuable to the agent and if A clearly produces greater value overall, then surely she should opt for A. What reason could she have to do otherwise? However, this aspect of the Hybrid View threatens to destroy a key element of moral autonomy. Many significant choices in real life are between options whose values are not only very difficult to calculate in practice, but possibly incomparable in principle. In such choices, the options do not appear to be 'equally valuable', even if neither is better than the other. If agents are always morally obliged to resolve such choices solely on the basis of impersonal value, then this denies them the opportunity to take account, in their deliberations, of the contrasting values embodied by the options. In particular, it looks as if few affluent agents will be permitted to even give serious consideration to parenthood, as they typically face choices analogous to Mary's. Yet, on many accounts of the value of autonomy, such deliberation should be a significant component of any worthwhile human life.

To defeat this objection, we must show how the Hybrid View could allow a more generous role for moral choice.

4.1.3. Four More Objections

Suppose we have resolved the autonomy objection, and constructed a Hybrid View that permits reproduction. In this section, we examine four related objections, which derive intuitively unacceptable results from the fact that the Hybrid View contains prerogatives without restrictions. While the Hybrid View permits agents to choose to pursue their personal projects at the expense of the overall good, it places no deontological restrictions on their pursuit of either personal projects or impersonal good.[9]

Each objection makes two claims. The first is that the intuitive problems faced by the Hybrid View are worse than analogous problems for Simple Consequentialism. The second claim is that the justification Scheffler offers for his Agent Centred Prerogative can also be used to construct a rationale

---

[9] For other objections to the Hybrid View, see ibid. 148–52, 238–41.

for Agent Centred Restrictions. The conclusion is that the Hybrid View is unstable. Once prerogatives are introduced, we are led inevitably to restrictions. Without restrictions, the Hybrid View is too permissive. (Each objection is based on one drawn from the literature, but I have adapted them to fit our interest in the ethics of reproduction.)

4.1.3.1. A Doing/Allowing Objection
Consider the following tale, based on one presented by Shelly Kagan.[10]

The Rich Uncle.   Suppose I want to have a child, and estimate that the cost of providing a decent life for that child is $100,000. If I cannot get $100,000, then I will abandon my plan to have a child. Consider two situations. In the first case, I don't have enough money myself, so I kill my uncle in order to inherit $100,000. In the second case, I already have $100,000, so I elect to spend it on my own child rather than give it to charity to save a stranger's life.

Kagan has argued that 'an Agent Centred Prerogative not only permits agents to *allow* harm, it will also permit agents to *do* harm in the pursuit of their non-optimal projects'.[11] The Hybrid View can thus permit acts of killing if and only if it also permits acts of letting die. If Agent Centred Prerogatives are to be any use at all, they must (at least sometimes) allow me to spend my money on myself rather than on saving the lives of distant others. In particular, any intuitively plausible prerogative will allow me to use $100,000 to provide a decent life for my child. Some acts of letting die must be allowed. So some acts of killing must also be accepted. Scheffler must permit agents to kill to advance their own personal projects at the expense of the general good.

Of course, Simple Consequentialism also allows some killing. However, Consequentialists have the defence that they only ever allow me to kill when this is necessary to bring about the best outcome. This response is unavailable to Scheffler, as he also permits killing when it produces a worse outcome, judged impartially, than not killing.

Scheffler describes this alleged feature of the Hybrid View as the 'symmetry condition', which arises because:[12]

it seems to follow [from the Hybrid View] that if it is permissible for a person to allow an n-sized harm to befall someone else in order to avoid a q-sized cost to himself, then it must, everything else equal, also be permissible for the person to inflict an n-sized harm directly in order to avoid a q-sized cost to himself.

---

[10] Kagan, 'Does Consequentialism Demand Too Much?'.   [11] Ibid. 251.
[12] Scheffler, 'Prerogatives without Restrictions' (1992), 380.

Scheffler admits that an Agent Centred Prerogative cannot, of itself, distinguish between various ways of pursuing personal projects. However, he argues that, in practice, there will be a difference. Doing harm is an act of commission rather than omission. It thus takes time and energy which cannot then be used in the pursuit of personal projects. By contrast, an act of allowing harm saves the agent time and energy, which can then be used in the pursuit of personal goals. Acts justified by Agent Centred Prerogatives will tend to be acts of allowing harm rather than doing harm.

Scheffler gives the example of starving inner-city inhabitants. By allowing them to starve, I am able to stay at home to work on my own personal projects. So this act may be justified by an Agent Centred Prerogative. Yet taking active steps to kill someone myself would leave me with even less, rather than more, time to devote to my projects. This act will thus not be justified by an Agent Centred Prerogative.

Scheffler's argument will work in many cases. Perhaps most harmful acts justified by Agent Centred Prerogatives will involve omission rather than commission. However, as Scheffler himself admits, it is implausible to claim that they all will. Situations are bound to arise where pursuit of my personal projects is best achieved by actively doing harm. Furthermore, acts of commission need not limit an agent's options. We can imagine a case where harming another person was the only way to open up a whole range of otherwise unavailable options. Indeed, our original tale seems to be just such a case.

4.1.3.2. The Forced Supererogation Objection
Consider the following tale.[13]

Amy's Dilemma.   Amy and Bob are scientists, working on a vaccine to cure a particularly virulent disease. Amy tells Bob that she is thinking of having children. If Amy becomes pregnant, then she will be unable to continue working with the radioactive materials in the lab. As no one else is available who has Amy's expertise, this would delay the development of the vaccine for several months. Several thousand people throughout the world die each month from this disease. Knowing all this, Bob reasons that, of all the actions available to him, the best consequences would result if he prevents

[13] Various ancestors of this objection are presented in Alexander, 'Scheffler on the Independence of Agent Centred Prerogatives from Agent-Centred Restrictions', 279–82; Harris, 'Integrity and Agent Centred Restrictions', 440–3; Hurley, 'Scheffler's Argument for Deontology', 123; and Myers, 'Prerogatives and Restrictions from the Cooperative Point of View', 147. For Scheffler's reply, see 'Prerogatives without Restrictions', 392. For more detailed discussion, see Mulgan, *The Demands of Consequentialism*, 154–5.

Amy from becoming pregnant. Bob attempts to persuade Amy not to have children. Amy replies that, for medical reasons, she must either have children now or never. She is aware of the implications for their research, but she still wishes to have children. Bob deliberately exposes Amy to a dose of radiation which leaves her infertile but otherwise unharmed. Amy never discovers what Bob has done. Unable to conceive, she continues her work in the lab and the vaccine is soon developed.

Let us assume that, under the Hybrid View, Amy is not required to sacrifice her chance to have children in this situation. She is permitted to make this sacrifice, but also permitted to have children. (If it does not yield this result, the Hybrid View will be very demanding.) However, the Hybrid View also permits Bob to perform the action with the best consequences. Bob is thus allowed to render Amy infertile, if this is the only way he can ensure that a vaccine is produced as soon as possible.

Indeed, Bob may still be permitted to sacrifice Amy's fertility even if he could have made a similar sacrifice himself instead, and even if that would have produced better consequences than sacrificing Amy. This is because, if Amy is sacrificed instead of him, the benefit to Bob, when multiplied by the weight he is allowed to give to his own interests, may well outweigh the small loss in impersonal value. Perhaps Bob is also thinking of having children. If he is to do so, he must undergo treatment for a medical condition. This treatment involves drugs which become highly toxic in contact with any radiation. If Bob is to have children, he must stop working in the lab. Suppose now that Amy and Bob's research only requires one of them to remain active in the lab. Bob exposes Amy to radiation, so that he can have children without delaying the development of the vaccine.

Alternatively, if Bob is not able to ensure the early discovery of a vaccine by sacrificing himself, then he may be *obliged* to sacrifice Amy. Bob's Agent Centred Prerogative only allows him to give disproportionate weight to the cost to *himself*, not the cost to Amy. Bob may be upset if he sacrifices Amy, but, unless he is extremely empathetic, the cost to him is obviously far less than the cost to Amy. So Bob may not even be allowed to spare Amy, even though Amy was not obliged to sacrifice herself.

The Hybrid View may thus permit (or even require) an agent to force another agent to make sacrifices which the latter is morally permitted to refrain from making. (Our previous tale was a special case of this objection. When I kill my uncle for my own benefit, I force him to make a sacrifice he was permitted to refrain from.)

Simple Consequentialism also permits (and sometimes requires) agents to force others to make sacrifices in pursuit of the impersonal good, as it contains no Agent Centred Restrictions. Indeed, some have objected that

Consequentialism always obliges agents to treat others as means in this way. However, its opponents allege that the Hybrid View is worse than Simple Consequentialism, for two reasons. Under the Hybrid View, the sacrifice Bob is allowed to force upon Amy is one Amy was not required to undergo voluntarily. By contrast, under Simple Consequentialism, if Amy's sacrifice does maximize the good, then Amy will be obliged to choose it herself. So Bob would merely be forcing Amy to do her moral duty. The second difference is that the Hybrid View sometimes allows Bob to sacrifice Amy even if this is not the optimal act available to him, whereas Simple Consequentialism always forbids the sub-optimal sacrificing of others.

4.1.3.3. The Commitments Objection
Once again, we begin with a simple tale.[14]

The Partnership.   Ant and Bee are friends, engaged in a cooperative venture which is a significant project for both of them: the conceiving and raising of a child. At time t, Ant's Agent Centred Prerogative permits him to embark on the project with Bee. Between t and t + 1, both Ant and Bee invest a great deal of time and effort in their project. Bee gives birth to a child, and puts her career on hold to raise the child. Ant goes out to work to support them all. At t + 1, Ant is permitted to continue with this project, assuming he still values it. However, Ant is also allowed to abandon the project, thereby abandoning Bee and their child, in order to pursue the impersonal good. One day, Ant goes to work for a famine relief organization in Africa, leaving Bee and the child to fend for themselves. Ant would also be permitted to abandon the cooperative project to pursue some new personal project of his own, even to enter into a new cooperative child-raising project with Spider, a sworn enemy of Bee's.

Under the Hybrid View, Ant has no special obligations to Bee to continue with their joint project. In the absence of Agent Centred Restrictions, Ant can never be obliged to behave sub-optimally, or to favour one personal project over another.

Simple Consequentialism also lacks special obligations. Indeed, if pursuit of the cooperative project is not optimal, then Ant will be *obliged* to abandon it. However, once again, the Hybrid View fares worse than Consequentialism. In the first place, it allows Ant to embark on the cooperative project, *because* of the significance that project will have in his life, and then it allows him to abandon the project, without any consideration for the

---

[14] An ancestor of this objection is presented in Harris, 'A Paradoxical Departure from Consequentialism', 91–2. Scheffler himself has recently presented a similar argument in favour of obligations derived from personal relationships (Scheffler, 'Relationships and Responsibilities', 2001).

significance the project has come to assume in the life of Bee. The Hybrid View thus allows agents to make commitments to others which they are then free to break, and then justifies this permission by reference to the significance of those commitments for the individual agent. By contrast, Simple Consequentialism's requirement that agents abandon personal projects is motivated solely by appeal to considerations of impersonal value.

The second difference between the two theories is that the Hybrid View permits an agent to abandon a cooperative project, not only in pursuit of the impersonal good, but also to pursue another personal project. The latter may even be less valuable to the agent than the abandoned project, so long as its impersonal value is correspondingly higher. This is the opposite of common sense. Breaking a commitment to further one's own interests seems much worse than breaking a commitment in pursuit of the impersonal good.

4.1.3.4. The Parental Obligations Objection
Consider the following tale, adapted from one presented by Gregory Kavka.[15]

The Slave Child Tale.   A couple in the developed world are planning to have no children. A slave trader from a society where slavery is legal offers them $100,000 to produce a slave for him. They want the money to pay for an overseas trip. Suppose they have planned the trip for decades, saved assiduously, but recently had their tickets rendered worthless by the collapse of an airline. Without the $100,000 they will be unable to take the trip. They sign the agreement, accept the money, produce the child, and deliver her into slavery.

This tale is clearly reminiscent of Kagan's uncle. Unless the Hybrid View is extremely demanding, it will permit the couple to keep $100,000, if they have it, rather than donating it to charity to save strangers from slavery. (Otherwise the Hybrid View would be very demanding on us all, as many thousands of people in the actual world continue to live in conditions tantamount to slavery.[16]) Because the Hybrid View recognizes no distinction between doing and allowing, it must also permit them to create a new slave, no matter how bad life as a slave can get.[17]

---

[15]   See Kavka, 'The Paradox of Future Individuals'. Unlike our previous tales, Kavka's original is specifically concerned with reproduction. However, I have adapted it to apply to the Hybrid View, which is not Kavka's target.   [16]   Sen, *Development as Freedom*, 30, 113–15.

[17]   This last possibility would be a crucial departure from Kavka's original tale. Kavka assumes that life as a slave is worth living, because his target is a person-affecting theory according to which it is never wrong to create a new person whose life is worth living.

This new tale is even more troubling for the Hybrid View than Kagan's original, as commonsense morality tells us that parents are under especially strong obligations to provide adequate care for their own children. To many people, selling your own child into slavery merely to fund an overseas trip is a paradigmatic case of moral atrocity. The Hybrid View cannot accommodate such obligations, as it cannot make room for special obligations in general. Without radical revision, the Hybrid View cannot provide an acceptable account of the morality of reproduction.

4.2. Parental Prerogatives

The autonomy objection and the four restriction-based objections must be taken in turn. The latter arise only within a theory that has dissolved the former. (If our theory does not permit reproduction at all, there is no point in asking if it is too permissive.) Our first task is to ask whether the Hybrid View can defeat the autonomy objection.

A central feature of commonsense morality is that people are, at least in ordinary circumstances, permitted to have children. Commonsense morality thus endorses a Reproduction Prerogative. We begin by asking what scope this prerogative might have. We then ask how prerogatives are justified. I shall argue that, in a Hybrid View, any such prerogative must be justified in terms of the significance, to the agent herself, of the goals involved in reproduction. This leads us to ask what goals might justify a Reproduction Prerogative.

We explore the scope of a prerogative using our earlier example of Affluent, choosing between reproduction, adoption, and charity. One distinctive feature of Scheffler's Hybrid View is that it always permits the agent to maximize the good. In Chapter 1, I argued that, under any plausible value theory, neither adoption nor reproduction produces as much good overall as a life devoted to charity. Therefore, any Hybrid View must leave open a life devoted to charity. This leaves the following possibilities.

The Oxfam Obligation. Affluent has no prerogative. She is morally obliged to donate all her time and money to charity.

The Full Parental Prerogative. Affluent can pursue any of the three projects.

The Reproduction Prerogative. Affluent has a limited prerogative. She is permitted to pursue either reproduction or a life devoted to charity, but adoption is morally forbidden.

The Adoption Prerogative. Affluent has a limited prerogative. She is permitted to pursue either adoption or a life devoted to charity, but reproduction is morally forbidden. (We might refer to both the Adoption and Reproduction Prerogatives as Partial Parental Prerogatives.)

The Parental Prerogative is often taken to be an integral part of common-sense morality. Each of the other three options can be found in the literature. Simple Consequentialists endorse the Oxfam Obligation.[18] Analogues of the Reproduction Prerogative can be found in the bioethics literature, where those who seek to pursue parental projects other than conventional reproduction are sometimes portrayed as being unreasonably selfish.[19] The Adoption Prerogative has recently been defended by some moderate Consequentialists, as a less extreme alternative to the Oxfam Obligation.[20]

We need to separate arguments for a full Parental Prerogative from arguments for the disjunction of our two Partial Parental Prerogatives. Many arguments in this area conclude that agents must be free to engage in *some* parental project. It does not follow that they need the freedom to pursue *any* parental project they choose. In particular, we need to be especially wary of arguments from the general moral significance of parental projects to the permissibility of conventional reproduction.

Furthermore, much depends upon how broadly 'parental projects' are defined. For instance, suppose we define a 'parental project' as any project that involves any contribution to the nurturing of human beings. This would render it comparatively easy to defend a weak 'parental' prerogative, but leave a large gap between that defence and the case for a genuine Reproduction Prerogative. By contrast, a narrower definition might lessen the gap to the Reproduction Prerogative, but render it harder to defend any Parental Prerogative in the first place.

4.2.1. Justifying a Prerogative

In Chapter 3, I distinguished two components of well-being: needs and goals. This distinction is crucial to the resolution of the autonomy objection. The role of needs in moral theory is comparatively simple. Only goals have the flexibility to ground the kind of prerogative we are seeking. The moral significance of the distinction between needs and goals arises primarily

[18] For a recent Utilitarian defence of the Oxfam Obligation, see Young, 'Overconsumption and Procreation'. See also Munthe, 'The Argument from Transfer', 26–31.

[19] For an evaluation of such arguments, see Moore and Mulgan, 'Open Letter: The Ethics of Non-Commercial IVF Surrogacy'. In practice, such arguments are not typically opposed to the Reproduction project *per se*. Rather, they seek to establish that the Adoption project is superior to any non-standard form of reproduction.

[20] Munthe, 'The Argument from Transfer'; and Petersen, 'The Claim from Adoption'.

because the value of a goal depends upon how it is pursued, whereas the value of a need is not directly affected by the way it is met.

Our objection is that the Hybrid View underplays the significance of autonomy. Goals are the component of well-being more intimately linked to autonomy. Section 4.2.2 develops an argument drawing on these connections. The present section considers an attempt to defeat our first objection directly, by arguing that reproduction *is* distinctly better for the agent than the alternatives. For the moment, we seek to defend the Hybrid View without making any controversial value commitments. We ask later whether this attempt succeeds.

Scheffler presents the Agent Centred Prerogative as a response to the following features of human moral life: the separateness of persons; the independence of the personal point of view; the fact that morality governs the choices of human agents; and the significance of the personal point of view *to the agent*, over and above its value from an impersonal point of view. The prerogative thus 'constitutes a structural feature whose incorporation into a moral conception embodies a rational strategy for taking account of personal independence, given one construal of the importance of that aspect of persons'.[21] Scheffler's guiding view is that an adequate moral theory should leave human beings morally free to choose, build, and pursue their own goals, projects, activities, and relationships, even at the expense of overall value. All these justifications clearly draw on factors particular to goals rather than needs.

Many people attach great significance to reproduction, and consider their lives to be devalued if they do not get to reproduce. This might suggest that some people have a biological need to reproduce. However, it seems more likely that the significance of reproduction is to be explained in terms of goals. It is hard to think of a *basic* need which can only be met by parenting, especially as many non-parents have worthwhile lives. However, agents do have a basic need to pursue their goals. If reproduction is an important goal, then this may be sufficient to justify a prerogative.

Many people strongly desire to have children of their own. It is tempting to think that the very existence of this desire is sufficient to justify a Reproduction Prerogative. However, it is not clear that it should. The presence of a strong desire is certainly a very good reason to ensure that particular options are *practically* available to an agent. Within the Hybrid View, however, desires cannot simply be taken at face value. We need a convincing account of why reproduction is better, either for the agent or for others, than the alternatives. The presence of a strong desire is indicative of

---

[21] Scheffler, *The Rejection of Consequentialism* (1982), 67.

the presence of something valuable, but it neither proves the existence of that value, nor constitutes it. For instance, the satisfaction of a desire for a worthless object does not benefit the agent at all, aside from any benefit she derives from the pleasure of pursuit or from the exercise of her autonomy. I have argued at length elsewhere that a Consequentialist moral theory can best account for the real value of desires by according moral significance to the autonomous pursuit of independently valuable goals, and to the moral openness of significant life choices.[22] The rest of this chapter applies this line of argument to reproduction.

A prerogative based on the strength of the agent's desire would also be too inclusive in general, as it would permit any action the agent strongly desired, irrespective of its contribution to their well-being or to the value of the object of desire. It is thus preferable not to ground a Reproduction Prerogative on desire alone.

Suppose an agent faces a choice between two goals (G1 and G2) where G1 is a parental goal (i.e. either reproduction or adoption), and G2 is not. Suppose also that the successful pursuit of G2 would generate more overall value than the successful pursuit of G1. If the Hybrid View is nonetheless to permit the pursuit of G1, then this must be because of the value of that goal to the agent. Goals relating to parenthood might be valuable to an agent in three distinct ways.

1. *Pursuit Value.*   The *pursuit* of goal G1 is more morally significant to the agent than the pursuit of goal G2. Engaging in parental projects will develop many human capacities, such as nurturing, empathy, and caring. On many accounts, these are among the most significant of all human capacities. The process of engaging in reproduction (as opposed to other parental projects) also develops or utilizes physical capacities, most obviously the capacity to gestate.

2. *Achievement Value.*   The *achievement* involved in successfully completing goal G1 is more morally significant to the agent than the achievement involved in completing goal G2. Parental projects can lead to valuable achievements. The most obvious of these is that a successful parental project results in the children in question having a flourishing human life, which they would otherwise not have had. (Either because they would have had a much worse life, or because they would not have existed.) Reproduction offers the additional achievement of creating a new person.

3. *Availability Value.*   The *availability* of goal G1 is more morally significant to the agent than the availability of goal G2. (Alternatively, perhaps G2 itself is more valuable if G1 is also available.) The availability of parental

---

[22] Mulgan, *The Demands of Consequentialism*, 176–9.

projects also contributes to the development of personal autonomy. In a society structured around the institution of parenthood, the decision whether or not to rear children is one of the most significant life choices any agent can make. It is therefore very important for this choice to remain open. In a society attaching great significance to *biological* parenthood, the decision whether or not to *create* children is one of the most significant life choices any agent can face. Perhaps this choice too must remain morally open.

In this section we focus on pursuit and achievement value. The significance of reproduction varies with the agent's situation. For instance, if society attaches a high status to biological parenthood, then an agent who cannot pursue reproduction is deprived of this status. In a society where (for instance) motherhood is accorded more social significance than fatherhood (or, conversely, in which childless women are viewed with more suspicion than childless men), the impact of this loss may also vary according to the agent's gender.

We must be very careful not to place too much weight on such socially constructed losses, especially when considering moral permissibility. We need to leave open the possibility that our moral philosophy will produce a radical social critique. Perhaps our culture is founded upon morally indefensible practices. On the other hand, given the way our society is structured, these choices are morally significant for us, and for anyone living in any society remotely like our own. (The question of what might be significant in a society radically unlike our own, and of how that could be relevant to moral theory, is explored in Chapters 5 to 8.)

A full assessment of either the Pursuit Value or the Achievement Value of parental projects would require us to explore in detail the precise alternatives open to potential parents in any given society. For some people, many of the capacities and achievements of parents could also be produced (perhaps more efficiently) by other goals, such as a career in teaching. For others, the capacities and achievements of parenthood are not easily replaced by equally valuable alternatives.

My aim is not to provide a comprehensive account of reasons for reproduction. Although an overwhelming array of particular reasons for having children have been reported in the empirical literature, these can be grouped into three broad categories: instrumental, enjoyment and achievement, and genetic.[23] This categorization is based on two factors of central

---

[23] Caution is needed in interpreting the empirical data in this area '[because] having children is so culturally expected and overlaid with clichés that the answer to a more direct question or the first answer to a question may not be as true a reflection of the respondent's views as the responses he gives after he has had more of a chance to think about the topic': Hoffman and Hoffman, 'The Value of Children to Parents', 31.

importance to the Hybrid View: contribution to the agent's well-being, and potential replaceability by non-parental goals.

Our present interest is in the prerogatives of particular individuals. The empirical literature provides examples of the kinds of reasons people have for embarking on reproduction. It also helps illustrate the significance people may attach to those reasons. At this point in the argument, we are not directly interested in the prevalence or strength of particular reasons within society as a whole. (We will be more interested in such global information in the next two chapters, especially in the form of evidence regarding collective responses to changes in public policy.)

4.2.1.1. Instrumental Values
The instrumental value of parenthood can be further sub-divided into economic, religious, status-based, and group-based.

1. *Economic*.   The most studied reasons for having children are simple economic ones.[24] This is largely because most studies relate to poor people in the developing world, for whom economic reasons loom large. In some circumstances, children are valuable assets, providing cheap, often irreplaceable, labour and security in old age. For many poor people, in the absence of reliable credit and investment facilities or old age pensions, children may represent the only reliable way to ensure that one will be cared for in one's old age. A Reproduction Prerogative is comparatively easy to justify in this case, as the alternative is almost certain destitution.[25]

2. *Religious*.   An analogous instrumental value arises in some religious traditions, where children are needed to perform one's death rituals. Among Orthodox Jews, for example, sons are needed to say prayers for their dead parents. Certain groups in India need sons to 'carry the dead bodies of their parents and burn them with care'.[26] An agent who belongs to such a tradition will certainly *feel* that the cost of not having children is sufficiently high to justify a Reproduction Prerogative. Our own estimation of the significance of this cost will depend in part upon the attitude of our moral theory to controversial claims regarding the afterlife, and on the significance we attach to the agent's own interpretation of the costs she faces.[27]

---

[24] For an introduction to recent debates, see Sen, *Development as Freedom*, ch. 9. For more detailed discussion, see Section 6.6 below. The focus on the developing world is not a recent development. In the early 1970s, there were already 'better data on [economic] value among farmers for India, Ghana, and Taiwan than for the United States' (Hoffman and Hoffman, 'The Value of Children to Parents', 60).

[25] The most difficult case is where a person both (*a*) needs a child in order to provide for their own needs, and (*b*) is unable to provide that child with a life worth living. This issue is canvassed in Chapter 6.

[26] Hoffman and Hoffman, 'The Value of Children to Parents', 49.

[27] The issues of respect for divergent views of the afterlife is discussed in more detail in Mulgan, 'The Place of the Dead in Liberal Political Philosophy' (1999); and Mulgan, 'Neutrality, Rebirth and

3. Status-Based.   In many social contexts, having children greatly enhances a person's status. This is especially true for women. Indeed, becoming a mother may be the only way for a woman to qualify for the privileges of adult life. If the social status one would have to endure as a non-parent is sufficiently bad, then this factor may well be sufficient to justify a Reproduction Prerogative.

4. Group-Based.   If a nation's population is seen as too low, then people may desire to have children for the national good.[28] Also, members of disadvantaged ethnic or religious minorities may feel that having children is an effective way of helping their group against the oppressive majority.[29]

Attention to all these complex instrumental issues is vital to the development of adequate population policies, especially in developing countries, or in poorer communities within the developed world. As we shall see in Section 6.6, the appropriate public policy response is often to expand people's options, so that children are no longer so instrumentally necessary.

Our primary concern at this point is with the prerogatives and obligations of affluent people in the developed world. Economic reasons to have children do not loom large for such people. In general, 'the importance of the economic value of children declines with increased industrialization and urbanization, the rise of cash in place of subsistence farming, increased pressures to send children to school, and an increase in the educational level of the parents',[30] as well as improvements in social security for the elderly. Even among the poor, there is no evidence that children in the United States or in any other developed nation are raised for profit.[31]

In countries where overpopulation is a greater threat than underpopulation, group-based reasons would oppose any Reproduction Prerogative. Even in nations where underpopulation is a genuine issue, it is not obvious that having children is a more effective response than, for instance, devoting one's life to the advocacy of pro-natalist or pro-immigration policies. Similarly, the

---

Inter-generational Justice' (2002). For discussion of the connection between views of the afterlife and our obligations to future generations, see Mulgan, 'Valuing the Future' (draft MS).

[28] Evidence of this motivation was found in the early 1970s in Ghana and Kenya. (Hoffman and Hoffman, 'The Value of Children to Parents', 50.) Recently, attempts have been made to foster similar desires in some developed countries where the birth rate has fallen well below the replacement rate. In the contemporary developing world, of course, the national interest is more often identified with a *fall* in the birth rate (Section 6.6).

[29] In the United States this motivation has long been reported by several minority groups, especially African and Hispanic Americans (Hoffman and Hoffman, 'The Value of Children to Parents', 50). Similar attitudes also appear common in minority indigenous groups.

[30] Ibid. 58. For more recent confirmation of this observation, see Section 6.6.

[31] Ibid. 60. Commercial surrogacy arrangements might provide a very small exception to this general rule, but even there it is not obvious that economic motives are paramount.

individual strategy of having children does not seem an effective response to social discrimination, as compared to devoting one's energies to the struggle against oppression. (This is especially likely to be true if large families contribute to the low socio-economic performance of the group.) In any event, any prerogative justified in this way would, naturally enough, apply only to minorities. While it is possible that a majority of people belong to some minority or other, many prospective parents will not. A broader Reproduction Prerogative must be justified in some other way.

Reasons of religion and status are also less significant in the developed world. More generally, most people who defend a Reproduction Prerogative are unlikely to be satisfied with a permission grounded primarily on such instrumental considerations. Such a justification would imply that people without religious affiliations who already enjoy high social status are not morally permitted to have children. Furthermore, when such reasons do become relevant, this is usually in cases where more direct reasons might also justify a prerogative. In particular, those for whom religion or status provide a significant reason for having children are also likely to lack adequate alternative sources of the enjoyment and achievement values associated with reproduction. Accordingly, it is to this second class of values that we now turn.

4.2.1.2. Enjoyment and Achievement
Children are often a source of pleasure, stimulation, and novelty. Successfully raising a child is also a difficult, creative accomplishment. Many parents report it as their most significant achievement and their greatest source of satisfaction.

These are obviously very significant values. It may seem obvious that they justify a Reproduction Prerogative. However, we must note that the relevant measure of cost in the Hybrid View is not the amount of value contributed to a person's life by a particular goal. Instead, it is the *difference* between the value to that agent of a life containing that goal and the value of an otherwise similar life containing the equally successful pursuit of some alternative goal. For instance, suppose Affluent does opt for reproduction over either adoption or a life devoted to charity. No doubt her child contributes enormously to the enjoyment and achievement of her life. However, we must ask, not what her life would look like if we simply subtracted all the value provided by her child, but how her life would have gone, in terms of enjoyment and achievement, if she had opted instead for an alternative lifestyle.

The first thing to note is that the enjoyment and achievement associated with raising a child applies to both adoption and reproduction. Successfully raising an adopted child may well be just as satisfying, rewarding, enjoyable, or valuable an achievement as raising a child 'of one's own'. It is certainly not obvious that Affluent would have been any less happy had she opted for adoption. Indeed, given the very different kinds of achievement represented by reproduction and adoption, it may be impossible even in theory to say that one of these projects would have been definitely more valuable *to her* than the other.

The crucial difference between reproduction and adoption, of course, is that, when compared to the Oxfam project, the former involves a Different Number Choice while the latter is a Same People Choice. In one sense, they both involve the same achievement: a person enjoys a good start in life, which they would not otherwise have had. In another sense, however, the two projects involve two very different achievements: creating a person who then has a good start in life, or providing a good start to an already existing person. It is very hard to say, in the abstract, which of these is the more valuable achievement. On the one hand, there is something impressive in creating anything worthwhile. On the other hand, adoption reduces the amount of unmet need in the world, while reproduction does not.

Similar remarks apply to the comparison between the Oxfam project and parenthood in general. The satisfactions involved are very different, as are the achievements, but it is not clear that they are any more valuable to the agent in the case of parenthood. As Young observes, 'social scientists, as far as I know, have not proven that couples with children are, on the average, happier over the course of a lifetime than couples without children'.[32] (I argue below that, when we turn to consider availability value, this very possibility of incommensurability between different kinds of valuable achievements may itself provide the most promising defence of a parental prerogative.)

These general issues are well illustrated by one particular achievement and source of satisfaction. The parent–child relationship itself is often cited as a primary reason for having children. The benefits of such a relationship include the provision of affection not adequately provided by others, and 'opportunity to be altruistic because of the sacrifices the parent must make',[33] as well as the general satisfaction of participating in a successful close relationship.

---

[32] Young, 'Overconsumption and Procreation', 187.

[33] Hoffman and Hoffman, 'The Value of Children to Parents', 49. Aside from self-identification, the evidence for the prevalence of the first reason is a positive correlation between a woman's reported dissatisfaction with her marriage and her desired number of children (Hoffman and Hoffman, 'The Value of Children to Parents', 37 and 53).

The parent–child relationship obviously can be an extremely valuable relationship. And the creation and maintenance of successful close personal relationships is, on any plausible theory, a central component of the human good. But, as ever, we must compare the alternatives. For instance, the relationship between a child and her adopted parent is no less valuable *per se* that the corresponding relationship with a biological parent. So we still lack any ground for a Reproduction Prerogative over an Adoption Prerogative. Furthermore, affection can often be sought equally successfully in other relationships with already existing persons, and the actual world is not exactly lacking existing opportunities to be altruistic. The parent–child relationship is valuable in a particular way, but this does not show that a life containing such a relationship is more valuable than one containing other valuable relationships instead. Adoption also provides a better outcome all-things-considered. Unless life as a biological parent is *more* valuable, the Hybrid View cannot permit it.

In the real world, adoption may not be a realistic option for all potential parents. Even if the argument just presented goes through, it would not rule out a Reproduction Prerogative for those unable to adopt. However, few defenders of commonsense morality would be satisfied by this conditional defence, as those intuitions clearly suggest that reproduction is morally permitted even when adoption is an option.

4.2.1.3. Genetic Reasons
Our final class of reasons for having children arise only in the case of reproduction. These include the desire to continue one's genetic line, the desire to produce a child who resembles oneself, and the often cited desire to 'transcend one's mortality'. The first two reasons clearly support reproduction over either adoption or a life devoted to charity. We have thus found the right kind of reason to ground a reproduction prerogative. The main question is whether the values in question are sufficiently important to justify the amount of good the agent forgoes in pursuing reproduction.

Everyday conversation and popular debate suggest that genetic reasons are very significant to many people. However, these responses may reflect a general preference for parenthood, expressed against a background where having children 'of one's own' is the standard form of parenthood. The rational basis for this frequently stated desire is harder to pin down. Why should the creation of a child genetically related to oneself be seen as a more significant achievement than the successful raising of an unrelated child? In the absence of a convincing answer to this question, those seeking a secure reproduction prerogative may need to look elsewhere.

The use of genetic reasons to support reproduction encounters two specific problems. The first is that a desire for genetic descendants does not necessarily lend support to reproduction *per se*. If one's desire is to promote the existence of children genetically related to oneself, then in some cases it may be more efficient to assist one's siblings to have children, rather than having children of one's own. Nieces and nephews are not as close genetically as one's own child, but (genetically speaking) three nieces are better than one child. Considerations familiar from evolutionary biology teach us that, in some circumstances, the best available strategy may be to aim for the larger number of more distant relations.[34] For instance, the optimal strategy for an affluent Westerner might be to single-mindedly maximize her income in order to create financial incentives (or remove financial, or other, impediments) to encourage her closest relatives to produce as many children as possible. It seems very unlikely that those who cite a desire to continue their genetic line as a reason for having children would agree that their real desire would be satisfied by such a strategy. This suggests that their real reasoning is not accurately captured in purely genetic terms.

The second, more significant, problem is this. If we accept that genetic reasons are legitimate, they seem quite *sui generis*. It is thus hard to see how we could balance them against other kinds of reasons with any degree of accuracy. Yet any Agent Centred Prerogative based on achievement value requires such balancing: we must know how much *more* valuable the achievement of producing a genetically related child (and providing a good life for that child) is for the agent than the available alternatives. As we shall see in Section 4.2.2, this very element of incomparability may provide the basis for a more robust defence of the Reproduction Prerogative.

Having children is often described as a way of transcending one's mortality. Children thus provide an ersatz form of immortality.[35] Obviously enough, having children does not literally make one immortal. One might thus expect the ersatz immortality provided by children to appeal only to those who do not believe in genuine personal immortality. This would suggest that immortality is not a major reason for having children, as believers in genuine immortality seem, if anything, to have more children than non-believers.

[34] A good recent introduction to the issues is Sober and Wilson, *Unto Others: The Evolution and Psychology of Unselfish Behaviour*. For a taste of the controversies, see Dennett, 'Commentary on Sober and Wilson, Unto Others'; Gildenhuys, 'The Evolution of Altruism'; Jamieson, 'Sober and Wilson on Psychological Altruism'. For an earlier overview of the issues, see Sesardic, 'Recent Work on Human Altruism and Evolution'.

[35] A classic example is Dasgupta, *Human Well-being and the Natural Environment*, 229: 'Morality threatens to render the achievements of our life transitory, and this threat is removed by procreation.'

On the other hand, the ersatz immortality provided by children might be superior to genuine immortality. There is a considerable philosophical literature disputing the claim that genuine immortality is valuable. For instance, Bernard Williams has argued that a life of infinite duration is necessarily undesirable for a human being, as tedium will inevitably set in after a few centuries.[36] Immortality might thus be less valuable than its ersatz cousin (genetic reproduction), as the latter lacks the factor that renders genuine immortality undesirable. (Williams himself admits that a constant change of personality, or a lack of memory, would remove the tedium of immortality. He argues that this removal also deprives one of genuine immortality. Genetic reproduction might thus be superior to any possible form of genuine immortality.[37])

Unless talk of immortality is another way of referring to strictly genetic reasons for having children, the idea is presumably that having children is a way of leaving a mark on the world that endures beyond one's death. This is certainly true, and may well be a good reason for having children. Indeed, I argue at length elsewhere (building on Kant's notorious 'moral argument' for belief in personal immortality) that any worthwhile life must include some 'mortality transcending' projects.[38]

Unfortunately, this alone does not give reproduction a decisive advantage, for the simple reason that many other projects leave a similar mark. In particular, both adoption and a life devoted to charity can secure analogous forms of immortality, as could a life devoted directly to furthering the interests of future generations.

To characterize an achievement as akin to immortality, I must presumably believe that it involves the leaving behind of someone standing in a relation to my present self sufficiently like the relation between myself today and myself tomorrow. On most accounts of the moral significance of personal identity, what makes the latter relationship valuable is some form of psychological continuity, not any genetic similarity. Accordingly, the best proxy for immortality would be to leave behind someone who shares one's beliefs and values, irrespective of their genetic make-up.[39] For

---

[36] Williams, 'The Makropolous Case: Reflections on the Tedium of Immortality'.

[37] Of course, a defender of the value of genuine immortality will reply that, *contra* Williams, personal immortality need not be tedious—for instance, if it involves a transformed life in heaven. The philosophical debate then turns on whether such a life constitutes a continuation of my present life, rather than my being annihilated and replaced by someone better. In practice, believers in personal immortality typically have some alternative ground for believing in a permission (or, indeed, an obligation) to reproduce—such as divine command. The argument in the text does not address the coherence of this position, as it applies only to the use of personal immortality as a justification for the Agent Centred Prerogative.

[38] Mulgan, 'Valuing the Future' (draft MS). For a foretaste, see Mulgan, 'Two Parfit Puzzles' (2004).

[39] See chapter endnote B, p. 128.

instance, Plato argues that interpersonal love between friends provides a better approximation of immortality, as it involves intellectual rather than physical similarities.[40]

4.2.2. Availability Value

Despite their obvious significance, Achievement Value and Pursuit Value are insufficient, on their own, to ground the Agent Centred Prerogatives required by common sense. Consider the following argument against *any* departure from Simple Consequentialism. The project of maximizing objective value appears at least as valuable as any other, and an agent effectively pursuing that project would develop most of the genuinely valuable human capacities. She would also be able to take pleasure and pride in her achievement. Therefore, the value of any alternative project cannot justify a decision not to maximize the good.

Many people will reject this argument. They will deny that 'maximizing the good' would be sufficiently fulfilling to serve as the guiding project of a rich human life. However, so long as we concentrate on Achievement Value and Pursuit Value, a more moderate variant of the argument is quite compelling. For any agent contemplating parenthood, there will be some specific charitable project (such as 'devote one's life to helping the poor in country X') that would be rich enough to provide all the main personal values associated with parenthood.

Defences of a prerogative based on Achievement Value or Pursuit Value are thus doubly deficient. The immediate problem is that, as an agent's chosen project is typically not more valuable to her than some more other-regarding alternative, any such prerogative will be extremely limited. There is also a deeper problem. Even when a precise calculation of Achievement Value or Pursuit Value does justify a prerogative, it seems to do so for the wrong reasons. Intuitively, a key component of moral autonomy is the freedom to choose a less other-regarding project irrespective of whether it is more valuable to us.

Justifications based on Achievement Value and Pursuit Value miss the point of the autonomy objection. The thought behind the objection is not so much: 'These *projects* must be permitted because of their comparative value', but rather: 'This is the kind of *choice* that should be morally open.' Unless we believe that respect for autonomy itself requires the availability of a range of distinct valuable projects, we can never justify supplementing the Reason to Promote the Good with parental prerogatives (Section 1.6).

[40] Plato, *Symposium* 206c1–209e5.

Perhaps particular options should not be permitted unless they are independently valuable, but that value alone cannot be the sole justification for the prerogative.

The limitations of Availability Value and Pursuit Value are not only significant for the Hybrid View. They also sound the death knell for any attempt to rehabilitate Simple Consequentialism by appealing directly to the value of reproduction. For instance, 'indirect' Individual Consequentialism allows an agent to choose the decision procedure that produces the best consequences over the course of her life, even if it yields sub-optimal consequences on some particular occasion. Such a theory seeks to avoid the Demandingness Objection by arguing that the policy of always devoting oneself 100 per cent to charity will cause burnout, and thus not be an efficient long-term strategy for promoting the good. However, if a more balanced life devoted to charitable projects is as good for the agent as a parental life, then the optimal decision procedure will lead to the former life. So, even if it avoids the Demandingness Objection, indirect individual consequentialism cannot sanction parenthood.[41]

The best case for a parental prerogative will thus appeal to Availability Value. A key feature of human goals is that they derive their value in part from their having been freely chosen by the agent. (In contrast to basic needs, whose significance to the agent is independent of choice.) The significance of this feature is that, if goals are to be sufficiently valuable to justify an Agent Centred Prerogative, then they must reflect the agent's autonomy. If the agent is to be autonomous, then a range of options must be available to her.[42]

A worthwhile and integrated human life is possible only if one's major life choices are morally open. If the making of a given choice is essential to the full development of one's autonomy, then one must be morally permitted to make that choice. Furthermore, the availability of unchosen options may alter the *nature* of those options which are chosen, as well as their significance. There is a great difference between choosing a life without parenthood and having such a life chosen for you. In our culture, parenthood has considerable social significance. The decision whether or not to engage in it is thus a central life choice for most agents in our society.

The significance of availability depends on two factors.

1. The impact of the choice on the agent's life.
2. The extent to which the different options represent radically different kinds of value.

---

[41] On indirect Consequentialism in general, see Jackson, 'Decision-Theoretic Consequentialism and the Nearest and Dearest Objection' 462–72; and Pettit, 'Decision Theory and Folk Psychology'.

[42] I defend these claims at length in Mulgan, *The Demands of Consequentialism*, ch. 7.

In a choice between different amounts of the very same value (for instance, money), it may be very important for the agent to choose correctly, but the actual process of choice is of less importance. A good test here is to ask whether it would matter if a third party chose on behalf of the agent, so long as they got the same result. Consider the contrast between choosing a financial investment strategy and choosing a career. The former choice concerns a single value: money. Many agents are happy to delegate this choice to a qualified third party. So long as the returns are good, the agent loses little from not actually choosing herself. The elimination of inferior unchosen financial investment strategies would not bother the agent. By contrast, almost no one would give up the opportunity to choose their own career. No doubt this is partly because one would doubt that a third party would make the right choice. But it is also largely because different careers represent different values (different balances of status and enjoyment, incommensurable achievements, etc.), and thus provide an opportunity for the agent to develop and express her own values and autonomy. The process of making the choice oneself is at least as important as getting it right. The elimination of non-chosen careers would adversely affect the agent, as she no longer gets to choose.

Suppose we believe that agents should be able to 'freely choose' between parenthood and non-parenthood. Our first task is to ask what degree of availability unchosen alternatives must have for the agent's goal to count as freely chosen. There are several possibilities.

Practical Availability.   To be freely chosen, a goal must be chosen from a range of practically available alternatives.

Legal Availability.   To be freely chosen, a goal must be chosen from a range of legally permitted alternatives.

Non-Interference Availability.   A goal is freely chosen only if no one interferes with the agent's choice.

Social Availability.   To be freely chosen, a goal must be chosen from a range of alternatives regarded as legitimate lifestyle choices within the agent's society.

Moral Availability.   To be freely chosen, a goal must be chosen from a range of morally available alternatives.

Razian Availability.   To be freely chosen, a goal must be chosen from a range of morally available alternatives, and it must be the case that at least one of those alternatives was neither better than, nor worse than, nor exactly as valuable as the chosen goal.

In most Western countries, both forms of parenthood are legally available, as is non-parenthood. Third parties do not generally interfere directly in the choice between parenthood and non-parenthood. Social availability, as characterized here, comes in degrees. Although non-parenthood is certainly tolerated in Western society, it is often regarded as inferior to parenthood. So the two options are not equally socially available.

If we agree that both options should be practically available, then we may conclude that agents (and societies) have an obligation to ensure that everyone is able to engage in parenthood, and that suitable alternative lifestyles are also available. This might require considerable changes to existing social practices, especially rules governing adoption and artificial reproductive technologies.[43]

Later chapters explore the extent to which both reproduction and non-reproduction should be available in these first four senses. Despite their obvious significance, these questions are not our present concern. Only moral or Razian availability could be sufficient to justify a genuine Agent Centred Prerogative. This is simply because our present objection relates directly to the moral availability of the option of parenthood. Furthermore, as we shall see, the autonomy objection is at its strongest when the options involved are genuinely incommensurable. In that case, moral availability goes together with Razian availability.

The argument for moral availability is as follows. If my choice is determined by morality, then I do not genuinely exercise autonomy in making that choice. If I want to be moral, then I have no choice. The argument for Razian availability is similar. If one option is superior to all others, then my choice is determined by the balance of reasons. Therefore, I cannot genuinely exercise autonomy. If I want to be rational, then I have no choice. On the other hand, if my choice is not determined by the balance of reasons, but only because the options are exactly equal in value, then it makes no difference what I chose. Raz argues that, in this case, one cannot *valuably* exercise autonomy. A genuinely valuable choice thus occurs only when one is balancing incommensurable reasons. Autonomy can be meaningfully exercised only in the presence of incommensurability, which Raz defines as follows: 'A and B are incommensurable if it is neither true that one is better than the other nor true that they are of equal value.'[44]

If we agree that both parenthood and non-parenthood need to be morally available, then we will conclude that all moral agents have (at least) some weakened analogue of the Parental Prerogative. If Razian availability is also desired, then we must conclude, not only that both parenthood and

---

[43] We would, of course, need to balance the desire to extend the availability of parenthood against other social policy goals, especially those relating to the meeting of basic needs. These issues are explored further in Chs. 5–8 below.   [44] See Raz, *The Morality of Freedom*, 322.

non-parenthood are permissible, but also that the balance of moral reasons does not determine the choice between them.

Razian availability arises if and only if options are incommensurable. I have argued elsewhere that incommensurability is a significant feature of our experience of autonomy and decision-making, and that any intuitively plausible moral theory must accommodate it.[45] The best case for genuine incommensurability is when different options instantiate very different kinds of value. The choice between the Oxfam, Adoption, and Reproduction projects is a very promising example. Our exploration of reasons for pursuing either reproduction or adoption suggests these two projects involve quite different values. These values can also differ significantly from the values realized by successful pursuit of charitable projects. It is hard to accept that, in every case, one of these options is better than the others, in terms of its contribution to the agent's own life. If incommensurability is ever plausible, it is plausible here.

If the agent's autonomy is the ground of her reproductive prerogative, then this enables us to explain another theoretically puzzling feature of commonsense morality: the significance it attaches to parental autonomy. Most people believe that parents have considerable autonomy in their treatment of their children. This can partly be justified on instrumental grounds. Parents are likely to be especially motivated to care for their children's interests, and especially well placed to discern what will further those interests, so children's interests are best served by parental autonomy. However, commonsense morality often goes further, justifying parents in choosing particular lifestyles or values for their children when other equally valuable, or perhaps even more valuable, alternatives were available. Our analysis suggests that, if the justification for any prerogative is the agent's need to exercise her autonomy, then autonomous parenthood represents a more significant achievement than non-autonomous parenthood, even if the result is no better for the child. The agent's prerogative is thus more likely to permit parenthood which is autonomously pursued.[46]

4.2.2.1. Evaluating the Availability-Based Defence
The availability-based defence raises several questions.

1. Is it paradoxical?
2. Is it sufficient?
3. Is it compatible with Scheffler's own defence of the Agent Centred Prerogative?

---

[45] Mulgan, *The Demands of Consequentialism*, ch. 7.
[46] For related discussion, see Page, 'Parental Rights'; and Bigelow et al., 'Parental Autonomy'.

The defence of a prerogative on the grounds of availability value can seem somewhat paradoxical. A prerogative is needed because the option the agent wishes to choose produces less value overall than some other option. The argument then concedes that our preferred option is not more valuable to the agent. (If the two options represent radically different, incommensurable values, then neither is better or worse than the other.) The central claim is that, because the two options represent very different valuable lives open to the agent, respect for her autonomy requires that these options both be available. If our moral theory is to adequately respect autonomy, then it too must leave this choice open.

Many people find this line of reasoning suspect. They will doubt that the Reproduction Prerogative has been adequately established. In particular, those who do not believe in incommensurability at all cannot endorse this solution. Incommensurability is a very controversial notion: some philosophers find the very idea incoherent, while others regard it as an essential feature of any adequate account of practical reason.[47] If defenders of the Hybrid View do not want to rely on controversial value claims, then they have two options.

The first is to argue that the autonomy objection itself presupposes incommensurability. If one rejects incommensurability, then the autonomy objection dissolves as well. If Mary does not face a choice between incommensurable options, then the value to her of a life spent on charity work must be either better than, or worse than, or exactly equal to, the value to her of life as a parent. If the charity life is better for Mary, then obviously she ought to choose it. If the two are equal, then she ought to be guided by impersonal considerations and opt for the life of charity. If life as a parent is better for Mary, then we simply need to ask *how much* better, to see if her prerogative will extend that far. We saw in Section 4.2.1 that, in most cases, parenthood will not be more valuable than more other-regarding alternatives. Those who reject incommensurability but remain troubled by Sam's advice to Mary would thus owe us an explanation.

The second option for the Hybrid Theorist is to argue that, even if the intuitions behind the autonomy objection do not commit us to incommensurability regarding values, they will require us to include something analogous in our overall moral theory. For instance, we might reject incommensurability in our theory of impersonal value, but accept that, if their deliberations are to do justice to the true nature of the divergent values

---

[47] For a variety of perspectives on incommensurability, see esp. Chang (ed.), *Incommensurability, Incomparability, and Practical Reason*. See also Broome, 'Incommensurable Values', in Crisp and Hooker (eds.), *Well-being and Morality*; Griffin, 'Replies', 285–9; Griffin, *Well-being*, 75–92; Raz, *The Morality of Freedom*, 321–66.

involved, then agents must adopt a presupposition that the values embodied in their options are incommensurable. (This move has obvious affinities to our endorsement of the lexical level in Chapter 3.)

My aim in this book is to develop a moral theory that responds to a set of intuitions. The intuition behind the autonomy objection to the Hybrid View is not decisive. Simple Consequentialists, and others, may reasonably reject it. However, I regard this intuition as distinctive of a certain picture of morality, one that pays special regard to the significance of autonomy, and to the phenomenology of the deliberations of moral agents. A commitment to the incommensurability of values is one theoretical response to that picture, along with the lexical level. (The connection between the two notions of lexicality and incommensurability is explored more fully in subsequent chapters.) For instance, in *The Demands of Consequentialism*, I argue that the supposition that values are sometimes incommensurable is crucial to the development of a Consequentialist response to the Demandingness Objection.[48] If incommensurability is indeed necessary to defeat the Demandingness Objection, and if the two compulsion objections are instances of the Demandingness Objection, then the Hybrid Theorist is already committed to incommensurability, and can appeal to that notion to show that agents need not abandon reproduction.

Incommensurability thus opens up the theoretical possibility of a response to the autonomy objection. However, there are two reasons to doubt that incommensurability is sufficient to defeat the objection entirely. In the first place, there may be cases where autonomy seems significant but where incommensurability is harder to establish. Consider the following variant of our original tale.

The Second Forced Choice.   Mary ignores Sam, and has a child. A few years later, the opportunity to devote her life to charity arises again. Mary can combine this new offer with caring for one child, but any more children would make it impossible for her to accept. Mary would quite like another child, but is unsure which option is better for her. She turns to Sam for advice. As before, he tells her she has no prerogative, and must take the job.

This new choice does not pit parenthood against non-parenthood. Rather, it compares a life with two children and a life with one. All the values associated with parenthood are present on both sides. It will thus be much harder to establish that Mary's choice involves incommensurable options, such that her autonomy requires that she be morally free in making that choice.

---

[48] Mulgan, *The Demands of Consequentialism*, ch. 7.

A second problem for the availability-based defence is that incommensurability alone is not sufficient to justify either a claim of Moral or Razian availability. Respect for autonomy is unlikely to require that every choice involving incommensurable options must be morally open, irrespective of the impersonal good at stake. For any such choice, there will be some other choice situation that is equally incommensurable for the agent, but where less total value is at stake. Leaving the latter choice morally open might provide sufficient room for autonomy. Perhaps Mary can valuably exercise her autonomy so long as she is able to choose between having one child and having none, even if the choice between one and two children also involves some incommensurability.

These are not knockdown blows for the availability-based defence. We could argue that Mary's second choice *does* involve significant incommensurability, or even bite the bullet and deny that there is a moral permission to have more than one child.[49] The strength of the commonsense intuition that people are permitted to have (at least) two children suggests that Hybrid Theorists will favour the first option. They might claim that, because each child is a different person, and because of the impact of family dynamics on the personalities of children, the decision to have another child *always* involves significantly incommensurable values. Alternatively, a Hybrid Theorist who rejects incommensurability might defend the weaker claim that, while the choice between one and two children is not strictly incommensurable, agents need to see it as being so—perhaps because only an agent who regarded each child as embodying an incommensurable value would be able to appropriately value her own children as distinct individuals.

As these claims are not obviously implausible, I propose to accept, at least for the sake of argument, that reproductive decisions typically do involve incommensurable values—or whatever else plays the same theoretical role in our account of value. This concession enables us to explore the resources of the availability-based defence more fully: a task that will occupy the remainder of this chapter We begin by asking whether this defence can be incorporated into Scheffler's original Hyrbrid View. This will lead us to a pair of revisions to that view.

4.2.2.2. Scheffler and Availability

One obvious question for the availability-based defence of prerogatives is how it fits into Scheffler's own formulation. Suppose an agent (Xavier) has only three options available to him: P (his preferred act), O (the optimal act in terms of impersonal value), and B (sub-optimal in terms of impersonal

---

[49] For a defence of the claim that couples should have only one child, see McKibbon, *Maybe One*.

value, but better than P). The choice between P and B involves incommensurability. In Scheffler's formulation, Xavier is

permitted to perform P, provided that there was no alternative (A) open to him, such that (1) A would produce a better overall outcome than P, as judged from an impersonal standpoint giving equal weight to everyone's interests, and (2) the total net loss to others of his doing P rather than A was more than M times as great as the net loss to him of doing A rather than P.

B is one of the available candidates for A. As B is incommensurable with P, it follows (by definition) that there is no net loss to Xavier in doing B rather than P. If B produces greater impersonal value, then it must be preferred to P. Therefore, Xavier cannot possibly have a prerogative to do P.

Let us see if we can justify a prerogative in such a case, without departing from Scheffler's formulation. The first move is to distinguish between B-chosen-freely-over-P and B-morally-compelled. (For the purpose of this argument, B counts as 'morally compelled' even if B was chosen over O when *this choice* was morally open. The crucial question is whether P was also morally available.) The appeal to the value of autonomy is designed to show that B-chosen is much better for the agent than B-compelled. There are then two steps to establish that Xavier is permitted to choose P.

The first step is to establish that Xavier *does* have a prerogative to opt for B-chosen. We now compare O, B-chosen, and B-compelled. Assume that B-chosen and B-compelled have the same impersonal value—less than the impersonal value of O. Let the difference between the impersonal value of B-chosen and B-compelled and the impersonal value of O be N1. (*Ex hypothesi*, O is the only option with greater impersonal value than B-chosen.) Let W(P) be Xavier's well-being if Xavier performs P. Similarly for W(O), W(B-chosen), and W(B-compelled). The availability-based defence will apply if the following two claims are true.

1. [[W(B-compelled) minus W(O)] multiplied by M] is less than N1.
2. [[W(B-chosen) minus W(O)] multiplied by M] is greater than N1.

According to (1), Xavier has no prerogative permitting B-compelled. By contrast, (2) implies that Xavier does have a prerogative permitting B-chosen. (Both conditions are necessary. If (1) is false, and Xavier has a prerogative permitting B-compelled, then the availability-based defence is unavailable, as the availability of P is not needed to ground the availability of B.)

The second step is to prove that, if B-chosen is permitted, then P is also permitted. We might begin by comparing P, B-chosen, and B-compelled. To simplify, assume that B-chosen and B-compelled have the same impersonal value, and that the difference between that value and the impersonal value of P is N2. The availability-based defence will apply if the following two claims are true.

3. [[W(P) minus W(B-compelled)] multiplied by M] is greater than N2.
4. [[W(P) minus W(B-chosen)] multiplied by M] is less than N2.

According to (3), if P and B-compelled are the only relevant options, then X has a prerogative permitting P. On the other hand, if we replace B-compelled with B-chosen, X has no direct prerogative permitting P. However, if X is permitted to opt for B-chosen, then P must be indirectly permitted, as B-chosen can only be available if P is permitted. (Furthermore, the basic claim of the availability-based defence is that both P and B are only genuinely valuable to the agent if freely chosen. P will only be sufficiently valuable to justify a prerogative if it is P-chosen, where this means 'P chosen instead of B when both were morally available'. But P-chosen certainly must be paired with B-chosen.)

This argument looks like a plausible instance of a Scheffler-style justification. However, closer inspection reveals its peculiarity. The problem comes from the role of the second half of the argument. The comparison between P, B-chosen, and B-compelled is meant to establish that, if the choice were between P and B-compelled, then P would be permitted. However, the notion of a choice between P and B-compelled makes no sense. If P is permitted, then the alternative must have been B-chosen. The real lesson of the second comparison is that, if B-compelled is the relevant version of B, then the agent has no prerogatives at all.

The second comparison thus cannot contribute to the defence of a prerogative regarding P. All the work is done by the first comparison, where there is no mention of P. P enters the equation not by reference to the cost to Xavier of not doing P, but via the cost to Xavier of giving up the option of doing P—B is valuable only if chosen instead of P. (Any attempt to directly justify a prerogative to opt for P-chosen over B-chosen in terms of the cost to Xavier of not doing P will fail, for the reasons already outlined in Section 4.2.1. There is no possible value of M such that the cost to Xavier of doing B-chosen rather than P-chosen, when multiplied by M, exceeds the difference in impersonal value between B-chosen and P-chosen. We therefore cannot translate the availability-based argument into Scheffler's formula.)

The availability-based defence is a significant departure from the letter of Scheffler's Hybrid View. The latter focuses on the cost to the agent of not performing a particular action, while the former invites us to broaden our view, and take account of the value to the agent of choices between several actions. So long as we concentrate solely on the personal and impersonal value at stake in a particular isolated pair-wise choice, rather than on the contribution of the choice itself to the agent's life, we cannot make sense of the availability-based defence.

Once we have begun to broaden our view, it will be tempting to continue: to move from evaluating choices to evaluating whole lifelong patterns of choice. Scheffler's constant 'M' no longer guides our moral thinking. We thus need to restructure our Hybrid View. Fortunately, such a restructuring may also enable us to resolve our second cluster of objections, where the Hybrid View produced highly counterintuitive results. To see how this might be so, we leave Scheffler's particular formulation, and return to the general motivation for the Hybrid View.

4.3. Constrained Prerogatives

Scheffler's guiding view is that an adequate moral theory should leave human beings morally free to choose, build, and pursue their own goals, projects, activities, and relationships, even at the expense of overall value. This leaves the crucial question: What constrains this freedom? One extreme view would allow the agent completely unconstrained moral freedom to pursue her own goals. She may choose any goal, and pursue it however she wishes. At the other extreme, the Simple Consequentialist contends that the agent's freedom to pursue her goals is entirely subject to the overriding goal of maximizing value. The moral moderate, such as Scheffler, seeks a freedom for moral agents which is constrained but not empty.[50]

There are three possible ways to constrain a prerogative.

Range Constraints. These limit the range of goals agents are permitted to pursue. For instance, agents might be allowed to pursue only goals developing valuable human capacities.

Method Constraints. These restrict the ways agents pursue their goals. A method constraint might be global, applying to the pursuit of all goals. For instance, an Agent Centred Restriction such as 'Do not kill' restricts the methods available to agents in pursuit of any goals. Alternatively, a method constraint might be particular, applying only to the pursuit of some class of goals. For instance, specific rules such as 'Only reproduce within heterosexual nuclear families' restrict the pursuit of a particular set of goals.

---

[50] For definitions of the notion of a moderate moral theory, see Scheffler, *Human Morality* (1992), 6; and Kagan, *The Limits of Morality*, 4–5. For a defence, see Scheffler, *Human Morality*, 98–114. For a critique, see Kagan, *The Limits of Morality*, 47–80.

Weight Constraints.   These limit the weight agents are permitted to give to their own goals, as opposed to the general good. As with method constraints, a weight constraint can be either global or particular. A moral theory might include a variety of different weight constraints, each governing a different class of goals.

In his original discussion, Scheffler focuses exclusively on the third form of constraint. He offers a simple blanket form of this constraint, with all agents permitted to give a certain weight to all their goals. The range of goals available, and the method of pursuit, are totally unconstrained. This focus on weight is the reason Scheffler cannot accommodate the availability-based defence. Furthermore, to avoid our cluster of objections, we need both range and method constraints.[51] In particular, we will be interested in the relationship between the two. Perhaps some permissible goals can only be pursued in certain ways. If these are the only permissible goals, then those method constraints will come close to Agent Centred Restrictions.

It might seem that a suitable weight constraint is sufficient to accommodate the different values of different goals. If Goal G1 is more valuable to the agent than Goal G2, then the weight constraint will permit the agent to pursue Goal G1 to a greater extent than Goal G2. This suggests that range constraints are unnecessary. Similarly, if a goal is less valuable (or not valuable at all) if pursued in an inappropriate way, then the weight constraint will discount it accordingly. This suggests that method constraints are unnecessary.

However, things are not so simple. The arguments in the previous paragraph assume that the moral significance of a given goal is proportional to its contribution to the agent's well-being. Yet strict proportionality between personal value and moral significance is not always appropriate. Perhaps some components of an agent's well-being have greater significance in certain contexts than other equally valuable components. In particular, if the justification of the Agent Centred Prerogative turns on the importance of certain features of human agency, then components of well-being closely related to those features may generate stronger prerogatives than equally valuable components contributing to other features of a flourishing human life. For instance, the Agent Centred Prerogative may privilege goals developing one's autonomy over goals which merely exercise that autonomy, even though the latter may develop other valuable capacities. Also, the choice between goals may have significance over and above the significance of the goals themselves, considered in isolation.

---

[51] In *The Demands of Consequentialism*, 148–52, I also advocate an amendment to Scheffler's original weight constraint.

To deny the need for range and method constraints is thus to claim that all choices involving personal goals make an equal contribution to the development and flourishing of human agency. This is a very strong claim. Indeed, one of my principal aims in *The Demands of Consequentialism* was to establish that this claim is, at best, highly implausible. Different goals are morally significant in very different ways. Accordingly, we should regard range and method constraints as genuine possibilities, and examine arguments supporting them.

In this book our interest is in obligations to future generations, not in moral theory more generally. We want to know, not whether the Hybrid View incorporates constrained prerogatives in general, but whether it includes a plausible constrained prerogative governing reproduction, as well as plausible principles governing other aspects of our relations with future generations. Our discussion of the comparative merits of values associated with pursuit, achievement, and availability suggests that the way goals are pursued, and especially the way they are chosen, will be especially significant in relation to reproduction. If method constraints are ever appropriate, it is here.

We may need to borrow our account of these additional constraints from an extant moral theory. In particular, I argue in Chapters 5 and 6 that the best constraints are provided by Rule Consequentialism. Indeed, only by incorporating Rule Consequentialism can the Hybrid View provide an adequate justification for, or account of, reproductive prerogatives. We return to the relationship between Rule Consequentialism and the Hybrid View in Chapter 11. First, however, we must establish that method constraints are necessary to avoid our cluster of intuitive objections, and ask if they are sufficient for this task.

4.3.1. *Constraints and Obligations*

Our second cluster of objections suggests that the intuitive costs of any Hybrid View that permits reproduction will be too high. How might proponents of the Hybrid View respond?

One option is to deny that the Hybrid View has these alleged counter-intuitive implications. As we saw in Section 4.1.3.1, Scheffler himself has replied to Kagan partly along these lines. As a general strategy, this move seems dubious. The odd results alleged against the Hybrid View are not accidental. They stem from a basic structural feature of the theory, namely its rejection of Agent Centred Restrictions. It is thus very unlikely that the Hybrid View can avoid conflicting with the general intuitions underlying such restrictions, even if some particular counter-examples can be dissolved.

A second response is to defend the Hybrid View in spite of its counter-intuitive results. After all, as Scheffler himself acknowledges, the intuitive appeal of Agent Centred Restrictions was never in doubt.[52] It is thus hardly surprising that a theory without restrictions has some intuitively unattractive features. The crucial question is whether we can find a rationale for Agent Centred Restrictions. Scheffler argues that we cannot, and that restrictions should thus be rejected. If restrictions have no rationale, then the present objections to the Hybrid View can be safely ignored. The problem with this strategy is its high intuitive cost. The Hybrid View would thus be inferior to any theory that could offer a plausible rationale.

A third strategy would seek to use our four objections to construct a rationale for some restriction on the behaviour of agents pursuing their prerogatives. We could then amend the Hybrid View by building restrictions into the structure of the theory. If it can be done in a principled way, this will be the most satisfactory response to our present objections. So we focus on this third response.

We begin by asking which particular restrictions would dissolve our present objections. Some examples might be the following: (a) agents are obliged not to harm innocent persons; (b) agents should not abandon their commitments, especially when they were permitted to originally make those commitments; (c) agents should not undermine the interests of others with whom they are engaged in morally sanctioned cooperative ventures; (d) agents should not abandon their children, and must provide for their basic needs. Each of these restrictions will probably be non-absolute, admitting some exceptions such as promise-breaking to avert disaster. (Even the obligation to provide for the needs of one's own children may admit some exceptions, as when the only way to avoid detection by the secret police is to suffocate a crying baby.)

Do the scenarios presented in Section 4.1.3 provide a rationale for these restrictions? Many of those who discuss such thought experiments have argued that they do.[53] One common form of argument is as follows.

1. Some Agent Centred Prerogatives are self-defeating without Agent Centred Restrictions.
2. A moral theory must include Agent Centred Prerogatives if it is adequately to recognize the significance of moral agency. (This is Scheffler's own rationale for the Agent Centred Prerogative.)

---

[52] See Scheffler, *The Rejection of Consequentialism* (1982), 83; and Scheffler, 'Prerogatives without Restrictions' (1992), 390.

[53] See Harris, 'A Paradoxical Departure from Consequentialism'; Kagan, 'Does Consequentialism Demand Too Much?'; Murphy, 'The Demands of Beneficence'; and Schueler, 'Consequences and Agent-Centred Restrictions'.

3. Self-defeating prerogatives are not sufficient for the recognition of agency.

4. Therefore, an acceptable moral theory must include some Agent Centred Restrictions.

There are many different versions of this argument. In the present section, we focus on its general form. Initially, this argument seems very convincing. It seems to diagnose the problem created for the Hybrid View by its lack of restrictions. However, things are not so simple. We seek a rationale for restrictions, not merely a restatement of their intuitive plausibility. It is not always clear precisely what a rationale amounts to in Scheffler's terminology.[54] However, it is clear that if we seek a rationale for departures from Simple Consequentialism, then appeals to value or disvalue are not sufficient. We cannot defend Agent Centred Restrictions merely by appealing to the value of the agency those restrictions safeguard. Such appeals cannot justify the claim that agents must refrain from performing an act of type X even when doing so would minimize the overall number of acts of type X. For instance, if murder is bad, then why should an agent refrain from murder when the result is more murders than would have occurred if she had murdered someone herself? Yet, the whole point of an Agent Centred Restriction is that it forbids agents from performing actions of a certain type even when the result is an increase in the overall number of acts of that type.[55]

We must therefore ask if the argument we are considering really is strong enough to provide a genuine rationale for Agent Centred Restrictions. Let us focus on the claim that prerogatives without restrictions are self-defeating. In what sense is it 'inconsistent', 'paradoxical', or 'self-defeating' for a moral theory to include prerogatives without restrictions?[56] The idea behind such phrases seems to be as follows. Prerogatives serve to protect or promote the agent's freedom to live her own life. Agent Centred Restrictions are necessary both to safeguard that freedom and to lend it appropriate meaning. As an example of the first role, without restrictions the Agent Centred Prerogative and the Reason to Promote the Good combine to permit agents to undermine and interfere with other agents' pursuit of personal projects. As an example of the second role of restrictions, if you do not pursue your projects consistently with the commitments embodied in those projects, then the projects will not be significant enough to justify an Agent Centred Prerogative.

[54] See e.g. Conee, 'On Seeking a Rationale', 605–9.

[55] This objection to value-based rationales is emphasized by Scheffler in his introduction to Scheffler, *Consequentialism and its Critics* (1988).

[56] For these expressions, see Harris, 'A Paradoxical Departure from Consequentialism'; and Kagan, 'Does Consequentialism Demand Too Much?'.

Four questions arise at this point:

1. What would these constraints on parental prerogatives actually look like?
2. Do they provide all the intuitive benefits of full Agent Centred Restrictions?
3. If not, can the Hybrid View consistently incorporate full restrictions?
4. Can the Hybrid View consistently incorporate constraints without becoming overly demanding? (For instance, will the rationale for constraints also justify a general obligation to assist others in the pursuit of their personal projects—on the grounds that my failure to assist you may render your Agent Centred Prerogative practically worthless to you, just as much as any active interference with your projects?)

I shall conclude that constrained prerogatives are not sufficient for an adequate moral theory.

4.3.2. The Structure of Parental Prerogatives

The nature of the constraints on any prerogative will obviously depend on the justification offered for that prerogative. Our second cluster of objections only arise at all once the autonomy objection has been resolved. (If there is no parental prerogative, there is no point exploring the constraints on that prerogative.) In reply to the autonomy objection, we saw that any justification will need to rest on the moral significance of goals, and their connection to autonomy. However, any argument based on autonomy and/or Availability Value must also begin with the claim that parental projects are valuable in themselves. Even on the availability-based defence, the chosen project must be valuable to the agent, as otherwise choices involving that project will lack the required significance. By exploring the conditions under which these projects are valuable, we may find some suitable constraints. We take each of the two key parental projects in turn.

The most obvious feature of reproduction is that it is essentially other-regarding. While an agent's motivation for embarking on the project may be primarily self-concerned, the project itself centres on someone else. To reproduce is to create a new agent. (Or, at least, to create a new potential agent.) Furthermore, many intuitive arguments for the availability of reproduction rely explicitly on its other-regarding nature. One common defence of reproduction is that it fosters certain other-regarding human capacities, or that it creates a valuable personal relationship. To pursue reproduction without due regard for the interests of the newly created agent is inconsistent with this justification of one's Agent Centred Prerogative. An acceptable moral theory would not permit an agent to pursue reproduction in this way even if this would produce a greater amount of good, both for the agent herself and overall.

Similar considerations apply to adoption, which is very similar to reproduction. In particular, the principal justifications for the two prerogatives are similar. Both projects acquire their deepest moral significance from the value of the social relationship between parent and child, and the independent value of the child's life. Adoption thus also loses its justification if it is pursued in a way inconsistent with the value of that parental relationship. The Adoption Prerogative will be subject to method constraints similar to those which govern the Reproduction Prerogative.

The principal difference between the two projects is that adoption does not bring an additional person into existence. It may thus be morally permissible to adopt a child even though one will be unable to guarantee her a good enough life, or even to meet all of her basic needs, as the alternative is even worse for the child. Indeed, it is in such cases that adoption often seems most praiseworthy, as when people voluntarily adopt a severely disabled child. By contrast, there cannot be anything praiseworthy in deliberately creating a child knowing that her life will fall below the zero level. (In Section 1.2, I suggested that this is one of the few decisive intuitions in this area.) The crucial difference between the two cases, of course, is that the alternative to adoption is that the needs in question go unmet, whereas the alternative to reproduction is that the needs never come into existence.

The claim is not that non-other-regarding ways of pursuing adoption or reproduction will be wrong because they produce a less valuable result overall. After all, the whole point of the prerogative is to justify agents opting for impersonally sub-optimal projects. Rather, the objection to such pursuit is that, if pursued in a non-other-regarding way, parenthood could not represent a genuinely valuable achievement for the agent herself. As the value to the agent herself is what grounds the prerogative, it follows that such projects are not permitted.

Consider two stark examples of improper parenting.[57]

The Slave Child Tale.   A couple in the developed world are planning to have no children. A slave trader from a society where slavery is legal offers them $100,000 to produce a slave for him. They want the money to pay for an

---

[57] These tales are taken from Kavka, 'The Paradox of Future Individuals', and Okin, *Justice, Gender and the Family*, 74–88.

overseas trip. They sign the agreement, accept the money, produce the child, and sell her into slavery.

Okin's Matriarchal Nightmare.   In a society based exclusively on absolute (Libertarian) property rights, mothers are deemed to have the right to do whatever they want with (or to) their children. Mary, who lives in such a society, has a child in order to keep it in a cage for a few years before eating it.

Neither of these parental projects seems acceptable. How might the Hybrid View account for this? The answer cannot simply be that these ways of bringing up children are sub-optimal in impersonal terms. After all, the basis for the Compulsory Non-Reproduction Objection in Chapter 1 was the observation that most forms of reproduction lead to sub-optimal outcomes. A more plausible answer is that, to be acceptable, sub-optimal behaviour must be sanctioned by a legitimate Agent Centred Prerogative. The Agent Centred Prerogative governing Reproduction Projects is principally justified by appeal to the significance of the agent's capacity for care in the context of a parent–child relationship. The parental strategies adopted in our two tales do nothing to develop those capacities. Indeed, they are not ways an agent who possessed such capacities to any reasonable degree would behave. To pursue the Reproduction Project in these ways is thus inconsistent with the underlying justification of the very prerogative which permits reproduction in the first place.

The same argument applies even if an agent, while not actively mistreating her child, fails to accord that child's interests any greater weight than the interests of everyone else in the world. If you treat your child as just another utility container, then you might as well not have that child in the first place. After all, if your interest is in filling utility containers, then there are more efficient ways of doing this. Your engagement in the Reproduction Project will be morally justified if and only if you have a special attachment to your child. This attachment will generate specific obligations to that child. If your project is to be covered by the Agent Centred Prerogative, then you must pursue it within the bounds set by those obligations.

We could cast this argument in Kantian terms. The justification of the Reproduction Project is that it is a valuable achievement for the agent. This achievement consists in the exercise of the agent's capacity to treat other people as an ends-in-themselves. Reproduction is therefore only legitimate if it is pursued in a manner which treats the resulting children as ends-in-themselves. (We have just seen that many reasons for having children treat those children as means to some end: economic security, social status, affection, satisfaction, achievement, etc. We must recall that Kant's dictum that rational agents always be treated as ends-in-themselves does not rule out using children as means, so long as we treat them at the same time as ends-in-themselves. Section 1.5)

A parent's special obligations to her child may conflict with her other goals. For instance, if the Reproduction project results in the existence of a child with special needs, then the agent's special obligations to that child may require her to sacrifice her own non reproduction projects. At the extreme, the special obligations generated by the Reproduction Project may require an agent to sacrifice her own life to protect her children. We can explain even this extreme obligation in terms of the Agent Centred Prerogative. Reproduction is only valuable if one undertakes it on the understanding that it places one under such strong obligations. Hence, it is only permissible if so undertaken.

Any plausible Reproduction Prerogative will be subject to stringent method constraints. If one is ever permitted to reproduce, then one can only do so by placing oneself under specific obligations to those one creates. We now ask if those constraints are sufficient to dissolve our objections to the Hybrid View.

4.3.3. The Limits of Constrained Prerogatives

I have assumed thus far that the agent's motivation for having a child is to pursue the project of raising a child. In this case, any Agent Centred Prerogative will be constrained, as the project must be pursued in a valuable way. However, on the Hybrid View, there is a significant gap between a constrained prerogative and a full Agent Centred Restriction. In particular, any constraints established so far would not apply if the creation of a child serves to maximize the good, or even if it serves as a means to some entirely separate personal project.

Recall the Slave Child Tale. Suppose that the couple in question are committed Simple Consequentialists. They desire to maximize their income—not to undertake a world trip, but in order to donate as much as possible to charity. They calculate that their best option is to produce as many children as possible and sell them to the slave trader. This will provide sufficient extra income, compared to any alternative occupation, to outweigh any negative impact on the children. This course of action is clearly justified by the Hybrid View, as it always allows agents to follow the Reason to Promote the Good.

This particular result only places the Hybrid View in the same boat as Simple Consequentialism. But there may be worse to come. I suggested in

Section 4.3.2 that, in the original Slave Child Tale, the couple's behaviour will not be sanctioned by the Reproduction Prerogative, as it does not constitute a valuable way of being a parent. However, this is not sufficient to prove that producing a slave child is not permitted, as it may fall under some other prerogative. For instance, consider the case of very poor parents whose only chance to live a non-impoverished life is to produce and sell a slave child. Any moderate moral theory must regard living a non-impoverished life as sufficient ground for a prerogative. This project is clearly a valuable one, and it appears that the way it is pursued does not in itself negate *that* value. So the creation of a slave child should be permitted here.

Indeed, even our original slave tale seems unaffected by this argument. After all the basis of the couple's claim was not that their Agent Centred Prerogative would permit reproduction, but merely that it would permit the project of embarking on a world trip rather than devoting $100,000 to saving a child from slavery. If we decide that this original project was not sufficiently valuable, then we can substitute another, worthier, project. Unless our moral theory is extremely demanding, there must be some project, more ambitious than subsistence, that is sufficiently valuable to outweigh the Reason to Promote the Good.

To avoid these results, defenders of the Hybrid View would now need to argue that any otherwise valuable project loses its value if pursued by means directly harmful to an innocent person.[58] However, this will be much harder to establish when the agent's relation to that innocent person plays no constitutive role either in the project or its value. Why is a world trip valuable when pursued at the expense of an existing slave child, but not when pursued at the expense of one's own, specifically created, slave child? Without a foundational distinction between doing and allowing, the Hybrid View seems unable to answer this question. Accordingly, the Doing/Allowing Objection remains untouched. If we are to dissolve this objection, we must look elsewhere.

Another problem is that the argument of Section 4.3.2 covers only some of our objections, not all of them. Suppose we could establish that a Reproduction Prerogative always constrains an agent's treatment of her own children. This relates only to the Parental Obligations Objection. It will

---

[58] A proponent of the Hybrid View has other options here. She might bite the bullet, and argue that, in such extreme circumstances, the creation of a slave child might be permissible. Alternatively, she might reject the example altogether, on the grounds that, as our current aim is to construct an intuitively plausible account of the obligations of affluent people in the developed world, it is inappropriate to bring in examples involving destitution. However, both these moves are distinctly sub-optimal, as they sacrifice either intuitive appeal or completeness. It is thus better to continue our search for a more intuitive, more complete moral theory.

not help with the Doing/Allowing and Forced Supererogation objections, where the problem lies in the agent's treatment of third parties who are not involved in her Reproduction Project.[59] To extend our reply to cover those objections, we would need to argue that the Reproduction Project is not valuable if it is pursued in a way that does not respect the autonomy of third parties. Constraints on the pursuit of reproduction due to the effect of certain actions *on the value of reproduction itself* look like internal constraints flowing from the nature of the project. By contrast, a distinction between doing and allowing, or any other constraint against harming others in the pursuit of one's projects, looks like an external constraint flowing from an independent moral principle. At this point it looks as if independent moral considerations based on respect for the autonomy of others are doing all the work, and the apparatus of the Hybrid View becomes a spare wheel.[60]

Constrained prerogatives are thus unlikely to be sufficient. We will need full-blown restrictions. Yet we have seen that even quite limited constraints are difficult enough to defend. The further step to full restrictions is significantly more controversial, as we shall now see.

4.3.4. Restrictions

The case for full restrictions, like the case for constraints, begins by asking what must be true if my Agent Centred Prerogative is to make a worthwhile contribution to my life. If I lived in a world where everyone interfered with my activities, either to promote the good or to pursue their own interests, then it would be very difficult for me to live my life. Furthermore, if I felt free to abandon my commitment to others (and my other personal projects) on a whim, then no doubt I would find it very hard to have a rich emotional life.

However, these observations are not sufficient to justify an Agent Centred Restriction. They both appeal to familiar Consequentialist reasons why it

---

[59] The argument of Section 4.3.2 could perhaps be extended to cover also the Commitments Objection, if we grant that reproduction is only valuable if pursued in a way that places one under obligations to one's co-parent. This will be more controversial than the corresponding claim regarding one's child. If one uses one's co-parent solely as a means, does that really devalue one's achievements *qua parent*? Furthermore, even if abandoning one's child or partner is inconsistent with the prerogative on which one embarked on the Reproduction Project, it is not clear that this is an objection *at the point* when one is considering abandoning that project. The prerogative one appeals to at that time is grounded in the value of the alternative project one wishes to pursue, so the value of one's Reproduction Project seems irrelevant. (Indeed, if one's inclination to abandon it reduces the value of one's Reproduction Project, then this seems to support the claim that one is allowed to abandon that project.) Finally, this move, even if successful, would still leave the Doing/Allowing and Forced Supererogation Objections unanswered.

[60] In his response to Kagan, Scheffler himself defends a no-harm constraint on the Agent Centred Prerogative (Scheffler, 'Prerogatives without Restrictions', 387–95.) However, this solitary departure from the basic structure of the Hybrid View seems somewhat ad hoc.

is desirable for people to act or deliberate in certain ways. They thus seem more likely to justify, for instance, laws against interfering with other people's projects, or deep-seated dispositions not to interfere, rather than a full-blooded moral restriction. How much security would I, or those with whom I collaborate, get from knowing that my interference with them would be *wrong*, if it is already common knowledge both that I am reliably disposed not to interfere and that the law would punish me if I did? How much security could anyone get from the knowledge that my interference would be wrong because it would violate a Non-Consequentialist Agent Centred Restriction, rather than because it would be inconsistent with the best Consequentialist decision procedure? In other words, can we justify an Agent Centred Restriction *honouring* the value of non-interference, rather than various Consequentialist strategies designed to *promote* non-interference?[61]

A case for Agent Centred Restrictions cannot simply appeal to the desirability of certain patterns of behaviour or disposition. Instead, it must focus on the particular features of each special class of valuable projects. Yet, as we saw in previous sections, in the case of reproduction, this more particularized route also offers the possibility of justifying, not full-blown restrictions, but instead more specific constraints on the Agent Centred Prerogative, specially tailored to the values in question.

Furthermore, any attempt to move to full-blown restrictions in the Hybrid View would face one additional (potentially devastating) objection. We can see this by asking the following question. Why does the apparent fragility of prerogatives without restrictions justify only an Agent Centred Restriction forbidding interference with other people's projects, and not also a correspondingly strong obligation to provide others with the necessities to pursue their projects, or to assist them with that pursuit? After all, if affluent people are pursuing Agent Centred Prerogatives, then their failure to radically redistribute resources will render practically worthless the prerogatives of those who lack sufficient resources to meaningfully pursue worthwhile projects. In such a situation, Agent Centred Restrictions will only worsen the plight of the destitute, in two ways. The first is that restrictions morally prohibit the destitute from taking the necessary resources by force. Thomas Nagel makes a similar point when he argues that, given the present state of the world, poor people would be able to reasonably reject any set of principles allowing the rich to avoid donating large amounts to famine relief.[62]

---

[61] For the distinction between honouring and promoting, see Pettit, 'Consequentialism'.

[62] See Nagel, *Equality and Partiality*, ch. 4; and Nagel, 'One-to-One'. See also Mulgan, *The Demands of Consequentialism*, 229–33; and endnote D to Chapter 11 below.

The second way restrictions harm the destitute is addressed by Scheffler himself under the heading of 'the distributive objection'. This 'challenges the idea that members of affluent societies have specific responsibilities to their associates that they do not have to other people'.[63] The thought is that, even if our moral theory imposes such obligations on everyone, the overall impact will clearly be to the benefit of the affluent, as their special obligations to one another will ensure that their own disproportionate share of resources is devoted even more disproportionately to themselves. Against a background of unequal resource distribution, the recognition of special obligations serves to exacerbate inequality.

Scheffler also makes the point that, if special obligations arise in the context of valuable interpersonal relationships, and those obligations serve the interests of both parties, then it is not accurate to classify such obligations as 'burdens' or 'restrictions'.[64] In particular, the special obligations requiring the affluent to assist one another do not restrict their agency in the same way that a prohibition preventing the destitute from seizing the resources of the affluent restricts the agency of the destitute. Indeed, the obligations of the affluent and the prohibitions on the destitute both combine to serve the interests of the affluent over the interests of the destitute.

If we merely appeal to the badness of being unable to live a meaningful life, then we will be unable to distinguish between active interference with the lives of others and passive failure to provide them with essential resources. To justify restrictions without falling into over-demandingness, we must show that interference with others is morally wrong, even in situations where a failure to provide resources is morally acceptable. It is not clear how this can be done without abandoning Scheffler's Hybrid View. (Our motivation for embarking on the Hybrid View was to limit the demands of our positive obligation to help others. If we accept that failure to assist is wrong whenever interference is wrong, then our moral theory will be extremely demanding.)

The results of introducing full-blown restrictions within the Hybrid View framework will thus be highly controversial. One explanation for this failure is that the Hybrid View seeks to determine an agent's prerogatives in isolation from background social conditions. While this analytic purity is desirable to some degree, it may ultimately prove untenable. In particular, we have already seen that the Hybrid View flounders because it lacks a robust distinction between doing and allowing. Perhaps attention to a broader context will enable us to ground such a distinction, in a suitably Consequentialist way.

---

[63] Scheffler, *Boundaries and Allegiances* (2001), 85.   [64] Ibid. 90.

4.4. A Collective Perspective

Our exploration of the Hybrid View has been inconclusive. The Hybrid View has some resources to construct and constrain parental prerogatives, but these resources seem insufficient either to ground the broad prerogatives of common sense, or to provide intuitively necessary restrictions. Perhaps Affluent will be permitted to adopt, or even to have one child of her own, and perhaps her treatment of her own child will be governed by some parental obligations. But fully robust parental obligations, or any obligations to third parties, seem beyond the Hybrid View as originally formulated.

The idea that any coherent Consequentialist theory might fail to permit reproduction may seem bizarre. If our value theory accords a central place to human well-being, then the continuation of humanity becomes a necessary precondition for even the possibility of future value. If no one reproduces, there will be no human well-being at all beyond the immediate future. So the consequences of everyone doing as this, allegedly Consequentialist, theory says they ought, would be a disaster in Consequentialist terms. This strongly suggests that Consequentialists should endorse at least a permission to reproduce.

This defence of the reproduction prerogative is not available to either Simple Consequentialism or the Hybrid View. Such theories explicitly adopt an individual perspective. They ask what each individual should do, given that others will continue to behave as they currently are. Given that most others will continue to reproduce, whether they ought to or not, each individual agent knows that, whatever she chooses to do, the next generation will contain more than enough people, and the social fabric will continue. Each agent is then obliged to act in a particular way, even though the result of all acting that way would be a disaster.

Versions of Individual Consequentialism—such as the Hybrid View or Simple Consequentialism—cannot appeal to any collective justification. Yet there surely is something to the thought that modes of behaviour should be assessed collectively rather than individually. In particular, reproduction, along with broader issues of our obligations to future generations, seems ideally suited to a collective treatment, as the impact of individual decisions depends so much on the behaviour of others.

We have seen that Scheffler's Hybrid View cannot provide an adequate account of this part of morality, and needs to be supplemented with a collective perspective. However, if the best form of Individual Consequentialism must incorporate some collective elements, then perhaps it would be simpler to abandon it altogether, and embrace a fully collective theory. Surely a purely collective theory would be more elegant than some semi-collective Hybrid View. Accordingly, we now turn to the collective strand of the Consequentialist tradition, and the most prominent theory within that strand, namely Rule Consequentialism. (Rule Consequentialism has another advantage over the Hybrid View. Even if it can accommodate our basic intuitions, the Hybrid View is only able to do so by relying on some very controversial value claims, especially regarding the significance of incommensurability. If Rule Consequentialism can endorse those intuitions without helping itself to any controversial value claims, then this gives it a comparative advantage over the Hybrid View, as it leaves fewer hostages to theoretical fortune.)

Unfortunately, we shall see in Chapter 10 that Rule Consequentialism also fails. Neither the individual nor the collective strand of Consequentialism on its own has the resources to offer a plausible account of reproduction (and of our obligations to future generations) embedded in a moderately demanding theory. At this point, the Hybrid View will return, as one component in the best Combined Consequentialism (Chapter 11).

Endnotes

A. For elaboration of Scheffler's view, see: Scheffler, 'Agent-centred, Restrictions, Rationality and the Virtues' (1985); Scheffler, 'Morality's Demands and their Limits' (1986); and Scheffler, 'Prerogatives without Restrictions' (1992). Scheffler also discusses related issues, though often from a different perspective, in both *Human Morality* (1992) and *Boundaries and Allegiances* (2001). For discussions of Scheffler's Hybrid View, see: Alexander, 'Scheffler on the Independence of Agent-Centred Prerogatives from Agent-Centred Restrictions'; Bennett, 'Two Departures from Consequentialism'; Conee, 'On Seeking a Rationale'; Harris, 'A Paradoxical Departure from Consequentialism'; Harris, 'Integrity and Agent Centred Restrictions'; Hooker, Review of S. Scheffler, *Human Morality* (1993); Hurley, 'Scheffler's Argument for Deontology'; Hurley, 'Getting our Options Clear: A Closer Look at Agent-Centred Options'; Kagan, 'Does Consequentialism Demand Too Much?'; Mulgan, 'A Non-proportional Hybrid Moral Theory'(1997); Mulgan, *The Demands of Consequentialism* (2001), ch 6; Murphy, 'The Demands of Beneficence', 274–7; Myers, 'Prerogatives and Restrictions from the Cooperative Point of View'; and Schueler, 'Consequences and Agent Centred Restrictions'.

B. The most obvious way to establish the credentials of genetic reproduction as an analogue of immortality would be on the basis of a genetic account of personal identity. It is certainly common philosophical practice, especially in the future generations literature, to follow Parfit in regarding my actual genetic make-up as a necessary condition for my personal identity across possible worlds. (If my parent's had not met, there would be no one existing with my genetic make-up—therefore *I* would not exist.) However, I am not aware of any serious attempt to defend individual genetic continuity—in the absence of any physical or psychological continuity—as a criterion of what is morally significant about personal identity. Suppose you tell me my body is about to be destroyed. You then tell me that, after my imminent annihilation, my genetic code will be used to create a new body housing a person with none of my memories or character traits. I do not think I would find this information the slightest bit comforting.

Another popular criterion of personal identity is physical continuity. This is typically combined with psychological continuity. I am the same person I was yesterday because thoughts psychologically connected to those I had yesterday are being supported by a brain physically connected with the brain that supported yesterday's thoughts. (For a good recent discussion, see McMahan, *The Ethics of Killing*, ch. 1.) On this view, personal immortality is impossible, in the absence of miracles. It is hard to see how any relation a person had with their descendants could be directly analogous to this type of physical continuity.

5

Rule Consequentialism

Historically, the principal Consequentialist alternative to Simple Consequentialism has been Rule Consequentialism, which can be initially characterized as follows: an act is morally right if and only if it is called for by a set of rules whose acceptance by everyone would result in at least as good consequences judged impartially as any other.[1]

Rule Consequentialism has considerable intuitive appeal. It seems to make only reasonable demands, as a relatively small percentage of the combined income of the well-off should be enough to meet all the needs of everyone on earth. It is also natural to see moral philosophy as the search for the optimal set of moral rules, and to expect those rules to produce the best consequences. Rule Consequentialism also seems fairer than Simple Consequentialism, as it does not require an agent to do more than her 'fair share' in promoting the good, even if others fail to do theirs.

The Collective approach, represented by Rule Consequentialism, is especially worth exploring in the morality of reproduction.[2] We have already seen that various forms of Individual Consequentialism, such as Simple Consequentialism or Scheffler's Hybrid View, cannot adequately

[1] For the best recent presentation of Rule Consequentialism, see Hooker, *Ideal Code, Real World* (2000). For further elaborations of Hooker's theory, see his 'Rule Consequentialism' (1990); Hooker, 'Rule Consequentialism' (2004); 'Rule-Consequentialism and Demandingness: A Reply to Carson' (1991); 'Rule-Consequentialism, Incoherence, Fairness' (1994); 'Compromising with Convention' (1994); 'Rule-Consequentialism and Obligations toward the Needy' (1998); Hooker, 'Ross-style Pluralism versus Rule-Consequentialism' (1996); 'Reply to Stratton-Lake' (1997). For discussions of Hooker's theory, see Carson, 'A Note on Hooker's Rule-Consequentialism'; Miller, 'Hooker's Use and Abuse of Reflective Equilibrium'; Mulgan, 'Ruling Out Rule Consequentialism' (2000); Mulgan, 'Rule Consequentialism and Famine' (1994); Mulgan, 'One False Virtue of Rule Consequentialism' (1996); and Stratton-Lake, 'Can Hooker's Rule-Consequentialist Principle Justify Ross's Prima Facie Duties?' For other discussions of Rule Consequentialism, see Brandt, 'Some Merits of One Form of Rule-Utilitarianism'; Brandt, 'Fairness to Indirect Optimific Theories in Ethics'; Gibbard, 'Rule Utilitarianism;' Hooker, (ed.), *Rationality, Rules and Utility* (1993); Hooker, Mason, and Miller (eds.), *Morality, Rules and Consequences*; Lucas, 'African Famine: New Economic and Ethical Perspectives'; Lyons, *The Forms and Limits of Utilitarianism*; Moore, 'The Utilitarian Ethics of R. B. Brandt'; Schaller, 'A Problem for Brandt's Utilitarianism'; and Wagner Decew, 'Brandt's New Defense of Rule Utilitarianism'.

[2] For other forms of Collective Consequentialism, see Mulgan, *The Demands of Consequentialism* (2001), ch. 4.

accommodate the fact that, unless reproduction occurs at an appropriate level across society, the very future of human well-being is jeopardized.

Given its initial plausibility, it is worth asking whether Rule Consequentialism is a plausible moral theory. This is one of the central questions of the rest of this book. After a brief introduction to contemporary Rule Consequentialism, we begin with the individual morality of reproduction. What rules regarding reproduction will the set of rules recommended by Rule Consequentialism contain? How, if at all, will Rule Consequentialism constrain people's freedom to reproduce? We focus on the two failings of the Hybrid View: its inability to accommodate either reproductive freedom or parental obligations. I argue that Rule Consequentialism fares better. Along the way, we must address the objection that reproductive freedom threatens the future of humanity. I argue that Rule Consequentialism can avoid this objection, but only by extending its scope to cover public policy as well as individual morality.

The basic idea of Rule Consequentialism is quite simple. We begin by looking for the optimal set of rules, the 'ideal code'. We assess each possible set of rules collectively, asking what would happen if everyone accepted that set of rules. The ideal code is the set of rules such that the consequences of everyone accepting them would be better than the consequences of everyone accepting any other set of rules. (A crucial question, as we shall see, is precisely what it means to 'accept' a set of rules.) We then assess acts indirectly. The right act in any situation is the act dictated by the ideal code. I shall sometimes speak of the possible world where everyone (or nearly everyone) accepts the ideal code as 'the ideal society'. This phrase should always be interpreted in light of Rule Consequentialism.

Variations on this simple Rule Consequentialist theory are usually motivated by particular objections. We will concentrate on a recent version of the theory developed by Brad Hooker. However, my aim is to explore the resources of Rule Consequentialism in general, not just of Hooker's particular version. Except for one or two brief comments, Hooker himself does not apply his theory to future generations. Indeed, I can find no detailed Rule Consequentialist account of either individual reproduction or intergenerational justice.[3]

5.1. Justifying Rule Consequentialism

Those who defend Rule Consequentialism often place great weight on its intuitive plausibility. Hooker, for instance, goes so far as to say that 'the best

---

[3] One key issue is canvassed more fully in Section 6.4 below.

argument for Rule Consequentialism is that it does a better job than its rivals of matching and tying together our moral convictions'.[4] These convictions operate at various levels. They might relate to moral ideals, general moral rules, or particular moral judgements.

It is important to realize that the defenders of Rule Consequentialism do not see their theory as merely providing a list of plausible moral judgements. They also present it as explaining, underpinning, and justifying those particular judgements. Rule Consequentialism aims to offer a principled rationale for plausible moral rules. Hooker explicitly acknowledges this when arguing for the superiority of Rule Consequentialism over Ross-style pluralism.[5] It is thus legitimate to test Rule Consequentialism against hypothetical examples as well as actual cases, as this enables us to evaluate its rationales.

One might ask how Rule Consequentialism *explains* particular moral rules. There are several answers a Rule Consequentialist might give.

1. The simple fact that a moral theory ties together our intuitions, and derives them from an underlying principle, is sufficient justification for those intuitions, irrespective of whether that principle itself is intuitive, or provides any explicit explanation for those intuitions.

2. Rule Consequentialism ties together, not only intuitions regarding particular cases and general moral rules, but also intuitive abstract moral ideals. In particular, Rule Consequentialism represents a marrying of two compelling ideals: the idea that morality is about the promotion of the good, and the notion of universalizability (captured by the common moral thought: 'What if everyone did that?'). Rule Consequentialism shows how these ideals are related to particular judgements, thus providing a justification for those judgements.

3. If we have independent reason to believe that morality is a collective project, involving the promotion of an identifiable good, then showing that Rule Consequentialism supports certain acts *constitutes* a demonstration that those acts are morally required or permitted. Similarly, to show that a rule is contained in the ideal code thus *is* to explain why it is morally binding. This demonstration would have the same force as a proof that morality consisted in the promotion of good by an individual agent or that morality consisted in following the Categorical Imperative. Rule Consequentialism would thus offer justification and explanation on a par with those claimed by Simple

    [4] Hooker, *Ideal Code, Real World* (2000), 101. See also Hooker, 'Rule-Consequentialism, Incoherence, Fairness' (1994), 29.

    [5] Hooker, *Ideal Code, Real World*, 105–7; and 'Ross-style Pluralism versus Rule Consequentialism' (1996), 543–6.

Consequentialism or Kantianism. (The significance of these comparisons is that the objection that Rule Consequentialism cannot provide moral justifications is often put forward by proponents of these other theories, who argue that they can provide a justification.)

Hooker himself relies on the second style of justification, focusing on the overall intuitive appeal of Rule Consequentialism. I myself believe that a stronger justification, of the third type, is available. However, I postpone the exploration of this possibility until Chapter 11, where I argue that, once we seek a deeper rationale for Rule Consequentialism, we find that only some areas of morality lend themselves to a collective treatment, and thus that Rule Consequentialism cannot be the whole of our moral theory.

5.1.1. Intuitively Plausible Principles for Reproduction

Hooker's argument for Rule Consequentialism appeals to its comparative intuitive plausibility. We need to ask three questions:

1. What are the inuitively plausible moral rules governing reproduction and obligations to future generations?
2. Would these form part of the Rule Consequentialist ideal code?
3. Can Rule Consequentialism's competitors accommodate these principles?

In this section, I present a range of intuitively plausible principles, and explain how competing moral theories have difficulty accommodating them. If Rule Consequentialism can accommodate them, then this is a significant point in its favour. The list of principles largely recaps our previous discussions of the morality of reproduction.

5.1.1.1. Reproductive Freedom

Perhaps the most striking feature of commonsense moral thought in this area is a widespread commitment to reproductive freedom. People should be able to decide for themselves whether or not, and in what way, to reproduce. This commitment is partly a belief that no outside agency, especially the state, should interfere with such choices. In the terminology introduced in Chapter 4, a range of options should be practically and legally available. Our commitment to reproductive freedom also reflects a belief that reproductive choice is morally open. There is no obligation to have children, nor an obligation not to. If one does opt to reproduce, then one is morally free to choose with whom one will reproduce, given that any other person contributing to the reproduction consents, and that one has no prior commitments that preclude one's reproducing with that person at this time.[6] Parents are entitled to considerable freedom regarding the upbringing of their children. If the state adopts a population policy, then it should pursue that policy non-coercively.

As we saw in Chapter 4, a commitment to reproductive freedom can reflect a belief that choices between radically different alternatives, such as reproduction and non-reproduction, are characterized by widespread incommensurability. There is often no single right answer, so it makes no sense for any outside party to seek to impose one. However, this intuition need not reflect belief in incommensurability. Even those who are sceptical about incommensurability typically attach considerable significance to reproductive freedom. For such people, the fact that the standard version of the Hybrid View can only defend reproductive freedom by invoking incommensurability is a strike against that theory. I shall argue that Rule Consequentialist is more robust than the Hybrid View here, as it can defend reproductive freedom without appealing to incommensurability.

5.1.1.2. Permissibility of Sub-optimal Reproduction
It is morally acceptable to reproduce even if any child one has will have a life which is far from perfect. For instance, even in a society where wealthy children have more opportunities than the children of the moderately well-off, the latter are under no obligation not to reproduce. Similarly, it is permissible to reproduce if one knows that any child one has will suffer some mild affliction, and if one cannot otherwise have children.

5.1.1.3. The Asymmetry
Most people agree there is no obligation to have children, even if one would be creating people whose lives were extremely worth living. Almost everyone also agrees there is an obligation not deliberately or knowingly to create lives not worth living. This strong asymmetry is a very basic feature of commonsense morality. Recall the tale of the Selfish Parents, who deliberately create a severely disabled child simply to explore their own capacity for other-regarding behaviour (Section 1.2). Almost no one finds this morally acceptable. It is also wrong to reproduce if one cannot ensure that one's child's basic needs will be provided for. If one cannot provide for those needs oneself, then it is wrong to reproduce in the absence of a reliable social safety net.[7]

---

[6] I am grateful to Brad Hooker for helpful reformulation of this principle.

[7] Some argue that, even in the presence of an adequate safety net, it is wrong to create children whose needs one cannot meet oneself, as one thereby imposes a burden on the rest of society. (Gauthier, 'Political Contractarianism'.) Gauthier's position is much more controversial than the view defended in

Furthermore, as I argued in Section 1.4, many people also believe it is wrong gratuitously to create a child with (even mild) disabilities, when one could have just as easily (i.e. at no greater cost to oneself) created a perfectly healthy child. This intuition is not universal, but it represents a distinctive commitment of any broadly Consequentialist approach to our obligations to future generations.

The obligation to ensure that children's lives are worth living is not limited to their parents. Third parties should intervene to protect children from being harmed or abused by their natural parents, and to ensure that basic needs are met. In modern liberal democracies, it is widely believed that this obligation falls upon the state. The failure of government agencies to protect children against violent parents is viewed very harshly by the public.

Commonsense morality seems to accept some degree of social relativism here. A certain level of well-being might be unacceptable in New Zealand, but regarded (by people in New Zealand) as acceptable for people in the developing world. We don't blame parents in Afghanistan or sub-Saharan Africa for producing children whose lives fall well below the level we would consider acceptable in our own country.

5.1.1.4. The Acceptance of Risk
Most people accept that it is permissible to reproduce even if there is some chance that one's child will have a life not worth living, and even if one has only the vaguest notion of either the magnitude of that chance or the awfulness of various possible lives. (Similarly, almost everyone thinks it permissible to drive, even though there is always some risk of killing an innocent person.) The level of risk considered acceptable by commonsense morality in any given society typically tracks that associated with 'normal circumstances'. It is assumed that ordinary cases of reproduction involve an acceptable level of risk. Reproduction becomes ethically problematic only when it involves abnormal risks. As with the notion of a minimum acceptable level of well-being, commonsense morality seems to accept some degree of social relativism here. A certain level of risk might be unacceptable in New Zealand, but regarded as acceptable for people in the developing world—both by those people themselves and also by people in New Zealand.

5.1.1.5. Conditional Obligations
People have no obligation to have children. However, if you do have children, then there are many things you are obliged to do for them. Similarly,

the text, as it concerns individuals' relationship with society more than their relationship with their child. (For Gauthier's theory in general, see Section 2.1 above. For a critique of his particular published views on reproduction, see Mulgan, 'Reproducing the Contractarian State' (2002).)

almost everyone agrees that we all have definite obligations to future people in general. We ought not to harm them, unnecessarily deplete resources they might need, etc.

5.1.2. Accommodating and Balancing these Principles

Several features of this list are significant. Each principle, taken in isolation, is intuitively compelling. Any plausible moral theory must either accommodate that principle, or provide a very strong argument to undermine it. On the other hand, our intuitive principles are in obvious tension with one another. In particular, our commitment to reproductive and parental freedom conflicts with the idea that everyone has an obligation to avoid harm to children. For instance, some of the most difficult conflicts in any pluralistic society arise when parents in a minority group wish to treat their children in ways the majority considers to be harmful, such as very strict discipline, limited education for girls, female genital mutilation, etc. Our commonsense intuitions provide no clear way to resolve these conflicts.

Many contemporary moral and political theories have real trouble making sense of this array of obligations and permissions. Simple Consequentialism, for instance, cannot easily accommodate reproductive freedom, and is notoriously unable to account for the asymmetry. If adding an extra life improves the value of an outcome, then the agent is obliged to add that life. To accommodate the asymmetry, Simple Consequentialists would need to adopt asymmetric value theories, whereby extra worthwhile lives do not add value but extra lives below the zero level reduce value.[8] A commitment to Simple Consequentialism also explains why the Repugnant Conclusion is so feared, as agents would then be obliged to choose the Z-world over the A-world, or even to turn a thriving A-world into a Z-world.

By contrast, person-affecting views have trouble accommodating generalized obligations to future people, or the idea that it is wrong gratuitously to create a disabled person whose life is barely worth living. Recall Parfit's tales where present policies create future people who are worse-off than ourselves instead of different better-off people, or the individual case of a mother deliberately choosing to have a child with a minor disability when she could just as easily have a perfectly healthy child (Section 1.3). In all these cases, so long as future people have lives worth living and would not have existed otherwise, it is hard to see how person-affecting theory can fault anyone's actions. Person-affecting theories often seek to accommodate

---

[8] For good critiques of this strategy, see Heyd, *Genethics*, 59–60; and Parfit, *Reasons and Persons*, ch. 18. See also the works cited in Ch. 1 n. 12 above.

such cases by accepting counterintuitive technical accounts of what constitutes a harm or benefit to a particular person.

Finally, we saw in Chapter 4 that, even with extensive modifications, the Hybrid View has difficulty explaining the significance of reproductive freedom, and is unable to make sense of the full range of obligations that commonsense morality ascribes to parents in regard to their children.

I shall argue that Rule Consequentialism can both accommodate and explain all the intuitively plausible principles on our list. It also provides a principled and appealing account of how to balance them. Our main task is to demonstrate how, and in what form, our principles feature in the Rule Consequentialist ideal code. A crucial starting point is Hooker's observation that the question to which Rule Consequentialism is the answer is not 'what if everyone did that?' but rather 'what if everyone felt free to do that?' Hooker himself explicitly, if very briefly, applies this distinction to the morality of reproduction.

Suppose my nephew tells me he refuses to have children. If everyone refuses to have children, the human species will die out. This would be a disastrous consequence. But it is irrelevant to the morality of my nephew's decision. What is relevant is that everyone's feeling free not to have children will not lead to the extinction of the species. Plenty of people who do not feel obligated to have children nevertheless *want* to—and, if free to do so, will. Thus, there is no need for a moral obligation to have children. Neither is there any need for a general moral obligation to have heterosexual intercourse.[9]

Before we begin, however, we must address some old objections to Rule Consequentialism, as these serve to explain current formulations of the theory. (Sections 5.2 and 5.3 largely recap a longer discussion in *The Demands of Consequentialism*, while new material is introduced from Section 5.4.)

5.2. Distinguishing Rule Consequentialism from Simple Consequentialism

Perhaps the most obvious objection to Rule Consequentialism is the following.

The Partial Compliance Objection.   Because it chooses moral rules on the basis of what would happen if everybody complied with them, Rule Consequentialism gives undesirable results in situations of partial compliance, where not everyone conforms with the rule in question. For instance, assume I am living in Sweden prior to 1967. I decide it would be

---

[9] Hooker, *Ideal Code, Real World* (2000), 177.

best if everyone drove on the right-hand side of the road. As a Rule Consequentialist, I begin to drive on the right-hand side, even though everyone else drives on the left. The results are not pleasant.[10]

To avoid this objection, Rule Consequentialists usually say that the optimal rules include clauses of the following form: Do x, unless doing x will lead to great disaster because everyone else is not doing x, in which case do y (where y avoids disaster). The rule for Sweden would be: Drive on the right unless driving on the right will have disastrous consequences because everyone else is driving on the left, in which case drive on the left.

This move leads directly to another objection, due to David Lyons.[11]

The Co-extensionality (or Collapse) Objection.   Rule Consequentialism collapses into Simple Consequentialism. It will be best for everyone to obey rules of infinite complexity telling people to maximize utility in each particular situation. This is an extension of the disaster-avoidance clause, where any failure to maximize the good counts as a disaster.

To avoid this objection, Rule Consequentialists seek a middle ground between overly simplistic rules and infinitely complex ones. Many contemporary formulations of Rule Consequentialism are driven by the need to differentiate the theory from Simple Consequentialism. One common response is to distinguish between 'following a rule' and 'accepting a rule'. The Co-extensionality Objection is said to apply only if Rule Consequentialism is built on the former notion, as there are limits on the complexity of the rules a community can accept. For instance, Brad Hooker distinguishes two forms of Rule Consequentialism.[12]

Compliance Rule Consequentialism.   To find the optimal rule set we ask what would happen if a given set of rules were always *complied with* by everyone.

Acceptance Rule Consequentialism.   To find the optimal rule set we ask what would happen if a given set of rules were *accepted* by everyone. For Hooker, to accept a set of rules involves 'not just the disposition to comply with these rules ... [but] also the disposition to encourage others to comply

---

[10]   See Gibbard, 'Rule Utilitarianism', 217; and Hooker, 'Rule Consequentialism' (1990), 74.

[11]   Lyons, *Forms and Limits of Utilitarianism*, 133. For critical discussion, see Feldman, 'On the Extensional Equivalence of Simple and General Utilitarianism'; Goldman, 'David Lyons on Utilitarian Generalization'; and Horwich, 'On Calculating the Utility of Acts'.

[12]   See Hooker, *Ideal Code, Real World*, 75–80; Hooker, 'Rule-Consequentialism, Incoherence, Fairness' (1994), 21; and Hooker, 'Rule Consequentialism' (1990), 67.

with them, dispositions to form favourable attitudes toward others who comply with them, dispositions to feel guilt or shame when one breaks them and to condemn and resent others' breaking them, all of which dispositions and attitudes being supported by the belief that they are justified.'[13] Hooker focuses on the cost of inculcating the set of rules in the next generation. The costs of acceptance include both transitional costs of moving from our present code to the ideal code and ongoing costs once the code has been internalized.

Hooker argues that these two alternatives recommend different sets of rules, as the acceptance of a rule by a population has consequences over and above compliance with that rule. Also, some people might accept a rule even though they do not always comply with it; while others might comply perfectly with a rule they do not accept. For instance, many people accept, on some level, more demanding principles regarding donations to charity than they can bring themselves to comply with fully; while social or legal sanctions often produce compliance without genuine acceptance.

Hooker argues that Acceptance Rule Consequentialism is superior to the compliance-based theory. He offers two basic arguments. The first is based on the connection between moral motivation and acceptance. Hooker argues that for the Rule Consequentialist 'compliance is not the only thing of importance. We also care about people's having *moral concerns*. So we had better consider the costs of securing not only compliance but also adequate moral motivation. From a Rule Consequentialist point of view, "moral motivation" means acceptance of the right rules.'[14]

This argument also helps to explain why Rule Consequentialists are especially interested in rules. The acceptance of rules is closely linked to disposition and moral character. In Hooker's theory, 'accepting rules is a matter of having certain associated motivations and beliefs, indeed of having a certain character and conscience'.[15] On this view, Rule Consequentialism is similar to a Consequentialism whose prime focus is on dispositions, motives, or character. Some might question this account of what it is to accept a rule. For our purposes, the more significant question is whether the resulting Rule Consequentialism fares better or worse than a theory founded on any alternative account of rule following.

As ever, this comparison rests primarily on the comparative intuitive plausibility of the two approaches. This brings us to Hooker's second argument: that Acceptance Rule Consequentialism produces better judgements about particular cases than the compliance form of the theory. In

---

[13] Hooker, *Ideal Code, Real World*, 76. See also Brandt, 'Some Merits of One Form of Rule-Utilitarianism'.   [14] Hooker, *Ideal Code, Real World*, 76.

[15] Hooker, 'Rule-Consequentialism, Incoherence, Fairness', 21.

particular, the move from compliance to acceptance is designed to solve the Demandingness Objection as well as the Collapse Objection. These two objections are clearly related. If Rule Consequentialism does deliver the same results as Simple Consequentialism, then the two theories will obviously be equally demanding. If Simple Consequentialism is unreasonably demanding, then so is Rule Consequentialism.

Rule Consequentialism could also collapse into Simple Consequentialism in the particular case of reproduction. This will occur if the ideal code includes a rule such as the following: have children if and only if this will maximize utility. This rule is equivalent to Simple Consequentialism, and is extremely demanding. In particular, it will almost never permit reproduction, for the reasons outlined in Section 1.6. One central task for Rule Consequentialists is to show how their ideal code avoids such a rule.

5.3. Contemporary Rule Consequentialism

We will focus on Brad Hooker's most recent formulation of Rule Consequentialism.

Hooker's Rule Consequentialism.

An act is wrong if and only if it is forbidden by the code of rules whose internalization by the overwhelming majority of everyone everywhere in each new generation has maximum expected value in terms of well-being (with some priority for the worst off). The calculation of a code's expected value includes all costs of getting the code internalized. If in terms of expected value two or more codes are better than the rest but equal to one another, the one closest to conventional morality determines what acts are wrong.[16]

The key feature of this account is the shift from compliance to acceptance, or 'internalization'. Several aspects of Hooker's use of this notion are significant.

1. We are interested, not in what would happen if a set of rules were internalized by everyone, but rather in the results of internalization by an *overwhelming majority*. Hooker explains and justifies this move as follows:

We should not imagine that the code's internalization extends to young children, to the mentally impaired, and even to every 'normal' adult. A moral code should be suited to the real world, where there is likely to be, at best, only partial social

---

[16] Hooker, *Ideal Code, Real World*, 32.

acceptance of, and compliance with, any moral code. An adequate ethic must provide for situations created by people who are malevolent, dishonest, unfair, or simply misguided . . . a moral code needs provisions for dealing with non-compliance.[17]

While admitting that it is difficult to specify precisely what an overwhelming majority is, Hooker stipulates internalization by 90 per cent of the population.[18]

2. When assessing the costs and benefits of internalizing a code of rules, we are to imagine that 'moral rules are inculcated pretty much as they are now—that is, by family, teachers, and the broader culture'.[19] We are not to imagine any centrally coordinated mass indoctrination.

3. The costs of inculcation are those associated with teaching a code to a *new* generation, and maintaining their allegiance to that code. We do not ask what would happen if we tried to teach the new code to a generation of adults who had already internalized a different moral code. We put such transition costs to one side.

Two other broad features of Hooker's Rule Consequentialism are significant. The first is the focus on expected value, rather than the actual consequences of internalizing a code. This is in line with a general trend in contemporary Consequentialist thought, whereby acts are evaluated in terms of expected value rather than actual consequences.[20] The second is the adoption of what Hooker dubs 'wary rule Consequentialism': the use of closeness to conventional morality as a tie-breaker.[21] This move obviously increases the probability that the recommendations of Rule Consequentialism will be in tune with conventional morality.[22]

I follow Hooker in formulating Rule Consequentialism in terms of acceptance (or internalization) rather than compliance. For ease of expression, I shall sometimes speak of 'full compliance', 'partial compliance', and 'non-compliance' with the ideal code. These expressions should always be interpreted as shorthand for varying degrees of internalization of that code.

Before we proceed to the morality of individual reproduction, and beyond to future generations in general, we must explore three general features of Rule Consequentialism: its value theory, its degree of collectivism, and its approach to uncertainty.

---

[17] Ibid. 80.   [18] Ibid. 84.   [19] Ibid. 79.
[20] Mulgan, *The Demands of Consequentialism*, 33–4.   [21] Hooker, *Ideal Code, Real World*, 114–17.
[22] For a discussion of what to do when two codes are equally close to conventional morality, see Mulgan, *The Demands of Consequentialism*, 67 n. 27.

5.4. Value Theory

Any complete Rule Consequentialism needs a complete account of value. Hooker himself bases his Rule Consequentialism on a particular account of value, evaluating codes using 'expected value in terms of well-being (with some priority to the worst-off)'.[23] However, my aim is to remain as agnostic as possible regarding value. I hope to show that Rule Consequentialism can yield intuitively plausible results without departing from the value theory sketched in Chapter 3.

My strategy can be illustrated using the example of equality or fairness. The Total View is notoriously insensitive to distribution. A very unequal distribution of twenty-one units of well-being trumps a perfectly equal distribution of twenty units. This leads to a standard objection to Simple Consequentialism: that it can require the sacrifice of those who are worse off to provide benefits to those who are better off. The morality of reproduction provides a stark example: should we create a person whose life is not worth living to increase the welfare of those who are very well off already? (Suppose we create people with a specially designed genetic make-up that both enables them to produce an enzyme that has distinct medicinal value to others and gives them a short life of unrelenting agony.) Because of its tight link between value and right action, Simple Consequentialism can only avoid these counterintuitive results by abandoning the Total View. Similarly, we saw in Chapter 4 that the Hybrid View addresses similar objections by leaning heavily on controversial claims about the incommensurability of values.

Rule Consequentialists can take this route, but they have another option. The code of rules that maximizes total value does not tell us to maximize total value on each occasion. Instead, it will include many of the rules of commonsense morality: do not kill, do not lie, do not steal, keep promises, etc. (This claim is the basis of all attempts to differentiate Rule Consequentialism from Simple Consequentialism.) Perhaps the best code will combine a reluctance to use others as means with a tendency to give priority to the interests of the worst-off. If it also includes parental obligations (Section 5.7), then someone who had internalized such a code would not feel free to create a life not worth living for instrumental reasons.[24]

---

[23] Hooker follows many contemporary Consequentialists, and others, by expressing a concern for equality in terms of priority to the worst-off rather than pure egalitarianism (Section 3.7.4). This is to avoid the 'levelling-down objection' to egalitarianism. If we attach independent value to an equal distribution, then a policy that blinds sighted people is, in one respect, a good thing, as it produces equality with respect to sight.

[24] The discussion in the text does not address the separate case of creating a life *well worth* living for instrumental reasons—such as when parents deliberately have a child to provide a suitable donor for a

The two versions of Rule Consequentialism (one based on the Total View, the other Hooker's own version) thus may not be very different in their practical recommendations. Indeed, given the large amount of uncertainty surrounding any Rule Consequentialist calculation, the ideal codes of the two theories may be indistinguishable.

My agnostic approach has three basic advantages.

1. It affords Rule Consequentialism a wide appeal, as it can be accepted by proponents of any one of a broad range of particular value theories.

2. It allows us to respond appropriately to our own uncertainty regarding value theory—especially over the future course of debates about value in the ideal society. (I argue in Section 8.1 that this represents a marked superiority of Rule Consequentialism over Rawls's constitutional liberalism.)

3. Finally, if they do affect the ideal code, then departures from the Total View to address particular objections to Rule Consequentialism may have negative intuitive impact in other areas. For instance, I argue in Chapter 10 that the real obstacle facing Rule Consequentialism is that, in the actual world, it may require too much deference to the interests of the worst-off. A shift to a more egalitarian value theory can only exacerbate this problem.[25]

Chapter 3 endorsed one important departure from the Total View as a necessary feature of moderate Consequentialism: the introduction of a lexical level. Section 3.7 canvassed several ways a moderate Consequentialist might incorporate a lexical level: as a component of the impersonal value theory, as an a priori commitment of practical reason, as a psychological necessity for human beings, or simply as the most psychologically effective way for a code to ensure that human beings promote the good.

One significant advantage of Rule Consequentialism is that it largely removes the need to decide between these options. For instance, Section 6.2 argues that the lexical level features prominently in the content of the ideal code in regard to reproductive freedom, while later chapters highlight the comparative advantage of an ideal code incorporating a context-dependent lexical level. While these arguments are obviously strengthened if lexicality is built into our foundational value theory, they both go through on the

transfusion to an existing sibling. In popular debate, this type of creation is often criticized as illegitimately using the new child as a means. As I argued in Section 1.5, this is an unnecessarily strict mis-reading of Kant.

[25] Other innovations in value theory might have even more unwelcome consequences. For instance, if Simple Consequentialists respond to the threat of injustice by adopting a value theory that allows the creation of a single life not worth living to trump any benefit to those who are better off, then they cannot allow any reproduction under uncertainty. Rule Consequentialists who follow this lead would meet the same fate. (For further discussion, see Heyd, *Genethics*, 59–60; and Parfit, *Reasons and Persons*, ch. 18. See also the works cited in Ch. 1 n. 12 above.)

much weaker assumption that the adoption of a lexical level is psychologically natural for human beings. If people cannot be effectively taught a non-lexical code, then a lexical code will be the best way to maximize non-lexical value. Rule Consequentialism can thus help itself to the practical benefits of a lexical level while remaining agnostic regarding impersonal value theory. (The main problem that lexicality poses for Rule Consequentialism is in relation to demandingness, to which we return in Chapter 10.)

As the lexical level plays a key role in subsequent chapters, it is worth pausing to explore the argument for its inclusion. To take the hardest case, suppose we deny that the lexical level is required by our foundational value theory, by Kantian transcendental arguments, or by psychological necessity. Human beings could be taught a non-lexical moral code. Why shouldn't they be?

Our Rule Consequentialism must avoid the Repugnant Obligation Conclusion, dissolve the Demandingness Objection, and ground a range of permissions to favour one's own interests, goals, and perspectives. Each of these desiderata introduces a lexical element into the ideal code.

The standard Rule Consequentialist response to the Demandingness Objection, and to most other standard objections to the Simple Consequentialist, is that it is inefficient to require agents to always seek to view the world from the perspective of impersonal value, or to attempt to impartially maximize the good. Things go better overall if agents give priority to their own interests, goals, and perspectives. This chapter and the next extend this defence to cover the morality of individual reproduction, and subsequent chapters extend it further to cover obligations to future generations more broadly. I argue that, when considering their own lives, and especially the lives of their descendants, those who have internalized the ideal code will set thresholds below which they do not want those lives to fall.

The ideal code does not require agents to develop fully fledged moral theories or complete impersonal value theories. However, nor does it recommend that they be unreflective automatons. Agents who have internalized the ideal code will realize that, when they pursue their own goals at the expense of the impersonal good, and especially when they set thresholds (or privilege goals without a precise calculation of the foregoing cost) they are acting as if there were a morally significant difference in kind between what they pursue and what they forgo, such that the former is not reducible to any available amount of the latter. I shall refer to this realization, and the patterns of behaviour that accompany it, as 'the adoption of a lexical level'.

There are several respects in which this is not strictly equivalent to the adoption of a lexical level as traditionally defined in contemporary Consequentialist value theory.

1. Those who have internalized the ideal code need not adopt any complete impersonal value theory.

2. Indeed, they may believe (perhaps for the reasons sketched in Chapter 3) that no complete value theory can be formulated (or at least, not one that includes a lexical level and/or is compatible with an intuitively appealing morality); or they may believe that the task of formulating such a theory is best not attempted.

3. Most of the elements of the ideal code that I characterize in lexical terms will admit of exceptions. The permission to favour one's own goals or perspectives can be outweighed in exceptional circumstances. What is adopted is thus typically not a lexical level, but merely an extra weighting for certain goods over others, together with a disposition not to generally seek commensurabilities between those different goods.

4. Several elements of the ideal code use these quasi-lexical levels in competing ways. We therefore need to balance these different lexical levels. This context-dependence, which was introduced in Chapter 3, is not something that can be easily cashed out in impersonal value theory, but finds its home in the deliberations of those who have internalized the ideal code.

Instead of saying that those who have internalized the ideal code often 'adopt a lexical level', I should perhaps say that they 'knowingly act in a manner best explained by supposing that they adopt something broadly analogous to a quasi-lexical threshold of some unspecified sort'. However, in the interests of brevity, I will continue with the former expression— although the underlying looseness of expression should be borne in mind.

This use of the lexical level is perhaps clearest with respect to the Repugnant Obligation Conclusion. Suppose we attempted to teach the next generation a moral code requiring them always to favour Z over A, and to reject the very idea of a lexical level. The result, even if such a code could be taught, would be a world of agents who regard all values as strictly commensurable, and in particular regard the values of their own lives and goals as capable of being outweighed by a sufficiently large increase in very minimal pleasures for creatures capable of nothing higher. This would not (only) be the impersonal value theory such agents would endorse in moments of philosophical reflection. It would also be the perspective from which they act.

Similar remarks apply to other potential departures from the Total View. The previous chapter introduced the possibility of widespread incommensurability above the lexical level. Given the psychology of human beings, and especially the way they deliberate, it is very beneficial overall if agents are encouraged to respect one another's autonomy and to exercise and value their own autonomy. The latter may include deliberating as if their choices involved options whose values are incommensurable. For Rule Consequentialism, these empirical factors may produce the intuitive results that, in other theories such as the Hybrid View, require that either incommensurability or the intrinsic value of autonomy be built into our impersonal value theory. The ideal code will be designed to ensure that people live above the lexical level, but it may make no sense to strive for perfection or 'maximum well-being' above that level. If a moderate set of rules would guarantee that (almost) everyone will be above the lexical level, then it would be counter-productive for the ideal code to advocate 'maximization'. (Similarly, the inclusion of a context-dependent lexical level in the content of the ideal code provides many of the practical benefits of the explicit introduction of holistic evaluations of possible histories: Sections 3.7.4, 7.6, 8.2.)

Of course, none of this implies that Rule Consequentialists should not build prioritarianism, lexicality, incommensurability, the intrinsic value of autonomy, or holistic evaluations into their impersonal value theory; or that those who favour such a value theory should abandon Rule Consequentialism. The main aim of Chapters 5 to 8 is to establish the intuitive appeal of Rule Consequentialism. Putting aside the problem of Demandingness, any of these departures from the Total View would enhance that appeal.

5.5. Unifying Rule Consequentialism

Rule Consequentialism avoids the Collapse Objection by appealing to human fallibility. Simple Consequentialism would be the best code to teach to perfect rational agents. Each distinctive feature of Rule Consequentialism can thus be seen as a response to some particular feature of human fallibility. Once we recognize this, we can provide a unified explanation (and justification) for what otherwise appear to be a set of unrelated ad hoc departures from Simple Consequentialism.

To compare possible codes of rules, we imagine the consequences of teaching each code to the next generation.[26] Even if our teaching is assumed to be more or less perfect, it does not follow that the next generation

---

[26] This may seem to go against the letter of Hooker's formulation of Rule Consequentialism. However, Hooker's focus on the cost of inculcation clearly suggests that we are evaluating *our attempts* to inculcate potential codes, rather than assuming that inculcation will succeed.

will perfectly learn, internalize, or act upon, any particular code. We must ask what would be the expected consequences of our teaching that particular code to a generation of humans. The more complex, demanding, or counterintuitive the code, the higher will be the likely rate of (*a*) failures to internalize the code at all, (*b*) failures to fully internalize the code, or (*c*) failures to act appropriately in response to the code. For any particular code, the extent of successful internalization and appropriate application will vary for different rules. For instance, we might see a very high level of internalization of a rule prohibiting murder, along with a much lower degree of response to a demanding rule regarding charitable donation.

This new characterization avoids the arbitrariness involved in choosing a particular percentage, and then asking what would happen if that percentage of the next generation internalized the code. We also avoid the artificiality of assuming that the internalization of a code is largely an all or nothing thing. (This assumption is not explicit in Hooker's formulation, but it is implicit in the idea of imagining a society where 90 per cent have internalized the code while the other 10 per cent have not.)

Some specific features of the Rule Consequentialist ideal code are motivated by particular human failings. Rules requiring agents to act impartially may be necessary to correct the natural human tendency to favour our own interests, and those of our nearest and dearest. Rules requiring agents to respect the autonomy of others may be necessary to correct the natural human tendency to think that we know what is best for other people.

The two most obvious formulations of consequentialism are individual ('What would happen if I did this?') and universal ('What would happen if everyone did this?'). Contemporary Rule Consequentialism opts for something in between. It has a scope that is collective, but not universal. How might we justify both the decision to go collective, and the choice of any particular non-universal level of collective compliance or acceptance? The most satisfactory explanation will be one where the precise level of collective acceptance flows from the underlying reason for adopting a collective approach in the first place. This section develops one such explanation.

Rule Consequentialism reflects a picture of morality as a task given, not to individual human beings taken in isolation (as in Simple Consequentialism), or to the set of all individual human beings (as in a fully universal version of Consequentialism), but to a particular group or community of human beings. The question it responds to is not 'What if everyone did that?' but 'What if *we* did that?' More generally, Rule Consequentialism asks us to imagine that we are choosing a moral code to govern our community. This explains the focus on teachability. It also provides a natural explanation for the non-universal character of Rule Consequentialism. The most natural interpretation of the idea of a community choosing moral rules for itself is one where the community acknowledges that not everyone will comply, and that even in the most assiduous community compliance will never be perfect.

Several things could be said in support of this collective approach.

1. Historical. The classical utilitarians focused on the best advice to give to a monarch, or other government, regarding legislation, and on the choice of moral principles to encourage within a society. (Bentham is the pre-eminent exponent of the first approach, and J.S. Mill of the second.) Our collective approach is thus continuous with the central concerns motivating the Consequentialist tradition. This does not mean that this is the correct Consequentialist approach, but it does suggest that it is worth exploring further.[27]

2. Foundational or Meta-ethical. We might have independent reason for regarding morality as a collective project, as opposed to an individual or universal one. Chapter 11 further explores the collective credentials of morality.

3. Intuitive Appeal. The particular form of Rule Consequentialism that flows most naturally from our collective justification also does the best job of tying together our considered moral judgements. Establishing this is the principal task of Chapters 5 to 9. This intuitive appeal reinforces the foundational case. One explanation for the intuitive appeal of our formulation of Rule Consequentialism is because it reflects a compelling picture of morality.

The collective justification for Rule Consequentialism has several advantages:

1. It can help explain a focus on a particular community. Rule Consequentialism is bedevilled by questions of scope. Do we seek rules to be internalized by everyone in our society, everyone in the Western world, everyone on Earth, or all sentient creatures in the universe? Many Rule Consequentialists acknowledge that an intuitive code is much more likely to result from a narrow scope, such as confining attention to our society, but that anything short of universal scope seems arbitrary. From the perspective of a choice between the individual and universal interpretations of Consequentialism, this arbitrariness is hard to avoid. However, if our focus

---

[27] The general historical precedent cited in the text is largely independent of the more specific question of whether, in their account of individual morality, particular classical utilitarians were adherents of Act or Rule Consequentialism. (Crisp, *Mill on Utilitarianism*, 102–5.)

from the very beginning is on the moral task of some particular community, then our narrower formulation is no more in need of justification than the even narrower formulation of the Simple Consequentialist, who focuses on my individual moral task. (I return to these issues in Chapter 9.)

2. As human beings belong to different levels of community (family, local, national, global), this justification raises the possibility that different levels of collective assessment may be appropriate for different moral contexts. If we ultimately decide that no single moral theory, based on a single focal point, is adequate, then the present justification thus provides an account of how to go about combining different foci. I sketch one such possibility in Chapter 11.

3. I argue in Chapter 9 that the appropriate level of collective assessment depends largely on the strength of bonds between individuals, and the extent to which the most valuable projects available to them are collective. These factors are themselves likely to change over time, especially under full compliance with the ideal code. The focus of Rule Consequentialist assessment would thus itself shift through time. Paradoxically, any particular version of Rule Consequentialism seeks to render itself redundant, by widening the scope of concern of those who have internalized it, and thus opening the way for a broader Consequentialist assessment. Our moral task is to create a world where *we* are no longer the principle focus of our own moral evaluations.

4. On the other hand, there are limits to this expansion of Rule Consequentialist focus, as there are corresponding limits to the extent to which is either practical or desirable to broaden the concerns and projects of individual human beings. A perfectly global Rule Consequentialism is neither possible nor desirable.

We return to the justification and scope of the collective focus in Chapter 9. In the mean time, we focus on our own community. We assume that we are seeking rules to be internalized by 'our community'.

The next six chapters explore the content of Rule Consequentialism. The remainder of this chapter sketches the basic features of Rule Consequentialism. Chapter 6 outlines an individual morality of reproduction, centred on the establishment of a prima facie case for a constrained reproductive freedom. Chapters 7 to 9 explore broader issues of intergenerational justice, asking whether these undermine the prima facie case established in Chapter 6. Chapter 10 addresses the demands of Rule Consequentialism as they relate to, and are affected by, reproductive and intergenerational ethics, especially in the context of partial compliance with the ideal code. (Our idealization to widespread compliance in the *next* generation does not rule out the possibility of widespread non-compliance with the ideal code in the more distant future, especially if circumstances change so that the demands of compliance increase significantly. The introduction of future generations thus increases the significance of partial compliance effects within Rule Consequentialism as a whole. We return to this particular issue in Sections 9.3.2 and 10.3.)

5.6. Rule Consequentialism and Uncertainty

All human choices are made under uncertainty. Uncertainty impacts on Rule Consequentialism in two distinct ways.

1. We, as moral theorists, operate under uncertainty when choosing an ideal code to apply to the real world. This uncertainty has two dimensions. We do not know what would happen if some particular code were taught to, or internalized by, some particular group. We are also uncertain how to evaluate different possible futures. Even if we knew exactly what would happen for every possible code, we still might not be sure which code would produce the most valuable outcome.

2. Moral agents who have internalized the ideal code will often be making decisions under uncertainty. Any plausible moral code must tell them how to respond to the uncertainty they face.

We begin with our own uncertainty. The first challenge comes from a common objection to Rule Consequentialism. Our uncertainty is so great that we have no idea what the consequences of teaching any particular code would be. It is thus impossible for Rule Consequentialism to offer us any guidance.[28] This is especially damning for those, like Hooker, who defend Rule Consequentialism primarily in terms of its intuitive appeal. If we have no idea what the theory tells us to do, we cannot say if its injunctions are intuitively appealing.

A first reply is that, in a particular case, we might be confident that one code is better than another, even if we could not possibly put any definite value on the consequences of teaching either code. To give an extreme example, we can be sure that a code encouraging agents to kill anyone who disagrees with them would have worse consequences than one containing the rules of commonsense morality.

However, in most cases, it is probably correct that we cannot easily compare the consequences of teaching two complete codes. The Rule Consequentialist's strongest reply to the present objection is to deny that this matters, as we can often be confident that the ideal code will include

---

[28] This argument is forcefully presented by James Griffin in his *Value Judgement*, 103–7; and Griffin, 'Replies', 303–10, (replying to Crisp, 'Griffin's Pessimism', and Hooker, 'Impartiality, Predictibility, and Indirect Consequentialism', 2002).

some particular rule, or at least a rule of a certain general type, even if we cannot specify the full contents of the ideal code. In many of the most interesting cases for moral philosophy, we have a strong prima facie reason for thinking that a certain type of rule, if widely internalized, would produce significant positive results, and we also have reason to believe that no alternative rule would offer any compensating benefits. Indeed, our case for an individual morality based on reproductive freedom will take precisely this form. Given the nature and situation of human beings in any feasible future, a suitably constrained principle of reproductive freedom provides significant benefits that are not available under any alternative set of rules. I then argue that no alternative to reproductive freedom has any advantage in terms of other valuable consequences. Reproductive freedom is certainly not perfect. Indeed, we cannot even guarantee that a code containing such a rule will produce acceptable consequences. However, we can be confident that the expected value of pursuing any alternative code would be less.

The primary interest of Rule Consequentialism is in rules, not complete moral codes. Rule Consequentialism never directly asks us to identify the ideal code—it only tells us to identify (and act on) particular rules contained in that code. If we can identify the rules without fully specifying the code, then Rule Consequentialism can offer useful advice.

Our own uncertainty does not prevent us from knowing something about the ideal code. However, that uncertainty can affect the content of the code we choose. For instance, we might respond to our own uncertainty regarding value theory by preferring an ideal code that encourages agents to explore and question the values prevalent in their society, rather than casting a particular set of value claims in stone. Chapters 8 and 9 present additional reasons for expecting Rule Consequentialism to recommend a code that is adaptable in this way.

One question concerning all decisions under uncertainty is whether we should seek to maximize expected value, or instead chose a more risk-averse decision procedure. Should we adopt a risky code that, so far as we can tell, maximizes expected value, or instead opt for a code with lower expected value that more reliably avoids catastrophe? I am personally inclined to believe that, when choosing a moral code for teaching subsequent generations, some degree of risk aversion would be rational. However, I do not believe that, as a matter of fact, we face a choice between maximizing expected value and avoiding catastrophe. For reasons that will hopefully become clear over the next two chapters, the general features that make an ideal code likely to maximally promote overall value in favourable circumstances also give it the flexibility to respond most effectively in extreme, potentially catastrophic, circumstances. Our own limited information and powers of prediction combine with general features of human nature and motivation, and with aspects of our value theory (especially the significance of autonomy), to suggest that, whatever our attitude to risk, we ought to choose the broadly liberal ideal code sketched over the next five chapters.

We turn now to the second role of uncertainty. How will the ideal code advise agents to deal with the fact that they are unable to predict precisely the consequences of their own actions? In general, there are several possibilities:

1. Instruct agents to maximize expected utility.
2. Instruct agents to follow some other specific mechanical decision procedure.
3. Build into the ideal code a set of rules which, while not necessarily directly referring to uncertainty, have the effect of guiding agents appropriately when they are uncertain.

The first two options are unlikely to be feasible. The simple fact is that agents are never sufficiently well informed to know what would maximize expected value in any particular situation. Advising them to seek to perform some complex mathematical calculation before acting is unlikely to be efficient. Indeed, the case for believing that Rule Consequentialism does not collapse into Simple Consequentialism is itself an argument for the flexible approach over the mechanical.

I do not propose to pursue the problems of uncertainty further at this point, though particular cases of uncertainty will return to plague us later on (Section 8.2). We should note, of course, that uncertainty is not a problem peculiar to Consequentialism. All moral theories must accommodate it one way or another. (For instance, we saw the problems uncertainty creates for Gauthier in Section 2.1.) Instead, we begin our examination of the Rule Consequentialist account of the individual morality of reproduction.[29]

5.7. Parental Obligations

In Chapter 4 we found two principal faults with the Hybrid View: it could not accommodate either reproductive freedom or parental obligations. Our principal task in this chapter will be to show that Rule Consequentialism avoids these two failings, especially the first. We begin by establishing that the ideal code constrains the behaviour of parents toward their children, and toward third parties. This section is relatively brief, as it mostly

---

[29] For a fuller discussion, see Hooker, *Ideal Code, Real World*, 136–41; Mulgan, *The Demands of Consequentialism*, 58–9.

applies general results familiar from previous discussions of Rule Consequentialism.

5.7.1. *Doing, Allowing, and the Ideal Code*

We begin with the general question of whether the ideal code might include a distinction between doing and allowing. Some such distinction is necessary if the code is to incorporate special obligations without also placing agents under very onerous obligations to assist others. As we saw in Section 4.1.3.1, Shelly Kagan claimed that the Hybrid View produces absurd results in many everyday situations because it cannot distinguish between actively doing x and passively allowing x to happen. This makes it particularly important to ask whether Rule Consequentialism fares any better.

Rule Consequentialism may seem no better placed than Simple Consequentialism to accommodate a distinction between doing and allowing. After all, like other forms of Consequentialism, Rule Consequentialism is primarily interested in what happens, not in how it comes about. The optimal set of rules is selected solely on the basis of consequences. However, as its proponents are fond of pointing out, Rule Consequentialism is not so simple. The ideal code is not designed to be implemented by perfect Utilitarian calculators, but to be taught to (and internalized by) fallible, finite creatures such as ourselves. The ideal code is thus constrained by human psychology, and by current institutions and practices. It may be that, whatever a perfectly idealized set of rules would look like, the best rules we (or creatures like us) could be taught include many of the Non-Consequentialist distinctions of commonsense morality. Indeed, this closeness to commonsense morality is often cited as one of the principal virtues of Rule Consequentialism, especially in comparison to Simple Consequentialism.

The limits of human development are almost certainly such that the costs of attempting to eradicate a tendency to distinguish morally between doing and allowing would outweigh the benefits. The strength, near universality, and resilience of intuitions supporting that distinction strongly suggest this. The ideal code of rules will differentiate between doing and allowing. A society where people refrain from interfering with one another's pursuit of goals is likely to enjoy a higher level of well-being than one whose inhabitants regard such interference as no worse than a failure to assist others in the pursuit of their goals.

Rule Consequentialism is also superior to the Hybrid View in its ability to acknowledge the significance of special obligations (Section 4.1.3.3). Suppose we are choosing between two competing codes of rules. One includes special obligations while the other does not. (Let us call these the Restrictive Code and the Permissive Code respectively.) We must compare the consequences of accepting each code. In a world where the Permissive Code was accepted, people would find it very difficult to pursue their goals, as they would be unable to rely upon others to fulfil any promises or undertakings on which those goals relied. By contrast, people who lived under the Restrictive Code would have confidence in one another's promises. Pursuit of goals would thus be much more widespread and ambitious. This considerable advantage is sufficient to outweigh any disadvantages of the Restrictive Code. Accordingly, Rule Consequentialists would recommend that code over its rival. More generally, as Hooker notes, 'on the whole, the consequences will be far better if there are generally accepted rules forbidding physical attack, torture, theft, promise-breaking, lying, and the like. Indeed, at least minimum forms of these rules are indispensable to society.'[30]

5.7.2. Person-Affecting Elements

Special Obligations typically take a person-affecting form. They tell us how to treat particular individuals, rather than urging us to promote impersonal value. One way to explore the role of special obligations within Rule Consequentialism is to ask whether the ideal code will include any person-affecting rules. In particular, will it encourage agents to treat Same People Choices differently from Different People Choices, or will it incorporate the No Difference View? I shall conclude that, although those who have internalized the ideal code will have a broadly person-affecting approach to morality, the actual rules governing reproduction in that code will be consistent with the No Difference View. One strength of Rule Consequentialism is that, unlike most rival accounts, it explains the intuitive strength of both the person-affecting approach and the No Difference View. (Section 1.7.)

There are several reasons to expect the ideal code to include person-affecting elements.

1. Intuitive Appeal.   Person-affecting principles have considerable intuitive appeal, especially in Same People Choices. The morality of everyday life deals primarily with such choices. When we evaluate competing codes, one crucial feature is their comparative teachability. If person-affecting explanations are more natural for Same People Choices, then the ideal code is likely to include such explanations.

This argument implicitly assumes that person-affecting views would seem as 'natural' to someone who had internalized the ideal code as they do to us. This assumption is potentially controversial. However, the ideal code definitely must

---

[30] Hooker, *Ideal Code, Real World*, 126.

include many rules directing agents to take direct account of the interests of particular others, as the general acceptance of such rules produces great benefits.[31] It seems reasonable to assume that the successful inculcation of such person-affecting rules will produce a natural psychological tendency to think of (at least some broad areas of) morality in person-affecting terms.

2. The Unity of the Ideal Code.   The ideal code is not a set of isolated rules for distinct prepackaged sections of everyday life. We thus cannot consider rules regarding reproduction in isolation. Other things being equal, we should expect rules regarding reproduction to cohere with rules for other moral choices. Because reproduction is a comparatively small part of the ideal code, we should expect this coherence to result from other rules influencing, colouring, or helping to interpret the rules regarding reproduction, not vice versa. If the ideal code has a person-affecting flavour in general, then those who have internalized the code are likely to have a person-affecting-tinted interpretation of the rules regarding reproduction.

3. Transparency Not Necessarily a Virtue.   Rule Consequentialism is interested in results. If the ideal code produces better results if people (mistakenly) apply rules designed for Same People Choices to Different People Choices, then Rule Consequentialism will applaud this mistake. There are several reasons why such a mistake might be beneficial.

1. If the ideal code is primarily person-affecting, then the addition of radically different moral rules for reproduction will carry significant inculcation costs. It will be better if people can apply similar rules, and treat reproduction in a person-affecting way.
2. If the ideal code is primarily person-affecting, then those who have internalized the code may well go wrong when they realize they are faced with Different People Choices, as they will be too lenient on themselves. In particular, they may feel they are permitted to create any child whose life is even barely worth living, as the standard person-affecting criterion of wrongness will not object to any such act of creation.[32]

We could conclude that the ideal code cannot be person-affecting in its treatment of reproduction. Alternatively, we might conclude that the ideal code will work better if people do not realize that person-affecting principles break down in Different People Choices. In general, person-affecting views are only implausibly permissive in Different People Choices once the

---

[31] Ibid. 136–41.

[32] More sophisticated person-affecting theories can avoid this result. However, the discussion in the text concerns the role of simple person-affecting *rules* within the ideal code, not the plausibility of sophisticated forms of the person-affecting view when presented as complete moral theories. (See Ch. 1 n. 12 above.)

agent realizes she is dealing with a Different People Choice. Person-affecting views work perfectly well in Different People Choices so long as the agent believes she faces a Same People Choice. Recall Mary, choosing between having a child in winter or in summer (Section 1.3). If Mary mistakenly believes that the Summer Child and the Winter Child are the same person, then her adherence to the person-affecting view will lead her to conclude (rightly) that she ought to create the happier child.

4. Narrow versus Wide Person-Affecting Views.   The preceding approach raises the general problem of esoteric morality, whereby a moral theory can only work if people are seriously mis-informed about morally relevant facts. Perhaps it is implausible to expect the inhabitants of the ideal society to make this sort of elementary philosophical mistake. An alternative suggestion is that the ideal code might combine person-affecting rules for ordinary inter-personal relations with quasi-person-affecting rules for reproduction. The latter would be formulated by substituting 'the child you would have' into the standard person-affecting moral principles.[33] The ideal code could thus exploit the fact that simple analogues of the person-affecting view work comparatively well in many Same Number Choices.

This composite person-affecting view officially treats Same People Choices and Different People Choice as equivalent. In practice, however, those who have internalized the ideal code might differentiate the two types of choice, because strictly person-affecting sentiments will pervade their moral outlook. Suppose such an agent is faced with a Partial Same People Choice—one where the future population contains some people who will exist whatever the agent does, and others whose existence depends on the present choice. An agent who has internalized a person-affecting moral code may give more weight to the interests of those who will exist whatever they do than to the potential well-being of someone whose existence is contingent on their choice. To someone who had internalized the ideal code, the well-being of particular identifiable people looms larger than aggregate well-being.

We must distinguish the *behaviour* of those who have internalized the ideal code from the *content* of that code. Person-affecting elements not included in the content of the code might affect behaviour in several ways. People who have internalized the ideal code might not want to do, or feel comfortable doing, certain things which are technically permitted by that code. In practice, when it comes to balancing their interests against those of others, they might well set themselves a higher threshold in Same People Choices than in Different People Choices. At the level of moral reflection, however,

---

[33] Rahul Kumar has recently sketched a response to the Non-Identity Problem along these lines, building on a Contractualist foundation. (Kumar, 'Who Can be Wronged?')

they might still recognize the No Difference View, and feel the same degree of moral freedom in the two cases.

In my full discussion of reproductive freedom in Section 6.2, I argue that those who have internalized the ideal code will not *want* to create children whose lives are below the zero level. I also argue that they would *not feel morally free* to create such a child. The contrast with the present case may seem arbitrary, but there are good Rule Consequentialist reasons for insisting on it. We must distinguish three types of case where it is desirable that most people not do x.

1. It is desirable that no one do x.
2. It is desirable that some people do x, so long as most people don't.
3. It doesn't matter whether some people do x, so long as most people don't.

Creating lives below the zero level is an instance of (1). Not having children, by contrast, is presumably an instance of (3). Certain forms of heroic devotion to a cause might be examples of (2). It is good to have some people showing such devotion, but the social fabric would collapse if everyone did the same.[34]

If it is desirable that no one do x, then we need an ideal code which forbids and censures x. This is a more effective way to minimize the performance of x than a code which permits x. Recall that we do not assume full internalization of the ideal code (Section 5.3). We thus cannot assume that no one in the ideal society *wants* to do x, even if no one who has internalized the ideal code would want to. If some people want to do x, then only a code which forbids and censures x will have a reasonable chance of preventing them.

However, forbidding and censuring have costs, both to individuals who wish to do x and to others. In particular, suppose we follow Raz and regard any removal of an option as a (prima facie) loss of autonomy, unless the option removed is bad in itself.[35] Forbidding and censuring will thus not be appropriate in cases where there is no loss of overall value if a small minority continue to do x. In such cases, we will prefer an ideal code which permits x. (On the other hand, it is reasonable to assume that, if it is better that no one does x, then x is not a valuable end, and does not aim at any valuable end. Removing the option of doing x is thus not a reduction of autonomy.[36])

[34] This reinforces our earlier conclusion that Individual Consequentialists cannot solve the Demandingness Objection simply by arguing that the right action is whatever would follow from the set of motives (or the code of rules) it would be best for the agent to have (or follow) over the course of her own life, taking the actual behaviour of others as given. Given the behaviour of others, the best way for me to promote the good over the course of my life is to follow extremely demanding rules, even if things would go much worse if everyone else did the same (Section 4.2.2). (See also Mulgan, *The Demands of Consequentialism*, ch. 2, esp. Section 2.5.)   [35] See Raz, 'Incommensurability and Agency'.

[36] It may appear that my moralized Razian view of autonomy renders Rule Consequentialism circular. (The purpose of the ideal code is to determine what is morally permissible. Yet we cannot compare competing codes until we have determined which projects are morally permissible, as only then can we

The crucial question is whether those who have internalized the ideal code will feel morally free to behave in a certain way. If they will, then such behaviour is permitted by the ideal code. Otherwise it is not. I am inclined to feel that, whatever intuitive qualms they may have about the No Difference View, those in the ideal society will feel morally free to act in accordance with it. So long as one does not violate one's other moral obligations, acting in accordance with the No Difference View would thus be permissible.

Suppose a person from the ideal society, who has a person-affecting world view, meets someone who internalizes the No Difference View and acts accordingly in Different People Choices. I am suggesting that the former might regard the latter as *psychologically* different from a typical inhabitant of the ideal society, but in a morally neutral way. They might acknowledge that such a person was *morally more consistent* than a typical inhabitant of the ideal society, where this is neither a good nor a bad thing. They might even regard such a person as *virtuous*, in an odd kind of way. Indeed, there are many other possible reactions here, subject only to the following pair of constraints.

1. Ordinary people are under no obligation to be like these peculiar people, and
2. the latter are under no obligation to be like ordinary people.

As in many other areas, the ideal code may accommodate a wide range of degrees of consistency between one's moral phenomenology and one's 'official' moral beliefs. This provides another illustration of the resilience of the ideal code. A code requiring rigid links between content and behaviour would be much harder to teach to a broad human population.

I have argued that, for Same People Choices, the ideal code will largely appeal to narrow person-affecting rules. However, such rules might be replaced with quasi-person-affecting rules even for some strictly Same People Choices. For instance, consider the example of leaving a bomb in a forest to detonate tomorrow, or to detonate and kill the first person to enter. We clearly want the ideal code to forbid this, and the most natural explanation is a general rule against causing gratuitous harm to other people. In this particular case, the agent's reasoning should be as follows. 'There is a person who will be harmed by my actions, namely the first person who comes along, therefore I should not plant the bomb.' Things will go better overall if the ideal code does not permit people to escape this obligation by pointing out that there is no presently existing person of whom we can say definitely that *they* are the person

know which projects are valuable.) However, this circle is avoided if we can find an account of the notion of 'valuable ends' which does not presuppose a theory of right action. We can then specify the value to be promoted without circular reference to the content of the ideal code. In line with my general agnosticism regarding value theory, the development of a full account of valuable ends would take us too far afield.

who would be harmed. Moral theorists can construct non-person-affecting accounts of moral obligation in such cases. These may be the most satisfying in some abstract theoretical sense. However, the quasi-person-affecting solution may be easier to teach, as it is a natural extension of the person-affecting views the ideal code employs for most other areas of everyday life.

5.7.3. Different Number Choices

How will the ideal code deal with Different Number Choices in individual morality? Standard person-affecting views clearly break down here, and there is no obvious or natural way to extend the person-affecting view to Different Number Choices. The ideal code will need different rules here. This may be a good thing. If there is no natural person-affecting approach to Different Number Choices, then the ideal rules regarding such choices will not conflict with the person-affecting intuitions of those who have internalized the ideal code. Specific rules for Different Number Choices are explored in the next chapter.

As an illustration, the Lexical Reproduction Rule defended in Section 6.2 below could be broken down, somewhat artificially, into two separate components, one dealing with a Different Number Choice ('shall I reproduce?'), the other with a Same Number Choice ('how should I reproduce?'). The Lexical Reproduction Rule uses a quasi-person-affecting principle for the Same Number Choice. For the Different Number Choice, the Lexical Reproduction Rule departs from both Simple Consequentialism and a pure person-affecting view. The former would require reproduction if and only if it maximizes utility, the latter would permit any reproduction above the zero level. By appealing to constrained reproductive freedom, this rule avoids both of these unpalatable extremes.

5.7.4. Parental Obligations Proper

Having seen that Rule Consequentialism includes person-affecting elements, it remains to ask if it is likely to endorse an account of parental obligations reasonably close to common sense. An emphasis on the value of autonomy is central to both our account of the ideal code in general, and our defence of reproductive freedom in particular. This suggests that a key desideratum of any ideal code is that it ensure that all children develop the capacity to meaningfully exercise autonomy in their adult life. Parents will be placed under obligations to meet the developmental needs of their children, and enable them to make the most of whatever opportunities are available in their society.

One might think it would be better to place such obligations on all adults, not just on parents, as this would maximize the benefit to children. The ideal code is likely to include a modest general obligation to meet the needs of others. We explore the strength of this obligation in Chapter 10. However, such a universal obligation is no substitute for specific parental obligations. The basic reason is that our ideal code must be successfully inculcated in the majority of the next generation. People will be psychologically resistant to any code incorporating very strong obligations to assist strangers. (This is the cornerstone of the Rule Consequentialist reply to the Demandingness Objection, to be explored in Chapter 10.) The ideal code can include a universal obligation to assist all children only if that obligation is comparatively weak. If such a weak general obligation exhausts the obligations of adults to children, then the needs of children will not be very effectively met, especially as one of the developmental needs of a human child is the formation of strong reciprocal attachments with particular adults.

By contrast, there are two reasons to think that people could be taught a code incorporating much stronger specific obligations to one's own children. The first reason is that human beings do seem to display a strong inclination to protect and nurture their own children. Such inclinations on their own are unlikely to be sufficient. They should be supplemented by an obligation to assist one's children. However, the prevalence of psychological inclinations should make it easier to inculcate a set of parental obligations that is much more demanding than any general obligation.

The second key factor is that, in general, it should be easier to inculcate conditional obligations (which must be voluntarily assumed) rather than unconditional obligations. An obligation to aid all children falls on everyone regardless of choice or inclination, whereas an obligation to care for one's own children falls only on those who choose to become parents. Very demanding specific obligations are likely to seem fairer than equally demanding general obligations. It will thus be easier to teach the former than the latter. (This also reinforces the case for reproductive freedom within the ideal code, as it will be easier to inculcate demanding parental obligations when these are combined with moral freedom regarding the decision to reproduce.)

I conclude that Rule Consequentialism can incorporate parental obligations. The principal remaining concerns are how demanding such obligations will be, and how they will be balanced against other obligations contained in the ideal code. In particular, opponents of Rule Consequentialism frequently allege that its overall pattern of obligations will be either too lenient or too demanding. We return to these questions in Chapter 10.

6

Reproductive Freedom

6.1. Compulsory Reproduction Revisited

Rule Consequentialism seeks a code of rules to maximize value. Rules regarding reproduction obviously affect the number of future people, and the size of the population is one factor affecting the total value of a possible outcome. So Rule Consequentialists must address the issue of optimal population size. How many future people should there be? It looks as if Rule Consequentialism must give a very demanding and unpalatable answer to this question.

We are operating with a traditional Consequentialist value theory, where the addition of extra lives worth living always increases total value. Other things being equal, the population should be as large as possible. If it incorporates such a value theory, then Rule Consequentialism tells us to strive to produce as many children as we possibly can, even if their lives are barely worth living. The maximum feasible fertility rate for a human population is usually estimated at between 13 and 17 children per adult woman.[1] Unconstrained reproduction at this rate would lead to a vast increase in the population. Whatever we may think of the underlying value theory, the resulting theory of moral action can seem both extremely demanding and intrinsically morally repugnant.

Our first reply is to deny that, as a matter of fact, the best Consequentialist value theory yields these results in the actual world. Our value theory only implies that it is desirable to maximize the population if other things are equal. In the actual world, other things are far from equal. Limitations on resources, and other problems resulting from overcrowding, almost certainly prevent even the Total View from advocating a population explosion. In practice, anything approaching Parfit's Z-world is not ecologically sustainable.

Furthermore, I argued in Chapter 3 that the best Consequentialist value theory may depart from the Total View by incorporating a lexical level. Environmental constraints suggest that the global population cannot grow too much (if at all) without a serious negative impact on the average quality

---

[1] Jolly and Gribble, 'The Proximate Determinants of Fertility', 81.

of life over the long run. Any value theory designed to avoid the Repugnant Conclusion will not countenance unconstrained population expansion nearly as often as the Total View. Rule Consequentialism need not recommend population growth if the result would be that everyone fell below the lexical level. Even if the Z-world and the A-world are both feasible, an ideal code may aim for the latter not the former.

A second reply is that the ideal code will not generally include purely maximizing rules. The code must be teachable to, and internalizable by, the next generation. This puts severe limits on the complexity or psychological demandingness of its rules. The best feasible outcome is not the best logically possible outcome, and the optimal rules probably will not even aim directly at the best feasible outcome. The code that maximizes value is unlikely to be a code that tells agents to maximize value. For instance, a rule requiring every woman to have as many children as she possibly can, while simple enough to grasp, would almost certainly be prohibitively difficult to inculcate in a broad population, especially as it would run directly counter to the general liberal tenor of the ideal code, as we shall see in Sections 6.2, 6.6, and 7.2.

The ideal code will thus not advocate the maximum feasible level of fertility. However, if we seek any particular precise population size, then we will still need a very prescriptive rule regarding reproduction. For instance, to achieve a population of precisely six billion (or precisely ten billion, or any other specific target), a considerable degree of coercion might be required. (Actually, it is far from clear that any rule, however rigid, could ensure that a precise population target was achieved, given the unpredictability of the natural processes involved.) A restrictive rule might also be necessary if we sought the precise maximum population consistent with (almost) everyone living above some specific target, such as the lexical level or the zero level.

On the other hand, the next few sections establish a strong prima facie case in favour of reproductive freedom. If this case is sound, then the ideal code will favour a freely chosen lower rate of reproduction over a higher rate imposed by coercion or moral obligation. Given the significance of autonomy, a world where five billion people enjoy broad reproductive freedom could well be better than a world where six billion people enjoy otherwise equivalent lives without reproductive freedom. If the denial of reproductive freedom is the only way to get a population of six billion, then the ideal code will not aim for the larger population.

We thus cannot assume that Rule Consequentialism seeks any precise population target. The next generation must be large enough to support the present generation in its dotage, and to provide cultural continuity. It must be small enough not to overburden the environment. Between these two extremes lies a wide range of possible population sizes. We should interpret the ideal code, not as seeking to achieve a particular optimal population size, but as seeking to avoid a population which is too large or too small. Depending on the circumstances of a particular society, some modest population increase may be desirable. I defer further discussion until Section 8.2.3, where I will argue that the specification of precise population targets should occur in public debate within the ideal society, rather than built into the ideal code in advance. (This is one obvious point where further departures from the Total View, such as explicit holistic evaluation of different possible futures, would reinforce our defence of Rule Consequentialism.)

Rule Consequentialism thus sets itself a comparatively modest goal. I shall argue that the ideal code should permit a wide range of reproductive options, and accommodate significant reproductive choice. The empirical evidence suggests that, in a stable society where women are provided with adequate education and a wide range of opportunities, a sustainable birth rate can be achieved.[2]

6.2. Rule Consequentialism and Reproductive Freedom

The cornerstone of my Rule Consequentialist account of the morality of reproduction is a commitment to reproductive freedom. Section 6.2 establishes a prima facie case in favour of such freedom. Rule Consequentialism advises us to follow a code of rules whose internalization by everyone would maximize value. Initially it seems obvious that the rule regarding reproduction will be something like the following.

The Simple Reproductive Imperative.   Have a child whenever that child's life would be worth living.

If the population has a finite optimal level (or an optimal *range*), perhaps due to resource constraints, then we might amend this slightly to yield the following rule.

The Conditional Reproductive Imperative.   Reproduce if and only if (*a*) the population is below its optimal range; and (*b*) your child's life would be worth living.

Rules such as these deprive everyone of reproductive choice. If the population is below the lower limit of the optimal range, then we have an obligation to

---

[2] For summaries of the evidence here, see Sen, 'Population: Delusion and Reality'; and Sen, *Development as Freedom*. For other references, see the footnotes accompanying Section 6.6 (nn. 22–30).

produce any possible (barely) happy child. If the population is above that level, then we are forbidden to do so. As many people regard reproductive choice as a basic value, this is a highly counterintuitive result.[3]

There are two ways to make room for reproductive choice. The first is indirect. In our actual situation, the way to produce the optimal population in the next generation is for some to reproduce while others do not. (Or, perhaps more accurately, at least some must reproduce and it must not be the case that everyone has as many children as they can.) Some but not all of the possible members of the next generation must become actual. The way to maximize the total happiness of the next generation is to create the happier possible people and leave uncreated those who would have been less happy. Suppose that n is the optimal number of people in the next generation. We then imagine the possible people arranged in descending order of quality of life, from 1 to m, where m is the number of possible people (m is obviously much greater than n). Rule Consequentialism will then recommend the following rule.

The Ordered Reproductive Imperative.   Have a child if and only if the value of that child's life is at least as great as the value of the n-th possible person on our ordered list of possible people.[4]

This rule leaves no direct role for choice. However, as a matter of fact, children are much more likely to be happy if their parents wanted to have them. Most of the happier possible people will be those whose parents wanted them, while most of the unhappier possible people are those who would have been unwanted. In practice, then, this rule will generally tell people to have children if and only if they want to.

This connection between reproduction and choice is too contingent. Those who could make comparatively good parents will still be *obliged* to reproduce even if they do not wish to. Commonsense intuition, reinforced by the considerations advanced in Chapter 4, suggests that, if at all possible, we should seek a more direct role for reproductive choice. The easiest solution is to argue that the ideal code would include the following rule.

The Simple Reproductive Choice Rule.   Reproduce if and only if you want to.

We begin with general reasons why the ideal code might include a rule similar to this one. We then move on to ask what particular form that rule might

---

[3] Even in extreme circumstances, the ideal code is very unlikely to include obligations to reproduce for other reasons, as such obligations are an inefficient way to guarantee any given optimal population. (See Section 6.6.)

[4] The discussion in the text is obviously an oversimplification, and requires an artificial way of enumerating possible people. Nothing of substance turns on this oversimplification, as the rule requiring such enumeration is rejected on other grounds.

take, and how it would be applied. If the ideal code is to be plausible, then this simple rule will need to be constrained.

The advantages of reproductive choice are obvious. If the members of the first generation are able to choose for themselves whether they will have children, then this will improve the quality of their lives. Given the significance of autonomy, the particular significance of being morally free to make major life choices, and the significance of this particular life choice, this additional value is not negligible, as we saw in our discussion of the Hybrid View in Chapter 4. The significance of reproductive freedom both justifies a general prerogative permitting sub-optimal reproduction, and explains why the Rule Consequentialist ideal code is likely to favour reproductive choice.

There is a more general point here. Autonomy can be significant for both instrumental and intrinsic reasons. Autonomy is intrinsically good for an individual, because it is an independently valuable component of a worthwhile life.[5] Autonomy is instrumentally valuable because it greatly enhances an individual's likelihood of successfully achieving other valuable ends. The ideal code is thus likely to have a strong liberal component.[6] A liberal code is both more efficient in its operations and easier to teach. One strength of Rule Consequentialism is that it does not rest its case for individual moral freedom solely on the intrinsic value of autonomy.

Reproductive freedom is thus significantly better for the present generation than any alternative. It can only fail to maximize well-being if some alternative approach produces a significantly greater total well-being for the second generation, or subsequent generations. There are several reasons why this is unlikely. The first is that happier parents who have chosen to have children are more likely to provide a good life for their children. A second reason relates to the nature of goals. Before an individual is born, it is very hard to evaluate precisely how valuable his or her life will be. It is almost impossible to tell which of two possible future people will have the better life, once we have been assured that each will be provided with the basic necessities of life, including the necessary background conditions for the successful pursuit of goals. (If we believe in genuine incommensurability, then such comparisons may be impossible in principle, and not just in

---

[5] If our value theory incorporates holistic evaluations of the life of a community, then autonomy might also be intrinsically valuable at a societal level, because autonomous deliberative processes are an independently valuable component of a good communal life. Once again, departures from the Total View would reinforce the conclusions reached in the text.

[6] Riley, 'Defending Rule Utilitarianism'. The connection between Consequentialism and liberty is most famously associated with J. S. Mill. For good contemporary introductions to the debate, see Riley, *Mill on Liberty*, Ch. 7; and Crisp, *Mill on Utilitarianism*, Ch. 8.

practice.) If there is a form of reproductive choice which can ensure that these conditions are met, then it is very unlikely that any alternative principle produces an increase in value for the next generation sufficiently large to outweigh the loss of freedom for the first generation. I am confident that we can construct such a principle, as part of a broader liberal code.

We should also note that the disvalue of any loss of reproductive freedom would fall on each subsequent generation in its turn, and not just on the first generation. This raises the general issue of intergenerational continuity. We must assume that the ideal code, as taught to the next generation, includes rules for what they will teach their own children. The code is chosen because it maximizes well-being across all generations. A code denying reproductive freedom to all generations would be very undesirable, unless it produced some much greater benefit. It might also be very hard to teach such a code to the second generation, once they had seen the negative effects of a lack of reproductive freedom on their parents.[7]

6.2.1. *Constraining Reproductive Freedom*

Our intuitive objections to the Hybrid View (Section 4.1.3) showed that a principle of total reproductive freedom is too permissive. It would allow people knowingly to create children with horrific lives, or to have children solely in order to sell them into slavery for monetary reward. Any morally acceptable principle of reproductive freedom must be constrained.

These constraints will be of two types, addressing two key questions.

1. When are agents permitted to have children?
2. How are parents permitted to treat their children?

These two questions are obviously related: whether one is permitted to have a child may depend, in part, on whether one would be able to treat that child appropriately. We addressed the second question in general terms in Section 5.7. Our focus now is on the first question.

At a bare minimum, agents should only be permitted to reproduce if the life they are creating can reasonably be expected to be worth living. Can Rule Consequentialism accommodate this result? Why should we expect the ideal code to include constraints on reproduction? We begin our inquiry with the following very limited constraint.

---

[7] The ideal code could include a rule of the following form. 'Do x, but teach the next generation to do y (where x and y are quite distinct).' However, such a rule would be very difficult to internalize in a whole population. Even if the first generation did internalize the rule, their attempt to teach the next generation to do y while doing x themselves would be unlikely to succeed.

The Zero Reproductive Choice Rule.   Reproduce if and only if you want to, but only if your child's life will be above the zero level.

If the ideal code contains only the Simple Reproductive Choice Rule, with no constraints, then some people will create people whose lives are not worth living. This has a negative impact on total well-being. Rule Consequentialism will thus endorse some constraints unless these have some countervailing negative consequence. The negative effect of any constraint is the loss of reproductive freedom. All constraints on reproduction limit the choices of potential reproducers.

The particular loss of freedom involved in the Zero Reproductive Choice Rule is unlikely to be very morally significant. Most people will still retain a wide range of reproductive options. They can still choose whether, and to a large extent in what way, they will reproduce. Furthermore, the option which is removed is an intrinsically undesirable one. Creating people with worthwhile lives is a very worthwhile project. I argued in Section 4.2.2 that the importance for autonomy suggests that the decision whether or not to embark on such projects should be morally open. By contrast, creating people with lives below the zero level is intrinsically undesirable. If the valuable exercise of autonomy consists in the choice between competing projects which are themselves independently valuable, then the Zero Reproductive Choice Rule does not impact negatively on autonomy.

The problematic case for this constraint concerns people who wish to have children but are only able to have children whose lives would be below the zero level. The Zero Reproductive Choice Rule effectively deprives such people of the option of reproduction. Rule Consequentialists have two options at this point. The first is to hold that the constraint imposed by this rule does not apply to such people, as the disvalue of their loss of reproductive freedom outweighs the possible disvalue of allowing some subzero lives. This line of argument seems implausible. For the reasons stated above, losing the option of creating people whose lives are not worth living does not impact negatively on autonomy. The real loss of autonomy is caused by whatever it is that deprives some people of the option of creating worthwhile lives. Once this deprivation has been suffered, permitting those people to create lives below the zero level is not a solution.

This suggests a second response. If the creation of children whose lives are not worth living is not a worthwhile project, then embarking on that project does not improve the quality of one's life. Nor does it enhance one's autonomy to leave morally open the decision whether or not to embark on it. A moral rule prohibiting such reproduction thus has no negative effect. The only way genuinely to enhance the autonomy of people with such limited reproductive options is to give them the ability to have children with worthwhile lives. This suggests that, other things being equal, Rule Consequentialism will strongly advocate support for, and research into, alternative methods of reproduction. Alternatively, it might recommend that society be organized so as to improve the lifestyle options available to those unable to have children of their own. One central aim of the ideal code is to ensure the availability (both practical and moral) of a wide range of valuable lifestyle options. (We return to public policy in Section 6.6.)

Some might argue that a *rule* against having children whose lives are not worth living would be redundant, as no one would be tempted to do so anyway, especially not if they have been raised in the ideal society. As we saw in Section 5.7.2, objections of this kind misinterpret the status of the ideal code and the nature of its rules. For the Rule Consequentialist, the crucial question is not 'Would those in the ideal society want to do x?' but rather 'Would they feel morally free to do x?' Someone who had internalized the ideal code would not just have no desire to create a child with a sub-zero life. They would also recognize that it would be wrong to do so. This would be seen most clearly in their response to someone who did create such a life. An inhabitant of the ideal society would not be likely to regard such a person as merely someone with eccentric desires. If someone who had internalized the ideal code would not feel morally free to do x, then Rule Consequentialism says that x is forbidden.

6.2.2. *More Stringent Constraints*

Rule Consequentialism will not permit agents to create people whose lives are not worth living. We must now ask whether the ideal code will include a more stringent constraint. Perhaps agents will only be permitted to have children whose quality of life is greater than x, where x is above the zero level.

There are several arguments in support of more stringent constraints. If a more lenient constraint would lead to overpopulation, then a prohibitive constraint may be the best way to achieve an optimal population level while maximizing average happiness. In light of the value theory presented in Chapter 3, and bearing in mind the potential looseness attached to the expression 'lexical level' as foreshadowed in Section 5.4, we will be especially interested in the following rule.

The Lexical Reproduction Rule.   Reproduce if and only if you want to, so long as the child you create will live above the lexical level.

From now on, we will focus on this rule, unless otherwise stated. Our first task is to ask why the ideal code might include the Lexical Reproduction Rule instead of the Zero Reproductive Choice Rule.

If most people in the ideal society are able to create children whose lives are above the lexical level, then this extra constraint will add value without significantly diminishing reproductive freedom. Although not as bad as creating children whose lives are not worth living, the option of creating lives between the zero and lexical levels is clearly sub-optimal. For those who can create lives above the lexical level, the really morally significant choice involves, not the decision whether to create a life above or below that level, but rather whether to create lives above the lexical level as opposed to not reproducing at all. So long as *this* choice is left morally open, autonomy is not significantly compromised. The main effect of removing the sub-optimal option is that some people will have happier children than they might otherwise have had. The net impact on well-being is thus positive. On the other hand, some people who have internalized the Lexical Reproduction Rule instead of the Zero Reproductive Choice Rule might respond by not having children at all, rather than having children who live below the lexical level. We are operating with a value theory on which the addition of extra lives worth living typically increases aggregate value. So this change would make things worse.

To evaluate the Lexical Reproduction Rule we thus need to know how people would respond to the removal of the particular option of creating people whose lives fall between the zero and lexical levels. Many will be unaffected, as they would not have chosen the lesser option anyway. Of those who would have opted for sub-lexical reproduction under the more permissive Zero Reproductive Choice Rule, some will choose supra-lexical reproduction instead. Others may opt not to reproduce at all. Of these two changes, the first seems to enhance overall well-being, while the second reduces it. We thus need some idea how prevalent the two responses will be. The higher the threshold below which reproduction is forbidden, the more likely it is that people will respond by declining to reproduce at all.

Proponents of any constraint more stringent than the Zero Reproductive Choice Rule face a potential dilemma here. If very few people would be attracted to sub-optimal reproduction, then the benefits of the new constraint are limited. We must then ask whether it is necessary to complicate the ideal code in this way. In general, there is a strong prima facie case against the addition of new rules. Every extra clause increases the cost of inculcating the ideal code, and reduces the likelihood of compliance. This reluctance to add extra rules is essential if Rule Consequentialism is to avoid the Collapse Objection (Section 5.2). On the other hand, if sub-lexical reproduction would be a common choice, then any constraint more stringent than the Zero Reproductive Choice Rule will meet with considerable psychological resistance. It will thus be very difficult to get such a constraint internalized by most people. At some point the costs of inculcation will outweigh any benefits.

More stringent constraints on reproduction face a further problem. For any value of x between the zero level and the lexical level, there will be some people who can have children whose lives are worth living, but are unable to create anyone whose life exceeds x. A rule forbidding the creation of people with lives worth less than x deprives such people of any chance to reproduce. As before, we have two options. We might accept that such people are not allowed to reproduce. This option only seems plausible if this additional restriction is necessary to avoid overpopulation. Alternatively, we might argue that the original Lexical Reproduction Rule does not apply to such people. Instead, they should obey the following rule. (So should every-one else, though for most people the following revision is identical to the original Lexical Reproduction Rule.)

The New Lexical Reproduction Rule.   Reproduce if and only if you want to, so long as the child you create will live above the lexical level. Unless you are unable to have a child who will live above the lexical level, in which case you may create if and only if (*a*) the value of your child's life is greater than x (where x is between the zero and lexical levels); and (*b*) you could not have given any child of yours a better life.

This seems the appropriate option for Rule Consequentialists to take here. Unless this amendment would lead to overpopulation, it is hard to see any negative effects. Lowering the threshold enhances the autonomy of this group of potential parents, and the lives of their children are worth living. The alternative is a world where autonomy is reduced and no extra lives are added. These extra lives may be well below the average for their society. However, even if there are times when the creation of below-average lives is undesirable in itself, this does not seem to be one of them. (As we shall see in Section 6.2.3, condition (*b*) is actually too strong. However, some condition of this type is necessary to avoid having people gratuitously create lives well below the lexical level.)

We need to ask why these additional lives would be below the lexical level. Suppose the lexical level is defined in terms of the successful pursuit of valuable goals, as suggested in Chapter 3 (and supported by Chapter 4's discussion of the significance of such pursuit). If an adequate social framework exists within which people are able successfully to pursue valuable goals, then any normal person can live above the lexical level if provided with an adequate start in life. If social conditions prevent some people from accessing the opportunities provided by the framework, then a rearrangement of those social conditions will almost certainly enhance overall well-being. The ideal code is thus likely to be designed to ensure that everyone has access to the social framework of opportunities. This suggests that people will live below the lexical level only if their physical or cognitive limitations cannot be remedied by any feasible rearrangement of social conditions. Our value theory implies that the addition of such lives, considered in isolation, would increase total value. However, given the significance of autonomy within the ideal code, this additional value would not be sufficient to justify an *obligation* on potential parents to create such children. The ideal code will thus leave the decision to individual potential parents. (If there is no general obligation to reproduce, then there will not be an obligation in this particular case.) So the ideal code is not too far from conventional morality.

A common reason why many people have lives below the lexical level in the contemporary Western world is because their parents fail to provide them with a good start in life. If their parents are able to provide a good start, then the New Lexical Reproduction Rule clearly requires them to do so. If one knows in advance that, although one could provide a good start for one's children, one will fail to do so, then the situation is less clear. Obviously, if I know that I will leave my children below the zero level, then I ought not to reproduce, under any plausible constrained principle of reproductive freedom. If I know that I will do a fair job of raising my children, so that they live between the zero level and the lexical level, then it is tempting to assimilate my situation to that of someone who cannot give their children a better start in life. However, there are sound Rule Consequentialist reasons for distinguishing the two cases. A complete code of rules will tell agents whether or not to treat their own predictable (and perhaps even unpreventable) future failure to behave properly as morally distinct from external factors impacting on the consequences of their actions. A code which tells agents not to excuse their future failings in this way may produce better consequences overall—as wishful thinking and a reduced sense of responsibility might lead too many people to fail to take adequate steps to improve their character or future behaviour. Accordingly, someone who had internalized the ideal code might read the New Lexical Reproduction Rule as forbidding one to create people who, as a result of one's own future parental failings, will have lives below the lexical level. (Such failings would arise even under perfect full compliance, as successful compliance with parental obligations may be beyond the capacities of some parents.)

On balance, in spite of these difficulties, I am inclined to believe that the ideal code will adopt the New Lexical Rule, combined with parental obligations (to children who already exist.) There are three general reasons to include these constraints and prohibitions.

1. Those who have internalized the ideal code are not saints. They will often be tempted by sub-optimal inclinations. If the code included no prohibitions, such inclinations would always lead to sub-optimal actions (Section 5.7.2).
2. Prohibitions provide security to third parties that they will not suffer at the hands of those who, for all they know, may have sub-optimal inclinations. In this case, the third parties are children, who need to know that their parents feel morally bound to raise them above the lexical level if at all possible. Psychologically, it would be hard to combine the belief that one had an obligation to raise one's existing children above the lexical level with the belief that one was morally free to gratuitously create a child who would live below the lexical level. The most stable combination will thus involve the Lexical Reproductive Rule.
3. Even in the ideal society, some people will have inclinations contrary to those of someone who had internalized the ideal code. To prevent such inclinations leading to undesirable behaviour, it is desirable that such people know that, because the action is forbidden by the ideal code, it would be morally censured (at least) by other agents.

6.2.3. Maximizing Reproduction

We can imagine even stronger constraints, urging people to create the best possible lives. These constraints are implausible if they would prevent some people who are unable to create extremely worthwhile lives from reproducing at all. A maximizing rule is plausible only if cast in the following form.

The Conditional Maximizing Rule.   Reproduce if and only if you want to, so long as (a) the child you create will live above a certain minimum threshold (which will be between the zero and lexical levels); and (b) you create the happiest child you can.

Whether a particular act of creation is morally acceptable will thus depend largely on the nature of the alternatives, not just on the intrinsic value of the life created.

The arguments supporting this new rule are comparatively obvious. It seems to maximize the well-being of the next generation. Every parent will have the happiest children they could have had. The rule seems to achieve this by leaving reproductive freedom intact. Everyone who is able to have children whose lives would be worth living is morally free to choose between reproduction and non-reproduction. In the area of reproductive freedom, this is the most significant decision, as it most clearly involves a choice between genuinely valuable, but radically different lifestyles.

There are several arguments against this new rule. Some will argue that it leaves too little reproductive freedom. Such freedom should not be limited solely to the decision whether or not to reproduce. It also covers a range of decisions regarding how to reproduce, and what sort of life one wants for one's children. A rigid rule requiring one to maximize the well-being of one's children removes this freedom. Such a rule is also extremely demanding, as it will impose enormous burdens once a child is born. There are no other circumstances where the ideal code is likely to require any agent to maximize someone else's welfare regardless of the cost to herself. While it does seem reasonable to place parents under special obligations to their children, the obligation to maximize well-being may seem extreme. (We return to the demands of the ideal code in Chapter 10.)

The extreme demands of this rule count against it at an intuitive level. They also suggest that it will not form part of the ideal code. Extremely demanding rules are very difficult to inculcate in the population as a whole. The costs of inculcating such a rule may well outweigh the benefits. Even if people could be taught such a rule, the consequences of their acting on it might well be undesirable. If their only choices are an extremely demanding form of reproduction or no reproduction at all, many people will opt for the latter. This suggests that the next generation may be too small. The ideal code could respond by placing a moral obligation on some people to reproduce. However, this would make the ideal code even more demanding. If one is only permitted to reproduce if one provides one's child with the best possible life, and if some people are required to reproduce, then the demands of Rule Consequentialism threaten to approach those of Simple Consequentialism.[8]

6.2.4. *Uncertainty*

All human choices are made under uncertainty. Reproduction is no exception. No potential parents can predict with certainty the well-being of any child they might have. There is always some possibility (however remote) that

---

[8] The Conditional Maximizing Rule may also be redundant. If incommensurability is widespread, then it may not be true, of a range of possible lives above the lexical level, that one is the best. To accommodate this possibility, we might amend the rule as follows: *The Revised Conditional Maximizing Rule.* Reproduce if and only if you want to, so long as (a) the child you create will live above a certain minimum threshold (which will be between the zero and lexical levels); and (b) you could not have created a child with a substantially better life. In practice, incommensurability and uncertainty may combine to leave this principle equivalent to the New Lexical Reproduction Rule.

one will have a child whose life falls below the zero level, perhaps due to an untreatable genetic condition which cannot be detected in advance.[9] If lives below the zero level reduce value, and lives above zero add no value, then no act of creation is ever permitted if there is *any* chance it will produce a life not worth living. As this risk is ever present, Simple Consequentialism can accommodate the asymmetry only by forbidding reproduction.

Rule Consequentialism can easily avoid this result. The consequences of everyone refraining from reproducing would be the extinction of the human species. The consequence of everyone feeling free to reproduce even if there is a slight possibility of having a child whose life is below zero (or a higher probability of a child below the lexical level) is a world where most people live above the lexical level, some live between zero and the lexical level, and a tiny number fall below zero. On the theories of value we are working with, the latter is the better world. (As we saw in Section 3.3, value theories that avoid this result fall foul of the Reverse Repugnant Conclusion.) Unlike Simple Consequentialists, Rule Consequentialists need not resort to asymmetric value theories to accommodate the asymmetry.[10]

To accommodate uncertainty, we could amend our rule regarding reproduction as follows.

The Expected-Value Lexical Reproduction Rule. Reproduce if and only if you want to, provided the *expected value* of your child's life is above the lexical level. If you are unable to have a child whose life has an expected value above the lexical level, then you may create if and only if (*a*) the expected life value for your child is greater than x (where x is between the zero and lexical levels), and (*b*) you could not have created a child with a substantially better life.

However, it is almost certainly not feasible to advise agents to constrain their reproductive freedom by reference to expected value calculations, for reasons sketched in Section 5.6. Such a rule simply cannot be followed. It is thus much more likely that the ideal code will include a rule such as the following.

The Flexible Lexical Rule. Reproduce if and only if you want to, so long as you are *reasonably sure* that your child will enjoy a life above the lexical level, and *very sure* that the risk of your child falling below the zero level is *very small*.

This rule is, of course, very vague. In practice, much will turn on the interpretation of the emphasized phrases. However, I argued in Section 5.6 that

---

[9] This raises serious problems for Simple Consequentialist attempts to accommodate the asymmetry by appealing to an asymmetric value theory. For further discussion, see Heyd, *Genethics*, 59–60; and Parfit, *Reasons and Persons*, ch. 18. See also the works cited in Ch. 1 n. 12.

[10] This is not to say, of course, that Rule Consequentialism itself is incompatible with prioritarianism, as Hooker's own theory shows.

such elements of vagueness are a strength rather than a weakness in the context of an ideal code. (See also Section 6.4.2.)

Having established the general form of the best case *for* reproductive freedom, we turn now to the case against.

6.3. The Ideal Code and Child-Rearing

Several areas of the ideal code will affect or interact with the rule regarding reproduction. The most obvious overlap is with rules regarding child-rearing and education. The ideal code is conceived of as a complete moral code, governing all aspects of life. It will thus cover such issues as the significance of parenthood, the distribution of child-rearing responsibilities, and the structure of families. The practices of any society in this area obviously impact on people's decisions regarding reproduction, and greatly affect the lives of their children.

The previous section established a strong prima facie case for reproductive freedom. Consideration of wider social issues might undermine this case in two distinct ways.

1. A change in background social conditions might open up other equally valuable alternative lifestyles not involving reproduction. This would reduce the significance of the choice between reproduction and non-reproduction, and thus undermine the moral significance of reproductive freedom.
2. The need to ensure an optimal population size in all future generations might generate a strong case for coercive policies regarding reproduction. If reproductive freedom is inconsistent with the maintenance of an optimal population, then this could well outweigh any positive case for reproductive freedom.

We begin with the first potential threat. In many ways, the case for reproductive freedom is stronger against a background of social services and support networks than in their absence. Such services and networks significantly reduce the possibility that reproductive freedom will lead to some people having lives not worth living. The ideal code is likely to produce such support services, as they clearly promote the interests of children. (While this reinforces the case for reproductive freedom under full compliance, it also increases the distance between the ideal society and the actual world. As we shall see in Chapter 9, this makes it much harder to tell what Rule Consequentialism demands of *us*, and to be confident that its demands are moderate.)

On the other hand, some ways of providing support for children and parents may undermine one of our key arguments in favour of reproductive freedom. Consider the following two possible extremes.

The Parental Extreme. All children are raised exclusively by their biological parents. In this world, the alternative to reproduction is to deny oneself any ability to develop any of the human excellences relating to nurturing.

The Social Extreme. All social parenting is undertaken equally by all adults, without any distinction between those who are biological parents and those who are not. In this world, the alternative to reproduction deprives one only of the gestational and other purely biological aspects of parenthood.

The availability of reproduction is much more significant in the Parental Extreme than in the Social Extreme, as the choice one makes here has a far more wide-reaching impact on the overall shape of one's life. In the Social Extreme, a life without reproduction is also a life without any real involvement in the raising of children. Both in everyday debate, and in our form of Rule Consequentialism, one of the main arguments for reproductive freedom is based on the significance of autonomy (Sections 4.2 and 6.2). That argument assumes that the decision whether or not to reproduce is morally significant. This claim may be largely undermined if the ideal code recommends the Social Extreme. We would then need to ask whether those who have internalized the ideal code will regard reproduction as a significant choice. Will they regard parenthood as significantly different from non-parenthood?

Some political theorists seek to sidestep issues of family structure and the domestic division of labour by confining their theory to a public or political realm, leaving the family outside politics.[11] Rule Consequentialism cannot sidestep these issues. It must admit the possibility that the ideal code would recommend family structures radically different from our own. In particular, we might expect those who have internalized the ideal code to show considerably more concern for the plight of the worst-off children than is the norm in any Western society. Our value theory creates a strong presumption that the ideal code will be designed to ensure that no lives slip below the zero level. Anyone who had internalized such a code would be disposed to support charitable organizations caring for disadvantaged children, to vote for public officials implementing child-centred policies, and to accept some curtailment of reproductive and/or parental freedom to enable the state (or other reliable agencies) to protect children at risk.

Rule Consequentialism is often presented as a moderate alternative to Simple Consequentialism. This is ironic, as it actually has the potential to be

---

[11] For a devastating critique, see Okin, *Justice, Gender and the Family.*

far more radical. The Simple Consequentialist only asks me to imagine possible variations in my own actions and their consequences. Everything else is kept constant. The Rule Consequentialist, by contrast, invites us to imagine all possible variations of *everyone's* behaviour. This threatens to lead us to a social world unlike anything we have ever known.

We explore these broader features of the ideal code further in Chapters 6 to 10. Our immediate concern is that the ideal code may be so radical that our case for reproductive freedom will be undermined. Fortunately, several factors limit the radicalness of the ideal code.

1. The most significant is that we must imagine the code being internalized by a society of ordinary human beings, with all our psychological and cognitive limitations. Since Aristotle, many philosophers have argued that, whatever its abstract merits, the Social Extreme is not a possibility for ordinary human beings. On this view, it is no coincidence that all successful human societies give parents and other close relatives a significant role in child-rearing. The cost of inculcating the rules required for the Social Extreme would be prohibitive. Our knowledge of human beings suggests that, however a society chooses to arrange to care for its children, most people will still regard reproductive decisions as a significant choice for creatures such as ourselves.

2. The autonomy of potential parents is only one of our grounds for favouring reproductive freedom. The other is that the combination of reproductive freedom and strong parental obligations is the most efficient way to meet the developmental needs of children. As Roger Crisp notes,

> children are brought up within traditions and cultures, and all the traditions and cultures that have yet developed among human beings have embodied partiality. Parents, teachers and others in society establish special relationships with children which make it possible to bring them up to be rational. It is hard to imagine a system of education which did not rest on such partialities, or to imagine partialities and attachments which could be shed once the capability to think rationally were achieved.[12]

3. Recall that our primary aim is only to find the best code to inculcate in the next generation. We are interested in the impact that our teaching a particular code to the next generation might have on the welfare of all subsequent generation, including any alterations in the content of their moral code and the way it is interpreted. But the code Rule Consequentialism will ultimately tell *us* to follow is the code we teach to the next generation, not

---

[12] Crisp, *Mill on Utilitarianism*, 106.

the endpoint of a process of moral evolution within the ideal society indefinitely into the future. The content of the moral code operating in the ideal society many generations down the track is relevant to our determination of the desirability of any given code, but the fact that the far distant code seems strange does not show that Rule Consequentialism's advice *to us* will be counterintuitive. (Indeed, in Chapter 8, I argue that the very possibility that the moral code of the ideal society can be expected to evolve in the future increases the intuitive plausibility of Rule Consequentialism, by grounding a Rule Consequentialist defence of open-ended democratic decision-making processes.)

4. A further factor is Hooker's wary Rule Consequentialism: the use of closeness to conventional morality as a tie-breaker. This clause, especially if combined with widespread uncertainty and/or incommensurability, suggests that the ideal code will be relatively close to conventional morality. Perhaps there is no radical alternative which we could reasonably expect to provide greater aggregate well-being than the status quo.

This raises the obvious question: what *is* the conventional morality with respect to family structures? Hooker's formulation seems to presuppose that conventional morality is a unified framework. As James Griffin has pointed out, this seems overly optimistic in general.[13] It is especially optimistic regarding reproduction and future generations. Modern societies contain a wide range of distinct, and incompatible, views about reproduction and 'family values'. The best solution is to settle on a set of very general uncontroversial principles, which Rule Consequentialism must accommodate if at all possible. We have seen that, at least as regards individual reproduction, Rule Consequentialism succeeds here, while most of its rivals fail. Under a refined version of Hooker's scheme, only closeness to these uncontroversial aspects of conventional morality would count, and then only as a tie-breaker. Other aspects of 'conventional morality' may be clearly sub-optimal from a Rule Consequentialist point of view. If so, Rule Consequentialism is justified in rejecting those conventions.[14] (In the terminology of Chapter 1, we might say that wary Rule Consequentialism need only be guided by decisive intuitions.)

5. Even if the ideal society would contain institutions radically different from our own, the ideal code's general rules regarding behaviour within existing institutions may still be comparatively close to our own. As ever, we must distinguish between what those in the ideal society would do, and

---

[13] Griffin, 'Replies', in Hooker and Crisp (eds.), *Well-being and Morality*.

[14] I am not sure how this proposal relates to Hooker's original notion of 'wary Rule Consequentialism'. However, the modifications I suggest seem necessary if Rule Consequentialism is to retain the potential to critize the status quo.

what the ideal code tells us to do in our situation. (We explore this point further in Section 10.4.)

I conclude that, while we must be aware of the impact of broader social conditions on the interpretation of the ideal code, those conditions are very unlikely to directly undermine the case for reproductive freedom. While we cannot know exactly what the ideal society would look like, we can be confident that it would be a place where reproductive freedom has very significant intrinsic value for most agents. We now ask if reproductive freedom involves indirect costs sufficient to outweigh this important benefit.

6.4. Reproductive Freedom and Population Size

On the face of it, it seems wildly unlikely that any given reproductive freedom rule will yield any particular population size. The Lexical Reproduction Rule says nothing directly about how many children each person should have. Under such a rule, the population size depends very largely on the details of people's preferences. It would be a miraculous coincidence if those preferences just happened to yield the replacement rate, or any other desired rate of population increase.

If reproductive freedom rules cannot guarantee that the population will remain within the optimal range, then it is doubtful that the ideal code will include such rules. This section explores the connection between reproductive freedom and population size. I conclude that, while reproductive freedom is not inconsistent with the attainment of any desired population range, it is likely to be inadequate on its own. We must turn to the public policy of the ideal code for an adequate response.

6.4.1. Can Freedom Guarantee Population Size?

We begin with a simple argument that reproductive freedom *does* reliably yield an appropriate rate of population increase. Any mortal species which fails to reproduce at (at least) the rate required for replacement will die out very quickly. This creates a prima facie case that evolutionary pressures will have left human beings with a strong psychological propensity not to fall below a replacement level of reproduction. Human beings will also be disposed not to reproduce too fast, as creatures which reproduced at too fast a rate would overburden their environment and also die out. The population will remain within the optimal range.

Unfortunately, this argument fails. The fact that the behaviour of our ancestors was once in long-term equilibrium does not guarantee that our present behaviour is sustainable, even in the short term. The conditions of human life have changed radically in recent times. Two changes are especially significant. The first is a reduction in mortality rates. Traditional ethical codes do not directly govern the number of adults to be produced in the next generation. At most, they offer guidance regarding the number of children one should aim to have. When mortality rates are high, an injunction to have as many children as possible could be necessary to ensure an adequate number of adults. If the psychological or social norms underlying that injunction remain constant when mortality rates fall, the result may well be an unsustainable population explosion. The history of Western nations over the past two hundred years suggests that, when infant mortality rates fall, patterns of reproductive choice eventually change to bring the population back toward equilibrium. But there is certainly no a priori reason to assume that this will always happen in time. The later equilibrium will be at a higher population level, which may not be ecologically sustainable in the long term.

The second crucial change is the unavailability of uninhabited areas to expand into when the population grows. Population pressure has been a major cause of most human migrations. Almost everyone alive today is the descendant of groups which outgrew their local environment and moved to new pastures. This strategy worked very well for a long time, given the largeness of the earth, the smallness of the initial human population, and their limited ability to affect local environments. Only very recently have we run out of other places to go.

Most significantly, this argument addresses only population size. The simple decision whether to reproduce does not exhaust the morality of reproduction. There is certainly no a priori reason to expect full compliance with other aspects of the ideal code dealing with the treatment of children or with broader social arrangements. *Homo sapiens* might have survived indefinitely without a social framework sufficiently sophisticated to enable anyone to rise above the lexical level, or even the zero level. Partha Dasgupta suggests that hundreds of millions of people currently live well below the zero level: 'disenfranchised, malnourished, and prone to illness, but surviving'.[15] Although they live in societies where infant morality rates are high and life expectancies low, many of these people manage to reproduce, and to raise children who

---

[15] Dasgupta 'Savings and Fertility: Ethical Issues', 116. See also Ng, 'What should we do about Future Generations?' Dasgupta himself uses the fact that such people strive to keep themselves alive as evidence that the notions of 'a life worth living' and 'a life above the zero level' are not identical, as the context of the passage quoted in the text makes plain. 'A person whose life is barely worth living has a *very low, negative* living standard. She is one of the wretched of the earth, and there are hundreds of millions of such people today, disenfranchised, malnourished, and prone to illness, but surviving, and tenaciously displaying that their lives are worth living by the persistence with which they continue to wish to live.' (For more on the zero level, see Section 3.3.)

themselves reproduce. A human society might thus survive indefinitely even though everyone lived well below the zero level. If they followed the Lexical Reproduction Rule, these people would no longer reproduce.

We must conclude, then, that there is no good reason to be confident that reproductive freedom, in the context of any plausible ideal code, will guarantee a population within the optimal range. If some other rule *can* guarantee an optimal population, then this will be a very significant strike against reproductive freedom. Before examining alternative rules, we first ask if reproductive freedom is even consistent with the maintenance of an optimal population. If it is not, then any alternative rule which is consistent will have a potentially decisive advantage.

6.4.2. Is Freedom Inconsistent with Optimal Population Size?

The ideal code must maximize expected value across a plausible range of possible futures. In particular, it must respond appropriately to the possibility of significant fluctuations in human living conditions. Suppose we are designing the ideal code to be taught to the first generation. That ideal code must be robust, designed to ensure the survival of the moral community, and the maintenance of the population within the optimal range, across a wide range of possible futures. The original Lexical Reproduction Rule seems inadequate here. If conditions improve, then too many people will reproduce, as they will find it much easier to create a child whose life is above the required threshold. Even more seriously, a deterioration in conditions would mean that no one reproduced, as no one would be able to create a life above the threshold.

There are two possible solutions. The first is to retain the original Lexical Reproduction Rule (in whatever formulation we finally choose in light of the complexities examined earlier in this chapter), but add an explicit reference to the optimal population size. Reproduction becomes obligatory if the population is too small, and is forbidden if it is too large. (Call this the *Disaster Avoidance Solution*.) The second option is to build reference to changing social circumstances into our description of the conditions under which reproduction is permitted. This seems to guarantee a population within the optimal range, even if social conditions change markedly or in ways we cannot now predict. (Call this the *Relativized Solution*).

Both solutions aim to ensure that the human species will not die out if there is some catastrophe in the future. So long as compliance with the ideal code remains high, enough people will always reproduce, even if they are unable to provide their children with an acceptable life from the standpoint of the first generation in the ideal society.

The Relativized Solution is superior to the Disaster Avoidance Solution. Even under full compliance, the Relativized Solution produces better consequences. There are two relevant possibilities. The first is that, even in the ideal society, there is always a possibility of environmental or other catastrophe. The future prospects for human life may take a sudden turn for the worse. Either the Relativized Solution or the Disaster Avoidance Solution would then come into play. If the ideal code contains the Disaster Avoidance Solution, then the creation of children whose lives would not previously have been regarded as acceptable will be seen as an undesirable emergency measure. If our ideal code adopts the Relativized Solution, by contrast, then this pattern of reproduction will be seen as a part of normal ethical behaviour.

In such a situation the Relativized Solution is easier to comply with, psychologically healthier, and likely to produce a better-adjusted next generation. Instead of believing that their lives are unacceptable, but required for the future of the human race, this first post-catastrophe generation will see their lives as worthwhile in their context, however much they may regret some features of that context.

We seek a moral code to teach the next generation. However, the consequences of teaching any given code extend to later generations. We should assume that the ideal code is taught, not just to the first generation, but to subsequent generations as well. It seems undesirable to bring the next generation up to regard their entire life situation as a catastrophic situation where the normal moral rules do not apply, especially as the new environmental conditions may persist for some time.

Our second possible scenario is the opposite of the first. In a world of full compliance with the ideal code, in the absence of catastrophes, the quality of life can be expected to improve dramatically, not just in the first generation, but over subsequent generations. Not all improvements in social conditions will take place immediately. If the ideal code is chosen to maximize well-being overall, then it will include an emphasis on investment and research designed to produce long-term benefits.

Our two rules come apart in this possible future. Under the Relativized Solution, as social conditions improve, the interpretation of the lexical level will become more demanding. Each generation of potential parents will thus feel obliged to provide a higher quality of life for their children, so long as they are able to do so. By contrast, those adopting the Disaster Avoidance Solution, with its non-relativized interpretation of the lexical level, will continue to set a lower threshold, even once a much higher quality of life is almost universally attainable. This difference has two negative consequences.

1. By setting a lower threshold that parents feel obliged to achieve for their children, the Disaster Avoidance Solution is likely to lead to lower

expectations of quality of life in subsequent generation, and thus to a lower overall level of well-being.

2. At some point in the future, the lower threshold may well lead to over-population, as the cost of morally acceptable reproduction to potential parents is much less than it would have been under the Relativized Solution. (The Disaster Avoidance clause then comes into play, once again depriving potential parents of the option of morally sanctioned reproduction.)

Some general considerations about Rule Consequentialism also favour the Relativized Solution. Consider two possible rules regarding reproduction.[16]

Mechanical Rule.   Create if and only if the life you create is worth more than c, or has the following specific features . . .

Flexible Rule.   Create if and only if the life you create is *well worth living*.

The value of flexible rules is that the general terms they contain may be applied differently in different situations. These rules are thus much more versatile than mechanical rules. This feature plays a similar role to the traditional disaster avoidance clause, by avoiding an absurd rigidity in partial compliance situations (Section 5.2 and Ch 9.) Flexible rules are also useful under full compliance when circumstances change—a common theme of Chapters 7 to 9.

The shift to flexible rules reflects the fact, stressed by Hooker,[17] that rules need to be applied to particular cases, and that such application requires judgement and sensitivity. To determine what we should do, we need both a set of rules and a judgement applying those rules to our situation. Our set of rules is the Rule Consequentialist ideal code. Whose judgement should we use to apply that code? It may seem obvious that we can only use our own judgement. However, things are not so simple. Should we apply the rules in the optimal code as we ourselves would apply them? Or should we seek to apply those rules as they would be applied by someone who had been brought up in a society where they were commonly accepted? These two procedures may produce quite different results.

I shall now argue that Rule Consequentialism must refer to the judgements of those living in the world of the optimal code, as well as to their rules. The main reason is that the distinction between rules and judgements is (at best) vague. Given any complete description of the beliefs, actions, and

---

[16] The distinction between mechanical and flexible rules is introduced in ch. 3 of Mulgan, *The Demands of Consequentialism*, where the latter bear the less informative label of 'subtle rules'. (I owe this change in terminology to an anonymous reader.)

[17] Hooker, *Ideal Code, Real World* (2000), 88; and 'Ross-style Pluralism versus Rule Consequentialism', (1996) 543–6.

judgements of the inhabitants of any society, there will be many different ways to categorize their moral system in terms of abstract rules and particular judgements. Some of these categorizations will be more natural than others, but there may be no unique set of rules and judgements capturing their morality. If we keep rules and judgements together, then this indeterminacy does not matter very much. However, if we seek to separate the rules of a society from judgements applying those rules, and then replace the latter with our own judgements, we must make an arbitrary choice. The consequences of widespread acceptance of a set of rules depend crucially upon how they are applied. A given set of rules will be optimal only because it is applied in a certain way. It thus seems odd for a moral theory to select a set of rules because of the consequences of one method of application, and then instruct us to apply those rules in a completely different way. Such a theory would be very ad hoc.

I conclude that the Rule Consequentialist criterion of rightness should be as follows:

> an act is right if and only if it would be judged to follow from the optimal set of rules by someone who had internalized those rules and had grown up in a society where such internalization was the norm.

In our present comparison, the Relativized Solution is a flexible rule, while the Disaster Avoidance Solution is more mechanical. A general preference for flexible rules over mechanical rules thus favours the former.

A second general argument for the Relativized Solution comes from value theory. I argued in Chapter 3 that Consequentialists who seek to use value theory to avoid the Repugnant Conclusion will adopt a lexical level suitably relativized to the agent's situation. In the context of such a value theory, the phrase 'reproduce if and only if your child's life will be above the lexical level' lends itself automatically to a relativized interpretation. For someone who has internalized the best Consequentialist value theory, the most natural interpretation of the Lexical Reproduction Rule thus already incorporates the Relativized Solution.

The Relativized Solution is not a peripheral addition to the Lexical Reproduction Rule. Our current rates of unprecedented technological advancement and unprecedented impact on the natural environment suggest that the quality of life available to future generations will be very different from today. It is possible that technological improvement and environmental degradation will exactly balance out, but this seems unlikely. It is much more likely that one or other will predominate, and one of the two scenarios discussed in this section will eventuate. The expected value of an ideal code thus depends very heavily on its ability to respond appropriately to either scenario. (We shall return to the question of the comparative likelihood of the two scenarios; see Sections 7.8, 8.2.)

Circumstances can change over generations, as well as within the same generation. The ideal code must respond to such long-term changes. There are two ways to accommodate this possibility. The first is to adopt a Relativized Solution regarding reproduction, indexed to the state of society. The second is to change the ideal code with each new generation. The second option is not inconceivable. Perhaps each generation would appoint a Rule Consequentialist commission to draw up a new moral code to be taught to the next generation. However, any such procedure has obvious drawbacks. A moral code is much easier to teach if it is passed down across generations with a high degree of continuity. This suggests, once again, that the relativized code will win out.[18]

All these suggestions are very speculative. However, they are not entirely ad hoc. The Relativized Solution wins out because it is better suited to human psychology, seems more fair, and fits in with the appropriate value theory. We could also defend the Relativized Solution by appealing to Hooker's Wary Rule Consequentialism. This solution is certainly closer to conventional morality than the Disaster Avoidance Solution.

6.5. Prescriptive Rules

Our approach thus far has been to picture an agent making a series of isolated decisions regarding reproduction. This is artificial. The ideal code is meant to guide agents in planning their lives, not in a series of unrelated one-off choices. For most people, the primary decision here is, not so much whether to reproduce at time t, but how many children to have over the course of their life. To borrow a distinction from Garrett Cullity, the ideal code must examine reproductive rules 'aggregatively', not 'iteratively'.[19] This shift in perspective makes room for a potential rival to our reproductive freedom rules.

If the ideal code aims to ensure that the population stays within a certain range, then one obvious set of rules would have the following form.

Numerical Reproduction Rule.   Have x children over the course of your life.

For instance, if we aim for the replacement rate, then we might set x equal to 2. For manageable short-term population growth x might be made equal

---

[18] The Relativized Solution thus provides a more elegant and practical approach than that suggested by Jonathan Riley, who argues that the ideal code will evolve and change over time, and thus must include rules enabling it to be updated in each generation (Riley, 'Defending Rule Utilitarianism'). If the ideal code contains flexible rules, this updating occurs automatically.

[19] Cullity, 'Moral Character and the Iteration Problem'.

to 3. Numerical rules seem simple to learn and to follow. They also distribute the benefits and burdens of the task of producing the next generation equally.

Unfortunately, such rules are unsatisfactory. One serious problem is that, by severing any link between reproduction and preference, they will ensure that many people have either more children than they wanted, or fewer. If everyone has exactly two children, then both those who wanted none and those who wanted four will be unhappy. As we saw earlier, there are strong Rule Consequentialist reasons for avoiding this situation. In particular, the ideal code should aim to avoid the existence of unwanted children.

Furthermore, numerical rules cannot even accomplish the task for which they are explicitly designed. Suppose our target is the replacement rate. The first thing to note is that not everyone can have children, even if they try. It seems inefficient for the ideal code to place agents under obligations they cannot fulfil: this would merely cause distress, and perhaps a reduction in respect for an impossible moral code. So numerical rules should actually be phrased as follows.

Numerical Rule Two.   Aim to have two children over the course of your life.

If everyone follows this rule, then the birth rate is likely to fall *below* the replacement rate. Not everyone will succeed in having two children. So the birth rate will be less than two children per adult woman. Yet the replacement rate is above 2. Even in the ideal society, not all children will live long enough to reproduce themselves.[20]

One might think these negative factors will be counterbalanced by several factors pointing to a higher birth rate: contraceptive failure by parents who already have two children, multiple births, and non-compliance. However, these factors are unlikely to be sufficient. Those who have internalized the ideal code will take their parental and reproductive responsibilities seriously, and will be careful to avoid any pregnancy they regard as morally wrong. The ideal society is likely to include reasonably effective family planning education. Contraceptive failure is thus likely to be extremely rare. Non-compliance is certainly relevant, but it is at least as likely to point in the opposite direction, with some people who do not desire to have any children refusing to reproduce. (And perhaps avoiding public censure by pretending to have been unable to.) Multiple births may be a factor, but it would be an

---

[20] The gap between the replacement rate and a birth rate of 2 depends on rates of child and adolescent mortality. In the developed world, the replacement rate is usually only marginally above 2. The ideal society would probably have even lower morality rates, but even there the replacement rate will be higher than 2.

astonishing coincidence if their statistical frequency exactly matched what was required to achieve the replacement rate.

If we retain numerical rules, and hope to avoid a population decline, then perhaps we should move up to the following rule.

Numerical Rule Three.   Aim to have three children over the course of your life.

After all, given what has just been said, we certainly should not assume that this rule would lead to an actual birth rate of 3. Under-compliance and inability to comply are bound to be more prevalent for this rule, while over-compliance will be less likely. So we should expect an even greater shortfall than with Numerical Rule Two. Therefore, Numerical Rule Three might well yield the replacement rate.

Given the range of factors involved, and the difficulty of extrapolating from existing data to precise patterns of behaviour under full compliance with any particular ideal code, we cannot say definitively that Numerical Rule Three would *not* yield the replacement rate. However, it would be an extraordinary coincidence if it did. It would be better if Rule Consequentialism did not need to rely on such extreme serendipity. It might well yield an unsustainably high rate of population increase.[21]

Numerical rules fail to guarantee that the population will remain within the optimal range. This removes any advantage of numerical rules over reproductive freedom rules. Yet this is not enough to vindicate the latter— we must still ask if they could form part of an ideal code that resolves the population problem.

6.6. Public Policy

Reproductive freedom is not inconsistent with the achievement of an appropriate population size. However, reproductive freedom alone cannot guarantee that we will meet that goal. The Relativized Solution is inadequate. Fortunately, as we have just seen, numerical rules fare no better. Indeed, the two approaches face the same problem. Nor is this a coincidence, as there is good reason to think that any rule governing individual morality will face that problem. The birth rate is a collective feature of a society, not

---

[21] This discussion is very significant for some Kantian moral theories. Kant's Categorical Imperative, on some interpretations, rules out any reference to the agent's empirical desires, or any other empirical circumstances, in the formulation of moral rules. Reproductive freedom rules would fail this test, as they explicitly refer to the agent's desire to have (or not have) children. Any such Kantian theory would thus be restricted to numerical rules, as only these can genuinely be willed as universal laws for a community of purely rational agents. If numerical rules are inadequate, as the discussion in the text suggests, then this is a serious blow to Kantian moral theory (Section 1.5).

a property of particular individuals. Uncoordinated individual action cannot hope to deliver a desired birth rate, unless circumstances are so bad that we need either maximal reproduction or no reproduction at all. It is much more likely that what is required is a gradual small increase or decrease in the birth rate. This calls for a coordinated shift in public policy to slightly alter people's incentives or inclinations. Even flexible rules are not flexible enough. Collective problems call for collective solutions. The ideal code must look beyond individual morality to the political realm. Two things follow.

1. It is no objection to an individual morality of reproductive freedom that it cannot guarantee an optimal population size.
2. If it is to be included in the ideal code, any reproductive freedom rule must be compatible with the most effective collective approach to the problem of population size.

6.6.1. *Why the Ideal Code Needs Public Policy*

Desirable individual moral dispositions are not sufficient to safeguard the continuation of the ideal society. We must turn to public policy. Fortunately, the ideal code must include public policy for more general reasons. So there is nothing ad hoc about using it to solve the population problem. Public policy is needed to cope with both non-compliance and coordination problems.

Even in the ideal society there is a certain degree of non-compliance with the ideal moral code. Non-compliance has two key sources.

1. Imperfect Idealization.   Rule Consequentialism idealizes to widespread compliance, not perfect full compliance. Even in the ideal society, some people have not internalized the ideal code, and cannot be relied on to act in accordance with it. The ideal code must include sanctions or other incentives for these people.

2. Imperfect Internalization.   We imagine the ideal code being internalized by ordinarily fallible human beings. Even people who accept the code cannot be relied on always to act in accordance with it, especially when doing so would be contrary to their own personal interests.

The code must therefore respond to non-compliance. It cannot simply rely on individuals to obey all moral rules voluntarily. In some cases, informal sanctions will be most effective. In other cases, however, the most efficient way to enforce compliance with the ideal code will be some form of institutionalized sanction.

In addition to non-compliance, public policy is also needed to solve coordination problems. In any complex society, there are many problems where a variety of solutions are available, and the choice between them is essentially arbitrary. It is more important that we all follow the same code of rules, than that we follow any particular code. (In game theoretic terms, we often face coordination problems with multiple equilibria.) It doesn't matter whether we all stop on red lights or on green. But it does matter that we all obey the same traffic conventions. The ideal code must provide a way to resolve these coordination problems.

We are imagining a code of rules, not for a small technologically primitive society, but for the next generation in our own post-industrial world. In that context, centralized institutions are often the best solution for these enforcement problems. A world where all take the law into their own hands, or try to select coordination equilibria on an ad hoc basis, will be worse than one where an efficient set of institutions provides coordination.

It may seem that these solutions could be built directly into the ideal code, in the form of particular rules governing particular coordination problems. This procedure is unsatisfactory. In particular, it assumes that those who design the ideal code are able to predict all the coordination problems likely to arise in the ideal society, and to determine adequate solutions to those problems. This assumption is implausible. We have only a very general idea of what life will actually be like in the ideal society, and we have no way of predicting the coordination problems that may result from social or technological developments, or environmental changes. Under full compliance with any moral code designed to maximize human well-being in the long run, technological advances are likely to be even more common than in the actual world, especially in areas leading to social changes.

These familiar considerations are especially significant in relation to future generations. We cannot hope to inculcate an individual moral code that responds well to all possible future global problems relating to environmental and population policy. Such problems call for coordinated collective solutions based on a careful evaluation of complex empirical data, much of which is simply not available this far in advance.

If the ideal code is to work effectively, then it must include general principles for solving coordination problems as they arise. The ideal society must have some way to choose public policy. It is reasonable to expect a flexible political system to produce better consequences than a rigid set of rules for particular cases. The ideal society needs public institutions.

On the other hand, even if enforcement is sometimes handed over to institutions, many aspects of the ideal code will not be subject to those institutions. A moral code allowing third parties to enforce all of an agent's moral obligations is likely to be extremely cumbersome, and to leave far too little room for moral autonomy. Better results are likely if each person's practical autonomy exceeds their moral autonomy, so that people are left alone to do as they please, even when what they please may not accord with all their moral obligations. Furthermore, many obligations which are appropriately enforced by third parties are better enforced by informal social sanctions than by force.

6.6.2. How Public Policy Might Aid Reproductive Freedom

For our present purposes, the crucial question is whether public policy in the ideal society can combine with reproductive freedom to yield an acceptable fertility rate.

One very robust empirical result is that public policy influences population growth. In particular, in the developing world, increases in female literacy and female labour force participation rates are both strongly correlated with a sharp decline in the birth rate from unsustainable levels toward the vicinity of the replacement rate.[22] There are several causal explanations for this correlation. One is primarily economic. As we saw in Chapter 4, in poor, rural, underdeveloped economies, children have significant economic value. This value is reduced by such diverse factors as compulsory schooling, the provision of free school lunches, urbanization, the introduction of social security (especially old age pensions), and more profitable employment opportunities for adult household members (Section 4.2.1.1). The general benefits of economic and social development, in terms of increased life expectancy, material prosperity, and opportunities for the exercise of autonomy, are such that, other things being equal, we should expect the ideal code to encourage economic development. Such development has a strong negative impact on fertility rates.

Reducing the economic value of children is not the only, or even the most significant, way to reduce the birth rate. The most effective route is via the empowerment of women, especially through increased literacy and opportunities for employment outside the home. The most popular explanation for these correlations is that, as women's education and opportunities

---

[22] For useful surveys, see Sen, *Development as Freedom*, chs. 8 and 9; Dasgupta, *Human Well-being and the Natural Environment*, ch. 6; Dasgupta, *Well-being and Destitution*, ch. 12; and Jolly and Gribble, 'The Proximate Determinants of Fertility'. See also Murthi, Guio, and Drèze, 'Mortality, Fertility and Gender Bias in India'; Caldwell et al., 'The Bangladesh Fertility Decline'; Cleland et al., *The Determinants of Reproductive Change in Bangladesh*; Bongaarts, 'The Role of Family Planning Programmes in Contemporary Fertility Tranisition'; Greenhalgh, *Situating Fertility*; Barro and Lee, 'International Comparisons of Educational Attainment'; Bongaarts, 'Trends in Unwanted Childbearing in the Developing World'; Easterlin, *Population and Economic Change in Developing Countries*; Birdsall, 'Economic Approaches to Population Growth'; Cassen et al., *Population and Development*; Jeffrey and Basu, *Girls' Schooling, Women's Autonomy and Fertility Change in South Asia*.

increase, they achieve a greater influence in household decision-making, with the result that they are able to choose to have fewer children. Greater influence also enables women to ensure adequate nutrition for their children.

Full compliance with the ideal code thus could enable a developing society with an unsustainably high birth rate to reduce its fertility. However, some will argue that the same reduction can be more effectively, and particularly more quickly, achieved by a coercive public policy. If this were true, it would undermine the reproductive freedom of the ideal code. The moral freedom to control one's reproductive decisions would have little meaning if the ideal code sanctioned coercive state interventions. Furthermore, some will argue that, even if a combination of reproductive freedom and liberal public policy suits the developing world, it is not appropriate for the quite different problems facing developed nations. We address these two objections in turn.

6.6.3. Why Coercion Doesn't Work

Coercive policies regarding fertility have been adopted in many countries. The Chinese government's one-child-family policy is a striking example.[23] Our emphasis on autonomy creates a strong prima facie case against coercive public policy.[24] If non-coercive means are available, then they are to be preferred. (In particular, if, as I argue in Section 8.1, the ideal code embodies democratic decision-making, then it is very unlikely that coercive measures will be freely adopted unless there is no alternative.) In some cases, however, it is tempting to think that policies based on reproductive freedom will not reduce the birth rate sufficiently quickly.

In a number of countries, the impact on fertility of an improvement in education and opportunities has been more complicated than the simple negative correlation presented in Section 6.6.2. Some studies have found that, while *large* increases in education for women do reliably reduce fertility, small increases in female education can actually lead, at least temporarily, to an *increase* in the birth rate.[25] The most likely explanation is that, even when

---

[23] Sen, *Development as Freedom*, 219–21.

[24] Furthermore, coercion is especially undesirable in some social circumstances. In China, for instance, the one-child family policy has exacerbated an existing trend toward sex-selective abortions, leading to a significant distortion of the sex ratio in the population as a whole. (Sen, *Development as Freedom*, 221.)

[25] Jolly and Gribble, 'The Proximate Determinants of Fertility', 89, found this second pattern in Burundi, Kenya, Liberia, Mali, and Ondo State. See also Cochrane, *Fertility and Education*; Cochrane, 'Effects of education and urbanization on fertility'; Dasgupta, *Well-being and Destitution*, 355–6; and Hess, *Population Growth and Socioeconomic Progress in Less Developed Countries*. Dasgupta notes that the prevalence, and even the existence, of this second pattern of the impact of female education on fertility is controversial. In the text, the existence of this pattern is granted for the sake of argument. Obviously, if the pattern does not exist, that merely strengthens our case for reproductive freedom.

the birth rate is as high as 7 or 8 children per adult woman, some social mechanism must be keeping the birth rate below its maximum possible level. These existing mechanisms can be undermined by an increase in education. If the increase is insufficient, then the traditional mechanisms will not be replaced by equally, or more, reliable alternatives. In many traditional societies in sub-Saharan Africa, for instance, the main factor keeping the birth rate below the maximum possible is a combination of prolonged breast-feeding and sexual abstinence following the birth of a child.[26] The evolution and persistence of such traditions may be due to their impact on the birth rate. However, breast-feeding and abstinence are not deliberately chosen because they reduce the birth rate. Rather, the motivation is a set of mistaken beliefs about the health needs of mother or infant. Small increases in female education tend to undermine these beliefs. This undermines the practices based on them, leading to an increase in fertility.

Proponents of coercion might argue that, in such circumstances, reproductive freedom will take too long to reduce the birth rate. If the population ever stabilizes, it will be at an unsustainably high level. This objection is unlikely to bother us at this stage of our inquiry, as full compliance with the ideal code should lead to a very significant increase in female education, sufficient to produce reductions in fertility even in the first generation. However, it does highlight the fact that partial compliance with the ideal code might have very undesirable effects—a fact that will return to trouble us in Chapter 10.

For our present purposes, the main objection to coercive policies is that, even if non-coercive policies cannot guarantee an acceptable fertility rate, there is no evidence to suggest that coercive alternatives could do a better job.

1. Even if coercion does affect behaviour, the resulting decline in fertility is not as sustainable as a similar decline resulting from education. This is because, as coercion largely leaves people's inclinations unchanged, the coercive policy must be continually maintained, and adapted to defeat people's determined efforts to avoid it. For instance, Sen quotes the architects of China's family policy as admitting that 'the birth concept of the broad masses has not changed fundamentally'.[27]

---

[26] This explanation is offered by both Jolly and Gribble, 'The Proximate Determinants of Fertility', 89, and Dasgupta, *Well-being and Destitution*, 355–6. In their analysis of data from twelve countries in sub-Saharan Africa, Jolly and Gribble found that the national average period of 'postpartum nonsusceptibility' ranged from 11.7 months for Kenya to 23.9 months in Ondo State (p. 74). They concluded that, 'In all of the . . . sub-Saharan African populations included in this analysis, except Zimbabwe, the proximate determinant having the greatest fertility-inhibiting effect is the postpartum nonsusceptible period.'

[27] Sen, *Development as Freedom*, 220.

2. Correlation is not causation. In particular, the reduction in the fertility rate in China has also followed significant improvements in education, health care, and female job opportunities. In fact, general development policy in China shares many of the features of the Socialist government in the Indian state of Kerala. Yet Kerala's fertility rate has declined even faster than China's, despite the fact that coercive policies are not followed in Kerala.[28]

3. The correlation between coercion and decline in fertility is not universal. For instance, many northern Indian states have followed very coercive family planning policies, yet they still have very high birth rates.[29] Coercion alone is certainly not sufficient to reduce the birth rate significantly. Yet once appropriate development policies are in place, there is no reliable evidence that coercion produces any additional reduction. Indeed, coercion may even undermine development. For example, evidence from India suggests that the use of coercive family planning policies can undermine the effectiveness of voluntary programmes.[30]

Even if we reject state coercion, or interference by other third parties, this still leaves the possibility of moral coercion. Why not endorse an obligation not to reproduce in developing countries, or an obligation to reproduce in developed countries? Aside from the general undesirability of a coercive moral code in this area, the challenge for proponents of this suggestion would be to formulate a *flexible coercive moral rule*, designed to produce whatever the optimal birth rate may happen to be in different circumstances. Population policy requires a collective response. This suggests that it must be addressed collectively, rather than individually. The failure of coercive policies suggests that the most effective way for the ideal code to achieve this is by a general moral disposition favouring reproductive freedom, together with public policy initiatives designed to create an incentive structure where that reproductive freedom will produce the desired birth rate.

An individual morality of reproductive freedom is thus not only consistent with the best approach to public policy—it actually reinforces it, as public policy based on changing people's incentives is more likely to be effective in a population whose moral code encourages people to consider themselves morally free to respond to those incentives.

[28] Ibid. 219–26. Kerala has been extensively discussed in the development literature. For a taste of the debate, see Jeffrey, *Politics, Women and Well-being*; Ramachandran, 'Kerala's Development Achievements'; Krishhan, 'Demographic Transition in Kerala'; Bhat and Rajan, 'Demographic Transition in Kerala Revisited'; Das Gupta and Bhat, 'Intensified Gender Bias in India'.

[29] Sen, *Development as Freedom*, 223.   [30] Ibid. 224.

6.6.4. *Underpopulation*

Many countries in the developing world face the threat of overpopulation. Some countries in the developed world seem to face the opposite problem. Reproductive freedom, combined with increasing employment opportunities and education for women, threatens to bring the birth rate unsustainably low. The ideal society is likely to correspond more to the developed world than to the developing. Accordingly, the real problem will be maintaining a high enough birth rate, rather than preventing overpopulation. This suggests that those in the ideal society will seek public policy initiatives designed to lessen the financial and other burdens placed on parents in order to encourage an increase in the birth rate. The development of such policies would be seen as a high priority in the ideal society. We cannot predict the precise details of these policies, but there seems no good reason to assume that they cannot be devised.

On the contrary, except in extreme circumstances, the birth rate in the ideal society, even in the absence of specially targeted policies, is likely to be fairly close to the desired level. Modest changes to the incentive structure should be sufficient to produce that desired rate. If the aim is slightly to increase the birth rate, these policies might include subsidies or tax breaks for parents, or subsidies on activities particularly undertaken by parents. If the aim is slightly to reduce the birth rate, suitable policies might include subsidies or tax breaks on activities likely to compete with parenthood. (For instance, if tertiary educated women have fewer children than less educated women, subsidies for tertiary study might reduce the birth rate.)

Owing to the significance of reproductive freedom, these measures are unlikely to be designed to prevent people from having children, or force them to have children. However, if the birth rate is too high, measures to discourage people from having more than two children might be considered acceptable. (We saw in Section 4.2.2.1 that the cost to the agent from settling for two children rather than three is almost always less than the cost involved in settling for no children rather than some.) Of course, these have to be balanced against the need to ensure that the needs of all resulting children are met.

A suitable combination of reproductive freedom and public policy support seems likely to bring the fertility rate into the optimal zone, and to keep it there. Furthermore, independent reasons to do with the welfare and development of children lead us to expect the ideal society to provide more facilities for young children, and thereby reduce the burdens faced by parents.

The preceding discussion is very vague. Indeed, throughout this chapter, I have emphasized the impossibility of predicting exactly what life would be like in the ideal society, especially beyond the first generation. (This impossibility is further highlighted several times in subsequent chapters.) We cannot hope to estimate the expected value of any proposed ideal code. This may seem a fatal blow for Rule Consequentialism. However, it need not be. Rule Consequentialism does not require us to have any idea of the expected value of a particular code. It merely requires us to establish that this code has at least as high an expected value as any competing code. Our proposed code combines reproductive freedom, strong parental obligations, and broadly liberal public policy. For each of these features, we have seen good reason to believe that any code lacking that feature will produce distinctly worse results over a wide range of plausible possible futures. By contrast, for none of our features is there any good reason to believe that its absence would produce valuable results. Reproductive freedom and parental obligations may not guarantee that the right number of children will be raised well by the next generation, but there is no reason to prefer any alternative code based on coercion. We don't know what the world will look like under our ideal code, but we can be confident that it would not be better under any competing code.

The specification of the ideal society is not an end in itself. Rule Consequentialism is not designed to sketch a detailed Utopian vision. Its primary purpose is to provide us with a code of moral rules. The underlying ideal code sketched in this book is surprisingly simple, as its response to different circumstances flows from flexible rules and public debate rather than mechanical rules. Rule Consequentialism does not seek a detailed map of the perfect road ahead. It merely asks for the first step. We can be confident that a certain set of flexible rules and dispositions is the correct first step along the right road, even if we have only the faintest idea where that road would lead.

6.7. Conclusions

I conclude that Rule Consequentialism can accommodate a plausible principle regarding reproduction. We still need a more detailed account of the notion of 'an acceptable life in our own society', as this would be applied by the inhabitants of the ideal society. In general terms, we can easily sketch the features of such a life. It will come as close as possible to life in the ideal society, and be characterized by the ability to live an autonomous life pursuing independently valuable goals. We may find it impossible to specify the precise degree of autonomy or value required for a life to qualify as acceptable. Fortunately, such specification is unnecessary. The ideal code is designed to ensure that the population remains within the acceptable range in all environments. The population will obviously not remain within the acceptable range for long unless most people regard themselves as morally free to reproduce. We can thus reasonably assume that any life not too far below the average in our own society should count as acceptable in our circumstances.

The ideal code thus reflects all of our intuitively plausible principles regarding reproduction. It incorporates an appropriate degree of reproductive freedom, including the permissibility of sub-optimal reproduction and the obligations of parents to care for their children. The ideal code also explains the asymmetry between the permission to refrain from having happy children and the obligation not to create wretched lives, and provides a moral foundation for our commonsense attitudes to risk. No other extant moral theory comes even close to delivering this combination of plausibility and explanatory power.

This concludes our preliminary investigation of the place of reproduction in the Rule Consequentialist ideal code. We have seen that Rule Consequentialism delivers an intuitively plausible account of the broad limits of reproductive freedom. We have also seen that Rule Consequentialism must cover public policy as well as individual morality. Our next task is to explore the public policy of the ideal society, especially as it relates to future generations.

7

Optimism and Pessimism

7.1. Intuitively Plausible Principles for Intergenerational Justice

Our focus on individual morality has led us to ignore many of the issues traditionally regarded as central to intergenerational justice. This decision has been deliberate, as one distinctive feature of our Consequentialist approach is its insistence on basing broader political obligations on a foundation of individual morality. However, we now address these broader issues, and ask how Rule Consequentialism might deal with public policy issues directly related to intergenerational justice.

A complete account of political philosophy, or even of intergenerational justice, is beyond the scope of this book. Instead, the next three chapters pick out a range of topical issues in contemporary political philosophy, and illustrates how a Rule Consequentialist focus on intergenerational issues contributes to each particular debate. (The topics are also chosen for comparative reasons, as they make it easier to compare Rule Consequentialism to its leading liberal rival, Rawls's liberal egalitarian account of intergenerational justice.)

For the morality of individual reproduction, we compared Rule Consequentialism to a list of plausible principles (Section 5.1). It is instructive to do the same for intergenerational justice. In this section I present a basic list of intuitively plausible principles of intergenerational justice, several of which are familiar from Chapters 1 and 2.

1. *The Minimal Principle.* The present generation must take some account of the interests of subsequent generations.

2. *The Accumulation Principle.* Each generation should (if possible) leave later generations better-off than itself.

3. *The No Worse-off Principle.* No generation should leave later generations worse-off than itself, if it can avoid this.

4. *The Non-Depletion Principle.* No generation should deplete resources which will be needed by subsequent generations, at least not without

providing adequate compensation in the form of new technologies or access to new resources. (As we shall see in Section 7.8, one key question for Rule Consequentialism is whether Principle (4) should be treated as merely a corollary of Principle (3), or whether it requires special consideration.)

5. The Collective Liberty Principle.   Each generation should be free to make its own public policy decisions, so long as these do not impose unreasonable burdens on those who come after.

5a. The Collective Reproductive Liberty Principle: a special case of (5).   Each generation should be free to make its own population planning decisions, so long as these do not impose unreasonable burdens on those who come after.

6. The Individual Liberty Principle.   Each individual should be free to make her own lifestyle decisions, so long as these do not impose unreasonable burdens on those who come after, or on her contemporaries.

6a. The Individual Reproductive Liberty Principle: a special case of (6). Each individual should be free to make her own reproduction decisions, so long as these do not impose unreasonable burdens on those who come after, or on her contemporaries, or on those she creates.

7. The Moderation Principle.   No generation is obliged to maximize either the size or the total happiness of the next, or any subsequent, generation.

The first four principles are clearly related. We begin with the claim that it is clearly wrong for one generation gratuitously to leave later generations worse off by unnecessarily depleting resources. Once we admit a prima facie reason not to leave later generations worse-off, it is hard to see how such a reason could have so little weight that it was always overruled by the needs or desires of the present generation. If it is wrong gratuitously to leave later generations worse-off, then it must sometimes be wrong to further our own interests by leaving them worse-off. If we accept the Minimal Principle, then we are almost certain to also accept the No Worse off Principle and the Non-Depletion Principle. The two Liberty principles and the non-Depletion Principle are also related, as liberty is a key component of any moderate moral theory.

Ideally a moral theory must accommodate our seven principles, explain their significance, and offer some guidelines for balancing them when they come into conflict. (In particular, the Moderation Principle and the two Liberty principles obviously have considerable potential to conflict with the Accumulation, No Worse off, and Non-Depletion principles.) If a moral theory cannot accommodate any particular principle, then its proponents owe us an account of why that principle should be rejected. Because the principles need to be balanced against one another, each can be thought of as coming in degrees (with the exception of the Minimal Principle itself). For every principle, there is a minimalist version that captures a decisive intuition. For instance, the minimalist version of the Individual Reproductive Liberty Principle captures the decisive intuition that individuals must enjoy some moral freedom in regard to reproduction. Acceptable political theories are then distinguished by the way they balance the non-minimalist versions of the various principles.

Simple Consequentialism easily accommodates the Minimal Principle. It also yields the Accumulation, No Worse-off, and Non-Depletion principles. However, it has trouble accommodating our other three principles. Simple Consequentialism places each agent in the present generation under an obligation to maximize well-being across all generations. Simple Consequentialism is thus very demanding. It contradicts the Moderation Principle and obliterates the two Liberty principles.

On the other hand, many non-Consequentialist political theorists have serious problems even accommodating the Minimal Principle, as they are built on person-affecting foundations. As we saw in Chapter 2, contract-based political theories also have particular trouble accommodating the Accumulation Principle.

The main purpose of the next three chapters is to show how Rule Consequentialism fares much better. It allows considerable deviation from strict maximization, as an overly demanding intergenerational rule could not be efficiently inculcated in the present generation. In Chapters 5 and 6, we discussed the significance of moral freedom in the ideal code. While political liberty is distinct from moral freedom, Rule Consequentialism's case for the former is built on its case for the latter (Section 7.2). Within Rule Consequentialism, the case for liberty can be justified either on instrumental grounds, or by appeal to the intrinsic value of individual autonomy, or, if our value theory admits holistic evaluations, by appeal to the intrinsic value of communal autonomy.

Yet the ideal code must include some obligations to future generations, and these must satisfy the No Worse off, and Non-Depletion principles. Rule Consequentialism also defends a moderate version of the Accumulation Principle, which typically has less weight than the other principles (No Worse-off, Non-Depletion, and Liberty), but is not always overruled by them.

We expect Rule Consequentialism to offer us some guidance about public policy regarding future generations. It is very difficult to predict the precise details of policy debate within the ideal code. Indeed, if such predictions were possible, then we could short-circuit that debate and copy our own public policies directly from the ideal society. However, we can make some general predictions. Under full compliance with the ideal code, we would naturally expect policy-formulating institutions to function considerably more effectively than they currently do. In particular, the ideal code is likely to include a disposition to pay particular attention to long-term consequences in developing public policy, as the advantages of such a disposition are compelling. In addition to general rules instructing us to vote, support legitimately constituted governments, obey laws which are not manifestly unjust, etc., the code will also include a number of specific injunctions to support particular policies designed to enhance overall well-being. While there may be considerable disagreement over precise institutional frameworks, the ideal society is almost certain to contain a significant majority in favour of policies designed to ensure that all children are able to develop as autonomous agents, and to ensuring the survival of the background social framework. The debates of the ideal society provide an ideal to which we might aspire.

Our discussions in Chapters 5 and 6 emphasized the flexibility of the ideal code. I extend this analysis in Chapters 7 to 9. The code will favour a combination of democratic public debate, public policy incentives, and individual moral freedom, over a set of specific moral obligations. To evaluate any proposed code, we must have some idea what public policy choices would be likely to result from the internalization of that code. However, those precise public policies are not built into the content of the code. When we ask how someone who had internalized the ideal code would act in our actual situation, the answer will be in terms of general dispositions to favour certain kinds of policy, rather than specific dispositions to follow some specific policy. (This flexibility is crucial to the Rule Consequentialist response to partial compliance objections, the subject of Chapter 10.)

Our task is to show that the ideal code delivers intuitively plausible principles regarding future generations. The case for this claim rests on two general features of that code.

1. Liberalism. Building on the case for moral freedom defended at length in Chapter 6, I argue that the ideal code leaves considerable room for individual and collective choice. On virtually any acceptable value theory, participation in collective decision-making enhances individual autonomy and well-being, both intrinsically and instrumentally. These facts establish a prima facie case in favour of collective liberty (Section 7.2).

2. Future Welfare. In any plausible Consequentialist theory, considerable weight is attached to the well-being of future humans. Rule Consequentialism chooses its ideal code by taking account of the impact of competing codes on the well-being of all human beings, including future people. This is, after all, why we should expect the ideal code to accommodate obligations to future generations. The benefits of the widespread inculcation of a general disposition to be concerned for the well-being of others (together with more specific dispositions to avoid harming them and to promote their interests and opportunities) are obvious. So long as these dispositions do not overwhelm the agent's concern for herself and/or her nearest and dearest, or lead her to violate particular obligations, or to interfere arbitrarily in the lives of others, then it is hard to see how they might have any negative consequences. Therefore, we should expect those who have internalized the ideal code to be disposed to take future welfare into account in their individual deliberations, and to carry this disposition over to their political lives.

The liberal aspect of the ideal code clearly ties in with our two liberty principles, while the emphasis on future welfare supports our first four principles. These two aspects are in considerable tension, as some freedoms for the present generation are incompatible with the welfare, or even the existence, of subsequent generations. Our main task will be to resolve this tension.

7.2. The Politics of the Ideal Code

This section explains the relationship between Chapters 5 and 6 and Chapters 7 to 9. Chapters 5 and 6 sketched and defended an ideal code for individual morality. This code has significant independent intuitive appeal. The next three chapters extend that code into the area of intergenerational justice. They do not simply apply the code of Chapters 5 and 6. It cannot be directly applied, as individual moral rules are not directly applicable to politics. Nor do Chapters 7 to 9 simply develop an analogous Rule Consequentialist account of political philosophy, independent of the moral code sketched earlier. Rather, my approach is to suppose that we do teach the ideal code, as depicted in Chapters 5 and 6, to the next generation. What would we expect that generation to think about politics? We imagine people who have internalized that code deliberating about the policies, laws, and procedures for their society.

There are several justifications for this approach.

1. It is different from the two traditional approaches to political philosophy that dominate contemporary discussions of intergenerational justice. Many Consequentialists, especially Simple Consequentialists, apply their account of individual morality directly to political questions. At the other extreme, liberals such as Rawls attempt to divorce their theory of justice from particular moral views. Because it differs from these traditional approaches, our approach has more chance of saying something new. It also avoids the pitfalls

associated with both approaches (Sections 1.6 and 2.2; for a critique of Rawls's liberal neutrality, see endnote C to Chapter 11.)

2. Overall, our discussion of public policy is less constrained by intuitions than our exploration of individual morality. Our intuitions are weaker in the political realm than with individual morality. Most public policy issues concern topics of such empirical complexity and controversy that we cannot be confident of any but the most general intuitions. Furthermore, our political intuitions can often be shown to rest on implausible empirical assumptions. In particular, I argue below that, in the actual world, most discussions of the Accumulation Problem—including Rawls's own account—require a degree of empirical optimism that would almost certainly be rejected (with regard to our actual situation) by anyone who had internalized the ideal code. As the most difficult questions for Rule Consequentialist politics arise precisely because of empirical threats to that optimistic picture, we should not expect our political intuitions to be a reliable guide when we most need them.

As our basic intuitions regarding personal morality are stronger than any particular intuitions we might have regarding public policy, we are entitled to use the former to correct (or flesh-out) the latter. I argued in Chapters 5 and 6 that a certain kind of Rule Consequentialism provides the best account of our intuitions regarding individual morality. It is thus not unreasonable to extend that Rule Consequentialist account into the area of public policy, even at some intuitive cost.

3. Our approach surely mirrors how the ideal code would actually be taught, learnt, and internalized. People first learn a basic code of individual morality. This gives them a general moral outlook, which they proceed, in later life, to apply to politics. As we judge competing codes by the costs of teaching them, we should expect the best code to regard individual morality as in some sense more basic than political morality.

4. By proceeding in this fashion, we do get a plausible ideal code for intergenerational justice. Or, more modestly, we get a code that offers useful advice on controversial questions—advice that is not clearly implausible. A society whose members have internalized the ideal code sketched in Chapters 5 and 6 would have as good a chance as any of flourishing indefinitely far into the future. This, in turn, provides independent support for that moral code. If our account of individual morality collapsed into incoherence or led to disaster when extended to intergenerational politics, then this would clearly be a very strong reason to reject it.

5. However Rule Consequentialism is structured, real-world compliance with those areas of the code dealing with intergenerational and international politics will be much lower than compliance with many areas of individual morality, especially the individual morality of reproduction. As we shall see

in Chapter 10, Rule Consequentialism is more confident of its verdicts the closer we are to full compliance. So this is another reason to begin from individual morality.

6. The gap between the real world and the ideal society of full compliance is relevant for several other reasons. The further the actual world is from full compliance, the harder it is to speculate about the details of the ideal society. We thus gain more insight into the political thinking of those who have internalized the ideal code by extrapolating from their code of individual morality than by trying to predict their political behaviour directly.

7. The further we are from full compliance, the more likely it is that Rule Consequentialism will offer a radical critique of our own institutions, and of the intuitions that accompany them. Of course, this also puts more weight on Rule Consequentialism to justify itself. The Rule Consequentialist explanation is that our approach to intergenerational and international politics is inconsistent with our basic intuitions regarding individual morality. The fact that we are closer to full compliance in regard to the latter is itself a reason for trusting them. Chapters 5 and 6 thus provide justification for a Rule Consequentialist departure from even our most considered intuitions in intergenerational and (especially) international politics.

8. Under partial compliance, the different strands of the ideal code will come apart. For instance, if actual world politics is very different from politics in the ideal society, then someone who has internalized the ideal code will be torn between a desire to follow better policies, and a disposition to follow the policies enacted in the society in which she finds herself. Under partial compliance, the main issue is the relative weight of various dispositions.

If we build up our Rule Consequentialism layer by layer, building our political morality on our individual morality, then we may find it easier to unpack the different layers, and discover which has priority (Sections 10.3 and 10.4).

In Section 8.1 I argue that, even in the ideal society, there will be considerable disagreement regarding public policy, and that we cannot hope to predict in any detail the policies adopted in the ideal society. It does not follow that Rule Consequentialism offers no guidance. We can attempt to model our decision-making procedures on those of the ideal society, even if we cannot predict the results those procedures would have there. Furthermore, even if they disagree about many of the details of public policy, people who have internalized the ideal code may share certain general attitudes. The purpose of this chapter is to explore those attitudes, seeking to bypass areas of disagreement by focusing on a higher level of generality.

For the moment, then, we identify the public policy priorities of the ideal society as those favoured by someone who has internalized the ideal code, as sketched in Chapters 5 and 6. Such a person has a general concern for the welfare of others, feels a special obligation to assist those with whom she stands in special relationships (including parental relationships), and a general obligation not to harm others. She also recognizes the significance of moral autonomy, and believes that, wherever possible, significant life choices (especially reproductive choices) should be left up to the individual. As I argued in Sections 5.7 and 7.1, it is natural to extend the scope of all these concerns to include future people (however far distant in time) as much as present people. Consideration of politics only supports this conclusion, as a code that encouraged, or even allowed, the present generation to ignore the interests of subsequent generations would obviously have very negative consequences.

Anyone who has internalized the ideal code will favour public policies designed to further the interests of future generations, not cause harm to present or future people, enforce and promote the fulfilment of special obligations to present and future people, and not compromise reproductive (and other) freedoms. As contributions to public policy, these generic remarks are neither surprising nor interesting. Their significance for moral philosophy lies in the fact that Rule Consequentialism's rivals have surprising difficulty generating such plausible banalities (Sections 1.4, 1.5, 1.6; Ch. 2). Also, the resources of Rule Consequentialism are not exhausted by the provision of platitudes. For the morality of individual reproduction, Rule Consequentialism delivered some quite specific results. The rest of this chapter asks if it can be similarly helpful in regard to public policy.

Aside from the general tendencies just listed, the feature of the ideal code that is most relevant to our present discussion is its detailed rules regarding the individual morality of reproduction. Someone who has internalized those rules will believe that, along with every other parent, she has an obligation to provide her own child with a life above the lexical level (wherever possible) and an absolute obligation not to create a child whose life is not worth living. She will also feel a very strong *inclination* to provide her own child with benefits above and beyond the lexical level, especially if she can do so without undue cost to her other projects, but will not feel *obliged* to do so. The principal theme of the present chapter is that this asymmetrical combination—of obligations below the lexical level and optional inclinations above it—will be carried over into the area of public policy. Someone who has internalized the ideal code will regard the No Worse-off Principle as generating strict obligations, whereas they regard accumulation as optional.

There are two reasons to expect such a person's attitudes to public policy to mirror her views on individual morality. The first is that the main arguments supporting the array of parental obligations and freedoms presented in Chapters 5 and 6 were based on balancing the relative value of individual autonomy against the importance of ensuring that basic needs and interests are met. Similar considerations naturally arise in politics. So we should expect them to be balanced in a similar way. (Just as, at a more general level, the case for including prohibitions on harming others, and a general concern for their welfare, in the ideal code clearly translates across to public policy.)[1]

Analogous arguments apply to both the individual and collective cases, leading us to expect similar results in the two cases. Furthermore, a key theme of Chapters 5 and 6 was the unity of the ideal code. As Rule Consequentialists, we do not develop an individual morality of reproduction in isolation and then proceed to develop a theory of public policy priorities in isolation, and then bring the two together. As the ideal code is internalized by human beings, it represents a single coherent moral worldview. We should thus expect the details of the individual morality of reproduction sketched in Chapters 5 and 6 to influence the attitudes to public policy of someone who has internalized the ideal code. In the absence of evidence to the contrary, we should expect the latter to mirror the former.

However, the public policy of the ideal code is not identical to its individual morality. In other words, those who have internalized the ideal code will not always support policies designed to enforce that code. There are several reasons for this.

1. Inefficiencies.   Force is seldom an effective way to get people to comply with any moral code. Persuasion and education are often better strategies. There is no reason to expect that those who have internalized the ideal code will be any less aware of these familiar facts than ourselves. If the attempt to enforce compliance is not an efficient way of promoting overall value, then they will not favour it.

2. The Liberalism of Interpretation.   Much of the ideal code consists of flexible rules, whose application to particular cases requires sensitive judgement in the interpretation of deliberately vague moral terms. For instance, familiar moral rules such as keep your promises, tell the truth, and do not steal, all come with the general caveat 'unless doing so is necessary to avoid

---

[1] One obvious exception, apart from those listed in the text, is that, in the individual case, we considered the objection that parental obligations are redundant as parents naturally care for their children. (Section 5.7.) Whatever its force in the individual case, this argument is clearly weakened by the translation to the collective level, as people's natural affection for future generations in general is much less reliable. (A factor that caused serious havoc for sentimental Contractarians, as we saw in Section 2.1.3.) If anything, the case for building public policy on a bedrock of obligations to future generations is thus stronger than the case for including parental obligations in the ideal code.

a disaster', where what counts as a disaster depends on both the situation and the rule.[2] Hooker's famine rule is another good example of a rule requiring judgement. In general, 'Rule Consequentialists are as aware as anyone that figuring out whether a rule applies can require not merely attention to detail, but also sensitivity, imagination, interpretation, and judgement.'[3] (Section 10.2.2.)

Those who have internalized the code are obviously aware of its features. Each person knows that his or her own interpretation of any given rule is but one of many. The only way to enforce such moral rules would be to enforce one particular interpretation. No one will want to be forced to act in accordance with someone else's interpretation of a moral rule, if it differs from her own. Recognizing that everyone else will similarly object to the enforcement of her interpretation, each person will not attempt to enforce it either.

3. Costs of Enforcement.   Even if most people agree on an interpretation of a moral rule, and even if enforcement would be possible, those who have internalized the ideal code will recognize that such enforcement will often undermine the value of the rule. One of the values promoted by many moral flexible rules, especially those governing reproductive freedom and the pursuit of other personal projects, is what Mill calls 'individuality', and is often today known as 'autonomy': the ability to live one's own life in accordance with one's own judgements and values. I argued in Chapters 4 and 6 that moral freedom is often necessary for genuine autonomy. But it is clearly not sufficient. One cannot meaningfully exercise autonomy unless a plurality of options is both practically and morally available. A law prescribing a certain pattern of behaviour obviously threatens both types of availability: illegal activities are unlikely to be practically available, and anyone who has internalized the ideal code will presumably have a strong general disposition not to feel morally free to break the law. So the enforcement of one interpretation of a flexible moral rule will often undermine either moral freedom or respect for the law.

The conclusion is not that the ideal society will be completely unregulated. Some moral rules require little interpretation ('Do not murder', 'Do not torture') and, even with the most flexible rules, interpretation will often be confined within certain broad limits. For instance, our discussion of reproductive freedom suggested that the prohibition on creating lives not worth living would be regarded as absolute. So this would be an appropriate object of public policy and legislation. The requirement to create a life above the

---

[2] Hooker, *Ideal Code, Real World*, 98–9.   [3] Ibid. 88.

lexical level requires much more interpretation, and is thus much less likely to be enforced. (In a similar vein, J. S. Mill argues that public debate and discussion are an essential part of each person's individuality.[4] The way we exercise our autonomy is, in part, by participating in public debate about how such autonomy should be exercised. Public policies enforcing particular lifestyle choices are obviously inimical to such debate. We return to similar issues in Section 8.1.)

Throughout the discussion of politics, as before, I aim to remain agnostic regarding our foundational value theory. However, the argument often appeals to elements included in the value theory of those who have internalized the ideal code. For instance, while our discussion in Section 5.4 left it open whether we should recognize incommensurability in our foundational value theory, we did subsequently conclude (in Section 6.2) that those who have internalized the ideal code will deliberate in a manner best explained by supposing that they regard the ability to make rational choices between genuinely incommensurable options as one of the most valuable aspects of human life. (I also note several places where additional departures from the Total View as our foundational value theory would assist the argument.)

Those who have internalized the ideal code also bring to politics a tendency to 'adopt a lexical level', as I loosely put it in Section 5.4. They often regard the achievement of a particular threshold as lexically more significant than further steps above or below that threshold, or act as if their own goals and interests were incommensurable with other values.

On the other hand, this tendency to lexicalize will be accompanied by a recognition that other agents are equally justified in adopting (possibly incompatible) lexical levels for their own deliberative purposes. As we shall see, one of the key challenges facing Rule Consequentialism in the political arena is to balance these inconsistent lexical interpretations, and the competing interests and divergent perspectives they represent.

One crucial element of public policy with respect to future generations is population policy. Rule Consequentialism seems set to be both demanding and counterintuitive here, due to the fact that, *ceteris paribus*, population increase adds value. However, I believe that the best Rule Consequentialist response to this challenge leans heavily on uncertainty and risk. Accordingly, I postpone all discussion of population policy until Section 8.2.3.

The details of politics in the ideal society, in general, are not our concern. Rather, we want to know how relations with future generations are dealt

---

[4] Mill, *Representative Government*. For a recent discussion, see Nelson, 'Open Government and Just Legislation'. (See also Section 8.1 below.)

with. The present chapter focuses on some features of the intergenerational context that threaten to exacerbate the difficulties such balancing entails, as well as greatly increasing the demands of Rule Consequentialism.

7.3. Growing up in the Ideal Society

A commitment to individual liberty and a concern for the promotion of welfare seem to conflict. We explore this conflict, beginning with an argument that public policy in the ideal society will have a different focus from that found in the actual world.[5] How well a person's life goes depends to a very large extent upon how he is nurtured during his early years. Different people are nurtured to wildly different degrees. This divergence is a very significant source of inequality in the quality of people's lives. This is the sort of inequality that Rule Consequentialists, especially those who endorse our account of the lexical level will regard as undesirable. Consequently, a just society will be one where, so far as is practicable, everyone is equally well nurtured during their early years.

We can explore this argument using Rawls's notion of the two 'moral powers', possessed by all moral persons.[6] (This is partly to facilitate the comparison with Rawls's own theory, as the argument of this section directly parallels Section 2.2.4.1.) One of these is the capacity for a conception of the good: the ability to form, follow, and revise one's individual doctrine of the good.[7] The other is the capacity for a sense of justice: the ability to cooperate with others in maintaining a just political society through fair terms of social cooperation.[8] Moral persons also have higher-order interests in the development and exercise of their two moral powers, and thus also in whatever is necessary for that development and exercise.[9] However the lexical level is defined, a life above that level requires the satisfactory development of these two powers.

Left entirely to their own devices, some human parents will not foster the moral powers of their children. Some hinder such development or even prevent it altogether. This will remain true to some extent even under full compliance—as we do not idealize to universal internalization of the ideal code, and as internalization does not produce perfect compliance. If the ideal code leaves child-rearing unregulated and unassisted by public institutions, some people will grow up, if they grow up at all, without a minimally adequate degree of moral power. We need to realize how bad the worst childhoods are. Perhaps some people flourish despite severe deprivation and

---

[5] The argument of this section is drawn from Moore and Mulgan, 'Growing Up in the Original Position'.   [6] Rawls, *A Theory of Justice*, p. 505.
[7] Rawls, *Political Liberalism*, p. 34.   [8] Ibid., p. xlvi.   [9] Ibid. 74.

parental abuse. Few flourish despite having been beaten to death by their parents. Those whose life begins with a disastrous childhood will be the worst-off members of society, and they will fall below the lexical level.

Given these facts, our ideal code should ensure, so far as possible, that everyone develops moral powers. This suggests that public policies within that society will be chosen to fit the following principle of justice, familiar from Section 2.2.4.1.

> *The Development Principle.*   Each person has an equal claim to a fully adequate scheme of equal conditions of early care, which is compatible with a similar scheme of such conditions for all.

A society governed by the Development Principle would be very different from any actual society, as many actual children fail to develop those powers. Accordingly, we are far from full compliance with this aspect of the ideal code. The Development Principle has two related implications:

1. It threatens to undermine our liberty principles.
2. It threatens to make the ideal code very demanding.

We begin with the first, drawing out analogies to real world conflicts over child-rearing.

Different groups raise their children in different ways. When is it legitimate for the state to interfere in such practices? The Development Principle suggests that, in a just society, the state will be obliged to intervene whenever cultural practices fail to guarantee the provision of a minimum degree of self-respect. The survival and self-respect of children take precedence over any considerations of parental freedom, or the value of cultural traditions.

Rule Consequentialism imagines that we teach the same moral code to everyone in the next generation. It also explicitly omits any costs associated with teaching a new code to people who have already internalized any existing moral code. One might therefore think that Rule Consequentialism has nothing to say about cultural diversity within a given society, as it assumes such diversity away. However, this does not follow. While we do imagine teaching a single code to the whole of the next generation, we do not suppose that generation to exist in a social or cultural vacuum. Our code is to be taught to people who themselves belong to a variety of cultural traditions. The ideal code must therefore include, *inter alia*, a characteristic set of attitudes to one's own cultural background.

My account of intergenerational morality and justice will appeal, at several crucial points, to the significance of committing oneself to projects extending beyond the end of one's own lifetime. These projects are unlikely to be entirely new. The most likely candidates for intergenerational projects will be those one inherits from previous generations. (I explicitly appeal to this possibility in Section 7.6 to defend the possibility of accumulation.) Therefore, those who have internalized the ideal code will feel some connection to their cultural traditions.[10]

Two things follow from the significance of cultural traditions.

1. It is not efficient for us to inculcate a moral code telling people to ignore their cultural traditions.
2. Those who have internalized the ideal code will be reluctant to institute public policies that conflict with people's cultural traditions.

Of course, whatever value they have, cultural traditions are far from the only things valued by those who have internalized the ideal code. It is unlikely that their commitments to such traditions would allow them to permit, for instance, the creation of lives below the zero level. It is more likely that cultural traditions, rather than trumping strict moral rules, will enter into the interpretation of flexible rules, especially into interpretations of the lexical level and of the notion of 'a worthwhile life'.

The ideal code thus supports liberal cultural diversity. The Rule Consequentialist test for any cultural affiliation will be: is it consistent with the internalization of the ideal code? Even within a liberal public policy, some interventions will be permitted. Some examples are obvious. Cultural traditions which sanction the sacrifice, starvation, and deprivation of children, under any circumstances, will be forbidden in the just society; as will traditions which permit potentially fatal physical punishment, or deny children the benefits of life-saving medical interventions. If they are to reach the lexical level, children must survive childhood. A just government would also prohibit practices which, although they guarantee survival, render it likely that many children will fail to develop adequate self-respect. Physical and sexual abuse clearly fall under such a restriction.

There are good reasons why the ideal code should leave many aspects of a child's care and education in the hands of their nearest and dearest. But the Development Principle shows that these reasons are defeasible, as the interests of the child take priority over those of the parents. One crucial task for any liberal account of justice for children is to discover when those defeasible reasons are actually defeated.

Given the importance of choosing good policies for children, those in the ideal society will favour social institutions which accord research into developmental psychology and educational theory a higher priority than,

---

[10] If we were to adopt a foundational value theory according any intrinsic value to the existence of diverse cultures or traditions, this conclusion would obviously be strengthened.

say, research into automobile technology. (To suppose otherwise is to suppose, implausibly, that those in the ideal society know that any public policy innovation is bound to fail children.) Unless they are confident that a free market for research delivers such priorities, they will favour significant taxpayer funding of research in this area.

Much of public policy concerns the allocation of scarce resources. We need to prioritize the needs and interests of different groups and individuals. Our new principle of justice provides a way to think about such prioritization. We give priority to children because of their vulnerability, and because those with the worst childhoods cannot reach the lexical level. Policies designed to meet the needs of disadvantaged children will thus take priority over policies aimed at children who are comparatively well-off.

Consider a stark choice. Suppose the price of raising every child above the lexical level is a subsistence economy in perpetuity. The resources needed to give all children a reasonable start would leave virtually nothing over for capital investment or technological development. Our ideal code seems set to become extremely demanding, even if we limit our concern to the next generation. (We return to distant future generations in the next section.)

We return to the general question of the demands of Rule Consequentialism in Chapter 10. Our present concern is whether the introduction of future generations unreasonably increases those demands. To this charge, the Rule Consequentialist has several replies.

1. In practice, the conflict between liberty and survival or welfare is often illusory. Policies prescribed by the Development Principle will not be economically crippling, especially under anything close to full compliance. Indeed, they may well have a positive economic effect in the long term. Turning at-risk children into well-adjusted adults, rather than leaving them to death, destitution, or crime, might well improve productivity, which, in turn, would provide more resources to ensure that every child reaches an adequate level of moral power.

In general, given the positive values associated with liberty, the ideal code will not require any individual, or any community or generation, to live in any particular way other than the way they choose, *unless* there is good evidence that they will choose a way of life with clearly inferior overall consequences. Such evidence is certainly not available in general, and there is good reason to believe that it will be lacking in most actual particular cases. As we saw in our long discussion of individual reproduction in Chapters 5 and 6, a strong commitment to individual reproductive liberty is often the most efficient way both to meet the needs of the next generation and to ensure a sustainable population across generations.

212 OPTIMISM AND PESSIMISM

2. However demanding Rule Consequentialism may be, its main rivals make even greater demands. Recall our discussion of a Rawlsian Development Principle in Section 2.2.4.1. We saw that the Development Principle will be selected in the original position, just as it is included in the ideal code of Rule Consequentialism. Indeed, the Development Principle will have lexical priority over the Liberty Principle. Social conditions of nurture should be sacrificed only for social conditions of nurture, and not for the sake even of basic liberties.

Owing to this lexical priority, the Development Principle is much more radical for Rawls than for Rule Consequentialism. Rawls's maximin orientation implies that the principle will instruct us to prevent *any* children from failing to develop their moral powers. This aim will have lexical priority over all other social policy goals. If the public policy demands of Rule Consequentialism seem harsh, the demands of a Rawlsian theory will be much harsher.

3. Our final Rule Consequentialist response is to deny that even highly counterintuitive implications need be fatal. The Rule Consequentialist case for the Development Principle highlights the tension between our most basic moral commitments (such as treating all human beings equally, protecting the most vulnerable, and ensuring that everyone enjoys at least a minimum level of opportunity and wealth) and the structure of most Western societies. The moral intuitions favouring the former are more solidly based than any political intuitions supporting the latter. So Rule Consequentialism may simply conclude that our political intuitions should be replaced by the Development Principle whenever the two conflict.

Intuitively, the Moderation Principle balances the two Liberty principles against the demands of the first four principles. Rule Consequentialism provides a more principled account of this balance than either common sense or any competing moral theory, as it will not be possible to efficiently inculcate any extremely demanding code in a broad population. Even though it involves a potentially radical departure from current public policy norms, a Rule Consequentialist Development Principle is thus much less extreme than its Rawlsian counterpart. I would submit that this aspect of the ideal code represents an intuitively plausible response (indeed, perhaps a compelling response) to familiar facts whose moral significance is often underplayed by contemporary moral theories

The gap between the ideal code and the real world does raise the spectre of extreme demands under partial compliance. We return to these in Section 10.4, where I argue that, owing to the way public policy is handled in the ideal code, partial compliance does not generate extreme demands in this case.

7.4. A Focus on Near Generations

Unlike some other political theories, Rule Consequentialism can easily allow for the possibility of obligations to distant generations. It need not appeal to the artificial device of constructing an obligation to distant future generations out of the reciprocal obligations of overlapping generations. This is a distinct advantage of a Consequentialist approach. In principle, each generation will have an eye to the distant future. The ideal code will thus include rules forbidding people from gratuitously performing actions which would have a devastating effect on members of a future generations. Planting a bomb in a forest where it will detonate in two hundred years is clearly wrong, simply because it harms a future person, and not because it somehow affects intervening generations (Section 5.7). This prohibition on gratuitous harm, being relatively inflexible, is likely to be carried over into the political realm (Section 7.2). So those who have internalized the ideal code will be very reluctant to support policies permitting anyone to harm future people.

It may seem that, once distant future generations are added, their interests will overwhelm those of the present generation. Most accounts of impersonal value theory are temporally neutral—a worthwhile life in 500 years' time counts exactly as much as an equally worthwhile life now. The interests of future people are thus exactly on a par with those of present people. If the conditions of life are constant across generations, then we can picture different generations as constituting a single human community spread out across time. Although we choose a code to teach to one small fraction of that community (namely, the first generation), we evaluate competing codes by examining their impact on the well-being of all generations. As the future people greatly outnumber the present generation, the interests of the former will swamp those of the latter. A code that imposes enormous burdens on one generation for small benefits to all subsequent generations will thus be superior, in Rule Consequentialist terms, to one that does not. In particular, the intrinsic value of autonomy to the present generation will not be enough to rule out coercive rules regarding reproduction.

On the other hand, a number of features of our Rule Consequentialist theory suggest that, as a matter of fact, the present generation will focus their attention primarily on what they bequeath to the next generation. The choice of an ideal code is constrained by the requirement of teachability. A code requiring one generation to make enormous sacrifices for subsequent generations would be perceived as unfair, and would thus be very difficult to inculcate successfully in the first generation.

In the case of a single generation, those who learn the rules are those who are affected by them. Any costs borne by everyone who has internalized a given rule is thus also borne by everyone who might benefit from that rule. This is why inculcation costs are so significant. In the intergenerational case, by contrast, those who learn the rules (the present generation) are a tiny subset of those who might benefit from them (all generations). Inculcation costs may thus seem negligible once future generations are introduced.

However, a demanding code has ongoing costs. Although the ideal code is taught only to the first generation, it will eventually be taught by them to subsequent generations. The loss of autonomy is thus suffered by each generation, not just by the first. On the other hand, if the ideal code told the first generation to teach a significantly less demanding code to subsequent generations, thus confining the loss of autonomy to one generation, then the code would be even harder to teach initially, as the intergenerational unfairness would be even more glaring. So the introduction of future generations does not reduce the significance of inculcation costs.

The ideal code cannot be fully impartial. Individual agents are permitted to give considerable priority to those with whom they stand in special relationships. Individuals in the present generation will stand in such relations with members of the next generation, with whom they overlap, in a way that they will not with members of far distant generations.

Two other factors, addressed at more length in Chapter 8, reinforce this focus on near generations. In general, our empirical uncertainty about far distant consequences is much greater than our uncertainty about near consequences (Section 8.2). So intervening generations will be much better placed to know how best to benefit a far distant generation than we are ourselves. Furthermore, even without empirical uncertainty, the possibility of moral progress suggests that it is better for the present generation to concentrate on leaving the next generation with a broad basket of resources to bequeath in their turn to subsequent generations, and to inculcate in that generation a disposition to care for the generation immediately following them, rather than to attempt to make any specific contribution to the well-being of far distant generations (Section 8.1.2).

Given these uncertainties, distant future generations will enter contemporary political debate only in a very general way. We must ensure that we leave our descendants sufficient resources, both material and cultural, to ensure their survival. As one need of human beings is for a culture containing a range of valuable goals, we must ensure that we leave behind such a culture, and the material resources to sustain it. So long as they meet this minimal requirement, it may be up to individual members of the present generation to choose the precise details of that culture and the goals it makes available. However, as the production and maintenance of the social framework is a collective enterprise, rather than the work of a single individual, some of these choices must be made by a generation as a whole, not by isolated individuals. (We return to the relationship between individual freedom and collective decision-making in Chapters 8 and 9.)

Rule Consequentialism thus supports both a practical political focus on the next generation, and the idea that each generation has an underlying obligation to leave the world in general in as good as possible a state for all subsequent generations. Instead of simply assuming that this should be our primary obligation, however, Rule Consequentialism explains why it is. Things will go best for all generations if we act in this way. Rule Consequentialism also explains why, in extreme circumstances, this tendency to focus on near generations might be overruled by obligations to distant future generations (Section 9.2.7).

7.5. Three Models

In Chapter 2 we saw that, aside from the general problem of generating *any* obligations with respect to future generations, the principal source of trouble for Rawls's political liberalism was the possibility that circumstances change across generations. The same is true for Rule Consequentialism. Setting aside the population question (to which we return in Section 8.2.3), the introduction of future generations *per se* does not greatly alter the basic form of the ideal code. Complications arise once we introduce the possibility that the conditions of life change across generations, so that later generations either can enjoy a much higher quality of life than the present generation, or cannot enjoy nearly as high a quality of life. (Especially relevant is the case where these changes in life conditions depend in part on the actions of the present generation: it is up to us whether, and to what extent, future generations will be better-off than ourselves.) The complexities flowing from this possibility are the main topic of this chapter. Our focus is on the general structure of the ideal code, not the details of particular policies. (Indeed, one of the themes of Chapter 8 will be that changing circumstances reinforce the need for flexibility in the ideal code, thus lending further support to a liberal interpretation. As a result, we cannot predict the actual policies of the ideal society. All we can expect from Rule Consequentialism is general guidance as to how to think about our obligations to future generations in a changing world.)

To structure our discussion, we distinguish three general sets of background assumptions one might bring to one's theory of intergenerational justice.[11]

---

[11] I owe this way of characterising approaches to intergenerational justice to a talk given by Henry Shue at the Australian National University in July 2001.

The Optimistic Model.   We will certainly leave future generations better-off than ourselves, and we ought to do so. The central question is how much better off we should leave them, and at what sacrifice to ourselves.

The Stasis Model.   We can leave future generations at least as well off as us, at some cost to ourselves. We ought to do so. However, we cannot make future generations better-off than ourselves.

The Pessimistic Model.   We cannot avoid leaving future generations worse-off than ourselves. By making significant sacrifices we can reduce the extent to which they are worse-off than us. The crucial questions are: how much worse-off are we allowed to leave them, and how much sacrifice should we make ourselves?

Only thirty years ago the optimistic model was taken for granted by political philosophers. As we saw in Section 2.2, for John Rawls the problem of inter-generational justice *is* the Accumulation (or 'just savings') Problem. How should each generation balance consumption to improve its own standard of living against investment to improve the quality of life of future generations?

After the oil shocks of the early 1970s, the realization that the standard of living of the developed nations currently requires the rapid depletion of non-renewable resources led some philosophers to replace the optimistic model with the stasis model. For instance, Brian Barry explored various intergenerational Lockean constraints on the appropriation and consumption of resources.[12] Even if the nature of our lifestyle makes it very difficult for us to ensure that future generations will always be better-off than we are, we should at least ensure that our depletion of non-renewable resources does not leave them worse-off than us, perhaps by compensating them with the provision of superior technology.

In recent years, debates over carbon emissions, greenhouse gases, ozone depletion, and the serious threat of climate change has brought the pessimistic model to the fore. It may already be too late to prevent future generations being worse-off than us. Furthermore, any feasible proposal to minimize the harmful effects of climate change will involve a major reduction in the standard of living of affluent people in developed countries. The pessimistic model raises many difficult and novel ethical and political questions.

We begin with the optimistic model, and the particular problems posed by intergenerational justice even on this scenario. This will lead us to consider the other two models, especially the pessimistic. I will argue that Rule Consequentialism fares comparatively well under all three models. In

---

[12]   Barry, 'Justice Between Generations'; and Barry, 'Circumstances of Justice and Future Generations'.

Chapter 8, we turn to the more realistic case where we do not know which model applies.

7.6. The Accumulation Problem

Rawls's discussion of the Accumulation Problem challenges any political theory to show that it neither permits too much accumulation (at the expense of present people), nor forbids accumulation entirely. These two goals are obviously in tension. To defend Rule Consequentialism, we must establish two claims:

1. The ideal code does not disregard the interests of the worst-off, or unjustly sacrifice them to assist the better-off.
2. The ideal code does not give *too much* weight to the interests of the worst-off, at the expense of enormous gains to everyone else.

The key to establishing these claims lies in the nature of the lexical level. If the present generation have internalized the ideal code, then they feel entitled to view the world from a perspective that privileges their own interpretation of the lexical level (Sections 5.4 and 6.4.2). They will thus think both that raising someone above the lexical level takes priority over improvements in well-being above that level, and that it is more important to try to raise current people above *our* lexical level, than to enable future people to strive to a higher lexical level.

This priority is reinforced if we adopt the essentially social account of the lexical level sketched in Chapter 3. If each particular lexical level is associated with a certain background social framework, so that no one can live above that level in the absence of that framework, then no one can live above a given lexical level in isolation. On the other hand, once such a framework is in place, people will only live below the lexical level if barriers are placed in their way, so it is almost always more efficient to raise more people above the lexical level than to benefit those already above it.

The Rule Consequentialist justification for these priorities parallels the standard case for all departures from pure impartiality in the ideal code. Concessions to partiality are required if the code is to be teachable to, and implementable by, finite human beings, and if it is to promote the welfare of such beings effectively. Human beings cannot maintain pure impartiality with respect to the lexical level throughout their deliberations. Any attempt to inculcate such impartiality would have undesirable effects.

The partiality justified by this argument has two dimensions. The present generation will give priority to their own well-being, interests, and preferences over the interests and well-being of others. This first priority takes many specific forms. Each individual gives priority to herself, her friends and family, her descendants, those of her contemporaries with whom she is engaged in cooperative projects or with whom she feels solidarity, those who are worse-off, and perhaps future members of her own community. Some of these priorities tell against accumulation, while others lend support to it. For instance, any priority given to one's own descendants obviously conflicts with priority to one's contemporaries. The general impact of priority is likely to tell against accumulation, as most of the preferences of those in the present generation will favour others in the present generation, especially against distant future generations.

Each person in the present generation will also give priority to the current interpretation of the lexical level over other interpretations. The combination of these two kinds of partiality suggests that, for the members of the present generation, the question 'Is the current generation above its own lexical level?' will take precedence over whether future generations are above future lexical levels.

Rule Consequentialism thus allows the present generation to accord some priority to themselves, especially to those who are below the lexical level. However, this priority is certainly not absolute. The current generation are aware that their interpretation is only one possible interpretation of the lexical level, and later generations have their own different (and, in some respects, superior) interpretations. Members of the current generation may still want future people, especially those to whom they feel particularly connected, to have aspirations that exceed their own.

Giving priority to one's own generation thus does not necessarily rule out a desire to accumulate for the benefit of future people. Indeed, there are several general reasons to expect accumulation.

1. Depending on the situation of early generations, capital accumulation may not require any significant sacrifice. To begin at the beginning, many hunter/gatherer societies are characterized by a relative abundance of leisure time. Devoting that spare time to the accumulation of cultural capital, which is then bequeathed to subsequent generations, requires no sacrifice from early generations.

This convergence of interests across generations is not just a feature of hunter/gatherer societies. Among the most valuable things any generation can bequeath to subsequent generations are a set of just, flexible, democratic institutions together with scientific and technological knowledge. The maintenance of just institutions and the advancement of technological research are also among the best ways to meet the needs and satisfy the preferences of those currently alive. Present investment in basic scientific research will benefit people in the future. However, these are not all *future people*. If research leads to a cure for cancer in forty years, then this benefits not only future people but also many currently existing people. In favourable circumstances, the present generation can ensure that future generations are better-off without forgoing anything for themselves. (This argument may seem to prove too much. Will the present generation favour scientific research ahead of meeting the basic needs of disadvantaged present citizens? We return to this question shortly.)

2. Most individuals in the present generation have powerful reasons to promote the improved welfare of some future people. Depending on our account of human well-being, the success of future people may itself improve the lives of those in the first generation, as that success is certainly intimately related to many of their most cherished projects. There is value in being the founding generation of a flourishing civilization. Accordingly, each generation can be expected to choose a higher level of investment than is strictly required. This will include individual investment for particular future people, contribution to specific institutions and projects extending into the future, and improving the general social framework of institutions and opportunities.

Both for individuals, and for the present generation as a whole, these projects conflict with concern for their worst-off contemporaries. (This conflict is especially pronounced in the international case, where the worst-off contemporaries are people in distant lands. See Section 9.2.)

3. Due to the context-dependence of the lexical level, the current generation may be satisfied with a certain quality of life, even as they strive to create a society where lives of that quality are no longer considered adequate. Their satisfaction with their own lot helps to explain why, even if those who have internalized the idea code will not feel *obliged* to make sacrifices to improve things for their descendants, they will voluntarily make (what they regard as) supererogatory sacrifices to assist future generations to aspire to a significantly higher quality of life.

4. The adoption of holistic evaluations of possible histories for a given society could also support a preference for accumulation, as such evaluations may value a society where well-being steadily improves over time more highly than one where it remains static or declines, even if the total well-being across the whole history is the same in all three cases. Even if our fundamental value theory rejects holistic evaluations, those who have internalized the ideal code might adopt them, in regard to either the lives of their immediate descendents, to the future fortune of their entire family line or community, or of humanity as a whole. Such evaluations would provide further stimulus for the beneficial combination of accumulation for future generations and present satisfaction with one's lot. (See also Section 8.2.)

I would suggest that the fact that voluntary accumulation is likely is sufficient to defend Rule Consequentialism. The decisive intuition here is that accumulation should not be forbidden. We may well accept a theory on which accumulation is both permissible and probable, even if it is not obligatory. I doubt that we have a strong intuition that accumulation *is* obligatory, especially when it involves sacrificing the interests of some of those who are comparatively worse off. Even if we do have such an intuition, it should be regarded as distinguishing rather than decisive. (By contrast, the No Worse-off and Non-Depletion principles are decisive. One of the key merits of Rule Consequentialism is that it explains this divergence.)

On the other hand, if our foundational value theory includes holistic evaluations of human history that accord sufficient weight to accumulation, then we may prefer an ideal code where accumulation is compulsory rather than optional. This seems to me the right result. It suggests that, while there is a decisive intuition that accumulation should be permitted, the intuition that accumulation is compulsory is a distinctive feature of a certain way of evaluating human histories.

The most difficult conflict is between the interests of future generations and the worst-off within the present generation. If we are reasonably close to full compliance with the ideal code, then the number of destitute persons is likely to be very small. It should thus be possible to meet all their basic needs, and to enable them to participate fully in the social framework of opportunities, while still leaving considerable resources available for scientific and cultural development. Furthermore, the presence of destitution and inequality might threaten the continued stability of the social framework. If so, then the best thing we could to *for future generations* would be to attempt to reduce destitution and inequality. (This is even more true if, as I argue below, those who have internalized the ideal code are very risk-averse when it comes to the future of a viable social framework (Section 8.2).)

However, some conflicts will inevitably remain, as some people have needs that are extremely difficult to meet. Suppose we must choose between the accumulation of capital for later generations and the provision of adequate opportunities to the most disadvantaged people currently living. Unlike Rawls's liberal egalitarianism, Rule Consequentialism does not give absolute priority to the worst-off (Sections 2.2, 5.4). Accordingly it can permit (indeed, perhaps require) some degree of accumulation even if this means that the social framework cannot be extended to absolutely everyone. For instance, the opportunity cost of extending a full range of social opportunities to the most severely disabled people, or of curing diseases which are extremely expensive to treat, may be too high.[13] As we saw in

---

[13] For Rawls's own attempt to solve the problem of the severely disabled, see Section 2.2.4.2.

Chapter 5, a code requiring everyone in a given generation to make extreme sacrifices to provide for the very worst-off will not be optimal (Section 5.4).

Many standard Rule Consequentialist arguments against a demanding code turn on the costs borne by those who have internalized the ideal code. One might think such arguments have no force in the present case, as what is sacrificed if we meet the needs of the worst-off present people is the interests of future people, not other present people. However, we should note two things:

1. Not all the arguments against striving to meet every need of the worst-off people are based on the cost to the agent. There is also the fact that, under any plausible value theory, a sufficient number of benefits to well-off people can outweigh the cost to the worst-off.
2. Meeting additional existing needs does impose a cost on present people, as the interests of future people that are thereby sacrificed are tied up with their own present projects.

This is an extremely difficult case. Either option can easily be made to seem intuitively implausible. How can it be acceptable to sacrifice the worse-off to provide benefits to the better-off? On the other hand, how can it be acceptable to allow a tiny benefit to a single worse-off person to trump any number of significant benefits to any number of better-off people? Hard cases such as this probably do not admit of any wholly satisfactory resolution. Rule Consequentialism cannot make such hard cases disappear. However, it does present a plausible account of the best way to balance the competing considerations. I argued in Chapter 2 that its leading rival fares much worse. Furthermore, the very fact that it highlights the difficulties inherent in the accumulation problem, rather than sweeping them under the carpet by bracketing them off from 'distributive justice', constitutes a distinct comparative advantage of Rule Consequentialism.

Rule Consequentialism can coherently allow for accumulation across generations. Under full compliance within the optimistic model, this accumulation will not generally be at the expense of disadvantaged members of the present generation. Full compliance with the ideal code should provide for the basic needs of most members of the present generation, and maintain an adequate framework within which to pursue valuable goals. This framework can then be bequeathed to future generations, along with an adequate store of natural resources. The pursuit of goals within the framework by each successive generation inevitably leads to improvements in technology, knowledge, and culture, thus raising the average level of well-being across time, without making anyone worse-off than they might otherwise have been. If we relax either of our two initial assumptions (the optimistic model and full compliance), however, then conflicts between the interests of presently disadvantaged people, our desire to aid future generations, and our pursuit of our own goals may become acute. We return to these two problems in Section 7.9 and Chapter 10.

The Accumulation Problem only arises under the optimistic model. We cannot ask how much better-off subsequent generations should be unless we can make them better-off. Our discussion has thus assumed the optimistic model. Our next two problems can also arise on the optimistic model, and it is under that model that we initially discuss them. However, these new problems are most troubling on the pessimistic model. Indeed, our discussion of them will bring out the reasons why this model has recently come to the fore.

7.7. Non-Renewable Resources

Non-renewable resources raise puzzles for many accounts of intergenerational justice, especially those based on the appealing notion that each generation should use only its 'fair share' of any given resource, or that resource use is only justified if one leaves 'as much and as good for others'. (Section 2.1.1). The puzzle is that, if the stock of a given resource is finite while the future population is (potentially) infinite, then each generation's 'fair share' of the resource is zero.

Rule Consequentialism easily permits the use of non-renewable resources. A moral rule forbidding anyone ever to utilize a given resource is clearly sub-optimal. So those who have internalized the ideal code will be inclined to permit utilization in at least some circumstances. The precise details of that utilization will, of course, depend upon a range of empirical considerations. In particular, we would need to know (a) what the resource is used for, (b) what would be the consequences of abandoning or severely restricting its use for the present generation, (c) whether the resource is more useful in some circumstances than in others, and (d) whether any substitutes are likely to be forthcoming.

The last issue is perhaps the most significant. In many actual cases, the appropriate policy for a non-renewable resource might be to utilize it fully for as long as it lasts, devoting some of the material and social capital thus generated to the search for alternative (preferably renewable) sources of energy or food.[14] Education and research are likely to be much better

---

[14] Indeed, if one could be sufficiently confident of success, this might even be the optimal utilization strategy for some renewable resources. However, for reasons outlined in Sections 8.1.2 and 8.2, running-down a renewable resource will generally be a last resort in the ideal society.

resourced under full compliance with the ideal code than in the actual world, so considerable optimism may be justified. Therefore, the fact that it involves the use of a non-renewable resource will not be a knock-down objection to a course of action. (However, this use of non-renewable resources increases the uncertainty surrounding our relations with future generations. See Section 8.2.)

If substitutes are unlikely to be forthcoming, then resource use must be rationed. One obvious approach is to restrict utilization to circumstances where the resource would be most useful. (Perhaps oil would be most valuable during an ice age, for instance.) However, this strategy is unlikely to prove efficient, as utilization may end up being constantly deferred. (Although even the policy of indefinite postponement could be appropriate in extreme circumstances, if a resource which present generations can do without might be needed to avert a future catastrophe. See Section 8.2.)

One solution to this dilemma is as follows. Under the optimistic model, anyone living in a society where the ideal code is widely internalized will expect average well-being to increase in each successive generation, owing to the gradual accumulation of technical expertise and other social capital. When distributing a non-renewable resource across generations, we are thus distributing across a set of groups whose well-being is (otherwise) unequal. In such circumstances, the most appropriate method is usually to weight our distribution in favour of those who are worse-off, as they are likely to obtain more significant benefit. Accordingly, the members of the present generation will utilize the resource, with each subsequent generation utilizing it to a lesser extent, until it is depleted. The precise details of the rate of utilization will depend, of course, on the nature of the resource itself. (What if the non-renewable resource is essential to well-being, so that we cannot live above our own lexical level without it? The short answer is that this possibility is inconsistent with the optimistic model, so we will return to it later.)

I conclude that, while they raise many difficult questions in practice, non-renewable resources pose no specific theoretical problems for Rule Consequentialism under the optimistic model. If there are patterns of use for any non-renewable resource that enable us, not only to preserve our own quality of life, but also to leave future generations better-off, then the problem of non-renewable resources is thus swamped by the Accumulation Problem. Particular problems arise in relation to non-renewable resources only if the scale of our reliance on those resources threatens the optimistic model. This could be because no substitutes are available, but it is more likely to be because our use of non-renewable resources has a negative impact.

7.8. Growth and the Environment

Suppose we discover that our use of resources has a negative impact on the environment—an impact that threatens the well-being of future generations. This possibility raises very serious intergenerational issues. Much depends upon the facts of the case. For the moment, we continue to operate within the optimistic model. Therefore, we assume that the present use of the resource facilitates technological advances which future generations could use to compensate for the environmental degradation. I shall argue that, even given this optimistic assumption, the use of the resource is not unproblematic.

Even if they are convinced of this account of the facts, those who have internalized the ideal code will still be wary of permitting resource utilization. Suppose the use of the resource at current levels will fuel economic progress, but destroy the last remaining population of a rare species of bird. The present generation estimate that the benefits of economic growth will outweigh the loss of the bird. There are several reasons why they might nonetheless still wish to preserve the bird and forgo the resource utilization. In such a case, the No Worse-off and Non-Depletion principles might come apart. The present generation will feel reluctant to violate the Non-Depletion Principle, even if they believe that they will leave future generations better-off overall.

Why might the present generation behave in this way? One argument would appeal to the traditional economic notion of an 'option value'. The bird might be much more valuable to future generations than we expect, as future generations will exploit some hitherto unsuspected feature of the bird. (Such arguments are often used to defend the preservation of plant and animal species as potential sources of new medicines. As a result, 'in recent years, it has been argued that projects protecting increasingly rare species ought to be discounted at a lower rate than other projects in the same risk category'.[15])

Option values are certainly significant. Suppose, however, they have already been accounted for. The option value of the bird has been balanced against the option value of a new avenue of pure scientific research made possible only by the proposed resource use. (It would be very difficult to estimate either option value with any precision, but suppose there is no reason to regard one as any greater than the other.)

Even if standard economic option values cancel out, those who have internalized the ideal code might *still* favour preservation, on the grounds of *moral option value*. The notion of a moral option value captures the possibility

---

[15] Dasgupta, *Human Well-being and the Natural Environment*, 190. (See also ibid. 137.)

that the comparative values assigned to different possible outcomes by future generations may differ from those we would assign ourselves. This potential for value change is relevant for two reasons. The first is that, as people's lives go better if they get what *they* value, we should want future people to be able to live according to their own values, whatever we might think of those values.[16]

More significantly, we must allow for the possibility that future generations will have *better* values than ourselves. This is especially likely under full compliance with the ideal code, as wide-ranging debate should improve the clarity of views about value. Such progress is even more likely if public attention is focused on a choice between two competing values. We should thus expect debate over the preservation of the birds to give future generations a clearer idea of the comparative value of a rare species as opposed to the benefits of economic progress. (See also Section 8.1.2.)

While it is interesting in theory, the notion of moral option value may seem unlikely to have any practical relevance. As we cannot predict the future course of debate over values, we cannot possibly know how the moral option value of one resource compares to that of another. So moral option values can never give us a reason to favour one course of action over another.

This pessimism is overstated. Of course we cannot predict the precise course of future debate in moral philosophy, any more than in science. (Indeed, our inability to make such predictions plays a key role in the defence of majoritarian democracy in Section 8.1.2.) However, we can make reasonable speculations. I limit myself to two.

Rule Consequentialism places great emphasis on autonomy, particularly moral autonomy. Those who have internalized the ideal code will regard the ability to make rational choices between genuinely incommensurable options as one of the most valuable aspects of human life (Sections 6.2, 7.2). They will thus be very wary of projecting into the future any argument based on the commensurability of different values, in case future generations come to regard the different resources as genuinely incommensurable, and greatly regret no longer being able to choose between them. (In addition, even if they grant the assumption that x and y are in principle commensurable, those who have internalized the ideal code will be very wary of allowing y to disappear on the basis of current judgments about the comparative value of x as opposed to y.)

---

[16] Given that people both enjoy and desire getting what they value, the claim in the text holds true on any theory of well-being that values either pleasure or preference-satisfaction, even if it does not explicitly value living in accordance with one's values. No plausible theory of well-being attaches no value to any of these three things.

The original argument from Section 6.2 is based on incommensurability between lifestyle choices. This is distinct from incommensurable values. However, the value of any lifestyle choice is related to the values realized by participation in that lifestyle. An agent is much more likely to face a choice between incommensurable lifestyle options if she inhabits a world containing radically different sources of value, in particular both cultural and natural values. So the present generation will be unwilling to prejudge the value of the existence of the birds for future generations.

A second source of information about moral option values is extrapolation from the recent history of debate about values in our own societies. That history points to an expansion of those values, in two key dimensions. The first dimension is that more different kinds of values come to be widely recognized. Pluralist accounts of value are now the norm, both in moral philosophy and in public debate. The second expansion is that the scope of our moral concern has expanded. Many of the most significant social changes of the last few hundred years have involved the extension to new groups of a moral standing initially reserved for an elite few. If such expansions were to continue in the ideal society, then the lives of birds might be accorded considerably greater value in the future than at present. Such extrapolations are very unreliable. However, as we shall now see, they are not necessarily any less reliable than predictions regarding the course of economic growth, on which the contrary argument is likely to rest.

The preceding discussion assumes that the economic benefits of technological investment are known to exceed the value of the environmental loss, at least according to current theories of value. This is in keeping with our focus on the optimistic model. However, environmental issues bring out the clearest case against that model. Rejection of the implicit values of the optimistic model (in particular, the assumption that all environmental losses can in principle be compensated by economic growth) often goes along with rejection of its empirical optimism. Opponents of the optimistic model argue that, even in terms of its own values, the model is implausible. In a recent survey of the literature on the relationship between economic growth and environmental degradation, Partha Dasgupta observes 'a cultural divide between growth economists and those who see the natural environment as playing an essential role in our lives'.[17] Growth optimists argue that technological progress and human inventiveness will always greatly outweigh any negative impact on the environment. Economic growth is thus confidently projected indefinitely into the future, irrespective of the rate of population growth. Ecological pessimists caution against placing 'such an enormous burden on an economic regime

[17] Dasgupta, *Human Well-being and the Natural Environment*, 131.

not much more than 250 years old'.[18] A good example of this division is the wide disagreement over the likely impact of climate change on the well-being and prosperity of future generations. If those in the ideal society are ecological pessimists (or even if they regard ecological pessimism as plausible), then they will be reluctant to bank on future growth outweighing definite up-front environmental loss (Section 9.2.7).

7.9. The Pessimistic Model

Having seen how Rule Consequentialism deals with the optimistic model, we now turn to the other two scenarios. We can quickly dispose of the stasis model. If we know that, while our reliance on non-renewable resources renders it impossible for us to leave future generations better-off than ourselves, we are still able to leave them no worse-off, then the ideal code will presumably tell us to satisfy the No Worse-off Principle and act to ensure a constant level of well-being for future generations. As I argued in Sections 7.3 and 7.4, in a world of constant well-being across generations, intergenerational justice raises no special issues for Rule Consequentialism.[19]

Unfortunately, the stasis model is very contrived. Given the complex array of variables involved, it is vanishingly unlikely that we could be confident both that *no* accumulation is possible *and* that we can satisfy the No Worse-off Principle. If we lose confidence in the optimistic model, then it seems inevitable that we will be led to the other extreme.

The pessimistic model raises very difficult moral issues for any theory. It is thus no particular objection to Rule Consequentialism that it will struggle to provide intuitively satisfactory guidance here. However, I believe that our version of Rule Consequentialism is especially well-equipped for the pessimistic model, at least compared to its rivals. Once again, the device of the context-dependent lexical level plays a key role.

The politics of the pessimistic model are in many ways similar to those of the optimistic model. In both cases those who had internalized the ideal code must balance their own projects, interests, and needs against those of their friends, their descendants, and their contemporaries. Many of the same considerations and priorities will apply. Our present interest is solely in differences. How will the shift from the optimistic model to the pessimistic model change political attitudes in the ideal society?

---

[18] Ibid. 130. For a more optimistic view, see Beckerman and Pasek, *Justice, Posterity and the Environment*.

[19] The theoretical interest of the stasis model, taken in isolation, is due primarily to the re-emergence of libertarian approaches to political philosophy, such as those of Nozick and Gauthier, on which even the No Worse-off Principle is difficult to justify. (Earlier discussions of these implications are Barry, 'Justice Between Generations'; and Barry, 'Circumstances of Justice and Future Generations'. See also Section 2.1 above.)

Under the pessimistic model, by definition, a decline in future well-being is inevitable, even under full compliance with the best feasible moral code. Our ideal code must include rules covering such decline. When discussing accumulation, I argued that those who had internalized the ideal code would most likely feel *permitted* to raise the well-being of future generations, even at some cost to themselves, but would not feel *obliged* to do so. By contrast, in the pessimistic model, the present generation *will* feel obliged to make (significantly greater) sacrifices to mitigate the decline in well-being for future generations

One reason for this difference is that, although they recognize the value of a constantly rising lexical level, those who have internalized the ideal code privilege their own lexical level when balancing the competing demands of their own projects, the needs of their contemporaries, and the needs of future generations (Sections 5.4, 6.4.2, 7.6). So they will have a much stronger motivation to avoid future decline than to promote accumulation. This conclusion is reinforced by the fact that decline will often interfere with a present person's own projects, as it disrupts continuity between generations, whereas a lack of accumulation does not generally have the same disruptive affect. The present generation will thus make significant sacrifices to limit the degree to which subsequent generations fall below the present lexical level.

In the case of an individual, there is a clear asymmetry between looking forward to losing what one has had and looking forward to the loss of a potential improvement or enhancement of one's quality of life. The former is more strongly felt as a loss—partly because it is much easier to visualize what is lost, and partly because the standard that one's future life fails to meet is already built into one's conception of oneself, and of what constitutes the value of one's life.

There is an analogous asymmetry when present people contemplate a decline in future quality of life as opposed to the loss of potential improvement, especially regarding the impact on the present generation's own interpretation of the lexical level. Reflecting on the possibility of future advances in well-being is unlikely to lead the present generation to raise their own aspirations for themselves. Knowing that future generations will adopt a higher interpretation of the lexical level will not lead us to adopt that interpretation for ourselves: partly because it is unattainable for us, partly because it is to some extent unimaginable (we do not know what the future lexical interpretation will look like), and partly because we are satisfied with meeting our own lexical level.

By contrast, the prospect of a sharp decline in well-being for their children or grandchildren will lead the present generation to reflect on, and perhaps revise, their own interpretation of the lexical level. In particular, if present people realize that their own lifestyle is unsustainable, they will focus their minds on finding the highest quality of life that is sustainable, and ask themselves if they can reinterpret the lexical level to accommodate that kind of life. A lower, or at least a less resource-intensive, interpretation of the lexical level would be both attainable and imaginable, so reinterpretation is more likely in the pessimistic case than the optimistic.

Suppose the present generation realize that, at some future date, all subsequent generations will inevitably fall below our current lexical level. If they adopted a simple lexical view, the present generation would adopt a policy of putting off that date as long as possible, thereby maximizing the number of future people above the lexical level, even if the result is much worse for more distant generations. (This is yet another instance of the potentially unattractive inegalitarianism of the Lexical View: it seems to urge us to maximize the number of people above the lexical level at the expense of those who cannot be raised above that level. Section 3.5.)

Fortunately, the context-dependent lexical level mitigates this result. It leads the present generation to prefer a strategy of slowly sinking lexical levels, where each generation has a chance to adjust its conception of the lexical level and strive to meet that new level (Section 6.4.2).

The Rule Consequentialist case for including such a disposition in the ideal code is comparatively straightforward. If resources are scarce, the best outcome is one where as many people as possible live above the lexical level, minimally defined. One reason the device of the context-dependent lexical level is incorporated in the ideal code is that, in favourable conditions, it enables a progressive increase in the threshold that each generation achieves. The flip side is that, if conditions decline, we want as many generations as possible to feel that both they and their descendants are living above the lexical level, as setting a lexical standard one cannot meet is a major cause of frustration and disappointment.

Similar considerations apply both to intergenerational justice under decline (where the privileged minority is the present generation) and to international justice in an unequal world (where the minority is affluent people in developed nations). We return to the international case in Chapter 9. However, there is reason to expect a stronger disposition to seek a more moderate sustainable interpretation of the lexical level in the intergenerational case, as future generations of one's own society are intimately connected to one's basic goals and accomplishments. The present generation may come to believe that their own lives go much worse if their descendants will be much worse off than themselves.

The crucial question, as ever, is the level of sacrifice demanded. In contrast to the case of accumulation under the optimistic model, there is no guarantee here that, even under full compliance, the demands of Rule Consequentialism will not be extreme. Much depends, of course, on how pessimistic our pessimistic model is. How much worse-off will future people be? However this is not a decisive objection to Rule Consequentialism, as it is not clear what level of demand or sacrifice is intuitively reasonable under the pessimistic model. On the other hand, the very fact that Rule Consequentialism is more demanding under the pessimistic models than the optimistic is itself intuitively plausible. In any event, we postpone full discussion of the demands of Rule Consequentialism to Chapter 10.

Rule Consequentialism delivers quite different advice in the three models. This is part of its intuitive appeal, but it leads to a serious problem. In reality, we do not know which of our three models applies. We suffer both from empirical ignorance (we do not know what future outcomes are possible) and value ignorance (we are not sure how to evaluate different possible futures). As its advice depends on what model applies, Rule Consequentialism owes us either a resolution of our uncertainty or an account of how to act in the face of it. As no moral theory could remove our uncertainty entirely, we now ask how Rule Consequentialism might deal with uncertainty.

8

Disagreement and Uncertainty

Our previous discussion made two simplifying assumptions: that we know the outcome of any particular policy, and that everyone who has internalized the ideal code will have the same political attitudes and make the same political decisions. In reality, decisions regarding future generations are plagued by disagreement and uncertainty. The dispute between growth optimists and ecological pessimists is a classic example (Section 7.8). Given the enormous complexities, it makes little sense to be confidently on either side of that debate.

The simplest way to deal with uncertainty is to ignore it. We examine various possible outcomes, and ask what a moral agent should do if she knows which outcome would result from each action. Our moral theory thus generates a series of conditional claims of the following form: 'If the consequences will be x, then do y.' The simplest way to deal with disagreement is to treat it as resulting from uncertainty, and then ignore it too. Once uncertainty is removed, all competent moral agents will agree.

This strategy is helpful when trying to clarify the nature and implications of a moral theory. However, as we saw in Section 5.6, it is inadequate as a general response to uncertainty. Uncertainty is a defining feature of human life, especially in regard to future generations. Any adequate moral theory must both respond to the uncertainty of moral theorists, and tell us how moral agents should respond to their own uncertainty. Uncertainty is especially significant for Rule Consequentialism, as the theory is built on departures from Simple Consequentialism motivated by human fallibility. One area where humans display their 'fallibility', as compared to perfect rational calculators, is in their responses to uncertainty. So we must ask how those who have internalized the ideal code might cope with uncertainty.

Uncertainty regarding future generations takes many forms. Suppose we do not know the carrying capacity of our planet (how many people it can sustain), the available store of non-renewable resources, the degree of renewability of many other resources, what future uses resources may have, or whether substitutes will be found in the future. We are unsure of the potential negative future impact of our current technology, lifestyles, and rate of utilization of resources, and of the likely impact of alternative lifestyles. We worry that our present lifestyle is seriously damaging the planet, but we cannot be sure that there is a significantly less damaging alternative available. We also do not know if our current rate of technological progress will one day prove to have been necessary to enable future generations to avoid some particular disaster.

If *we* could resolve our uncertainty regarding any of these factors, then this resolution would obviously have a significant impact on our political decisions, especially in regard to population policy and resource utilization. Suppose, however, that we cannot resolve our uncertainty, and must act in spite of it. Furthermore, within the present generation there is considerable disagreement concerning the likely consequences of different courses of action, and also regarding the values to place on different outcomes.

As Rule Consequentialists, we decide how we should act by asking how those who have internalized the ideal code will respond to disagreement and uncertainty. Two key issues are their attitude to disagreement and their attitude to risk. We take each in turn.

8.1. Disagreement and Democracy

How will public policy decisions be made in the ideal society? We might assume that, as everyone in that society has internalized the same ideal code, there will be unanimity regarding public policy. Unfortunately, this answer is too simple. Even in the ideal society, we should not expect complete agreement about the appropriate policies or institutions of government. While much real-world disagreement does result from moral differences, we should still expect disagreement in the ideal society for three basic reasons.

1. Much disagreement is not due to moral differences. For instance, people often disagree over complicated empirical questions. While those who have internalized the ideal code may pay more attention to these issues, there is no guarantee that disagreement would thereby disappear. (Consider the disagreements between ecological pessimists and economic optimists: both groups who have studied the relevant question in some detail.)

2. Those who have internalized the ideal code do not always agree about moral values. Different interpretations of flexible moral rules, especially due to cultural differences or different lifestyle priorities or different attitudes to risk, can arise and cause disagreement even under full compliance.

3. Even under idealized conditions of perfect full compliance, there is thus no compelling reason to expect unanimity regarding complex political

decisions. Further disagreement will result from the fact that not everyone has internalized as the ideal code.[1]

If we believe that many political questions are matters about which reasonable people genuinely disagree, then we should expect such disagreement to persist even if everyone has internalized the ideal code.[2] Of course, their disagreements may be different from ours. The question is whether they will be any less pervasive. Although many political theorists implicitly assume the absence of radical disagreement in any ideally just society, the history of political philosophy, and of Western democratic culture in general, does not support this assumption.

So the ideal society must find some way to resolve disagreements. Democratic procedures are likely to be favoured on both intrinsic and instrumental grounds. Democratic institutions are more likely to select public policies that promote aggregate welfare. (Furthermore, either our foundational value theory or the values espoused by those in the ideal society might view the ability to participate in decisions regarding the government of one's society as a central component of individual autonomy, and hence as directly enhancing well-being. Section 6.2.) Democracy reflects both individual and communal autonomy, and best promotes other valuable ends.

The instrumental argument for democracy is familiar in the Consequentialist tradition, going back at least to J. S. Mill (Section 7.2).[3] Amartya Sen's work on the prevention of famine provides a striking recent illustration of the general Consequentialist claim that democracy is the most reliable way to promote people's interests.[4] Sen argues that, in combination with a free press, democracy provides rulers with strong incentives to prevent famine, and that the practical result is that famines do not occur in democracies, whereas they do occur in despotic regimes in similar circumstances. More

---

[1] For other reasons why the ideal society may contain disagreements about morality, see Mulgan, 'Ruling Out Rule Consequentialism' (2000).

[2] For a robust defence of this diagnosis of political disagreement, and of its implications for democratic theory, see Waldron, *Law and Disagreement*.

[3] Mill, *Representative Government*. For a recent discussion, see Nelson, 'Open Government and Just Legislation'.

[4] For a recent survey, see Sen, *Development as Freedom*, 170–5. Sen summarizes his own conclusions as follows: 'It is not surprising that no famine has taken place in the history of the world in a functioning democracy, be it economically rich (as in contemporary Western Europe or North America) or relatively poor (as in postindependence India, or Botswana, or Zimbabwe). Famines have tended to occur in colonial territories governed by rulers from elsewhere (as in British India or in an Ireland administered by alienated English rulers), or in one-party states (as in the Ukraine in the 1930s, or China during 1958–61, or Cambodia in the 1970s), or in military dictatorships (as in Ethiopia, or Somalia, or some of the Sahel countries in the near past).' (ibid. 16). It is a sad irony that Sen lists Zimbabwe as a poor famine-free democracy. The disastrous consequences of the current transition from democracy to one-party state in Zimbabwe reinforces Sen's conclusions.

broadly, a positive correlation between democracy and a variety of indicators of well-being (including real net income per head, economic growth, infant survival rates, and life expectancy at birth) is well established in the empirical literature. Partha Dasgupta concludes a recent summary of that literature with the observation that '[t]he argument that democracy is a luxury that poor countries cannot afford is buried by the data, such as they are.'[5]

The debate over the merits of democracy takes different forms in the developing and developed worlds. In the former, the question is whether democracy is superior to despotic or authoritarian alternatives. The literature just cited strongly suggests that it is. However, despotism is no longer a live option for Western nations, nor is it likely to appeal as a candidate for the ideal society. In the developed world, the choice is between different forms of democracy. In particular, debate centres on the comparative merits of unfettered majoritarian democracy as opposed to a system where the legislature is constrained by an entrenched constitution interpreted by an independent judiciary. For the sake of simplicity, I shall refer to these as the Westminster Model and the American Model respectively. (Of course, all real-world democracies are much more complex than either of these simple models.) The choice between the two models is obviously most significant when the proposed constitution would restrict the majoritarian decisions of future generations, and we discuss it exclusively in this context.

In contrast to the debate between despotism and democracy, this more rarefied debate tends to be largely a priori rather than empirical. There is surprisingly little solid empirical evidence on the relative merits of the American and Westminster systems, especially from a Consequentialist perspective. In particular, although much of the philosophical literature favours the American model over the Westminster system, there appears to be no empirical evidence that, on balance, the former does a better job of promoting aggregate well-being, or any other aggregate measure, than the latter.[6]

---

[5] Dasgupta, *Human Well-being and the Natural Environment*, 75. See also ibid. 66–75; Dasgupta, *Well-being and Destitution*, 116–21, and the many works cited there. Recent studies of the correlation between democracy and national per capita income include Burkhart and Lewis-Beck, 'Comparative Democracy'; Londregan and Poole, 'Does High Income Promote Democracy?'; Przeworski and Limongi, 'Modernization: Theories and Facts'; and Barro, 'Determinants of Democracy'. As some of these titles suggest, the literature indicates that high incomes stand in a mutually supporting relationship with democracy. Economic growth is both a cause and an effect of the transition to democracy. (For more discussion, see Section 9.3.2.)

Of course, there are exceptions to these general correlations, but, as Dasgupta notes, 'There is no policy prescription flowing from such examples as Singapore and Hong Kong'. (*Well-being and Destitution*, 127). One significant group of apparent exceptions is discussed at length in Section 9.3.2.

[6] A recent excellent summary of the available empirical evidence is Shapiro, *The Moral Foundations of Politics*, 213–19. In particular, Shapiro highlights the lack of evidence of a link between the American

Nor is there any evidence the other way. Unlike the choice between democracy and despotism, this new choice cannot be so easily settled.

There are several reasons for this lack of empirical evidence. No doubt measurement problems play a role. While the contrast between democracy and authoritarianism is comparatively clear-cut, democratic regimes come in degrees. Even the most entrenched constitution can be amended by a sufficient majority (either in the legislature or in the population as a whole) and no actual democratic legislature feels free to completely ignore traditional constitutional values. It is thus no easy task to divide actual democratic states neatly between the two models. Furthermore, democratic nations of all stripes tend to have relatively good civil rights records, compared to despotic regimes, so the standard data might not be sufficiently sensitive to reveal any systematic differences between democracies. Finally, while transitions from authoritarianism to democracy (and vice versa) are quite common, transitions from one type of democracy to another are rare. Democratic nations tend to be strongly attached to their own system. One key source of empirical information is thus lacking in this case.

The attachment of citizens of democratic nations to their own system is itself a likely explanation for the lack of reliable empirical data on this issue. Many theorists seem to rest content with a priori demonstrations of the superiority of whatever passes for democracy in the land of their birth. In particular, the best critiques of either system tend to come from theorists who have grown up under one system and lived as adults under the other.[7]

In the present section I sketch a Rule Consequentialist case in favour of the Westminster system over the American. The philosophical literature on this comparison is vast, and I cannot hope to engage it all directly here. My aim is not to settle this debate, but merely to indicate what the introduction of an intergenerational Rule Consequentialist perspective might contribute to it. Section 8.1.1 assesses two common anti-majoritarian arguments, while Section 8.1.2 sketches a new Consequentialist argument for majoritarian democracy in the intergenerational context.

---

model and the protection of individual rights, both in the United States itself and also in other nations. (On the United States debate, see also Dahl, 'Decision Making in a Democracy'; Dahl, *Democracy and its Critics*, 188–92; Dahl, *How Democratic is the American Constitution?*, ch. 3; and Hirschl, *Towards Juristocracy*. On the alleged link between individual rights and the American model in other nations, see Hirschl, 'The Political Origins of Judicial Empowerment through Constitutionalization'.)

[7] I am thinking in particular of Jeremy Waldron's critiques of the American model from a Westminster (specifically New Zealand) perspective and Ronald Dworkin's critiques of the Westminster model from an American perspective (Waldron, *Law and Disagreement*; and Dworkin, *Freedom's Law*).

8.1.1. Rawls's Two Arguments

We will focus on two arguments from John Rawls.[8] Most arguments for the American model mirror one or other of these two arguments. Also, a comparison between Rawls's liberal egalitarianism and our Rule Consequentialism is an underlying theme of this part of the book. Rawls expresses two different attitudes to the choice between an entrenched constitution placing specific limits on future democratic deliberation, and an unfettered majoritarian democracy. In *Political Liberalism* Rawls admits that 'some will say that parliamentary supremacy with no bill of rights at all is superior to our dualist regime. It offers firmer support for the values that higher law in the dualist scheme tries to secure.'[9] He goes on to say that 'political liberalism as such, it should be stressed, does not assert or deny any of these claims and so we need not discuss them....[Rawls's] remarks on the [United States] Supreme Court are not intended as a defence of judicial review, although it can perhaps be defended given certain historical circumstances and conditions of political culture.'[10]

However, in a number of other places, Rawls explicitly argues in favour of the American model. He presents two basic arguments. (These arguments originate within Rawls's 'Original Position' framework. I have revised them for use in a Rule Consequentialist theory.)

1. The Argument from Basic Rights.   An entrenched constitution guarantees basic rights whereas majoritarian democracy does not.

2. The Sociological Argument.   'The greater educational role of a political conception in a constitutional regime may alter its political sociology so as to favour it over procedural democracy.'[11]

Some of Rawls's claims are more plausible when applied across generations. Majoritarian democracy obviously cannot guarantee that basic needs and liberties will be respected in perpetuity.

Rawls's arguments for the American model parallel his arguments for the two principles of justice over the principle of utility. Many utilitarian critics of Rawls accuse him of a double standard, on the grounds that he compares the worst-case scenario for utilitarianism with an ideal form of his two principles of justice.[12] A similar objection applies to many versions of the argument from basic rights. The worst imaginable excesses of majority

---

[8] Two recent explorations of Rawls's complex attitude to democracy are Cohen, 'For a Democratic Society', and Gutmann, 'Rawls on the Relationship between Liberalism and Democracy'.

[9] Rawls, *Political Liberalism*, 234.   [10] Ibid. 235, 240.

[11] Rawls, *Justice as Fairness: A Restatement*, 147.

[12] For an overview and references to the debate, see Scheffler, 'Rawls and Utilitarianism' (2001), 155 ff.

rule are contrasted with the ideal protection promised by an entrenched constitution. (One finds this most strikingly in tedious sophmoronic arguments beginning 'Of course, Hitler was elected ...'.)

Obviously enough, no constitutional system, on its own, guarantees anything. To take an extreme example, young girls in New Zealand do not enjoy an entrenched constitutional protection against female genital mutilation, whereas young girls in Senegal do. Yet the rates of female genital mutilation are considerably higher in Senegal than in New Zealand.[13] More generally, recent years have seen a high level of migration between New Zealand (a land with no constitutionally entrenched rights) and South Africa (a country with an entrenched constitution). The desire for basic security is often cited as a prime motivation for such moves. Yet the direction of emigration is the opposite to what any a priori argument from basic rights would lead us to expect.

These extreme examples remind us that the culture and circumstances of a nation count for more than constitutional formalities. An entrenched constitution can fail just as spectacularly as majoritarian democracy. The relevant comparison, for the purposes of Rule Consequentialism, is between affluent nations with established democratic traditions of different types. When we turn to such comparisons, we find no reliable evidence, either systematic or anecdotal, to support the argument from basic rights. To take the four countries I am most familiar with personally, there is no reason to believe that basic rights are not any more secure in Australia or the United States than in New Zealand or the United Kingdom.

Our present concern is with the comparative merits of the two systems under full compliance. The argument from basic rights would only be relevant if there were reliable evidence that a democratic system would be more likely to fail to protect basic rights even among people who had internalized the rest of the ideal code. This seems highly unlikely, as most purported cases of such failure involve the 'tyranny of the majority'—something which is especially unlikely when the majority have internalized the ideal code.

This brings us to Rawls's sociological argument. Rawls suggests that 'the greater educational role of a political conception in a constitutional regime may alter its political sociology so as to favour it over procedural democracy.' He explains the thought behind this argument as follows. 'The political sociology of a constitutional regime will differ from that of a procedural democracy. The conceptions of person and society are more fully articulated in the public charter of the constitution and more clearly connected with the basic rights and liberties it guarantees.'[14] In other words, basic

---

[13] I owe this striking example to Gerry Mackie.

[14] Rawls, *Justice as Fairness: A Restatement*, 146.

rights will be more secure under an American model, because people who grow up under such a system will more strongly identify themselves (and one another) as persons with certain inalienable rights. This argument, unlike the previous one, might apply under full compliance with the ideal code.

This is a difficult claim to disprove, but we should note three crucial points:

1. The argument rests on a quasi-empirical claim, for which no empirical evidence is provided, especially not by Rawls.

2. Following Rawls's a priori method, one could just as easily construct arguments for the opposite conclusion. Consider an argument based on J. S. Mill's defence of freedom of thought.[15] If certain options are placed off the political agenda from the start, then people's understanding of, and commitment to, the options that remain will be less well founded, and hence less resilient, than if the protection of basic rights had been a commitment that needed to be continually re-defended and re-affirmed. An alternative argument, closer to Rawls's own, might appeal to the sociological possibility that an entrenched constitution will have a dangerously infantilizing effect on future generations. Such a constitution removes the most basic political decisions, those regarding basic rights, from the hands of the people. People who have grown up under such a constitution may come to believe that their own judgements regarding basic rights are worthless, or at least unreliable, and that the protection of basic rights is nothing to do with them. They may thus be less likely to stand up for basic rights if these come under threat, or to object to a government that fails to respect their judgement as citizens.[16] It is anyone's guess which of these contrasting pieces of a priori political sociology is closer to the truth, especially under full compliance with the ideal code.

3. Rawls's argument assumes that we can identify in advance which basic rights and liberties should be removed from the political agenda in perpetuity. This questionable assumption brings us to the positive case for majoritarian democracy.

8.1.2. Moral Progress

Democratic decision-making has a specific advantage in the context of intergenerational Rule Consequentialist ethics. Our methodology in

---

[15] Mill, *On Liberty*, ch. 2.

[16] This last argument could, in principle, be tested empirically. Suppose the governments of two countries, following the American and Westminster models respectively, both deceive their citizens. To take an extreme case, suppose both governments tell the same half-truths to justify an unjust war fought for other reasons. The argument in the text predicts that the citizens of the Westminster country will be outraged, while those in the other nation will be more apathetic.

philosophical ethics assumes that ethical progress is possible. (Otherwise, why do moral philosophy at all?) Some changes in values thus constitute moral progress. In particular, if the values of those who had internalized the ideal moral code would differ in any way from our own, then we should definitely see this as an improvement in values, rather than a morally neutral change (Section 7.8).

This raises an interesting question. Should we seek

1. a moral code that maximizes what we now regard as being valuable, or
2. a code that maximizes what is actually valuable?[17]

In practice, there is usually no difference between the two. Our best guide to what is actually valuable is what, after due reflection, we currently take to be valuable. When we consider the appropriate response to value change in the ideal society, however, the two goals come apart. If we adopt the second goal, then we will place a high priority on the exploration of new values within the ideal society—a task that is largely irrelevant (or possibly even counter-productive) if we are following the first goal. Faced with this potential divergence, it seems clear that we should seek to maximize what is actually valuable.

Of course, if we knew now exactly how values would change in the ideal society, then this knowledge, together with the argument in the previous paragraph, should lead us reflectively to endorse those new values, and build them into the foundational value theory we use to evaluate the ideal code. Just as, if we knew exactly what scientific advances would arise in future, we could use this knowledge to equip the ideal code with specific rules for specific new technologies. Yet we lack such knowledge. We are dealing with a situation where, although we know that ethical change is likely, we cannot reliably predict its exact course. This is analogous to technological or scientific advancement—we know these are likely, but we cannot say exactly what advances will be made.

Our own uncertainty reinforces our preference for flexible rules, especially in relation to current areas of controversy in value theory. In particular, there is currently considerable controversy regarding the appropriate role for environmental and holistic values, especially their relative weight compared to individual human welfare (Section 7.8). For the sake of simplicity, we are concentrating on human well-being in this book. However, I do not want to put too much weight on one particular account of value. Rather

---

[17] For relevant discussion of this general choice between objective and subjective values in moral philosophy, see Mulgan, *The Demands of Consequentialism*, 32–4. See also Jackson, 'Decision-Theoretic Consequentialism and the Nearest and Dearest Objection', 462–72; and Pettit, 'Decision Theory and Folk Psychology'.

than presupposing some particular resolution of this controversy, we should aim at an ideal code where public policy will be based on the continuous re-evaluation of controversial values, undertaken during public debate in the ideal society. We should expect such debate to lead to a refinement in the society's conception of value. Public debate is necessary to develop people's values, as well as to allow the expression of existing values. Sen puts this point well: even in relation to economic needs 'our conceptualization . . . depends crucially on open public debates and discussions, the guaranteeing of which requires insistence on basic political liberty and civil rights.'[18]

Recall our central notion of the context-dependent lexical level. I have sometimes expressed this notion by saying that the lexical level rises and falls over time. This is a great oversimplification. The lexical level is not a particular point on some pre-existing scale of cardinal utilities. Rather, it is the result of a complex judgement of the relative merits of the diverse components necessary to constitute a worthwhile life. As society develops, the lexical level will evolve. Any interpretation of the lexical level reflects judgements about the relative significance of material components, measures of health status, basic liberties, modes of artistic and cultural expression, etc. As conditions fluctuate, new comforts, new dimensions of health, and new liberties will emerge and become salient, and their relative importance will vary enormously. To entrench any one set of priorities among these components of well-being is to arbitrarily prioritize, for all time, the current interpretation of the lexical level. Recall the conflict between ecological values and economic growth presented in Section 7.8. Future generations, especially if they are wealthier than us, might balance the values of ecological diversity and additional wealth differently from ourselves. So we should neither entrench our own interpretation ourselves (by building it into either our foundational value theory or our specification of the ideal code) nor expect those who have internalized the ideal code to entrench *their* preferred interpretation (by locking it into the constitutional arrangements they bequeath to future generations).

The adoption of an entrenched constitution is often likened to individual acts of rational precommitment. Ulysses ties himself to the mast to prevent his future self from succumbing to the lure of the sirens. Such precommitment makes sense only if one can be confident that one's future self will be less rational that one's present self. A common analogy here is with the 'advance directive' in medicine. An individual in middle age overrides the future wishes of his demented (or otherwise diminished) elderly self, perhaps by instructing his physicians to cease life-prolonging treatment under certain

---

[18] Sen, *Development as Freedom*, 148.

specified conditions, even if his future self expresses a desire to continue living.[19] In the case of a society spread across generations, a more apt analogy is with an adolescent wilfully binding his adult self to his present preferences, on the assumption that people over 30 have unreliable judgement. In this case, precommitment involves the arrogant assumption that, while all past change was progress, all future change is decay. (The connection between democracy and precommitment also has an international dimension, to which we return in Section 9.3.1.)

One might think that we could entrench a relativized provision: 'Everyone is entitled to a life above the lexical level'. However, even this broad requirement should not be entrenched. The main problem is one of scope. From a Consequentialist perspective, one of the great advantages of technological development is that it enables us to rectify previously incurable debilitating conditions, thus enabling more people to live worthwhile lives. This highlights a practical ambiguity in our simple provision. No doubt, ideally, every single person should be above the current lexical level. However, this is unlikely to be possible. There will always be some people whose condition is such that they cannot be raised above that level. In practice, each generation will face a continuum of interpretations of the simple provision, between the following two end-points.

1. Every single person should be above whatever is the highest level such that it is possible to raise every single person above that level.
2. Every 'normal' person should be raised above the highest level such that it is possible to raise every normal person above that level.

Neither of these simple interpretations is satisfactory. The second interpretation tells society to ignore completely the possibility of assisting 'abnormal' people with treatable disabilities. By contrast, the first interpretation would see vast resources devoted to tiny improvements in the lives of extremely disabled people, with no regard to the cost imposed on everyone else. To take a concrete example, suppose Bob is the most severely intellectually disabled person in his generation. Bob can never enjoy the intellectual level of a moderately educated 6-year old. However, every expenditure of additional resources on Bob's education will yield some small improvement. (Suppose these improvements decline exponentially.) The first interpretation forbids any spending on education designed to raise the intellectual level of normal 6-year olds, as the necessary resources must be diverted to Bob. (As we saw in Section 2.2.4, Rawls's theory fares even worse here.)

[19] For an excellent recent discussion, see McMahan, *The Ethics of Killing*, 455–93. For a discussion of whether Rule Consequentialism in particular permits euthanasia when a person's death would make her life go better overall, see Hooker, *Ideal Code, Real World* (2000), 177–87.

Each future generation must choose an interpretation of the simple provision between these two extremes. They will need to exercise political and moral judgement in balancing the interests of differently able groups of individuals. Therefore, the need for future interpretation cannot be eliminated. The only question is: Who will do the interpreting? In other words, the question is not whether future generations in the ideal society will have a collective liberty here, but how they will exercise that liberty.

It only makes sense to *entrench* such a provision if there is good reason to regard the judgements of future judges as somehow more reliable than the collective wisdom of future citizens. Nothing in the principles of majoritarian democracy prevents any particular generation from temporarily placing certain decisions in the hands of judges rather than ordinary citizens. So the question at issue is not: 'Are judges more reliable than citizens, with respect to decision x?' but rather: 'Are *we* better qualified than future people to decide who should decide x?' There is no justification for answering the latter question in the affirmative, especially in the context of the Rule Consequentialist ideal society.

When constructing the ideal code, we should not privilege our own particular values over the values endorsed by a majority in the ideal society in a given generation. Accordingly, the ideal code should be able to respond to whatever values that majority converges on, in whatever way they see fit. (Rule Consequentialism is thus more modest then Rawls, whose constitutional framework cannot so easily accommodate the possibility that future generations may know better than we do what is truly valuable.)

It may seem that we could at least entrench a basic rule such as 'Do not torture'. After all, how could future generations be right if they sought to depart from this? Those who have internalized the ideal code will certainly not want future generations to torture anyone. However, even here they will be reluctant to entrench, for several reasons.

1. What is the value of the entrenchment, over and above a strong commitment to avoid torture? Is there any reason to believe that an entrenched constitution would prevent torture, in a society where the government wanted to torture? After all, most governments that practise torture do so in secret, so the existence of an entrenched constitution would be largely irrelevant.

2. Even the prohibition on torture may not be absolute. Like all Consequentialists, Rule Consequentialists can *imagine* situations where torture might be permissible. Under full compliance, we have good reason to expect that future generations will consider torture only in those circumstances. Our preference that future generations not torture is really a preference that they never be in situations where torture is called for. Entrenchment

involves the illegitimate assumption that such circumstances will never arise.

3. Casual observation of contemporary Western public debate shows that a large number of practices can be described as 'torture' by someone or other. Entrenching a prohibition on torture might encourage future generations of lawyers to broaden the scope of the prohibition, thereby weakening future opposition to real torture. Entrenchment thus has costs that may well outweigh any advantages.

Our primary interest is in Rule Consequentialism's advice in the actual world, rather than the construction of the ideal society *per se*. Suppose we agree that someone who had internalized the ideal code would support democratic procedures. How will they deal with any particular actual disagreement? Under full compliance, or anything approximating it, they will participate in (or, at least, follow) public debate, seek to inform themselves about issues of the day, campaign for the policies they judge to be best, vote accordingly, and then defer to the results of the democratic process. After all, the justification for democratic procedures will be well known within the ideal society. Everyone will thus realize that they represent the optimal response to reasonable disagreement, and therefore they will be disposed to accept the results of such procedures in place of their own judgement.

One upshot of the arguments from disagreement and moral progress is that, although they generate a prima facie argument for some form of democracy, they probably also prevent any detailed specification of the democratic system that would be adopted by those who had internalized the ideal code. If a society in the actual world already has a well-established democracy, then it is unlikely that proponents of an alternative system can base their case on the details of the ideal democratic system. On the other hand, proponents of the democratic status quo can appeal to the fact that those who have internalized the ideal code will feel strongly disposed to support existing institutions, so long as these are reasonably just. We return to these issues in Section 10.4.

Under full compliance, the demands of these dispositions will not be too great, as things will go much better overall if most people are free to devote most of their time to activities other than politics. (Like most other modern liberal political theories, Rule Consequentialism does not regard the pursuit of political life as the primary source of value.) Under partial compliance, two questions become crucial.

1. How demanding are these dispositions, especially the disposition to campaign for one's favoured public policies?
2. Would someone from the ideal society respect our existing democratic processes?

We return to these two issues in Chapter 10.

8.2. Uncertainty and Risk

We turn now to the Rule Consequentialist response to uncertainty, especially concerning the question of whether we expect future people to be better- or worse-off than ourselves. What should we do if we do not know whether to adopt the optimistic or pessimistic model?

In Chapter 5, we decided, for the sake of argument, to follow Hooker and choose a code on the basis of the expected value of internalization of that code. Our theory itself is thus neutral regarding risk. However, as we saw several times in Chapter 5, it does not follow that those who have internalized the ideal code will themselves seek to maximize expected value. A generally risk-averse disposition may produce better results in the long run than an attitude of indifference to risk. Fallible human beings seeking to maximize expected value may miscalculate, or be tempted to overlook small risks, or be blinded by the possibility of large gain. Or, being satisfied with their lot, they may find a constant striving to maximize expected value unnecessarily stressful. (These lines of argument have obvious affinities with the traditional Rule Consequentialist defence of rules of thumb, special obligations, and agent-centred restrictions.) As we shall soon see, considerations from value theory also suggest that the best code will be one that ensures the continued survival of a functioning human society, even at the expense of a loss of expected value as judged by some more traditional value theory, such as the Total View.

One main lesson of Chapter 7 was that those who have internalized the ideal code will be more concerned at the possibility of a future decline in welfare than at the prospect of losing possible future improvements. This has several implications.

1. In forming their own views about probabilities, they will tend to be pessimistic.

2. In choosing a strategy based on their own subjective probabilities, they will tend to be risk-averse.

3. In the ideal society, the most natural diagnosis of widespread disagreement regarding the probability or scale of any potential catastrophe is that reasonable well-informed people disagree about complex matters. This diagnosis will lead those who have internalized the ideal code to be wary of placing too much weight on their own personal calculation of probabilities, and to give more weight to the views of those who have serious doubts about the safety of a given course of action than to the views of those who favour a more positive prognosis.

This argument may seem to contradict the conclusion reached in Section 8.1: that the appropriate response to disagreement should be majoritarian democracy. The reason it does not is that special constitutional or institutional mechanisms are not necessary to achieve the desired sensitivity to risk. Each individual who had internalized the ideal code would be inclined to pay particular attention to the views of those who are sceptical about a given policy, even if the individual herself initially favoured the policy. In a society where most people's deliberations follow this pattern, it remains rational for each to defer to the collective will as expressed in the outcome of the democratic procedure. Risk-aversion enters into the deliberations of each individual within a democratic society; it does not remove disagreement.

Before returning to the general question of decay as opposed to improvement, we address one specific issue requiring special treatment: the possibility of annihilation.

8.2.1. Annihilation

Under a range of not implausible empirical assumptions, several courses of action collectively open to the present generation of humanity might lead to the annihilation of the human species. These include, most obviously, the indiscriminate use of nuclear or biological weapons. They might also include more mundane activities, such as driving on freeways, burning coal, or using refrigerators. Avoiding such disasters could involve sacrificing key aspects of our current lifestyles, as well as refraining from using weapons of mass destruction. Even if we do not regard annihilation as a realistic threat, we still gain insight into Rule Consequentialism's attitude to risk by examining this extreme possibility.

Suppose we face a choice between two courses of action: safe and risky. The safe option ensures that a large number of people each have a life worth x, while under the risky option there is a p probability that the same number of people each have a life worth $x + y$ and a $[1 - p]$ probability that no-one exists. If we are maximizing expected total utility, then the safe option is preferable if and only if $p < x/(x + y)$.

Suppose $p > x/(x + y)$. For the sake of simplicity, assume that p equals 0.5 and y is greater than x. The riskier option thus has greater expected value. There are several reasons why those who have internalized the ideal code might still opt for the safer alternative. These turn on the fact that the difference between a world where everyone has a life worth x (the Happy World) and one where no one exists (the Empty World) is morally much more significant than the difference between the Happy World and a world where everyone's life is worth $x + y$ (the Very Happy World).

All the following arguments rely on two related features of the moral worldview of those who have internalized the ideal code: their value theory, and the priority they attach to their own projects.[20] The key fact is that individual human lives cannot be evaluated in isolation. The value of a life is affected by its social context, and by the person's relations with others. If the human race dies out, this may also lead us to re-evaluate the value of the lives both of the present generation and of those who existed in the past.[21]

1. Personal Projects.   A human community does not exist in its entirety at one particular time, or in one particular generation. It is spread across many generations. The value and significance of our present goals often presuppose the existence and well-being of future people. In some cases this is obvious, as the content of our goals refers explicitly to the future. More generally, the unstated assumption that our projects, communities, and culture will persist after our death is often required to make sense of the significance we attach to our goals. To see this, consider our response to science-fiction stories where the present generation discover that their world will be destroyed soon after their death. Our immediate reaction is one of dislocation and horror. Such scenarios seem to remove much of the point of ordinary human lives. Being part of ongoing cultural achievements adds to the value of an individual's life. This gives each member of the present generation a personal motive to ensure the continued survival of humanity.

2. Concern for Past People.   Similar considerations might generate an inclination to assist future generations, based on a sense of obligation to *previous* generations, especially those with whom we have overlapped and pursued joint projects. For instance, I might owe it to my parent's generation to ensure that their investment in the social framework of our society, from which I have benefited, is maintained for the next generation. In Section 2.1.2 I argued that such reciprocal obligations cannot provide an adequate *foundation* for a complete account of intergenerational justice. However, they may form part of the moral worldview of someone who has internalized the ideal code. We saw in Section 5.7 that the ideal code is likely to include general obligations to those with whom one has shared valuable projects. It would be natural to apply such obligations retrospectively where possible— if I can benefit my forebears, I should do so. This extension has no obvious negative impact, and seems to offer clear long-term benefits in the present

---

[20] The argument in the text assumes the standard value theory set out in Ch. 3: the Total View, possibly supplemented by a lexical level. Several possible departures from that value theory would reinforce the risk-averse character of the ideal code, especially if we introduced either an intrinsic value for the existence of civilization *per se* (over and above the contribution civilization makes to individual well-being) or an extra weighting for the lives and welfare of the worst-off.

[21] This brings us to the two issues of posthumous harms and duties to the dead. For some taste of the considerable literature on the former, see Feinberg, 'Harm and Self-Interest'; Feinberg, *Harm to Others*, 79–95; and Levenbook, 'Harming Someone after his Death'. On the latter, see Mulgan, 'The Place of the Dead in Liberal Political Philosophy' (1999); and Ridge, 'Giving the Dead their Due'.

case. So it is likely to be included in the ideal code. (The belief that one can benefit one's forebears, and the corresponding belief that one's descendants can benefit oneself, are themselves likely to produce good consequences, by encouraging people to engage in intergenerational projects. Accordingly, we might expect those who have internalized the ideal code to be especially receptive to these beliefs.)

3. The Lexical Level. If a life worth x is above the lexical level, then the similarity between the two populated worlds is lexically prior to any difference between them. Indeed, if both the X-lives and the X + Y-lives are lived in a worthwhile cultural context, and thus contain similar relationships, then we may doubt that life in the Very Happy World could really be *twice as valuable* as life in the Happy World. The possibility of extra value above the lexical level cannot be worth the threat of annihilation. Those who have internalized the ideal code will thus not think that the Very Happy World is twice as valuable as the Happy World. (Furthermore, if they believe in widespread incommensurability above the lexical level, then the idea that life in the Very Happy World is better than life in the Happy World may not even make sense to them.)

This argument is particularly strong if we assume that the present generation themselves enjoy life worth x, and that x corresponds to their interpretation of the lexical level, to which they will give priority (Sections 5.4, 6.4.2, 7.6, 7.9).

4. An Infinite Future. The possibility that humanity might have an infinite future also reinforces the preference for risk-aversion. Consider the following three possible outcomes discussed briefly by Derek Parfit.[22]

1. Peace.
2. A nuclear war that kills 99 per cent of the world's existing population.
3. A nuclear war that kills 100 per cent of the world's existing population.

Parfit argues that 'the difference between (2) and (3) is *very much* greater' than the difference between (1) and (2). Parfit's point is starkest if we accept that, under favourable conditions, the human race might enjoy an infinite future. The difference in value between the annihilation of the whole of humanity, and the annihilation of 99 per cent of the next generation is thus infinite, and dwarfs the difference between the latter and the survival of a full next generation. The risk of total annihilation is not worth any finite gain in expected well-being.[23]

---

[22] Parfit, *Reasons and Persons*, 453.

[23] The argument in the text may seem inconsistent with our general policy of ignoring infinite values (Ch. 3 endnote C). However, it need not be. Given uncertainty, it is generally reasonable to proceed on the assumption that any possible infinite values cancel one another out. The possibility of annihilating the human race is a rare exception, as the potential infinite value is all on one side of the equation.

5. Consistency with Reproductive Freedom. In the individual case, the ideal code favours reproductive freedom over any obligation to create. It may seem that, if extended to intergenerational politics, this would yield a willingness to allow the human race to die out. It is important to see why this does not follow.

In the case of an individual human being, it is crucial to distinguish a decision whether to bring someone into existence from a decision whether to end someone's existence. This tracks the distinction between a possible world where a particular possible person never exists, and one where she dies young. Even if the person's life goes well overall within the latter possible world, we still have a clear intuition that creating a person and then killing her is morally worse than opting not to create a new person. Rule Consequentialism accommodates this asymmetry by incorporating person-affecting restrictions into its ideal code (Section 5.7).

An analogous asymmetry arises in the case of a society. Compare the following three possible worlds.

The Empty World. No humans ever exist.

Short History. Human society flourishes from t0 until t1, when it suddenly ends.

Long History. Human society flourishes from t0 until well after t1. (Assume, that from t0 to t1, Long History is identical to Short History.)

Under most plausible value theories, and certainly under the theory explored in Chapter 3, Long History is clearly better than Short History, which is clearly superior to the Empty World. However, many people have a strong intuition that it would be much worse to opt for Short History over Long History at t1 than to opt for the Empty World over Long History at t0. Once the human race exists, we should do everything we can to ensure its continued survival. But no one was under any comparable obligation to create the human race in the first place.

Some might use this intuition to show that Long History cannot be better than the Empty World. (Just as, in the individual case, some use the asymmetry to show that adding an extra person with a valuable life never improves the value of an outcome. See Ch. 5 n. 8.) An alternative solution is to note that, as in the individual case, the Rule Consequentialist ideal code contains many elements besides a simple injunction to bring about the best available possible world. In particular, agents within the human society at t1 will have many projects and obligations whose content and value are intimately tied to the continuation of that society. The difference between

Long History and Short History may be less significant from an impartial point of view than the difference between Long History and the Empty World, but it is much more significant from the point of view of the agents involved.

By contrast, a choice between the Empty World and Long History bears little relation to any choice a real agent might face. Our intuitions in such 'Pure Genesis Choices' are blurred by our commitment to individual reproductive freedom in the (loosely) analogous individual case.[24] We strongly believe that individual humans should be free to decide for themselves whether to reproduce. We conclude that the addition of one extra worthwhile life does not increase overall value, and then extrapolate to the conclusion that the Empty World is neither better nor worse than Long History. The solution is to note the crucial element of cost involved in ordinary human reproduction, and the manifold obligations such reproduction involves. Our intuitions simply are not designed for costless creation, and thus are not applicable to it. (This is especially significant for Rule Consequentialism, whose entire *raison d'être* is to respond to human fallibility, and to accommodate the ways in which human beings are not perfect rational calculators.)

The appropriate analogy for the collective decision we are considering is not the decision whether or not to create a new person. It is the decision whether or not to end the life of an existing person. We saw in Chapter 5 that there are strong Rule Consequentialist grounds for expecting the ideal code to include a very strong prohibition on killing someone if his death would make his life go worse.[25] Analogously, we should expect the ideal code to include at least a very strong presumption in favour of the continued existence of humanity.

We can thus retain a plausible set of pairwise comparisons at the level of abstract value, while still admitting that there are special reasons for us to avoid the extinction of the human race. A commitment to individual reproductive freedom does not entail that those who have internalized the ideal code will feel free to end the history of humanity.

I conclude that, if they have internalized the ideal code, the present generation will strongly prefer the risk-averse policy. Furthermore, they would almost certainly not feel free to adopt risky policies, even if they wanted to. (The pursuit of annihilation is clearly something we want no one to do, even if they have unusual preferences.) Such policies are thus properly seen

---

[24] The phrase 'Pure Genesis Choice' is borrowed from Heyd, *Genethics*, 16.

[25] For references to discussions of euthanasia (both general and in relation to Rule Consequentialism), see n. 19 of this chapter.

as forbidden by Rule Consequentialism, and the ideal code will impose a very strong obligation to ensure the survival of humanity. Also, the value at stake is so significant that the ideal code may require extreme sacrifices to avoid any possibility of annihilation. The threat of annihilation exists even under full compliance. (For instance, an asteroid shower might threaten the very existence of the Earth.) The inclusion of a strong disaster avoidance clause thus increases the expected value of the ideal code. As the disaster in question threatens the value of everyone's projects, it seems reasonable to suppose that people could be taught a much more demanding disaster-avoidance rule here than in the case of disasters affecting people in distant lands. (We return to the issue of demands in Chapter 10.)

8.2.2. Less Drastic Decline

In addition to the absolute threat of annihilation, any human community faces a wide range of less dramatic possible fates. In particular, a social framework adequate to make possible the successful pursuit of valuable goals is a fragile achievement, which might be disrupted or destroyed.

A decline in overall well-being is obviously bad, and the ideal code will be designed to avoid, or at least mitigate, it. As we saw earlier, because they privilege their own lexical level, those who have internalized the ideal code have a stronger motivation to avoid future decline than to promote accumulation. To take another simplified example, suppose those who have internalized the ideal code enjoy a life worth x. They face a choice between the certainty that future people will also enjoy lives worth x, versus a risky option offering a 50 per cent chance that future people will have lives worth $x + y$, and a 50 per cent chance that they will have lives worth $x - z$ (where y equals z). They will prefer the secure bet to the gamble, even though both have exactly the same expected value. This preference would remain even if *(a)* the probability of the optimistic outcome is greater than 50 per cent; and/or *(b)* the rate of improvement of average well-being under the optimistic outcome would exceed the rate of decline of average well-being under the pessimistic outcome (that is, if y is greater than z).

On the other hand, those who have internalized the ideal code are not totally risk-averse, just as they do not give absolute priority to the worst-off. Accordingly, if the probability of improvement over decline is sufficiently high, or if the degree of improvement is sufficiently greater than the degree of decline, they will take the gamble. As ever, it is very hard to say with any precision how the notion of 'sufficiently greater' would be interpreted in either of these cases, especially as different people in the ideal society will favour different interpretations.

To illustrate this risk aversion, suppose the present generation is contemplating using a non-renewable resource in a way that would enhance economic growth at the cost of environmental degradation. Despite their best empirical investigations, they remain unsure whether the benefits of the former will outweigh the costs of the latter. The expected benefits of growth will need significantly to outweigh the expected loss of degradation before they will favour this policy. This reluctance is enhanced if there is a significant risk that degradation will leave future generations unable to reach the lexical level.

A more difficult case arises if the choice is starker. Suppose resource utilization is the only way the present generation can remain above the lexical level, but that such utilization will destroy the environment for future generations, leaving them unable to rise above the lexical level. In this case, the present generation face an unenviable choice. We saw in Section 8.2.1 that the ideal code may demand great sacrifices in order to ensure the survival of humanity. However, this argument is premised on the high value of human survival, an assumption which rests in turn on the ability of future generations to rise above the lexical level. If this assumption is false, and no future generations will ever rise above the present lexical level, then the present generation may reluctantly opt to live above the lexical level themselves, and then allow humanity to die out.

On the other hand, unless the damaging resource use actually threatens the existence of the human race, the devastating impact of a catastrophe on future welfare may well be temporary. Perhaps, after several generations of harsh, poverty-stricken struggle, social conditions might eventually improve to that point where a distant future generation can reach, and perhaps even surpass, the lexical level enjoyed by the present generation. In this case, both our foundational value theory and the values of those who have internalized the ideal code will prefer the continued existence of humanity to its extinction—assuming the number of generations enjoying a life above the lexical level is much greater than the number living below it.

If they knew that this would happen, then this would give the present generation a reason to prefer continued existence to extinction. It would also reduce their reluctance to opt for the resource use. However, that reluctance would not disappear. Insofar as the particular projects of present people involve the welfare of future people, these tend to be particular people in the next few generations. So, although it yields a more desirable long-term history for humanity, the negative impact of the temporary catastrophe will still loom large in the minds of present people.

Suppose, however, that those who have internalized the ideal code are simply unsure which of these general futures will eventuate. I would argue that they will have two seemingly contradictory attitudes to catastrophes of this kind. If the catastrophe can be avoided, their generally risk-averse disposition will lead them to overestimate the possibility of annihilation, or of a more bleak human future, and make great sacrifices to avoid the catastrophe. If the catastrophe is inevitable, however, those who have internalized the ideal code will be inclined to 'look on the bright side', and convince themselves that future generations will eventually rise above the lexical level. Like the adoption of the context-dependent lexical level itself, this optimistic response to catastrophe is desirable, and perhaps psychologically necessary, to avoid widespread despair (Section 6.4). The present generation must act on the assumption that their attempts to provide a better future are not futile, because this increases both their own well-being and their chances of success. (We should expect this optimism to be built into the ideal code as catastrophe is possible even under full compliance.) In the actual world, agents with both these dispositions may oscillate between extreme efforts to avoid catastrophe and optimistically proceeding as if everything were all right. The crucial question is the balance between the two conflicting dispositions under partial compliance. We return to those in Chapter 10.[26]

8.2.3. Population Policy

Suppose the present generation have two options: one offers a 100 per cent chance that the next generation will contain x number of people enjoying lives above the lexical level, while the other offers a 50 per cent chance that double that number of people enjoy lives above the lexical level, but also a 50 per cent chance that there will be no future people at all. Both options offer the same expected value. Once again, I will argue that the present generation will be risk-averse, and will prefer the certain survival of their community. In contrast to our earlier example, all the individuals in all outcomes are assumed, for the sake of simplicity, to have the same level of well-being, so the nature of the lexical level cannot justify risk-aversion here. However, all the self-interested reasons, and all the obligations owed to previous generations,

---

[26] There is an obvious parallel here with Kant's introduction of the postulates of God, divine grace, the intelligibility of human history, and personal immortality. I explore these parallels in a Consequentialist context in 'Valuing the Future' (draft MS).

as discussed in relation to our earlier example, are equally satisfied if the next generation has only x people rather than 2x. Accordingly, the world with 2x will not seem twice as valuable, and so the 50 per cent chance of attaining that future is not nearly sufficient to outweigh the risk of annihilation.

The present generation will adopt a cautious attitude to population policy. This is reinforced by uncertainty regarding the future carrying capacity of the earth, and also by the striking empirical fact that any society similar to those found in the modern developed world will find it very difficult to manage any *reduction* in population across generations, as this leads to an oversized elderly generation needing support. The present generation will thus not wish future generations to face the need to reduce the population. Accordingly, they will choose a population policy designed to ensure, first and foremost, that their community continues to survive, and that its future members enjoy comparatively unconstrained individual and collective choices. This goal will take precedence over any inclination to increase the size of the population.

8.3. Abandoning Democracy

To bring our two topics together, we must finally ask whether our discussion of risk aversion in Section 8.2 threatens our case for democracy in Section 8.1. Democracy cannot guarantee the survival of a viable human community. Could this risk justify the abandonment of democracy in favour of a more coercive political system? I shall argue that it could not.

It is tempting to assume that, for any conceivable future threat, it would be possible to design a political system that perfectly avoids that threat, by embedding certain measures in its constitution. There are two problems with this approach. The first is that constitutional entrenchment, just like democracy, is not infallible. We cannot guarantee that future generations will interpret their constitution so as to avoid some particular threat, any more than we can rely on democracy to achieve the same result.

The second problem with this approach is that different potential threats require different, and potentially conflicting, responses. Technological development fuelled by the utilization of non-renewable resources may be the best way to avoid some potential threats, but obviously this route exacerbates other potential threats. Once we look into the far future, the global social fabric faces a huge variety of potential threats, including natural forces, the environmental impacts of human lifestyles, tensions within individual countries, and tensions across national boundaries. There is no good reason to believe that the present generation could design a constitutional system which would do a better job of finding the appropriate balance of responses to future threats than open public deliberation at a later date. The range of possible threats thus reinforces the case for both a democratic decision-procedure and a cautious attitude to risk. It also justifies the Rule Consequentialist reluctance to seek more detailed moral conclusions than the complexity of the subject matter permits.

9

International Justice

If Rule Consequentialism is a complete moral theory, then it should offer advice in all areas of life. Life in the real world is not lived in isolated communities. A complete Rule Consequentialist theory must outline the obligations of one nation to another, and of individuals in one nation to individuals in another, and tell us how these are to be balanced against our obligations to others in our own nation, both present and future people.

A complete discussion of international justice is beyond the scope of this book. We limit our attention to a few specific questions, relating particularly to the intersection between international and intergenerational justice. The two topics are clearly related for the Consequentialist. In each case, we ask how the actions of a small group (the present generation, affluent people) impact on a much larger group (all future people, all contemporary people). In both cases, the interests of the larger group threaten to swamp those of the smaller, leading to a very demanding ideal code. The question of the overall demands of Rule Consequentialism will be postponed until Chapter 10. The present chapter explores the structure of the obligations the ideal code places on the present generation of affluent people regarding people in other lands.

9.1. The Scope of Rule Consequentialism

There is one crucial difference between the intergenerational and international cases. In the former, we can teach our code only to the next generation. The only way to get a code internalized by subsequent generations is as a consequence of teaching it to the first generation. By contrast, in the international case, there is no a priori reason why we should not seek a code to teach to everyone in the world, rather than just to the next generation in our own society. Yet our discussion has largely proceeded as if we were asking merely what code to teach to our own society. How can this parochial focus be justified? There are two basic possibilities.

1. We might defend, at a foundational level, the restriction of Rule Consequentialism to our own society. We could argue either that moral

philosophy itself has that narrow focus, or that the narrow focus reflects the particular role played by Rule Consequentialism within a broader moral theory. I return to this line of defence in Chapter 11. (One motivation for this pluralist approach is precisely the conclusion that Rule Consequentialism cannot cope on a global scale.)

2. We might argue that, although the Rule Consequentialist code applies to everyone in the world, that code allows each individual to give priority to members of their own community, and encourages them to operate within existing national and international institutions, even if these are not exactly as would be found in the ideal society. In particular, if they found themselves in a world of established nation states, those who have internalized the ideal code would feel inclined to operate within that framework. I explore this defence in Chapter 10, and in the rest of the present chapter.

In either case, we suppose that the ideal code leaves room for international ethics, as well as for global obligations owed to all individuals. The key question is how to think about balancing these two sets of obligations.

Contemporary philosophical discussion of international ethics is dominated by a dispute between nationalists (who argue that it is reasonable to favour one's co-nationals) and cosmopolitans (who argue that one's primary obligations are owed to all humanity).[1] In terms of that debate, our Rule Consequentialism proceeds from a cosmopolitan framework, but asks how much room can be made for nationalism.

Both nationalism and cosmopolitanism face difficulties. The former seems to place too much weight on morally arbitrary distinctions, while the latter threatens to be extremely demanding for anyone in the developed world. The fate of Rawls's theory of justice when applied to international affairs is instructive. Rawls's own approach is to confine his original egalitarian account of distributive justice to a single liberal democratic society, and offer a much more conservative account of international justice that presupposes a foundational moral distinction between nations.[2] Others, notably Charles Beitz, have attempted to apply Rawls's original Original Position

---

[1] The literature here is vast. For representative defences of cosmopolitanism, see Pogge, 'Cosmopolitanism and Sovereignty'; and Waldron, "What is Cosmopolitanism?"' A prominent contemporary defender of nationalism is David Miller. (See e.g. Miller, 'Nationality: Some Replies'; Miller, 'Holding Nations Reponsible'; Miller, 'In Defence of Nationality'; Miller, *Citizenship and National Identity*.) Yael Tamir and Will Kymlicka defend positions intermediate between pure cosmopolitanism and pure nationalism. (Kymlicka and Straehle, 'Cosmopolitanism, Nation-States, and Minority Nationalism'; Kymlicka, 'Multicultural States and Intercultural Citizens'; Tamir, 'Two Concepts of Multiculturalism'; Tamir, *Liberal Nationalism*.) For general discussion of the issues, see Brock, 'Liberal Nationalism versus Cosmopolitanism'; Dallmayr, 'Cosmopolitanism'; Scheffler, 'Conceptions of Cosmopolitanism' (1999); Weinstock, 'Is There a Moral Case for Nationalism?'

[2] Rawls, *The Law of Peoples* (1999), 11, 33.

framework at the global level, with quite radical results.[3] (As in the case of intergenerational justice, Rawls's use of maximin in the Original Position ensures that any such extension is much more radical and demanding than any form of Rule Consequentialism.[4])

9.1.1. Global Decision-Making

In one sense, our Rule Consequentialism is essentially an individualist moral theory—it tells me what I should do. If, as a Rule Consequentialist, I want to know what I should think about international ethics, then I ask what someone who had internalized the ideal code (as presented in Chapters 5 to 8) would think about international ethics. There are two key questions.

1. How would they think about international ethics in their own world of (largely) full compliance?
2. How would they think about international ethics in *our* world of (largely) partial compliance?

We leave the second question until Chapter 10. This chapter addresses the first.

How would those who had internalized the ideal code developed in earlier chapters approach international ethics? We begin by recapping their general ethical and political outlook. Their general ethical outlook includes the following elements: a general concern for all sentient beings; a feeling that it is acceptable to give priority to oneself, one's friends, one's children, one's collaborators; a set of specific obligations to avoid harm, to keep promises, to follow through on joint projects; and a range of specific obligations, especially parental. Their general political outlook includes: a strong preference for democratic decision-making and liberal politics; a generally risk-averse attitude; an *obligation* not to allow the quality of life to decline for future people, but only an *inclination* to raise their quality of life above one's own; and the belief that it is, at least in certain circumstances, reasonable to privilege one's own interpretation of the lexical level, even though one recognizes that it is only one interpretation among many.

The strongest dispositions of those who have internalized the ideal code will be to ensure the survival of humanity and the maintenance of an adequate social framework for future generations. Once that social framework is guaranteed, they seek to balance the following desires: to advance their own interests, to invest for future generations in their own society, to aid the destitute in other societies, and to invest for future generations in those societies.

---

[3] Beitz, *Political Theory and International Relations*.
[4] We return to Rawls's theory of international justice very briefly in endnote A of Ch. 9.

This raises the following questions for international ethics. Does the preference for democracy carry over to the global level? Does the preference for democracy extend to a preference that other groups be democratic? What kinds of international policies would someone who had internalized the ideal code support? Will they support group autonomy? How far will they favour the autonomy of their own group? How far will they respect the autonomy of other groups?

We begin with the case for democracy. This seems to carry over to the international arena, at least under full compliance. In particular, the standard instrumental arguments for democracy, outlined in Section 8.1, apply as much at the global level as at the national.

I suggested in Chapters 6 and 8 that the ideal code will support individual participation in collective decision-making for a number of reasons. Some of these carry over to global democracy. In particular, at least some individual participation in global decision-making is necessary to ensure that global decisions reflect the values and interests of individuals. Indeed, *this* argument for democracy is perhaps even stronger in the global case than it was within an individual country, as non-democratic decision-makers are even less likely to have the motivation and information necessary to take appropriate account of the interests of people in other nations. It is thus very unlikely that international institutions, rules, or policies developed in the absence of global democracy will adequately take account of the interests of the world's most vulnerable people, even if all those involved have internalized the ideal code and make an honest attempt to deliberate in accordance with it.

Anyone who has internalized the ideal code will thus favour some degree of global democracy. We may well ask what (if anything) such a person would make of our world of very powerful nation states and precious little global democracy. We begin by asking if they would recognize any role for nation states, or other similar foci of group partiality.

For Rule Consequentialism, as for any moral theory founded on a value theory acknowledging the equal worth of all human beings, the first question is whether we need a separate moral realm of inter-group ethics at all—as opposed to a global world where all obligations and interactions are ultimately between individuals. The content of the obligations of inter-group ethics, as well as their strength compared to other obligations, flows directly from our initial justification for according moral status to groups in the first place.

As ever, we could short-cut the whole debate by building the distinct value of groups into our foundational value theory. (Of course, unless this was our only value, we would still need an account of its relationship to the value of individual well-being, and to the values of holistic evaluations of possible histories of humanity as a whole, if our theory includes these as well.) Having noted this possibility, we set it aside. I seek to show that the recognition of groups makes sense even if our foundational value theory is group-blind. As in Chapters 5 to 8, the distinction between the foundational value theory we use to evaluate ideal codes and the value theory of those who have internalized the ideal code plays a crucial role. Even if groups are not recognized in the former, they may feature in the latter.

Our discussion thus connects to a central issue in the moral philosophy of international relations: the limits of state autonomy. Charles Beitz noted twenty years ago that the analogy between individuals and states is overused in the moral theory of international relations.[5] This is most striking in discussions of state autonomy, where such autonomy is often justified by direct analogy to the liberal commitment to the protection of individual autonomy. If states are like people, then the freedom of states is just as valuable as the freedom of human beings, and for the same reasons. Unfortunately, states are, in many ways, quite unlike individual human beings. As we shall see, our Rule Consequentialist framework provides a way to both justify and limit state autonomy.

The case for the recognition of groups begins from the limits of global democracy. While instrumentally necessary, participation in decision-making within a group containing the six billion inhabitants of our planet (or all the ten billion inhabitants it is likely to have in 2050[6]) may seem insufficient for other purposes. An individual's participation is likely to be far too indirect and insignificant to provide a sufficient sense of participation in 'her community'. Furthermore, the nature of global decisions is likely to be very general, with many specific decisions delegated to smaller groups, just as the domestic code leaves many decisions to individuals. If individuals are to be meaningfully autonomous, then they should be able to contribute to those decisions which most affect them. The best way to ensure this will be to grant local groups considerable autonomy. For Rule Consequentialism, while participation in local or national decision-making has both intrinsic and instrumental value, the justification of individual participation in global decision-making will be primarily instrumental.

Arguments for democracy based on the value to individuals of participation in decision-making, over and above the protection of their interests, thus point away from pure global democracy and towards a role for groups. Furthermore, most people's projects, goals, and interests are intrinsically

[5] Beitz, *Political Theory and International Relations*.

[6] This estimate is based on the median projections of the 2000 revision of the official United Nations population estimates and projections. (www.un.org/esa/population/unpop.htm)

connected to their groups, in a variety of ways that will emerge as we proceed. Any argument in favour of permitting partiality to oneself thus generates also an argument in favour of group partiality.

A person who has internalized the ideal code will thus support the recognition of groups in international politics. (In the real world, these might correspond to states, countries, or nations—or to smaller groups. For present purposes, we remain agnostic about the particular nature of these groups.) This recognition has several components.

1. Individuals are morally entitled to give priority to members of their own group over other groups.
2. The best system of international politics recognizes and legitimates this priority.
3. The best system of international politics allows groups considerable autonomy to determine their own affairs.

9.2. Justifying Group Autonomy

A major theme of our Rule Consequentialism is that it is both natural and desirable that people are disposed to give significant priority, not only to themselves, but also to those with whom they share the projects that define and shape their lives. These especially include projects that extend over time, to include both future and past generations. If we are teaching our code to the next generation in the actual world, then we must allow for the fact that most suitable projects will be embedded in a cultural context. That context often also has a national, or other group, focus. To recognize the significance, for individuals, of long-term projects, thus *is* to accord some significance to group identities.

Those who had internalized the ideal code will thus give (and will feel justified in giving) *some* priority to their co-groupies. They will favour policies permitting, and perhaps sometimes encouraging, group solidarity—both for themselves and for others. Also, they will recognize that, as people tend to make better decisions when dealing with matters of concern to themselves, the groups people identify with will often be a more appropriate level of decision-making than the global community. (One exception will be where global coordination problems render group-based decision-making ineffective; Section 9.2.7.)

This defence of group autonomy is familiar. It may also seem rather weak. Surely, for most individuals, most of their central life projects have nothing to do with their national identity. Fortunately, our Rule Consequentialism points to a deeper justification for group-based politics.

For any person who has internalized the ideal code, her own interpretation of the lexical level (a key feature of her moral worldview) is linked to the nature of her background social framework. We have seen several times that, in addition to privileging the interests of certain people, someone who has internalized the ideal code will privilege her own interpretation of the lexical level, especially when thinking of herself and her contemporaries. However, she also recognizes that future generations will have their own interpretation. I concluded that, while she recognizes that the impact of her decisions on future generations should ideally be judged against *their* interpretation of the lexical level rather than her own, she naturally attaches less significance to the question of whether future people are above their own lexical level than to the question of whether her contemporaries are above her lexical level. It is natural for such priorities and attitudes to carry over to comparisons between contemporaneous groups, insofar as they also have different interpretations of the lexical level. While judging her group against her lexical level, anyone who has internalized the ideal code will judge other groups against *their* interpretations—and be more interested in the former judgement than the latter.

As in the intergenerational case, this tendency to relativize lexicality has two key implications. The first is that the connection between one's personal projects, one's interpretation of the lexical level, and the social framework of one's group reinforces the priority to one's own group and its deliberations. If all projects depend on one's social framework, and include interpreting the lexical level, then even projects seemingly unrelated to the life of one's group are linked to that life at a deeper level. Also, if one is especially interested in a certain range of questions, then one will be more interested in the place where those questions are appropriate. In the intergenerational case, these effects are somewhat mitigated by connections between the social frameworks of different generations. If these connections are lacking between contemporary groups, then no analogous mitigation is possible.

Secondly, because interpretations of the lexical level are delicate and multifaceted, agents will hesitate to apply interpretations divergent from their own, especially if these are embedded in foreign background social frameworks. Therefore, the recognition that the politics of each group should be founded on its own interpretations of the lexical level leads to a strong disposition to allow each group to decide for themselves. In the intergenerational case, where the groups are generations, this produces a reluctance to constitutionally entrench the present generation's interpretation, and a desire to leave the choices of future generations as rich and open as possible (Section 8.1). Analogously, in the inter-group case, it will lead to a reluctance to impose uniform constitutional structures across groups, and a desire both to enable groups to manage their own resources, and to ensure that each has an adequate range of resources.

9.2.1. Property Rights

For an individual, a key component of moral autonomy is the freedom to determine the use one makes of one's own resources. (This includes moral freedom, but also political and legal liberty. These may diverge, as we saw in Section 7.2.) Analogously, a group's autonomy will include the right to determine how to use its own resources. We must first determine what each group's resources *are*. We begin by contrasting two extreme approaches to property rights.

The Communal Extreme.   All resources are owned in common by everyone on earth. All proceeds from the production and use of resources are shared equally.

The Libertarian Extreme.   Natural resources are owned by whoever finds them first. People have absolute property rights over everything they find, and over everything they produce.

The domestic ideal code would not include either of these rules. In Rule Consequentialism, this is due to both the instrumental value of such autonomy in terms of economic productivity and the intrinsic value of autonomy to each individual. The extreme redistribution required by the Communal Extreme will blunt incentives and create widespread inefficiencies. (Recall, as ever, that Rule Consequentialism does not idealize to perfect human behaviour.) Furthermore, the politics of the ideal society will not *enforce* all moral obligations. Our discussion of political liberty suggests that, so far as possible, those in the ideal society will be left to decide for themselves how much to donate to charity. On the other hand, the Libertarian Extreme, in practice, might leave some people to starve—or, at least, it would leave them without sufficient resources to thrive, even though others have a superabundance. The ideal code will steer a middle path, with moderate property rights constrained by obligations to assist others.[7]

Similar considerations apply at the global level. One difference is that, in practice in the actual world, the resources of a group are usually identified, at least initially, as those lying within its 'territory'. The association of groups with territories is a controversial one. However, for the sake of

---

[7] Mulgan, *The Demands of Consequentialism* (2001), 69–76.

simplicity, we assume that, at least for the next generation, attachment to groups identified partly on a territorial basis, together with the instrumental efficiency of such identification, would lead those who had internalized the ideal code to support policies recognizing the notion of 'a group's territory'. (Doubts about the legitimacy of territorial claims can be represented as constraints on the weight accorded to this notion.)

A global Communal Extreme would not provide adequate incentives to develop resources, and the coordination of global rights to all resources might be needlessly cumbersome. Two factors render these incentive failures worse in the global case:

1. As property is shared across all inhabitants of the earth, each person's share from any benefit they produce is even smaller than if the benefit were shared merely with their own group.
2. The first difference may seem insignificant, given the size of some groups. A more significant difference is that, insofar as people identify with their group, any benefit to their group is a benefit to themselves. This identification is largely lacking at the global level.

The opposite approach (a global Libertarian Extreme) would grant each group absolute property rights over any resources found in its territory. This could lead to a great inequality in the distribution of resources, whereby some groups would end up with far more than they need, while others would have an inadequate supply of resources. Furthermore, the two factors just mentioned exacerbate the likelihood of this result in the global case, as charity is thus much less likely to be an adequate solution for global problems. Obligations of assistance, though they may be weaker than in the domestic case, are more likely to require enforcement or institutionalization of some sort.

Those who have internalized the ideal code will probably favour global policies allowing each group considerable freedom to use resources found in its territory. However, in addition to the standard obligations on both individuals and groups to avoid harm, keep promises, pay debts, each group's freedom will be subject to two constraints.

1. Assistance.   If one group finds itself with a superfluity of resources, then it will feel obliged to assist other groups who have inadequate resources. This assistance might take the form of direct aid to deprived individuals in the poorer state, or financial or technical assistance to the government of a group, or contributions to an inter-group aid agency.

Such obligations are necessary to protect and advance the well-being and autonomy of individuals and groups. Individuals can only meaningfully exercise autonomy if their basic needs are met. A group can only meaning-fully exercise autonomy if the basic needs of its members are met. To ensure this, a group must have access to resources: land, fuel, building mater-ials, food, etc.

2. Conservation. A group may find itself in possession of a major share of a particular non-renewable resource. This raises familiar intergenerational issues within that group, as we saw earlier (Sections 7.7 and 8.2). It also raises inter-group intergenerational issues. As we saw earlier, those who had internalized the ideal code will feel a strong obligation to conserve the non-renewable resource for future generations in their own group. While the ideal code permits some partiality toward members of one's own group, we should expect a deep reluctance gratuitously to deplete resources that could be of use to present and future people in other groups.

Under full compliance, a range of factors limit the demands of these con-straints for each group and individual, thereby reinforcing their desirability. One obvious mitigating factor is the possibility of trade. If nations begin with different bundles of resources, they can enter mutually advantageous exchanges. These might be exchanges between individuals or between states. A state whose territory does not contain a certain necessary mineral can thus survive without aid.

Even if aid is required to redress extreme resource imbalances or natural disasters, a small contribution from wealthy groups would suffice. (Just as, in the individual case, a small percentage of the income of each wealthy per-son is sufficient to alleviate poverty.) Recent World Bank figures suggest that an economic reform tripling all incomes for the worst-off 20 per cent of the world's population would cost less than 1 per cent of the incomes of people in high-income countries.[8]

Rule Consequentialism provides a clear justification for these intuitively plausible general ideas. Any ideal code incorporating such ideas would produce better long-term consequences than either a communal or a libertarian code. The ideal code will allow each group to give themselves preferential treatment. We must now ask how we might expect them to exercise that freedom in particular cases, and balance it against their obligations to future generations.

9.2.2. Differently Affluent (Unconnected) Groups

The relationship between social frameworks and interpretations of the lex-ical level lends general support to group autonomy and partiality. It also has

---

[8] This calculation is based on figures from World Bank, *World Development Report 2000/2001*. 275.

particular implications where groups are at very different levels of affluence or development. In the intergenerational case, this involves the possibility of improvement or decline across generations. In the contemporary case, it is due to the separate histories of the different groups. For Rule Consequentialism, perhaps the key issue in inter-group ethics is the relation between these two cases: the intergenerational and the inter-group. We begin with the similarities.

Suppose the present generation of a group compare themselves to two other groups, both considerably better-off than themselves: a future generation of their own group, and a more affluent contemporary group. In both cases, while the present generation recognize that the other group operates with higher interpretations of the lexical level, and while they recognize that this is both natural and desirable, they are much more concerned to raise themselves above their own lexical level than to assist the other group to rise above theirs. With the future generation, I argued that the present generation would feel no obligation to provide such assistance, especially if it would involve significant cost to themselves, even though they might feel a strong inclination to do so. This absence of obligation will carry over to the contemporary case. A worse-off group will feel no obligation to assist the, from their point of view *supra*-lexical, aspirations of a group who are already much better off.

Suppose now that the present generation of our group compare themselves to two other groups, both much *worse-off* than themselves: a future generation of their own group who have suffered a catastrophe, and a contemporary group whose history and present circumstances are much less prosperous. In the intergenerational case, I argued that the present generation do feel an obligation to raise each future generation above, at least, that generation's own interpretation of the lexical level, and not merely an inclination to do so. Rule Consequentialism provides no reason why this obligation, too, will not carry over to the inter-group case.

We now turn to potential differences between the intergenerational and contemporary cases. These generate a series of reasons why the sense of both inclination and obligation will be both stronger and more precise in the former than in the latter. This is due to the connections the present generation feel between themselves, their projects, and their descendants.

In Section 7.6 I argued that, even though there is no obligation to pursue accumulation for the benefit of future generations, those who had internalized the ideal code will feel a very strong inclination to do so, as a combination of holistic evaluation of different possible histories for their group, a sense of obligation to past generations who sacrificed to make them better-off, particular concern for specific future individuals (especially their own descendants), and a commitment to specific ongoing projects, all support a strong desire to see future generations have higher aspirations than ourselves. The resulting inclinations may be sufficiently strong to outweigh even the (very difficult to meet) needs of some contemporary members of the group.

Analogous reasons are not likely to arise with regard to a better-off contemporary group. The crucial difference is that, in the intergenerational case, we strive for higher aspirations for future generations than for ourselves largely because such aspirations are inappropriate, unimaginable, or otherwise impossible for ourselves. They are aspirations that can only evolve over time, and are simply not currently available. By contrast, it is hard to imagine a plausible tale where a worse-off group wants another contemporaneous group to have higher aspirations without desiring them for themselves. If we believe that the higher lexical level has merit, then we will adopt it for ourselves. If not, then we will attach little weight to the other group's aspirations toward it.

Turn now to our two examples of worse-off groups. In the intergenerational case, the present generation feel an obligation not only to raise their descendants above whatever lexical level is appropriate to their straightened circumstances, but also to modify those circumstances to make that lexical level as high as possible. They feel obliged to minimize the intergenerational decline, not just to manage it. These reasons are similar to those operating in the case of accumulation, only each is stronger here, as decline is more destructive and more morally urgent than forgone accumulation.

A well-off group may feel some sense of inclination (or even obligation) to raise the aspirations of a completely unconnected worse-off group. However, this inclination will not have nearly the same force here as in the intergenerational case, as the manifold connections are not paralleled.

In addition to their added force, the present generation's inclinations take a more self-concerned form in the intergenerational case. Because their concern for future people is bound up with their partiality for themselves and their own projects, the present generation don't just want future generations to be well-off. They also want them to feel, and to be, connected to themselves. Therefore, in addition to wanting future people to have a more flourishing social framework and a correspondingly higher interpretation of the lexical level, they will also want that framework and that interpretation to be a continuation of the present framework and interpretation. Radical discontinuity between generations is undesirable, from the perspective of the present generation, even if it would leave future generations better-off.[9]

---

[9] The position explored in the text is analogous to McMahan's concept of identity-preserving concern for individuals. McMahan, *The Ethics of Killing*, 82–6.

Similarly, if decline is inevitable, the present generation will want to preserve for future generations those elements of their social framework and lexical interpretation that are most precious to, or distinctive of, themselves. By contrast, if one group sees another contemporary group embarked on a path of social improvement, they will be relatively uninterested in whether that path would lead to cultural similarity or divergence between the two groups.

9.2.3. An Illustration

In general, then, the present generation will give priority to future generations in their own group over unconnected contemporary groups. Perhaps the hardest conflict is when the present generation must choose between accumulation for their descendants and improvement for a worse-off contemporary group. In Section 7.6 I argued that the inclination favouring accumulation will sometimes outweigh even the needs of some contemporaries in our own group. Therefore, we should expect it to outweigh the needs of the worse-off members of unconnected groups even more often. How often, of course, it is difficult to say with any precision. (Of course, we should not conclude that the inclination to accumulate will always outweigh the interests of everyone in a worse-off group, especially if the latter group is especially numerous or especially needy.)

We now explore this tension between intergenerational and inter-group obligations using a simple imaginary tale.

A Tale of Two Groups. Two previously unconnected groups of space travellers are marooned on an island in a vast ocean on an otherwise uninhabited planet. The island contains two resources: oil and date palms. The date palms provide an adequate supply of nutrients to both groups. One group (the lucky people) are able to use the oil to run machines salvaged from their spacecraft. The other group (the unlucky people) are unable to make any use of the oil, having failed to salvage anything. As a result, the lucky people enjoy a high standard of living, while the unlucky people have a subsistence life. Fortunately, the machines salvaged by the lucky people include the technology to repair some machines in the unlucky people's ship. So both groups could enjoy a high standard of living. Unfortunately, the oil-driven machines pollute the water table, which adversely impacts on the date palms.

Suppose the lucky people have internalized the ideal code. What should they do? Should they share their technology and resources with the unlucky people? If so, at what cost to themselves or their descendants? Should they reduce their consumption of oil? Should the lucky people destroy their technology altogether, preventing anyone from using the oil? (After all, if oil is never used, the date palms are never damaged.)

Given our earlier discussion of property rights in the ideal code, we can assume that the lucky group will regard the technology on their ship as their property, but they will not conclude that they have an automatic moral right to do whatever they want with it. (For the moment, we assume that each group has plenty of oil on its side of the island, so that property rights in oil are not an issue. Later variants on our tale introduce issues surrounding such rights.)

Owing to the significance of individual and group autonomy, the enormous variety of possible empirical dilemmas future generations might face, and the unpredictability of future developments in technology, the ideal code will not prescribe the precise details of present or future energy usage. We focus on a single general question: Will the ideal code require the lucky to sacrifice to improve life for the unlucky?

Suppose the present generation of lucky people have already accepted a reduction in well-being due to the need to adopt sustainable policies. This sacrifice is comparatively easy to accept, as it directly provides long-term benefits for future members of one's own society, thus enhancing the value and meaning of the life of the present lucky people in a way that intergroup redistribution does not. I argued in Section 8.2 that the ideal code can be extremely demanding when the survival of one's community or its future well-being or liberty is at stake.

Once they have accepted this sacrifice, will the present generation accept sacrifices to aid the unlucky group? There are several competing considerations: some suggest that they will, while others suggest that they will not.

The overall conclusion of our previous abstract discussion was that the present generation of lucky people will be inclined to favour their own interests, and the interests of future lucky people, over the interests of the present unlucky people. The bias in favour of accumulation will be stronger here than in the intra-group case.

Suppose the present generation of lucky people conclude that a policy of equalizing consumption between the two groups (at a sustainable level) would either be impossible, or would involve too great a burden for themselves or their descendants. They will probably favour a policy involving a higher degree of intergenerational equality within each group than of equality between groups.

On the other hand, if they have internalized the ideal code, the lucky group will almost certainly feel a strong obligation to ensure that the unlucky people have sufficient resources to provide an adequate background social framework to enable their society to rise above the lexical level (minimally defined), so long as this does not impoverish the lucky people, or jeopardize their own social framework.

Much depends, not only on the relative levels of well-being of the two groups, but also on their absolute levels. Our version of Rule Consequentialism includes both a zero level and a lexical level, either in its foundational value theory or in the beliefs of those who have internalized its ideal code. Therefore, we must compare life among the two groups to these two levels. There are too many possibilities to consider them all here. Two questions will be especially significant for anyone who has internalized the ideal code. Is there a policy of sharing and conservation that enables (at least most members of) both groups to live above the lexical level? On the other hand, is there any policy that at least enables (almost everyone in) both groups to live above the *zero* level?

If there is a form of conservation that would enable both groups to live above the zero level, then it will count heavily against any policy that it would allow the unlucky people to fall below the zero level. We saw in Section 6.2 that the obligation to raise people above the zero level is likely to weigh very strongly with those who have internalized the ideal code. This obligation would be likely to trump most other moral reasons, except perhaps the need to ensure the survival of an adequate social framework to enable one's own group to remain above the lexical level. Under partial compliance, or in very unfavourable circumstances, this demand may become overwhelming (Section 8.2).

Suppose, on the other hand, that the lucky group have comparatively undemanding options where everyone will be raised above the zero level. Recall that one feature of the formulation of the lexical level used in our foundational value theory is that the gap between the lexical level and the zero level is comparatively small, in the following crucial sense: If a group has the resources to raise everyone above the zero level, then little additional material prosperity is required to raise everyone above the (minimal) lexical level.

Our foundational account of the lexical level is comparatively modest (Sections 3.4, 3.6). A life of basic autonomy, free from severe deprivation and disease, lived in a world of reasonably stable institutions, can exceed the lexical level. It is thus quite likely that, perhaps with some sacrifice from the lucky group, a non-environmentally disastrous level of resource consumption could provide such a life to both groups. Given the significance they attach to the lexical level, we might expect someone who had internalized the ideal code to have a very strong preference for this policy.

However, things are more complicated. Those who have internalized the ideal code adopt a context-dependent lexical level. As the two groups are at different levels of social development, they operate with different lexical interpretations. The lucky ones will privilege their own interpretation, but probably only with regard to themselves. They may be disposed to think that the most important thing is that each group remain above *its own* lexical level. Their motivation to raise the unlucky group above the *lucky* group's lexical level may be weaker. A policy of unequal resource utilization may thus be preferred, if it is the only option that enables both groups to remain safely above their own respective lexical levels.

The argument for this conclusion is as follows. In my discussion of the Accumulation Problem, I argued that each generation will both privilege its own interpretation of the lexical level, and be aware that other generations will have different interpretations (Section 7.6). As a result, they will judge the sacrifice required of them against their own interpretation, not against anyone else's. Something similar will happen in the international case. The lucky ones will judge the sacrifice required *of them* against their own lexical standard, but they may think it reasonable to judge any benefit forgone by the unlucky people against the lexical standard appropriate to the perspective of the latter group. Accordingly, they will not feel the same *obligation* that they normally would to raise other people above the lexical level.

We need to distinguish an *interpretation* of the lexical level from a broader notion I shall call 'the lexical threshold'. The former is a particular account of what a life needs to be like in order to reach the lexical level. Within any given group, different people will have different lexical interpretations, and one of the key roles of politics is to respond appropriately to these differences: respecting them where possible and resolving them where necessary.

Within any group the set of available interpretations of the lexical level is constrained by the social framework. That framework both makes interpretations imaginable and makes them feasible. If different groups have different social frameworks, then they offer different sets of lexical interpretations. If we were cultural relativists, we could leave it at that. The different sets are simply *different*. As Rule Consequentialists, we should not do this. However much they may respect individual and cultural differences, those who have internalized the ideal code are not wholesale cultural relativists. They will recognize that some sets of lexical interpretations are better than others. When considering the impact of their decisions on future generations, for instance, they aim to structure their society so that their descendants will have *better* interpretations of the lexical level, not merely different ones. If one group (G1) operates with a better set of lexical interpretations than another (G2), then we will say that G1 has a higher *lexical threshold* than G2.

A given interpretation of the lexical level might be good enough for G2, but not for G1: the interpretation reaches the lower threshold, but not the higher.

Three good examples of the notion of a lexical threshold are literacy, economic development, and life expectancy. While individuals and communities may differ in the comparative weight they place on these three factors, and while scholars may differ as to the precise empirical connections between them, a society which scores better with respect to these indices has available (if other things are equal) a *superior* set of interpretations of the lexical level. If other things are equal, literate, wealthy, long-lived people are better-off (in ways that transcend particular cultural values) than people who are illiterate, poor, and short-lived. Any disparity with respect to our three indices thus lead to a disparity in lexical thresholds. If an individual who has internalized the ideal code concludes that, in a particular case, disparate lexical thresholds are morally inappropriate, then she will seek to remove disparities of literacy, development, and life expectancy as well.

Within a group, one central aim of politics is to ensure that, even if different people opt for different lexical interpretations, they all choose against the same lexical threshold. The crucial question in inter-group ethics is whether we should tolerate different lexical thresholds for different groups. As the thresholds are linked to social frameworks, this turns on whether we should accept distinct social frameworks. When looking at an unconnected group, the lucky ones may think it appropriate to apply a lower threshold. In the context of the unlucky group, their lower aspirations are appropriate interpretations of the lexical level.

There is a further reason why the lucky group will be reluctant to equalize consumption. In any realistic situation, not every member of a particular group enjoys the same lifestyle or opportunities. Not everyone would be equally affected by a shift to conservation. In particular, there may be some among the lucky people whose lives depend upon the current pattern of oil consumption, and who would be unable to survive if there is *any* conservation. These might include both present people who require resource-intensive technologies to live, and future people who will suffer from medical conditions which will be cured only if technological advancement within the lucky society proceeds at its current oil-fuelled rate.

A code *requiring* some people to make such a sacrifice may be difficult to teach. In the intra-group case, the better-off in the present generation may feel connected to the worst-off, through joint projects and feelings of solidarity, especially as they all share the same social framework. Suppose such bonds do not exist between the two groups in our tale. Given the lack of connection between the two groups, it will be harder to get people to make a demanding sacrifice for another group than to get them to make the same sacrifice for future members of their own group. So we should expect the ideal code to be less demanding here than in the parallel case involving declining future well-being in their own society. Also, the fortunate members of the lucky group will be more reluctant to sacrifice their less fortunate fellows to assist the unlucky group, than to benefit their own descendants.

9.2.4. *The Significance of Connections*

We turn now to the differences between our simple tale and the real world of international relations. There are several key disanalogies, each of which may affect the appropriateness of various features of the proposed ideal code. In particular, bringing our simple tale closer to the actual world may increase the willingness of the lucky group to make sacrifices for the unlucky group.

One obvious difference is that the real world contains many groups, of varying sizes and strengths, arranged along a continuum from the most lucky to the least lucky. This creates problems of partial compliance. If most affluent countries fail to contribute as they should, the burdens placed by the international ideal code of those willing to comply may be extreme. We return to these issues in the next chapter.

The main source of the different attitudes of those who have internalized the ideal code in the intergenerational and inter-group cases is the lack of connections between the lucky and unlucky groups. Conversely, anything that creates connections between contemporary groups will bring the two cases closer together, and alter the strength and focus of the lucky group's obligations and inclinations regarding contemporary groups.

The most obvious source of connections is shared history. In our tale, the initial allocation of resources and technologies is completely a matter of brute luck. In the real world, things are not so clear-cut. The existing global distribution of resources, technologies, infrastructure, and even social and economic institutions, is the result, not merely of luck, nor of the virtuous industry of the lucky, but also of a history of unequal international inter-actions, which have often unjustly created or exacerbated inequalities.

The history of injustice underlying present inequality will affect the behaviour and attitudes of those who have internalized the ideal code. In particular, we can reasonably expect two complementary effects:

1. People in 'unlucky' groups will definitely not support policies permitting 'lucky' groups to retain the advantages of their past misdeeds to the extent that they might have permitted the retention of the fruits of brute luck or personal industry.

2. Those in 'lucky' groups will accept much more demanding obligations to unlucky people, if their advantages are neither entirely earned nor completely morally innocent.

In both cases, one explanation for the shift is familiar. The ideal code is likely, for a variety of reasons discussed in Section 5.7, to include a strong distinction between doing and allowing, and a wide range of person-affecting principles and obligations to particular individuals. Once one accepts these elements, it is natural also to accept that a person's obligations to rectify past injustices they have either performed or benefited from exceed their obligations to distant strangers with whom they share no previous connection. In particular, it is very natural to think one should at least be required to make a sacrifice equivalent to the extent of one's unjust benefit. (In one very relevant sense, giving up unjust benefits is not a sacrifice at all.)[10]

Suppose our two groups are not unconnected, but have interacted many times in the past. This could affect the attitudes of the present generation in several related ways. Past interactions may place individual members of the lucky group under particular obligations, either to the unlucky group as a whole, or to specific individuals in that group. We saw in Section 5.7 that, in the ideal code, obligations owed to particular individuals often trump both one's permission to pursue one's own projects, and one's general obligations and inclinations to meet the needs of others, promote their interests, etc. If enough particular individuals in one group come under such obligations to particular members of the other group, then this will materially impact on our relations with them at a political (that is, group to group) level.

One crucial question in inter-group ethics is whether present individuals can owe obligations due to harms their ancestors did in the past. For us, of course, the question is what someone who had internalized the ideal code would think. We are proceeding on the assumption that such a person feels a strong sense of group identity, and that this extends to both future generations and past generations. (If they do not feel this sense of identity, then the case for both partiality to one's own group and for global rules or policies recognizing group autonomy is largely undermined, and the global ideal code becomes directly cosmopolitan and very demanding.)

Those who have internalized the ideal code presumably know all this. Whatever their inclinations, they will recognize that, if they accept the benefits of group autonomy, then consistency requires them to accept at least

---

[10] The fact that the very question of the demands of beneficence presupposes a background of legitimate entitlements to resource-use is especially well canvassed in Murphy, *Moral Demands in Nonideal Theory*, ch. 3. For a discussion of similar issues in an international context, see Pogge, *World Poverty and Human Rights*, 196–215.

partial responsibility for the prior misdeeds of their group, even where they have not themselves directly benefited from those misdeeds. (In particular, even though they adopt a largely person-affecting moral code, they will not feel entitled to avoid all obligation to make reparations by appeal to non-identity-based arguments to the effect that, as the particular unlucky people wouldn't have existed without the prior injustice, they are owed nothing (Section 5.7).) Whatever their ontological status, if groups are sufficiently important to ground the recognition of group autonomy, then they are real enough to ground group-based obligations.

It is thus natural for those who have internalized the ideal code to extend their sense of individual obligation to the group level, and favour policies acknowledging the debts and obligations owned by their group to other groups because of past injustice, past promises, past agreements, etc.

A further consideration supports the acknowledgement and discharge of group debts by the present generation, and their reluctance to incur additional group debts. In several earlier chapters, I argued that moral autonomy is a significant component of a flourishing human life (Sections 4.2.2, 5.4, 6.2). The present generation will want their descendants to be able to flourish, so they will want to leave them as much moral autonomy as possible. They will want valuable lifestyle choices to be morally open to all future generations. However, the present generation know that, if they benefit themselves or their descendants by ignoring the plight of other groups affected by their present choices, then those very descendants, having internalized the ideal code themselves, will feel a very strong obligation to make significant sacrifices to rectify this ongoing injustice. To protect the moral autonomy of their descendants, as well as their material and environmental comforts, the present generation have additional reason to take responsibility now.

A further complication in the real world is that, in most affluent countries, many people subscribe (to varying degrees) to a more positive explanation of the discrepancies between nations, attributing them to the virtuous industry of themselves and their ancestors, and the opposite qualities in other nations.[11] One cause of disagreement with respect to international justice in the real world is disagreement about both the extent and the nature of historical interactions. For instance, those who believe that the plight of the destitute is (somehow) 'their own fault' are likely to be much less generous than those who believe that their plight is (somehow) 'our

---

[11] This view is also espoused by many liberal philosophers from affluent nations. For instance, in *The Law of Peoples*, Rawls offers the following opinion: 'I believe that the causes of the wealth of a people and the forms it takes lie in their political culture and in the religious, philosophical, and moral traditions that support the basic structure of their political and social institutions, as well as in the industriousness and cooperative talents of its members, all supported by their political virtues' (Rawls, *The Law of Peoples*, 108).

fault'. No doubt some disagreements regarding the impact of history would persist in the ideal society. However, given the significance of history for present obligations, we should expect those who have internalized the ideal code to be more concerned to get their historical facts straight than most affluent Westerners in the actual world. If we conclude that, as a result, their historical views would be different from our own in some definite direction, then this discovery may have distinct lessons for us.[12]

9.2.5. Aside on History in a Forward-Looking Code

As Rule Consequentialism is forward-looking, one might wonder why we should expect the ideal code to include *any* rules governing past injustices. Shouldn't all rules be geared to promoting future well-being? However, the ideal code will clearly tell agents not to perpetrate injustices in the future, and to provide appropriate reparation for any injustices they perform and/or benefit from. The benefits of including such provisions in the ideal code in regard to future injustices are obvious, unless we can be sure future injustices will not occur. Once these future-looking provisions are included, however, the ideal code will be much simpler, and presumably easier to teach, if it also tells agents to make reparations for past injustices they may discover themselves to have benefited from or committed. (As we have just seen, discovering that your group committed an atrocity, while not as bad as discovering that you committed it, is also not the same as discovering that it just happened, or discovering that it was committed by strangers.) So the ideal code will have rules for past injustices unless we can be sure that there will be no future injustice.

Yet the ideal code cannot eliminate future injustices, as it does not idealize to perfect future compliance. We must therefore accommodate the possibility that individuals who have internalized the ideal code will find themselves benefiting from additional injustices in the future. It will obviously be desirable for them to be disposed to use their benefits to rectify those injustices. Overall, the presence of historical injustice is thus likely to increase the degree of sacrifice considered reasonable by those who have internalized the ideal code.

9.2.6. History and the Lexical Level

A history of interaction also affects the relativities of the respective groups' social frameworks, and hence their interpretations of the lexical level. The

---

[12] In the actual world, some affluent people believe that their nation is successful because it has been chosen by God for special favour. I put to one side the question of whether such belief could survive scrutiny in the ideal society. (Although I hope to return to it elsewhere.)

assumption that different lexical interpretations are appropriate for different groups rests on the prior assumption that they have distinct social frameworks. Yet a social framework is not, for the Rule Consequentialist, some mysterious holistic entity. It is merely a pattern of interactions between individuals within a group. Two groups have perfectly distinct social frameworks if and only if their members *never* interact. In the real world, the distinction is therefore a matter of degree. The more interaction between two groups, the less plausible it is to see their social frameworks as distinct. In particular, if our interpretation of the lexical level regards as essential a feature of our lifestyle that is only available to us because of historical or present interactions with another group, then it is much less plausible for us to expect that very group to rest content with an interpretation of the lexical level that regards that lifestyle feature as optional. (The other group may choose not to pursue that lifestyle feature, but we should not proceed on the assumption that it need not be available to them. Were it not for them, it would not be available to us either.)

For instance, suppose G1 have a higher lexical threshold than G2 based on the following social differences: G1 have more leisure time, easier access to affordable commodities, stable liberal democratic institutions, better health care and sanitation, longer life expectancy. To see whether G1 can, when deciding what to sacrifice to aid G2, consistently both apply their higher threshold to themselves and at the same time apply a lower threshold to G2, we should ask how many of these advantages G1 would still be enjoying if either G2 did not exist or if G1's interactions with G2 were perfectly just. (To borrow Gauthier's terminology, are G1 taking advantage of G2? Section 2.1.1.) The more our social frameworks intertwine, and the more our own values presuppose the fruits of that intertwining, the more we should come to see not two groups, but only one.

Interactions between the two groups may also lead each group to readjust their views about their *own* lexical thresholds. The unlucky group, seeing how much better life is in the lucky group, will begin to ask why they should not adopt similar aspirations, and accordingly set much more ambitious interpretations of the lexical level, for themselves. An impoverished Chinese worker, slaving to produce toys for affluent Westerners, may wonder why she doesn't enjoy any leisure time or disposable income.

On the other hand, as happens when they contemplate the possibility of intergenerational decline within their own group, if the lucky group are continually confronted with people who adopt interpretations of the lexical level that are suited to less affluent circumstances, then this may lead them to regard as optional some elements of their own lifestyle that they previously regarded as essential to the lexical level.

History is thus highly significant for Rule Consequentialism, even though it is fundamentally a forward-looking theory. Given their strong disposition to give priority to people below the lexical level, much better-off groups who have internalized the ideal code will only feel free to accumulate for their descendants, and pursue their own luxurious projects, while leaving another group of their contemporaries much worse-off, if they have faith that it is morally acceptable to apply different lexical thresholds to different groups. If an appreciation of the historical and contemporary economic and social context of their world undermines that faith, then it will push members of better-off groups in a distinctly cosmopolitan—and thus more demanding—direction.

Even if there is no historical connection between the two groups, the possibility of future interaction may have some impact on the attitudes of the lucky group. Their disposition to feel concern for all human beings could lead them to adopt the cosmopolitan project of striving for a global social framework, or more particular projects aimed at improving the lives of some particular members of the unlucky group. Once someone who had internalized the ideal code had adopted such projects, she would soon find her well-being and her moral worldview tied up with the fate of the unlucky group, and she would develop personal obligations towards particular members of that group. This would bring her moral relations with the unlucky group closer to her relations with future members of her own group.

There is an interesting paradox here. If the present generation take steps to ensure that their social framework extends in the next generation to include the members of the unlucky group, then future generations of the unlucky will be part of the same community as the future generations of lucky people. There is thus a real sense in which the present lucky people are closer to the future unlucky people than to the present unlucky people.

9.2.7. Climate Change

One topical issue where precise empirical details are crucially relevant to the behaviour of those who have internalized the ideal code is climate change.[13] Suppose the present generation of affluent people in the developed world accept the following empirical claims:

1. Previous consumption of fossil fuels, predominantly by people in the developed world, is changing the global climate in ways that have

---

[13] For an introduction to the economic, ethical, and scientific complexities involved in climate change, or 'global warming', see Dasgupta, *Human Well-being and the Natural Environment*, 187; Gardiner, 'Ethics and Global Climate Change'; Gardiner, 'The Global Warming Tragedy and the Dangerous Illusion of the Kyoto Protocol'; Grubb, 'Seeking Fair Weather'; Kopp and Thatcher, *The Weathervane Guide to Climate Policy*; and Pearson, *Economics and the Global Environment*.

detrimental effects on future people, especially those in developing countries.

2. Current patterns of consumption of fossil fuels will cause additional climate change, with additional detrimental impact.

We have already defended the following claims about those who have internalized the ideal code:

1. They will be more disposed to make sacrifices to prevent declining well-being for their descendants than to obtain benefits for those descendants.
2. When the possibility of harm to subsequent generations arises, they will be risk-averse.
3. In international ethics, they will be more disposed to make sacrifices to rectify harms that they have caused than to provide assistance.

A necessary condition for the valuable exercise of autonomy is the presence of a background social framework providing a range of independently valuable goals. A healthy global ecosystem is a necessary precondition for the existence of any social framework whatever, whether within or between groups. As climate change threatens the viability of the global ecosystem, those who have internalized the ideal code will take it extremely seriously.

Obligations relating to climate change will have higher priority than almost any of the other intra- or inter-group obligations canvassed in this chapter. A full discussion of what those obligations will be is beyond the scope of this book. However, Rule Consequentialism does help to explain the real significance of climate change, and sketch some moral priorities for inter-group efforts to deal with it.

In the real world, of course, a persistent feature of climate change debate is disagreement over the empirical facts. Section 8.2 showed that those who have internalized the ideal code will be risk-averse in the face of such disagreement—adopting the pessimistic model, favouring policies designed to mitigate the worst feasible effects of climate change, and attaching a high priority to the acquisition of more reliable empirical information. The fact that climate change potentially involves catastrophe caused by human action strongly reinforces these conclusions. Those who have internalized the ideal code want their descendants to have lives that are both personally worthwhile and morally respectable. They will thus be especially concerned to avoid a future where, owning to their present behaviour, their descendants face extremely demanding obligations of reparations to people in other nations devastated by climate change. (Another striking feature of climate change in the real world is the extent of partial compliance with the behaviour we would expect from anyone who had internalized the ideal code. We return to this issue in Section 10.4.1.)

Rule Consequentialism does not definitively settle the behaviour of the lucky group in our simple tale, or in more complex real-life analogues. However, it does show how a complex range of factors are to be balanced. We now turn to a series of more specific international issues, where Rule Consequentialism supports some departures from conventional international practice.

9.3. The Autonomy of Other Groups

If the recognition of group autonomy by international politics is justified on instrumental grounds, then the scope of that autonomy is limited. Given our value theory, we justify group autonomy primarily by appeal to the value of individual well-being and autonomy. Therefore, the former is only desirable insofar as it enhances and respects the latter—for members of all groups. In particular, while we should expect someone who had internalized the ideal code to recognize and respect the autonomy of *other* groups, especially groups whose members are mostly worse-off than herself, that respect must be balanced against her direct concern for individuals within that other group, and especially her desire to avoid harming them and to ensure that they are able to live worthwhile lives.

To illustrate these issues, consider a variant on our original tale.

The Despot.   The unlucky group are ruled by a despotic leader, who stifles dissent, inhibits economic development, and curtails personal liberties. The lucky group have the power, thanks to their superior technology and economic influence, to intervene on behalf of individuals within the unlucky group, and to otherwise lobby the unlucky government.

Should the lucky group exercise that power? Should they recognize the government of the unlucky group as legitimate? In general, how much will the lucky group feel justified in looking inside the operations of the unlucky group?

For someone in the lucky group who has internalized the ideal code, the first question is whether it is appropriate for them to even have a view about what goes on in the unlucky group. A cultural relativist might argue that, as the two groups are distinct, and as their social frameworks and lexical interpretations are so different, it is not possible for anyone in the lucky group to say what should happen in the other group.

This argument has some force. Anyone who has internalized the ideal code will recognize that many political questions relate to interpretations of the lexical level, and are sufficiently interwoven with the relevant social framework particular to one group, that (*a*) it is very unlikely that judgements initially reached in relation to one group would carry over automatically to the other; and (*b*) it would be rash for someone in one group to make judgements about the other.

However, this cultural relativism has limits, as not all politics relates to contested interpretations of the lexical level. Two areas of politics, in particular, are more basic.

1. The politics of someone who has internalized the ideal code are built on the foundation of the individual morality of the ideal code, as sketched in Chapters 5 and 6. That morality contains many specific obligations, and many inclinations, whose specification is independent of the lexical level. The case for the political attitudes analogous to these obligations will thus carry over to other groups. These political attitudes include: a prohibition on gratuitous harm; respect for the very basic liberties and resources that are the necessary prerequisites for living above *any* lexical level; and a strong sense of obligation to provide everyone with the ability at least to live above the *zero* level if at all possible. If the lucky group see the rulers of the unlucky group violating any of *these* obligations, they are very unlikely to regard this as a morally neutral difference in cultural practices.

2. Recall the distinction between interpretations of the lexical level and the lexical threshold. The latter notion, although broad and vague, provides some cross-cultural comparison of the value of different forms of social organization. When evaluating competing policies in terms of their impact on themselves or their descendants, the present generation in the lucky group will often appeal to their impact on the lexical threshold rather than on individual interpretations, especially if the latter remain controversial. In particular, if a given policy offers a much higher lexical threshold than any alternative, then this will count heavily in its favour. Political arguments based on the lexical threshold can thus carry over to other groups, in a way that arguments based on specific interpretations of the lexical level cannot.

Those in the lucky group who have internalized the ideal code will thus have a range of views about the treatment that the members of the unlucky group are entitled to expect from their government. They might also have more general views about how the unlucky group should be governed. In Section 8.1, before comparing alternative forms of democratic government, we briefly reviewed the empirical literature comparing democracy with non-democratic government. We saw that democracy does a (statistically significant) better job of delivering on a wide range of measures of well-being, including the following: preventing famine, increasing real net income per head, promoting economic growth, reducing infant mortality rates, and raising life expectancy at birth. These factors are not elements of controversial interpretations of the lexical level. Rather, they are a combination of the basic necessities of life (not starving, not dying in infancy) and factors clearly positively related to the lexical *threshold* available to a group (economic growth, life expectancy). Accordingly, these arguments for democracy are group independent. In the absence of compelling evidence that democracy is not appropriate for the unlucky group, the lucky group will believe that the latter should become democratic.

Having established that the lucky group have views about life in the unlucky group, we must now ask how they might act on those beliefs. The individual case offers an instructive parallel. After all, those who have internalized the ideal code do not act on all their beliefs about how other individuals should behave. Nor, on the other hand, do they always refrain from doing so. They try to strike a balance. It will be the same in the inter-group case. The lucky group will aim to strike a balance between respect for group autonomy and a concern for the well-being of the other group and its members.

To explore possible constraints on the notion of group autonomy, we thus begin by examining the analogy with individual autonomy.

In the individual case, both common sense and the ideal code prescribe a general principle of non-interference with other people's actions, even where those actions are harmful to the person herself. On balance, a principle of non-intervention is likely to produce greater benefits (in terms of increased autonomy and security) than a code permitting constant interference (Sections 6.2, 6.4, 6.6). Freedom from non-intervention is the flip-side of moral autonomy. If those who have internalized the ideal code will feel free to make a particular decision for themselves, they are hardly likely to feel free to interfere when another agent faces the same decision. Furthermore, non-intervention extends further than moral freedom. As we saw in our discussion of political liberty, those who have internalized the ideal code will want to leave other agents free to do many things that they themselves would not feel morally free to do.

However, there are limits to this principle of non-intervention. In particular, we do feel justified in preventing self-harm when the person is clearly not behaving as a rational autonomous agent, such as when their actions are caused by drugs, brainwashing, psychiatric or mental illness, or even radical misinformation. (For instance, it is not a violation of moral autonomy forcibly to prevent someone from unwittingly ingesting poison.) It is easy to see why the ideal code will include such exceptions to the non-interference rule. In the ideal code, non-interference is not an end in itself. It is valued only insofar as it generally promotes well-being. The obligation not to interfere, like almost all other obligations in the ideal code, is only prima facie. In cases of obvious self-harm it competes with the obligation to assist others in dire need. While those who have internalized the ideal code may balance these competing prima facie obligations differently from ourselves, there is no reason to believe that they will always accord non-interference a higher status. Indeed, in cases of serious irrational self-harm, they might feel an *obligation* to 'interfere', not merely a permission to do so.

Just as an individual can fail to be autonomous, so can a group. In both cases, at least in the context of the ideal code, autonomy is not a purely descriptive concept: it has a clearly normative or evaluative dimension. Insofar as autonomy is morally valuable, a group following autocratic or dictatorial decision-making processes is not acting autonomously. Accordingly, respect for autonomy gives us no reason to respect such decisions, especially when the outcome is harmful to the group or its members. The relationship between individual and group autonomy gives group autonomy a certain externally observable moral structure that individual autonomy lacks. Therefore, failures of autonomy can be easier to diagnose.

If a despot seizes control of a state and silences all democratic processes, then respect for group autonomy does not require that we stand aside, or that we allow the despot to speak for the group. If no other group recognized despots as legitimate rulers, then the incentive to become a despot would be greatly reduced. So an anti-despot code of inter-group politics would probably produce more well-being, especially in relation to individual freedom, than any despot-friendly alternative code. (One particular instance of this gives rise to the resource privilege, discussed at length in Section 9.3.2.)

Of course, we must be wary not to diagnose a lack of autonomy too readily. In particular, our criteria should be primarily procedural not substantive. The individual case is instructive here. If we all felt free to interfere whenever another person failed to choose exactly as we ourselves would in their place, then no one would enjoy any real freedom at all. None of us would ever be sure that others were not about to intervene to 'save us from ourselves'. So the ideal code will not include any broad permission to intervene. Under any plausible ideal code, a lack of autonomy is typically displayed by *how* people decide, not by *what* they decide. The latter can, of course, be a relevant indicator of a lack of autonomy. If someone makes a seemingly inexplicable choice—opting for what no sane person would want—we are right to suspect some deficiency in their decision procedure. But this is merely circumstantial evidence of a failure of autonomy. If closer investigation reveals the decision to be fully autonomous, then we generally feel we ought to respect it. Such deference to the individual's own judgement makes good Rule Consequentialist sense, as cases where a third party genuinely is better informed as to a person's interests will be comparatively rare, especially in a world where most of one's interactions are with people who have internalized the ideal code.

Similarly, the ideal code will presumably not license every group to interfere whenever another group chooses differently. Furthermore, we must expect, as in the individual case, that a broad range of procedures will count as autonomous. The ideal code would not allow one group to impose its own constitutional peculiarities on others in the name of respecting their group autonomy. For instance, I argued in Section 8.1 that, from the perspective of the ideal code, democratic majoritarianism is preferable to an entrenched constitution. It does not follow from this that citizens of a genuine democracy will feel entitled to intervene in the internal affairs of another nation simply because the latter labours under an ancient and somewhat cumbersome entrenched constitution. While the argument favouring democracy over despotism is based on general features of human beings that hold constant across all societies, the arguments favouring majoritarian democracy over an entrenched constitution might seem more rooted in controversial claims peculiar to particular interpretations of the lexical level, especially those found in a liberal society. These arguments are thus much less likely to carry over from one group to another.[14]

As so often in the ideal code, the precise boundaries of the key moral concept are likely to remain vague here. We probably cannot determine exactly how anyone who had internalized the ideal code would interpret the notion of 'autonomous group'. However, it seems certain they will recognize a close connection between individual and group autonomy, so that democratic decision-making processes would count as more autonomous than despotic ones.

As in the individual case, the hardest situation is where a clearly autonomous decision procedure produces a clearly harmful result. In both cases, we may think this will be comparatively rare in practice. However, it cannot be ruled out. A fully autonomous individual may decide, on a whim, to starve himself to death or to chop off his arm. A fully democratic state may embark on economic or social policies which will clearly have disastrous consequences, or it may adopt policies highly detrimental to the interests of a small minority group, perhaps even trampling on their basic rights.

Many people have the intuition that the individual and communal cases should diverge here. The autonomous individual should be allowed to do as he pleases, whereas there are some things a group should never be allowed

---

[14] Rawls's arguments in favour of an entrenched constitution, by contrast, probably would have carried over if they had been successful, as they appeal to basic rights and social stability. (See Section 8.1.1.)

to do to its members, however autonomous the process of communal decision-making. There is good reason to expect the ideal code to reflect this distinction. The benefits of agents preventing others from autonomously harming themselves might well be outweighed by everyone's general loss of the enjoyment of their freedom if they know that everyone else feels free to interfere with someone's autonomy if they judge a serious self-harm to be imminent. By contrast, one central benefit of a rule permitting intervention if a state threatened the basic rights of its citizens would be an increase in ordinary people's sense of security. In a world of international full compliance with such a code, everyone would know their basic rights would remain secure, even if local autonomous procedures yielded policies which might threaten them.

This shows that, when the two are in conflict, the primary interest of the lucky group is with the results that democracy tends to promote and the rights it tends to protect, not with democracy itself. Therefore, if they were faced with a non-democratic regime that was very hostile to democracy, but could be persuaded to implement policies friendly to basic rights and economic development by suitable inducements, then the lucky group would favour this more pragmatic approach above the options of either attempting to impose democracy, or refusing to interact with a non-democratic group. (As we shall see below, the attitudes of democratic governments and their citizens can be a key determinant of the behaviour of non-democratic regimes regarding their own citizens.)

Suppose we have decided that another group is not autonomous, in the morally loaded sense used in the ideal code. There are several possible levels of response to this judgement:

1. The refusal to enter close ties with that group.
2. The refusal to trade with them.
3. The refusal to recognize their government.
4. The refusal to allow others to trade with them.
5. Direct interference with the groups affairs, either to change attitudes or to change the government.

Different standards of proof of 'lack of autonomy' will presumably be required to trigger each of these escalating responses. Our explanation of their general attitudes suggests that those who have internalized the ideal code will be most disposed to intervene with respect to practices that threaten the viability of a life above the zero level, or that violate absolute moral obligations. They will be least likely to intervene in complex political decisions where competing legitimate interpretations of the lexical level must be balanced. In general, as in the individual case, we should expect their interventions to be designed to assist the unlucky group in making its own autonomous decisions, rather than imposing particular judgements.

Another legitimate ground for intervention would be if the present generation of a particular state threatened the basic rights of welfare of their own future citizens. (In practice, such a threat is also likely to spill over, and threaten the future generations of other states, thus giving those states a self-concerned motive for intervention.) In terms of the analogy with the individual case, such threats are half-way between imprudence and immorality, depending on whether future people are regarded as members of the present community, or as threatened outsiders.

This is especially significant if, owing to increasing globalization, and increasing connections between the two groups in particular, future people in the lucky group are likely to share a common social framework with future people in the unlucky group. Judgements based on the interpretations of the lexical level adopted by the present generation in the lucky group might thus carry over, if not to the present unlucky group, then to their descendants. If the two groups will effectively become one through future connections, then the future generations of the unlucky group are, from the point of view of present members of the lucky group, future members of their own group. They will thus feel entitled to intercede on their behalf just as they would for their own descendants.

9.3.1. Precommitment

In both the individual and collective cases, an especially striking set of problems arises when an agent radically changes personality or values across time. Consider a psychotic person, for whom periods of sanity alternate with periods of psychosis. We typically characterize such a life in terms of psychotic episodes deviating from an underlying autonomous life, as distinct from someone who changes his mind frequently about basic questions of value. This has obvious implications for our treatment of the person during his psychotic episodes, and especially for the comparative weight we place on the wishes he expresses during those episodes, as opposed to wishes he expresses at other times about what we should do when he becomes psychotic.

Many people who suffer from periodic psychosis try to enact precommitment strategies, to ensure that when psychosis strikes they will be unable to act on their destructive (or otherwise undesirable) impulses. These strategies often require the cooperation of third parties. A mild everyday example is when you give me your car keys at the start of the evening, and make me promise not to return them if I judge that you are too drunk to drive, even if you ask for them. In more serious cases, patients might commit themselves to being hospitalized if psychosis strikes, knowing in advance that they will resist. An intermediate case might be Parfit's example of the radical young Russian landowner, who signs his property over to his wife to be distributed to the poor, and makes her promise not to return it to his later conservative self.[15]

Thomas Pogge has recently suggested an analogous measure for states.[16] A democratic state, fearing a military coup, might seek to initiate a precommitment strategy, to prevent any future military leadership from making decisions detrimental to the community's interests. Pogge's own suggestion is that the state enact an amendment to its constitution, announcing that debts incurred internationally by any future military leadership will not be honoured by subsequent democratic governments. Alternatively, a state might ask neighbouring states not to recognize any future dictator as competent to speak for their community. Or State A might enter a treaty with a powerful neighbouring state, or collection of states, whereby the latter undertook to intervene to protect State A's democratic constitution. Or an international agency might be set up to which individual states could grant national analogues of an enduring power of attorney, so that the state's assets would be held in trust during periods of non-democratic rule.[17]

Pogge's suggestion not only illustrates the analogy between the individual and group cases, but also highlights the fact that genuine autonomy often requires the support of other agents. In this case, a group cannot reliably safeguard its own autonomy without assistance from other groups. This assistance often takes a negative form. Other groups assist by not recognizing an unconstitutional regime, not trading with illegitimate heads of state, and not lending them money for which subsequent democratic governments will be held accountable. There are good reasons to expect someone who had internalized the ideal code to favour the policy of encouraging groups to enter and honour these precommitment agreements. In particular, the knowledge that dictators will not be recognized internationally would significantly reduce the desirability of becoming a dictator, thus reducing the likelihood of constitutional upheaval, and reinforcing group autonomy.[18]

---

[15] Parfit, *Reasons and Persons*, 327–9. [16] Pogge, *World Poverty and Human Rights*, 146–67.

[17] Pogge's suggestion is obviously related to the resource privilege, discussed in more detail in Section 9.3.2. The primary difference is that the present suggestion is aimed at people within the poor country itself, rather than at rich countries. In an international ideal code, the two suggestions could easily support one another.

[18] There is an intriguing parallel here with the individual case, where the fact that a precommitment strategy has been initiated, thereby reducing the potential harm of any psychotic episode, can sometimes also reduce the likelihood of such episodes. (I owe this observation to a conversation with John Dawson.)

The present defence of group precommitment sits uneasily with the argument against precommitment offered in Section 8.1. There are two key differences between the two cases.

1. In Section 8.1 the precommitment consists of the present generation favouring a minority of future people in their own society over the majority of future people in their own society. In Pogge's precommitment, the judgement of (the majority of) future people in another democratic society is preferred to the judgement of an unelected minority of future people in our own society. The general case for majority rule favours Pogge's precommitment, just as it opposed the distinct precommitment envisaged in Section 8.1.

2. Pogge's precommitment is especially offered to nations lacking stable or established democratic traditions. If the present generation know that their own democratic commitment is fragile, for whatever reason, it may be rational for them to favour the judgement of (the majority of) future people in a more stable democracy even over (the majority of) future people in their own nation. Borrowing constitutional measures from another democracy could provide an analogous form of precommitment—a way of tying future decisions in one's own society to the future jurisprudence of that other country. This could well be rational if one's own democracy is fragile or unstable. By contrast, it is hard to see why one established democracy would tie itself in this way to another.

The key difference between precommitment and other interventions is this. Owing to the overlapping social framework and the correspondingly closer lexical thresholds and interpretations, and to their involvement in one another's projects, the judgements of one generation in a group about what should happen to future generations in their own group are stronger, more detailed, and carry more weight than judgements made from one group to another. Therefore, it is appropriate to agree to intervene in support of specific judgements made autonomously within the other group, even when we would not have intervened to impose our own judgement. Once they have entered into an agreement of this form, of course, those who have internalized the ideal code will feel bound to intervene if the need arises, owing to their underlying sense that it is morally obligatory to keep one's contracts.

Pogge's precommitment has implications for the question of whether the present generation within any particular group should be held responsible for the actions of their predecessors. On the one hand, stable economic and social relations between groups over generations will be impossible if the present generation are unable to bind their successors in any way. If intergenerational contracts between groups were never binding, then no one would ever enter into them. On the other hand, Pogge's argument strongly suggests that the ideal code should not hold future generations of a group accountable for decisions made in the present generation without any reliable democratic process.

9.3.2. The Resource Privilege

To further illustrate both the relevance of empirical and historical factors for inter-group ethics and the complex notion of group autonomy, we now consider another variant on our original tale.

An Even More Unlucky Group.   Two unconnected groups land on an uninhabited planet. This time, the *unlucky* group have landed next to the only oil reserves and taken possession of them. As before, only the lucky ones have access to the technology and expertise necessary fully to utilize the oil resource.

One would expect this change to advantage the unlucky group. In fact, in the real world, the opposite is often the case. The problem lies with what Thomas Pogge dubs the 'international resource privilege': the fact that any-one gaining effective control over a geographical area is recognized as the sovereign of that area, and granted the right to appropriate and transfer any natural (or cultural) resources.[19] In the real world, owing in part to the tra-ditional over-reliance on the analogy between states and individuals, the international resource privilege is largely unconstrained by requirements of moral legitimacy or internal justice. In our terms, the rulers of (very) non-autonomous groups enjoy resource privileges.

As a result, nations with significant natural resources often lag far behind in terms of infrastructure and institutions. The presence of rich oil reserves, combined with the international resource privilege, provides a strong incent-ive to any would-be dictator. Foreign companies and consumers benefit from this situation, as the price of a resource is likely to be lower in the hands of a military strongman concerned only to finance his own opulent lifestyle and security forces, than if the resource were controlled by a democratic government accountable to millions of very poor people.

One might wonder what any of this has to do with Rule Consequentialism. After all, the negative consequences for poor countries result, in large part, from the corrupt and immoral actions of the elite in

---

[19] Pogge, *World Poverty and Human Rights*, 112–16.

those countries. Under full compliance with any plausible ideal code, such behaviour would presumably not occur, so the problem would not arise. Therefore, those who have internalized the ideal code will have no familiarity with such situations, and will thus have no advice to offer us.

There are three clear replies to this objection.

1. Imperfect Idealization.   As we do not idealize to perfect full compliance, we cannot rule out the rise of a corrupt elite in any given country. In our actual world, the wealth granted by oil reserves is so vast that it can enable a very small minority to control a whole country, especially if that country's economy is otherwise underdeveloped. Compliance with the ideal code by 90 (or even 99) per cent of the population would not be sufficient to prevent a poor country without established liberal democratic institutions from being overtaken by a military dictatorship. By contrast, in a wealthy liberal democracy, full compliance by 90 per cent of the population is a reasonably safe guarantee against a successful military coup. Furthermore, as I argued in Section 5.5, our comparative evaluation of competing codes must take account of the likely impact of those codes on future rates of compliance. One key factor here is the incentives associated with non-compliance. The wealth flowing from oil provides enormous incentives for non-compliance, thus making future non-compliance much more likely.

2. A Non-Complying Country.   At the international level, compliance by 90 per cent of everyone in the world is consistent with substantial non-compliance in one particular country. What if 90 per cent of countries comply with the ideal code while 10 per cent do not? An international ideal code should deal with this eventuality. (This is not as statistically unlikely as it may seem. Once non-compliance in state S reaches a certain threshold, S might become a magnet for non-compliers, enabling them to mount a coup. Once non-compliers are in power, they can easily attract fellow travellers to their country.) So our choice of the ideal code must accommodate the possibility that, even under full compliance, oil reserves will produce the same dire consequences as they do in the real world.

3. Broader Inclinations.   Even if the problems resulting from the resource privilege would not themselves arise under full compliance, it does not follow that the ideal code cannot assist us in dealing with them. The ideal code includes a range of specific moral obligations and general inclinations. These might be sufficient to determine the attitudes that someone who had internalized the ideal code would have when faced with the negative effects that Pogge highlights. This is especially likely if those effects constitute a harm for which the present generation in the lucky group would feel responsible.

The ideal code includes a general inclination to aid anyone in distress. Anyone who has internalized that code carries this disposition over to inter-group politics, where it supports a range of policies designed to raise the well-being of people in worst-off lands and to protect their rights (Section 9.2). One might think that these general dispositions exhaust the response of the ideal code regarding the resource privilege. The unlucky group are badly off, and the lucky group will feel some obligation to assist.

My principal aim in this section is to show that anyone who has internal-ized the ideal code will feel a much stronger and more specific sense of obligation in this particular case. Here it is crucial to note that, while cor-ruption and immorality inside a nation may often be a necessary condition for oil reserves to have undesirable results, it is not sufficient. Oil has no magic properties. What makes people rich is not oil *per se*, but the fact that wealthy industrialized nations need oil and will purchase it from whoever effectively controls it. If rich countries refused to recognize the rights of dictators to transfer resources, then oil would be worthless to dictators. So oil would cease to have profound negative incentive effects. This suggests that there are policies whose adoption by rich nations *alone* would avert the negative effects that oil reserves have in the real world.

As we shall see, the claim that the resource privilege harms the unlucky group can have a very significant impact on the lucky group's attitude to inter-group politics. Suppose someone in the lucky group, anxious to avoid potentially extreme demands, wants to reject this claim. There are two ele-ments they might wish to attack: empirical and moral. We consider both together. The most obvious response is to deny that the effects of the resource privilege are harmful, either by denying that they occur at all, or by denying that such effects as do occur constitute a *harm*.

One response would begin with the correlation between resource abundance and the lack of progress toward democracy. It would then deny that the latter constitutes a harm—on the grounds that the preference for demo-cracy is a cultural artefact of Western liberal society, and is thus not applicable when we are judging the impact of a policy on non-Western societies.

We addressed a more general form of this argument in the introduction to Section 9.3.1. I argued that, while those who had internalized the ideal code will regard democracy as desirable for all groups, this will primarily be for instrumental reasons. Even if the preference for democracy *per se* is rejected as culturally relative, the preference for economic growth, the absence of famine and poverty, and respect for basic rights will not be sim-ilarly rejected. The present relevance of this is that, in addition to the lack of democracy, resource abundance is correlated with both poor economic performance and an increased incidence of civil war.

The empirical relationship between resource abundance and poor economic performance is complex and multifaceted. Countries with significant oil reserves experience slower economic growth than comparable resource-poor nations. Developing oil-rich nations are also less likely to develop stable democratic institutions, and more likely to experience civil wars and political instability.

The correlation between resource wealth and slower growth is found in both developed and developing nations.[20] The general phenomenon is known as the 'Dutch Disease', after the experience of the Netherlands, where the discovery of significant gas reserves in 1959 was followed by a long period of economic stagnation relative to its neighbours.[21] One common explanation is that, as the export of resources becomes a significant component of GDP, labour and capital shift away from the manufacturing sector. This retards long-term growth because international markets for manufactured goods grow at a faster pace than markets for primary products.[22]

Although the name results from recent events, the Dutch Disease phenomenon has been long observed. Sachs and Warner point out that 'in the 17th-century, resource-poor Netherlands eclipsed Spain, despite the overflow of gold and silver from Spain's American colonies. In the 19th and 20th centuries, resource-poor countries such as Switzerland and Japan surged ahead of resource abundant economies such as Russia.'[23] Ironically, the Netherlands itself has thus been on both sides of the Dutch Disease comparison.

The negative correlation between economic performance and resource abundance is even more pronounced in developing countries, especially in Africa and the Middle East. This appears to be because, when democratic institutions are not firmly established, resource abundance is correlated with democratic failure and civil war, both of which further retard economic growth. By contrast, even if economic performance is adversely affected, Western nations with long-established democratic systems do not suffer political or civil instability when resources are discovered. Wantchekon illustrates this vividly by comparing the different fortunes of Nigeria and

---

[20] Sachs and Warner, 'Natural Resource Abundance and Economic Growth'; Sachs and Warner, 'The Big Push, Natural Resource Booms and Growth'; Leite and Weidmann, 'Does Mother Nature Corrupt? Natural Resources, Corruption and Economic Growth'; and Ross, 'The Political Economy of the Resource Curse'.

[21] Sachs and Warner, 'Natural Resource Abundance and Economic Growth', 2–7. Sachs and Warner also survey a range of other explanations for the Dutch Disease, and provide references to the extensive empirical literature.

[22] A second explanation, especially relevant to developing nations, is that 'richer countries are more protectionist regarding primary imports than regarding manufacturing imports'. (Sachs and Warner, 'Natural Resource Abundance and Economic Growth', 5).   [23] ibid. 2.

Norway following their respective discoveries of significant oil reserves in the 1970s.[24]

I argued in the introduction to Section 9.2.3 that, because it lowers the lexical threshold available across the whole social framework, rather than merely impacting on some interpretations of the lexical level, poor economic performance is a bad thing for any group. (Or, at least, it will be judged to be so by anyone who has internalized the ideal code—which for Rule Consequentialism amounts to the same thing.)

Resource abundance is also correlated with both high military spending and an unusually high incidence of civil war.[25] The presence of oil reserves provides a strong incentive to any would-be leader. In the absence of stable democratic institutions, incumbent regimes can use oil wealth to purchase political and military support.[26] Such regimes can then be overthrown only by military means. Once a regime becomes aware of this, of course, it will further increase its spending on the military.

The negative impact of civil war on a nation's economy and institutions is obvious. Military spending also has a negative impact on both economic development (because resources are diverted from economically more productive sectors) and on the transition to democracy (because higher military spending means a disproportionately powerful military, who can then resist any move toward a political system likely to involve less military spending.)

Aside from any instrumental effects on growth and democracy, civil war is very obviously a (cross-culturally) bad thing in itself, as it deprives many people of the most basic necessities of life (food, shelter, security, life itself.)

Proponents of an amended resource privilege will now argue that the lack of transition to democracy due to the wealth resulting from the resource privilege constitutes at least an indirect harm, as it exacerbates these other effects. The result of an unamended resource privilege is a vicious cycle, where civil war and poor economic performance both contribute to, and result from, the prevalence of non-democratic politics. In developing oil-rich countries, the three factors of low growth, poor transition to democracy, and civil war are thus mutually reinforcing.

At this point, a member of the lucky group seeking to avoid very demanding obligations might take a different tack. Suppose they agree that the other negative effects (war and poverty) are harms caused by the lack of the transition to democracy. They might then deny that the resource privilege causes that lack of transition. The real cause is cultural. The observed

---

[24] Wantchekon, 'Why do Resource Dependent Countries have Authoritarian Governments?'

[25] Collier and Hoeffler, 'On Economic Causes of Civil War'; Ross, 'The Political Economy of the Resource Curse', 13–15.

[26] Wantchekon, 'Why do Resource Dependent Countries have Authoritarian Governments?'

correlation between resource abundance and lack of democracy is merely a coincidence. It just so happens that most of the world's oil reserves are in territories occupied by groups whose culture is hostile to democracy and liberalism.

This cultural explanation is found in the empirical literature. Both the lack of economic development and the absence of a transition to democracy in oil-rich Middle Eastern states have been attributed to some feature of Islamic or Arab culture.[27]

The problem with the cultural explanation is that it cannot account for the fact that identical patterns are observed in resource-rich nations outside the Arab and Islamic worlds, most notably in sub-Saharan Africa. In a comprehensive analysis, Ross found that whether Islam is the dominant religion in a nation is not significantly correlated with economic or political performance, once we have controlled for the level of resource abundance.[28]

Of course, the fact that one particular cultural explanation fails to explain the absence of democracy does not show that the correct explanation appeals to the resource privilege. To be confident that it does, we need an explanation of the causal mechanisms leading from resource abundance, via the resource principle, to a lack of democracy and the accompanying low growth and other problems.

There are at least two possible explanations for the correlation between resource abundance and non-democratic regimes.

1. Modernization Theory.[29] 'Democracy is caused by a collection of social and cultural changes—including higher levels of urbanization, education, and occupational specialization—which in turn is caused by economic development.'[30] Once democracy is established, it supports further social and cultural changes along similar lines. This in turn leads to more economic development, and hence more social and cultural change, further reinforcing democracy.

One strength of the modernization model is that it explains the exceptions to the general correlation between economic development and democracy. When economic growth occurs in a way that bypasses the standard modernization process, democracy will not occur. This is why many resource-rich nations miss out on democratization and its flow-on economic benefits.

2. Rentier Effect. Studies comparing contemporary events with the emergence of democratic institutions in Western Europe suggest that

---

[27] Hudson, 'The Political Culture Approach to Arab Democratization'; Sharabi, *Neopatriarchy*.

[28] Ross, 'The Political Economy of the Resource Curse', 4.

[29] For a defence of Modernization theory, see Inglehart, *Modernization and Postmodernization*. For an empirical critique of the theory, see Ross, 'The Political Economy of the Resource Curse', 9–10.

[30] Ross, 'The Political Economy of the Resource Curse', 9.

a non-democratic regime can 'use its abundant resources to relieve social pressure that might otherwise lead to demands for greater accountability'.[31] If the populace receive expensive social services without being taxed, they are much less likely to demand accountable or representative government. It has also been argued that oil reserves enable a government to use its wealth to prevent the emergence of an independent bourgeoisie, arguably a key element in the development of democracy in Western Europe.[32]

Without significant oil reserves, industrialization would be necessary for any significant number of people in a developing country to enjoy the benefits of the modern world, such as cars, televisions, and modern medicine. Industrialization promotes economic growth, and the resulting processes of urbanization and increases in education and workforce participation lead to calls for democracy. People see that their endeavours are enriching the nation, and call for greater political participation. Oil reserves allow a sizeable elite to purchase the benefits of modernization, and distribute these to their supporters, without embarking on any process of modernization. The end result is that the society is worse-off than it would have been in the absence of oil reserves. It is also worse-off than it would have been if its natural resource had been one whose exploitation requires labour-intensive activity from the the local population. For instance, countries whose export earnings depend on agriculture are far more likely to experience the benefits of modernization.[33] Overall, 'rentier states' (those that 'receive substantial rents from foreign individuals, concerns, or governments'[34]) are 'less likely to become democratic and do a poor job of promoting economic development'.[35]

For our purposes, the crucial point of both of these (complementary) explanations is that the causal effect of resource abundance would not occur

---

[31] For the original studies of the emergence of democratic institutions in Western Europe, see Tilly, *The Formation of National States in Western Europe*; and North and Weingest, 'Constitutions and Commitment: The Evolution of Institutions Governing Public Choice in Seventeenth-Century England'. For the contemporary debate, see Ross, 'The Political Economy of the Resource Curse', 10–13.

[32] The claim that an independent bourgeoisie was crucial to the development of Western democracy is defended in Moore, *Social Origins of Dictatorship and Democracy*. In a recent summary of the literature, Ross notes that 'scholars examining the cases of Algeria, Libya, Tunisia, Iran and the Republic of Congo have all observed oil-rich states precluding the formation of independent social groups; all argue that the state is thereby blocking a necessary precondition of democracy' (Ross, 'The Political Economy of the Resource Curse', 12). As Ross himself notes, it is not clear whether such states are acting deliberately. (ibid. 13).   [33] Ibid. 19.

[34] Beblawi, 'The Rentier State in the Arab World', 51. See also Mahdavy, 'The Patterns and Problems of Economic Development in Rentier States: The Case of Iran'.

[35] Ross, 'The Political Economy of the Resource Curse', 7. The connections explored in the text are general, statistical correlations, not absolute rules. As Ross notes, 'there is nothing inevitable about the resource curse: states like Malaysia, Chile and Botswana have done relatively well despite their oil and mineral wealth' (ibid. 31).

if non-democratic regimes could not turn abundant resources into wealth with which to purchase Western goods and services. The recognition of the resource privileges of non-democratic regimes by affluent nations, both past and present, is thus a necessary causal contributer to the plight of the unlucky group.

Suppose someone in the lucky group still wants to avoid demanding obligations to the unlucky group. They might argue as follows. 'Although the unlucky group's plight is a result of interactions between the two groups in the past, it does not follow that we have harmed them. They might be worse-off than if we had behaved differently, but they are not worse-off than if we had never existed. The benefits of their overall pattern of interactions with our group (medicine; technology; aid; other goods, services, and ideas) exceed the costs. They are better-off than they would have been in our absence. So we owe them nothing.'

There are two basic replies to this objection. The first is that it is not obvious, as a matter of fact, that the inhabitants of poor resource-rich countries are better-off today than they would have been if the developed world had never existed. Such counterfactuals are extremely notoriously difficult to evaluate. I limit myself to two observations.

1. Some of the negative effects of the wealth caused by resource abundance are very severe, notably civil war. Those who are killed, starved, or dispossessed by civil war are obviously not compensated by any benefits from interaction with the developed world. If enough members of the unlucky group are affected in this way, then the overall impact on the group as a whole will be negative. This is especially true if we are evaluating things from the perspective that those who have internalized the ideal code adopt when considering another group—as they place a very high priority on the loss of the basic necessities of life and anything else that might place people below the zero level.

2. In the absence of the developed world, it is entirely possible that developing nations would have embarked on the path to economic development and democracy on their own. After all, this is what happened only a few hundred years ago to the Western European nations themselves. Compare the present situation of resource-rich African nations with the early modern period in Western Europe. Liberal democratic institutions in Europe typically grew out of conflict between absolute monarchs and their people. This conflict was often more financial than military. Rulers were forced to yield power because they could not afford to maintain their position without money; money could not be raised without internal taxation; and taxation was impossible without some degree of consent from the

people. Imagine how different the history of England might have been if the Tudor and Stuart monarchs had access to a vast source of external finance to hire foreign mercenaries. (As, indeed, several other European monarchs did, in the form of South American gold.) This is why, under the rentier and modernization models, the wealth gained from resource abundance enables non-democratic governments to create the trappings of economic growth without the political liabilities of an independent bourgeoisie and a capitalist economy. By operating the international resource privilege in its present form, Western democratic nations thus impose on some developing nations a constraint whose absence was a crucial factor in our own transition to liberal democracy.

Of course, it is impossible to say when or whether currently non-democratic states would have become democratic if the whole course of history had been different. But we cannot confidently say that they would not. (There is an obvious connection here to our rejection of the cultural explanation for the failure of democracy. If opposition to democracy were to turn out to be an intrinsic feature of Arab or Islamic culture, then this would lessen the likelihood of such a culture becoming democratic on its own. However, an outside observer might well have thought that opposition to democracy was a deep and intrinsic feature of late medieval European society, or even of English society late into the nineteenth century—especially if their primary informants were members of the ruling class.)

Given their indeterminacy, counterfactuals are an unsatisfactory basis for moral arguments either way. A more robust response is to point out that, for someone who has internalized the ideal code, the morally relevant question is not whether the unlucky group are worse-off than they would have been if the lucky group had never existed, but rather (*a*) whether the lucky group have wronged the unlucky group, and (*b*) whether the interactions between the two groups have undermined the claim that their social frameworks are distinct.

Recall that the ideal code contains many of the person-affecting constraints and obligations of commonsense morality. Faced with the empirical information outlined earlier, someone who had internalized that code would almost certainly hold that a policy of sharing the wealth generated by the natural resources found in the territory of the unlucky between the lucky group and a small unaccountable elite within the unlucky group, to the exclusion of all other members of the unlucky group, constitutes a wrong to those excluded people. The lucky group have failed properly to recognize the property rights of those members of the unlucky group. In general, the ideal code is likely to hold that, if we have wronged someone, then we must make some reparations for any other negative effects of that wrong, even if we neither intended nor foresaw those consequences.

Consider two intra-group analogies. Imagine a system of property rights that always allowed a person in a psychotic state to sell (or give away) all her possessions, and then refused to allow her to recover them once the psychosis had passed. This would clearly be inferior to a system protecting the person's property during her psychotic periods.

Suppose, knowing you are psychotic, I purchase your million-dollar house from you for ten dollars, and then refuse to return it when you recover. Whatever the rules of property in operation at the time, someone who had internalized the ideal code would clearly think I had wronged you. The analogous claim seems even more appropriate in the case of a group, where the non-autonomous state (i.e. despotism) is much easier to diagnose.

In fact, in the real world, the appropriate intra-group analogue of the resource privilege is even more striking. Imagine a moral code which always recognized the ownership rights of whoever effectively controlled a particular natural resource. If you discover oil in your backyard, and some intruders break into your house at gunpoint and drive you from your land, then this code would recognize them as the rightful owners of that oil.

The domestic ideal code will not incorporate this account of property rights. The negative effect of allowing thieves to benefit in this way would outweigh any positive benefits flowing from the fact that this code ensures that the oil ends up in the hands of someone determined to use it profitably. If I purchase your oil at a discounted rate from someone who I know to have taken it by force, then, once again, whatever the law might say, someone who had internalized the ideal code would surely think I have wronged you if I refuse to pay you something approximating a fair price. In the domestic case, this result is uncontroversial. It is not clear why it should be any more controversial at the international level.

In neither case would those who had internalized the ideal code think that they could avoid all moral responsibility by giving the owner some token payment for his property, and then argue that he is better-off than he would have been if no one had wanted his property at all.

To those in the lucky group who have internalized the ideal code, the plight of those in the unlucky group is thus a harm for which they are responsible due to a history of interactions from which the lucky group have benefited. If future interactions follow the same pattern, then the future plight of those in the unlucky group will be even more directly the responsibility of the present members of the lucky group. This has several obvious implications.

1. As the present plight of the unlucky group is a harm for which the lucky group are partly responsible, they will feel a very strong obligation to compensate the unlucky group for that harm, insofar as they can estimate it.

2. In particular, they will feel obliged to offer recompense at least equal to the extent of their own benefit from the history of unjust interactions. One practical first step would be to estimate the economic benefit to the lucky group of the lower energy prices they have enjoyed under the resource privilege. They will feel that they should give at least that much assistance to the unlucky group.

3. The institution of a just resource privilege for the future will be a very high priority for the lucky group in inter-group politics.

From a Rule Consequentialist perspective, the second crucial question, concerning the social framework, is even more significant. Whatever else their history of interactions may have done, they have linked the lucky and unlucky group together, in a way that undermines the claim that the two social frameworks are distinct. Once they become aware of it, the history of interactions must undermine the lucky group's willingness to operate with distinct lexical thresholds for themselves and for the unlucky group, especially as those interactions directly impact on the lexical thresholds available to the two groups. (In opposite ways: cheaper energy prices raise the lexical threshold of the lucky group, while the negative impact on the unlucky group greatly reduces their threshold.) As we saw earlier, the removal of the assumption that distinct lexical thresholds are legitimate has a very serious impact on the demands of the ideal code. It also makes it much harder to deny that the Rule Consequentialist case for democracy carries over to the unlucky group, which would further strengthen the case for amending the resource privilege.

I conclude that anyone who had internalized the ideal code would want the international resource privilege to be highly constrained. One possible constraint would be as follows. Only 'autonomous' governments would be allowed to transfer resources to foreign entities. Indeed, other states might be required to intervene to depose rights-threatening dictators, rather than entering sordid bargains with them. (We must bear in mind, of course, that the two are distinct. As the ideal code includes a strong distinction between doing and allowing, states and individuals will feel more obliged to avoid perpetrating harms, and to rectify harms they find themselves to have perpetrated, than to assist those whose needs they are not themselves responsible for.) These constraints on the resource privilege make it much more urgent for the lucky group to decide when to regard the unlucky group as 'autonomous'.

The amended resource privilege thus grounds a form of Pogge's constitutional guarantee—one that is available even to nations who have not precommitted themselves.[36]

Overall, Rule Consequentialism shows when and why empirical factors are relevant to political morality, and thus offers us some guidance in applying the lessons of the ideal society to our own situation.

Endnote

A. In earlier chapters, I compared our Rule Consequentialism to Rawls's liberal egalitarianism. Rawls's theory of international justice is not as well developed as his account of justice within a society. His account of the boundary between intergenerational and international justice is especially underdeveloped. Accordingly, instead of attempting a full critique of Rawls's account, I briefly illustrate one general problem he faces, to show the superiority of our more flexible Rule Consequentialist account. Rawls's account of international law—his 'law of people'—includes a duty of assistance (Rawls, *The Law of Peoples* (1999), 38). All liberal peoples must assist *burdened peoples* to estabilsh stable liberal institutions. (Burdened peoples are those who cannot currently establish stable liberal institutions, no matter how hard they try.) Rawls argues that this duty is comparatively modest, for two reasons. (1) The threshold for the duty is very low. Stable liberal institutions can be maintained even in a very poor country. Burdened peoples are thus comparatively rare, and the assistance needed to place them in a position where they could establish stable liberal institutions is slight. (2) The duty of assistance, like the obligation to save for future generations, is transitional. Once a liberal people can establish liberal institutions, the duty of assistance ceases. The maintenance of stable liberal institutions is then the responsibility of the people themselves (Rawls, *The Law of Peoples*, 106–8, 118–19).

Our discussions in Ch. 2 and the present chapter cast doubt on this optimistic picture, as they oblige us to replace an absolute interpretation of favourable conditions with a comparative one. We saw in section 2.2.4.2 that all generations must save. The just savings principle is not transitional. Nor is the duty of assistance. Section 9.3.2 shows that a comparatively poor people cannot establish stable liberal institutions, whatever their absolute level of wealth. Furthermore, our discussion of the context-dependent lexical level in Section 9.2 suggests that, in a world where peoples interact, the notion of basic needs will be continually adjusted upwards by the aspirations of wealthier peoples. As wealthier liberal peoples are always saving, the threshold liberal institutions must meet if they are to count as 'meeting everyone's basic needs'

---

[36] See chapter endnote A, p. 299.

is always increasing. Wealthier liberal peoples must always assist poor peoples to keep up.

Rawls regards even his own modest transitional duty of assistance as one of the two components of the law of peoples most likely to be violated (Rawls, *The Law of Peoples*, 126). The risk of violation is much higher for our more demanding comparative duty.

10

The Limits of Rule Consequentialism

We have seen that Rule Consequentialism can provide a compelling account of the morality of individual reproduction, and also offer guidance to public policy regarding future generations, at least in the idealized world of full compliance. If Rule Consequentialism coped equally well with other areas of morality, then it would be a plausible theory overall. Unfortunately, it does not.

I have argued at length elsewhere that Rule Consequentialism is not adequate as a complete moral theory, on a number of grounds.[1] I do not propose to rehearse the relevant arguments here. Instead, the present chapter focuses on a single problem for Rule Consequentialism: whether it makes unreasonable demands under partial compliance.

The possibility of partial compliance has three implications for moral theory.

1. Partial compliance greatly increases the amount of unmet need in the world, and exacerbates the likelihood of catastrophes that are either caused by, or could have been prevented by, human activity. This threatens significantly to increase the demands of Rule Consequentialism.

2. The notion of a context-dependent lexical level played a large role in the development of Rule Consequentialism in Chapters 5 to 9. If partial compliance in the actual world impacts on agents' background social framework, then it also impacts on their interpretation of the lexical level. If partial compliance means a society is worse-off in morally relevant terms than it would have been under full compliance, then it may also lower the lexical threshold appropriate when applying the ideal code to that society.

3. If partial compliance is a widespread feature of the actual world, then we must ask, not only how someone who had idealized the ideal code would deal with emergencies and catastrophes, but how they would respond to the fact that those emergencies result from partial compliance. Will they treat these differently from similar problems resulting from natural causes?

---

[1] Mulgan, *The Demands of Consequentialism* (2001), chs. 3 and 8.

Our principal question in this chapter is whether the second and third features of partial compliance counteract the first. Can we render Rule Consequentialism's demands more palatable either by reinterpreting the lexical levels and thresholds, or by focusing on the ideal code's attitude to partial compliance itself?

I have discussed the demands of Rule Consequentialism under partial compliance at length elsewhere. I do not propose to cover all the same ground again. Instead, I briefly recap the arguments of *The Demands of Consequentialism* and then ask how they are affected by the material presented in Chapters 5 to 9 of the present book. Does an intergenerational perspective make Rule Consequentialism more or less palatable under partial compliance?

The basic objection is that Rule Consequentialism will make implausible demands under partial compliance. This means both that some of its demands are unreasonably stringent, and also that the relative priority it accords to different moral demands is unacceptable. More specifically, I seek to establish the following claims.

1. Rule Consequentialism does make unreasonable demands under partial compliance with the ideal code in general.
2. The Rule Consequentialist account of the morality of reproduction, considered in isolation, is plausible even under partial compliance.
3. Partial compliance with other aspects of the ideal code threatens to undermine the plausibility of both the account of the morality of reproduction offered in Chapters 5 and 6 and the account of intergenerational justice offered in Chapters 7 through 9.
4. The implausibility of the general Rule Consequentialist account of the demands of morality is increased when those demands are set against the demands Rule Consequentialism makes regarding reproduction and future generations.

My overall conclusion is that Rule Consequentialism is not a plausible complete moral theory and that, so long as it presents itself as a complete theory, its account of reproduction and future generations is also inadequate. My solution, presented in the next chapter, is to limit the scope of Rule Consequentialism to one particular subset of moral choices.

The role of the next two chapters is to convince those who reject Rule Consequentialism as a general moral theory that the Rule Consequentialist account offered in Chapters 5 to 9 may nonetheless play a role in the best Consequentialist moral theory, or in a broader theory that combines Consequentialist and non-Consequentialist elements. As far as possible, I seek to develop the discussion without too much reliance on my own particular version of Combined Consequentialism, as outlined in *The Demands of Consequentialism*.

10.1. From Full Compliance to Actual World

The actual world is one of very partial compliance with some aspects of the ideal code of Rule Consequentialism. Before we can explore the significance of this partial compliance, we must examine its extent. I focus on several areas: obligations to distant strangers; public policy, especially regarding the welfare of children and environmental policy; and international politics.

Consider one key demand on our resources: the problem of poverty in distant countries. In defence of Rule Consequentialism, Brad Hooker has recently argued that, in a society where everyone follows the optimal code of rules, poverty would be eliminated if every affluent person in the developed world gave 10 per cent of her income to charity.[2] In *The Demands of Consequentialism*, I argue that we cannot share Hooker's confidence that Rule Consequentialism will make reasonable demands, even under full compliance.[3] However, here I will focus on partial compliance, where the problems facing the theory are much starker. Let us grant Hooker's assumption that, under full compliance, the ideal code requires the affluent to sacrifice approximately 10 per cent of their income. Unfortunately, internalization of any such rule is not widespread in our world. Almost no one in the developed world gives anywhere near 10 per cent of his income to relieve the plight of distant strangers.

We turn now to the broader issue of partial compliance with the ideal code as this impacts on the general obligations of the present generation to subsequent generations. I argued in Section 7.3 that the ideal code includes a commitment to the development of children's moral powers which exceeds anything found in contemporary public policy or morality. The ideal code would place a very high emphasis on social justice and the provision of services for the disadvantaged, especially disadvantaged children. It is hard to believe that current practices are optimal in this area. Even in affluent societies, there are many disadvantaged people who are much worse-off than practically anyone in the ideal society.

The ideal code requires support for public policy initiatives, not merely abstinence from harming others. It is not sufficient for me to develop the moral powers of my own children, and refrain from interfering in anyone

---

[2] Hooker, 'Rule Consequentialism' (1990), 72. As we shall soon see, Hooker has since abandoned this particular formulation. However, he seems to retain the assumption that Rule Consequentialism demands approximately 10% from the affluent.

[3] Mulgan, *The Demands of Consequentialism*, 67–87.

else's moral development. I must also seek to ensure that all children are able to develop their moral powers. We are thus a long way from full compliance.

This is not an isolated case. A number of general features of our society also make life here worse than life in the ideal society. The ideal society will include a wider range of support services, a better civic culture, a lower level of violence and crime, and a much greater opportunity to live a morally integrated life. The average expected quality of life in the actual world is thus significantly less than in the ideal society.

If the ideal domestic society depicted in Chapters 5 to 8 seemed somewhat optimistic, the subsequent picture of international affairs sketched in Chapter 9 is apt to appear fantastical. Whatever the flaws of domestic political arrangements in the developed world, they pale into insignificance beside the injustices of our present international arrangements. To begin at the beginning, international laws and institutions have a degree of democratic legitimacy which would be considered grossly inadequate in any domestic context. Unsurprisingly, the resulting laws are far removed from what we would expect any remotely democratic process to produce; and the world that results, once again unsurprisingly, is far further removed from the ideal global society than virtually *any* nation (whether developed, developing, or neither) is from the ideal domestic code. Even allowing that the ideal code imposes weaker demands for external aid than for domestic intergenerational aid, most countries probably come much closer to meeting the latter than the former.[4]

The ideal code will not require total redistribution. However, even under full compliance, it does place some demands on people in comparatively well-off groups. It is almost impossible that the pitiful percentages of GDP donated to genuine development assistance, or the token efforts at international reform currently on offer from wealthy countries would suffice. Anyone who had internalized the ideal code would demand considerably more than any group currently delivers. Our global community is a place of very very partial compliance.

Two aspects of international partial compliance are especially significant for our purposes: climate change and population policy. Partial compliance by other groups not only affects the need for development aid. It may also threaten the environmental sustainability of all gruops. Recall our first

---

[4] Thomas Pogge offers a striking illustration of the disparity between national and international norms using the imaginary nation of Subbrazil (Pogge, *World Poverty and Human Rights*, 100–1.) Subbrazil has an average income and distribution of income equivalent to those found in the world at large. It is thus equivalent to Brazil in terms of average income, but approximately three times as unequal, even though Brazil has one of the most unequal income distributions of any individual nation.

international tale from Section 9.2.3. Suppose the lucky group are divided into several sub-groups, most pursuing the policy of using an unsustainable amount of oil and refusing to share its technology with the unlucky group. Our sub-group is one of the few already following policies that would be sustainable if followed by all. If we abandon even that level of oil use (and opt instead for total abstinence), this will reduce the overall environmental degradation, at great cost to ourselves.

A possible real-world example of such a dilemma is widespread partial compliance with the ideal code (both domestic and international) with respect to climate change (Section 9.2.7). In a world of approximate full compliance, future climate change would be minimized, and strategies to alleviate its adverse impact would be vigorously pursued. The quality of life available to future generations would thus be much higher, and cover a broader range of valuable ends, than is likely in the actual world. Indeed, widespread partial compliance regarding climate change may transform our world from one where the optimistic model is appropriate to one best captured by the pessimistic model. As Rule Consequentialism makes such different recommendations under the two models, this shift is highly significant.

Under anything close to full compliance there is good reason to expect population policy largely to take care of itself. If most groups comply with the global ideal code, then almost everyone will have their basic needs met, including the need for basic education and the provision of a reasonable range of social opportunities. All the available empirical evidence strongly suggests that, in such circumstances, fertility rates will soon approximate the reproduction rate (Sections 6.6). Given the constraints imposed by limited global resources and environmental pressures, there is no good Consequentialist reason to desire a fertility rate significantly different from the replacement rate. The replacement rate is sustainable, but any significantly positive rate of population growth has the potential eventually to be environmentally catastrophic.

Under full compliance, there is no alternative to general reproductive autonomy which produces a better result. There is thus no justification for imposing any non-autonomous solution. Accordingly, the ideal global code will leave communities free to choose their own population policies; communities will leave individuals free to make their own reproductive choices; and the balance of individual choices will produce a stable population. The ideal code for reproduction, in an autonomous society, will be as presented in Chapter 6.

Unfortunately, we do not live in a world of full compliance with the relevant components of the global ideal code. Many nations fail to meet their domestic obligations to provide adequate education and opportunities to women, and many other states fail to provide adequate encouragement for those nations to do so. Partial compliance raises the threat of a population explosion.

This aspect of partial compliance poses two threats. The first concerns partial compliance within a developing country. If the rulers of such a country fail to adopt the appropriate strategies regarding education and development, then fertility rates may continue to be high. Furthermore, we saw earlier that, in some developing countries, small increases in the education levels of women lead to an increase in overall fertility rates, rather than a decrease. Fertility rates might rise if desirable policies were implemented in a half-hearted manner (Section 6.6.3).

Fertility rates in the developing world are also threatened by the partial compliance of *developed* nations. I argued in Section 9.3.2 that anyone who had internalized the ideal code will favour a constrained international resource privilege, designed to encourage the development of democratic regimes in developing countries. Suppose other developed nations continue to recognize the resource privileges of dictators, with the result that dictatorships flourish where they might otherwise have been replaced by regimes more accountable to the interests of the people. The implementation of policies necessary to reduce the fertility rate is thus rendered much less likely, and fertility rates remain high.

Both sources of partial compliance are found in the real world. As a result, global population continues to rise. Most demographers predict that the population will stabilize in the foreseeable future.[5] However, to generate a clear conflict in obligations, suppose that this stabilization either will not occur, or will not occur soon enough. The global population might 'stabilize', but at an unsustainably high level from an environmental perspective. Our nation's population policy is sustainable, both locally and globally. If everyone did as we do, there would be no population problem. However, given the behaviour of other nations, our present policy is not sustainable. If we continue as we are, then the earth will become overpopulated, and key environmental systems will collapse. However, if we unilaterally adopt a policy of (almost) universal non-reproduction, then the global population may eventually stabilize at a sustainable level. (As our nation is unlikely to be so pivotal, it is perhaps more plausible to assume that our abstinence would at least alleviate and delay the impact of environmental collapse.) Are we required to make that sacrifice?

On the other hand, we must not overstate the gap between the actual world and the ideal society. Our Rule Consequentialism does not idealize to

---

[5] This claim is true under most of the possible scenarios discussed in the 2000 revision of the official United Nations population estimates and projections. (www.un.org/esa/population/unpop.htm)

full compliance. Instead we imagine a world where the rules gain widespread acceptance, but are not accepted or followed by everyone. The ideal society thus contains a certain amount of crime and other antisocial behaviour. Otherwise the ideal code would contain no rules for dealing with wrongdoing by others. One might also argue that those portions of the ideal code relating to criminal activity are actually accepted by approximately 90 per cent of the population in the actual world, as most people do not participate in such activities. So we could be close to full compliance here. (Similarly, some aspects of the ideal global code do currently enjoy a considerable degree of compliance. For instance, aggressive warfare against other states is not practised on a regular basis by many modern states.) However, nearly universal acceptance of the ideal code in other areas, such as civic participation, political behaviour, and voting patterns, would presumably reduce crime and other violence considerably. (To deny this is to claim that no collective pattern of behaviour by the law-abiding majority could reduce crime.) The actual level of acceptance and compliance for programmes to meet urgent needs and maintain an adequate social framework for everyone falls far below 90 per cent. Individual members of the next generation in the actual world will face a harsh choice between pursuing their own individual goals and meeting the urgent needs of other members of their community. Such problems would not be faced by the vast majority of inhabitants of the ideal society. The actual next generation is thus much worse-off in highly morally relevant terms.

10.2. Partial Compliance

Partial compliance is a huge topic for Rule Consequentialism. Our focus is on the impact of partial compliance on the morality of reproduction and our obligations to future generations. Other areas of the ideal code are relevant only insofar as partial compliance with respect to them impacts on the operation of moral rules regarding reproduction and future generations. One question of particular relevance to us is how partial compliance impacts on the rules regarding reproductive freedom. We thus begin with partial compliance with the rule regarding reproduction itself.

10.2.1. Reproductive Partial Compliance

Recall our favoured rule regarding reproduction.

The Flexible Lexical Rule.   Reproduce if and only if you want to, so long as you are *reasonably sure* that your child will enjoy a life above the lexical level, and *very sure* that the risk of your child falling below the zero level is *very small*.

There are several reasons why partial compliance with this rule does not increase the demands of the ideal code. In the case of famine relief, partial compliance by others means that there is more work for the agent to do. It is possible for her to take up the slack left by others. No such possibility arises regarding reproduction. We cannot easily make sense of the thought that, because others are not doing their share of following the rule regarding reproduction, the agent herself should do more than her share.

It might seem that partial compliance will impact on the agent indirectly, by affecting the size of the next generation, thereby placing her under either an obligation to reproduce or an obligation not to reproduce. There are two reasons to doubt this. The first is that, as a matter of fact, in the actual world in developed countries, the population is not heading out of the optimal range.

This need not be because most people actually do comply with the ideal code. Deviations from full compliance can go in both directions. Perhaps some people reproduce who would not do so under full compliance, while others who would have reproduced under full compliance do not. Widespread non-compliance could produce the same population as full compliance. (For famine relief, departures from full compliance lie in only one direction. Over-donation to charity is not a major concern.)

Even if partial compliance did lead the population out of the optimal range, this would only affect an agent's permission to reproduce if the ideal code includes either a moral prohibition on reproducing if the population is too high, or an obligation to reproduce if the population is too low. In Section 6.6 I argued that the ideal code will rely on public policy incentives instead of such crude mechanisms. The ideal code thus leaves the agent free to have children (or not) if she wants to, irrespective of the level of compliance.

Unfortunately, constraints regarding the optimal population size are not the only limits on reproductive freedom in the ideal code. The code also contains constraints regarding the quality of life of the child one considers creating. Partial compliance with other areas of the ideal code makes it very likely that the average expected quality of life in the actual world is significantly less than in the ideal society.

Furthermore, partial compliance elsewhere in the ideal code may impact more directly on reproductive freedom. Our main concern is whether obligations to donate to famine relief will crowd out an agent's permission to reproduce. We have already established that, under full compliance, the ideal code will permit widespread reproductive freedom (Section 6.2). Accordingly, our problem only arises under partial compliance.

We begin with an explanation of why partial compliance with respect to the general demands of the ideal code might be relevant to reproductive freedom. This is followed by a brief summary of how Rule Consequentialism copes with partial compliance in two particular cases: famine relief and disaster avoidance. Our question is whether such partial compliance crowds out the agent's freedom to reproduce. We then turn to the potential impact of partial compliance elsewhere in the ideal code on the interpretation of the rule regarding reproduction, especially its notion of the lexical threshold. This interpretative impact has the potential to counteract the previous crowding-out effect.

Overall, it is hard to predict with any precision whether those who had internalized the ideal code would feel free to reproduce in our situation. However, one more definite conclusion does emerge from our discussion. Even under partial compliance, the ideal code offers an intuitively plausible account of the morality of reproduction, except when the general demands of other aspects of that code threaten to overwhelm the agent's reproductive freedom. If we could somehow constrain those demands, then Rule Consequentialism would emerge as intuitively plausible.

Would agents be required to give up their reproductive freedom due to partial compliance? We begin with two arguments that they would. The first builds on an interpretation of the notion of 'significant sacrifice' in the Rule Consequentialist rules governing famine relief. Reproduction requires resources. The ideal code contains many other rules governing the allocation of one's resources. This raises the possibility of conflict. As my resources are finite, I must decide between competing possible allocations. This requires some prioritization within the ideal code.

In the ideal society, such conflict will be limited. A small contribution from everyone (or nearly everyone) would probably be sufficient to alleviate famine and destitution, and to ensure the implementation of appropriate environmental and other policies. If reproduction were always overruled by these other demands on one's resources, then no one would ever reproduce. This would not be an optimal result. Nor would it be optimal if reproduction were permitted only in rare or exceptional circumstances. So the ideal code will include a permission to reproduce which is not generally overridden by other demands in the ideal society.

To say that reproduction is not generally overridden in the ideal society is not to say that it cannot be overridden in the actual world. (It is also not to say that it is not occasionally overridden even in the ideal society.) Most significantly for our purposes, a situation which arises only occasionally in the ideal society may arise very often, or even universally, in the actual world. If so, then reproduction may be always overridden for us. These problems arise because our world differs from the ideal society. That society is a world of (almost) full compliance with the ideal code. In the real world, by contrast, the ideal code is the object of (at most) very partial compliance.

Under extreme partial compliance, do the demands of famine relief undermine the reproductive freedom enshrined in the ideal code?

10.2.2. Famine Relief

We turn now to a brief summary of the Rule Consequentialist position regarding famine relief obligations. Under full compliance, the ideal code tells each agent to donate 10 per cent of her income to charity. The underlying rule could be mechanical (e.g. 'Donate 10 per cent'), but it is much more likely to be flexible. (As Hooker himself notes, 'Rule Consequentialism is implausible if it holds that how much I should contribute is completely insensitive to how much others are actually contributing.'[6]) Hooker offers the following formulation of the optimal rule regarding famine relief.

Hooker's Flexible Rule.   'Over time agents should help those in greater need, especially the worst-off, even if the personal sacrifices involved in helping them add up to a significant cost to the agents.'[7]

Hooker's flexible rule raises two main questions:

1. Would Rule Consequentialism really recommend it?
2. Is it relatively undemanding in the actual world?

We need to consider these two questions together. There are interpretations of Hooker's rule on which it is not unreasonably demanding. There are also interpretations under which it would be chosen by Rule Consequentialism. Unfortunately, no single interpretation meets both desiderata. The optimal form of the rule is unreasonably demanding in the actual world.

I argued in Section 6.4.2 that the internal logic of Rule Consequentialism requires us to attempt, as far as possible, to apply the ideal code as it would be applied by someone who had internalized it and who lived in a society

---

[6] Hooker, *Ideal Code, Real World* (2000), 164. Mulgan, *The Demands of Consequentialism*, 77–87.

[7] Hooker, *Ideal Code, Real World*, 166. Hooker also adds that 'The cost to the agents is to be assessed aggregatively, not iteratively.' The reason for focusing on aggregative cost is that 'small sacrifices, repeated indefinitely, can add up to a huge sacrifice' (ibid. 167). See also Cullity, 'Moral Character and the Iteration Problem'.) For instance, a rule requiring a one-off donation of $100 is not demanding, whereas a rule requiring such a donation every day could be extremely demanding. Elsewhere in his book, Hooker offers the following more mechanical formulation of the rule regarding aid: 'A rule requiring contributions of at least 1% to 10% of annual income from those who are relatively well-off by world standards' (Hooker, *Ideal Code, Real World*, 163).

where such internalization was the norm. We must ask how someone who had internalized the ideal code would interpret the phrase 'significant cost'. We saw in Section 6.4.2 that the judgements of those in the ideal society will often differ from our own. In particular, their interpretation of a notion such as 'significant (aggregate) cost' is likely to be significantly more demanding.

This conclusion is defended at length in *The Demands of Consequentialism*.[8] The basic idea is simple. In a world of full compliance with the ideal code, situations where the agent can produce a great good by a comparatively small sacrifice will be relatively rare. The cost of inculcating a rule is primarily a function of the demands it makes under full compliance. Therefore, a rule that applies infrequently under full compliance may be included in the ideal code even though its demands under partial compliance (where it applies much more often) are very high.

As cooperation is more widespread in the ideal society than in the actual world, opportunities for applying the flexible rule may be quite different in the two situations. Under full compliance, natural disasters will still occur, whereas disasters caused by widespread human moral failing will be less common. Our own commonsense judgements regarding obligations to aid others are more demanding regarding natural disaster than they are when disaster results from the misdeeds or inaction of others. (In the latter case, we feel that primary responsibility for alleviating the need falls on those responsible for its existence.) If those who have internalized the optimal code apply the flexible rule primarily in cases of natural disaster, and if their application of that rule makes plausible demands in those cases, then when they come to apply the rule to famine relief under partial compliance, the result will be very demanding.[9]

Flexible rules are harder to assess than mechanical rules. Our conclusions can only be tentative. It is anyone's guess precisely what the optimal rule regarding famine relief would actually tell us to do. At the very least, we have seen no reason to believe that Rule Consequentialism is not very demanding in practice, and considerable reason to believe that it is.[10]

To bring our two topics together, we must ask whether an inhabitant of the ideal society would regard the decision not to have children as a 'significant sacrifice'. In Hooker's formulation, the sacrifice is to be judged aggregatively, not iteratively. (For further discussion, see n. 7 of this chapter.) We must

---

[8] Mulgan, *The Demands of Consequentialism*, 67–87.

[9] See ibid 87–90, for Rule Consequentialist attempts to avoid this conclusion.

[10] Some might ask why we should be interested in the moral judgements of people (i.e. those in the ideal society) whose sensitivities are ill equipped for our moral world. The short answer is that the basic moral attitudes of those who have internalized the ideal code are very relevant to our moral situation, and that Rule Consequentialism therefore does offer some useful moral advice. For a longer discussion, see Mulgan, *The Demands of Consequentialism*, 83–7.

compare a complete life with children to a complete life without children. This removes one obvious defence of reproduction. We cannot say that deciding not to have children is too great a sacrifice for one particular day.

In this case, the aggregative measure of sacrifice is *more* demanding than some interpretations of the iterative method. There are many similar cases. For instance, the ideal code may require me to give up an inheritance, or turn down a lucrative morally dubious job. Judged as one-off sacrifices, each of these might seem very significant. The cost is less burdensome if spread over a lifetime. We thus cannot blithely assume that a shift from iterative to aggregative assessment renders Rule Consequentialism less demanding.

Our question probably has no definitive universal answer. We are unlikely to find either that not having children always is a significant sacrifice, or that it always is not. The significance of the sacrifice depends to a large extent on the nature of the individual person's life. It is affected by the strength of their desire for children, the availability of suitable alternatives, the social significance of reproduction, etc. We must confine ourselves to general remarks. Given our earlier discussion in Sections 6.4.2 and 10.1, we can say that, in general, an inhabitant of the ideal society operates with a very different notion of 'significant cost' than we do. They will regard as obligatory many sacrifices which strike us as clearly supererogatory. There seems no reason to expect this general feature of their evaluations not to carry over to the case of reproduction.

If those in the ideal society operate with more stringent moral views than us, then Rule Consequentialism will oblige many people in the actual world to opt for a life of charitable works over a life of parenthood. Even if those in the ideal society have only a slightly more stringent view than ourselves, they will expect the life of charity in some cases where we believe it to be optional. If their views are much more stringent than ours, then the ideal code will require this in many cases where we would regard such a sacrifice as morally unnecessary. In particular, the ideal code may not allow an ordinary affluent person in the developed world to reproduce.

This may seem to contradict the argument of Chapter 6, where I claimed that the ideal rule regarding reproduction would allow most affluent people in the actual world to have children. However, that earlier conclusion related to that particular rule considered in isolation from the rest of the ideal code. The permissions granted by the rules governing reproduction are always conditional on the assumption that the agent is not obliged to put her resources to another use. Unfortunately, if the ideal code covers the whole of morality, then an agent's prima facie right to have children could easily be swamped by her obligation to meet the needs of distant others. Our aim is to somehow contain the range of the ideal code, so that an agent's permissions are not crowded out by other obligations, and she is allowed to have children.

The crucial question is whether someone who had internalized the ideal code would feel free to reproduce rather than devoting her life to famine relief, when faced with the urgent demands of the actual world. Different features of the ideal code will push in different directions here. Our discussion of famine relief suggests that, as the situation we are considering would be comparatively rare in a world of full compliance, someone who had internalized the ideal code would be inclined to make a very significant sacrifice, and to forgo reproduction, to produce a great benefit. Under full compliance, this general disposition has obvious advantages, and does not threaten the continuance of humanity.

10.2.3. Annihilation

One particular source of moral demands is worth exploring separately: the possibility of annihilation or disaster. I argued in Section 8.2.1 that Rule Consequentialism can be extremely demanding when the survival of humanity is at stake. It can also require the present generation to make very significant sacrifices to ensure an adequate life for their descendants. Partial compliance threatens to increase these demands, as it makes catastrophe more likely. In the actual world, it looks as if Rule Consequentialism may tell me to devote my life to averting a potential environmental catastrophe in the future, perhaps by campaigning for a sustainable alternative to contemporary patterns of fossil fuel consumption, in order to prevent the potential catastrophe of global warming.

The Rule Consequentialist has several replies here. In the first place, it is not obvious that Rule Consequentialism will always require extreme sacrifices. The expected value of devoting my life exclusively to environmental concerns is very difficult to calculate. Admittedly, the potential payoff is extremely large. However, the probability that various courses of action will produce that payoff is very hard to estimate. Furthermore, we should note that we are comparing a life of exclusive devotion to environmental causes, not with a life of total apathy, but with a more balanced life involving some (possibly considerable) activism. The additional expected impartial value produced by complete devotion may not be as significant as it might initially appear. It is by no means clear that the ideal code would require a sacrifice from the agent if the probability of successfully producing any significant benefit is so hard to assess.

On the other hand, if I really *am* confident that I could save the world, or even significantly enhance the probability of survival for humanity, then it is not clear why I should not be required to do so, even at considerable cost to myself. Consider familiar fictional scenarios where the fate of an entire civilization or planet rests on one particular person. Our intuitions may be quite different here than in the case of famine relief. Significant sacrifices for the continued existence of humanity seem obligatory to a degree that equal sacrifices on behalf of the distant starving do not. These demands might include forgoing reproduction (or any other project) to focus on averting catastrophe.

The demands of the ideal code will be no different if the threat of annihilation results from partial compliance. If the survival of humanity is at stake, then great sacrifices will be required regardless of the cause of the impending disaster. The limits on the demands of the ideal code are then imposed by human nature. The code is as demanding as it is possible for human beings to internalize, but no more so. This does not seem unreasonable. When so much is at stake, agents should sacrifice as much as they can bring themselves to.

Rule Consequentialism explains and clarifies these intuitions. A more demanding code is required here, because of the vital significance of the value at stake, as a precondition for all other values. And the significance of that value, and its intimate connection to the goals and autonomy of moral agents, explain why it may be possible to inculcate a demanding rule.

Under full compliance, annihilation is a possibility, especially if we are expecting that the code will be handed down to future generations, so we must take it into account. If partial compliance in the actual world makes annihilation more likely (for instance, in relation to climate change), then such partial compliance makes the code more demanding, but not necessarily implausibly so.

A related argument against reproductive freedom appeals to the lexical threshold embodied in the rule sketched in Chapter 6. As we have seen, partial compliance means that many lives in the actual world will be below the level that would be considered acceptable in the ideal society. The ideal code could thus yield an obligation not to create, as an inhabitant of the ideal society would not create someone with such a deprived childhood. If they had internalized the ideal rule regarding reproduction, people who were in such adverse circumstances might not feel free to reproduce.

In addition to the general loss of well-being, those who have internalized the ideal code will also have in mind the demands of ideal code in a world of partial compliance. As I argued in Section 8.2, the present generation will want their descendants to be able to live lives that are both morally good and personally fulfilling. If the demands of the ideal code are too great in a world such as ours, then such lives may not be possible.

10.3. Defending Rule Consequentialism

If Rule Consequentialism is to be plausible, then it should not be unduly onerous in the actual world. If the ideal code contained an obligation to refrain from reproduction altogether whenever the quality of life for the next generation in the actual world is significantly less than in the ideal society, then it certainly would be very onerous in the actual world. Therefore, if we are to defend Rule Consequentialism, then we must deny that the ideal code contains such an obligation. The solution is to focus on the precise formulation and application of our rule regarding reproduction.

One key desideratum in choosing an ideal code is flexibility. In particular, the code must be able to ensure the continuation of the social framework even in very adverse circumstances. We should thus expect that those who have internalized the ideal code will feel free to reproduce whenever their situation is the norm in the context of the society they find themselves in. Without this disposition, the ideal could run the risk that, if circumstances change, no one will ever reproduce.

On the other hand, even if they feel free to reproduce in our world, those who had internalized the ideal code might be inclined to forgo reproduction, and make a great sacrifice, when they know that, due to the actual expected behaviour of others, the survival of humanity is not actually threatened. The crucial question is how they would balance these competing factors. We get some insight by exploring how the necessary relativity to context is instantiated in the ideal code.

The ideal code absolutely prohibits creating people whose lives will be below the zero level. It also tells us not to create people whose lives are below a certain threshold, *so long as* our options include the creation of people above that threshold. However, if every life in the actual world is below the threshold, then most of us do not have the option of creating people above that level. It may thus be acceptable for us to reproduce, so long as our children have lives worth living.

For the moment, let us assume that life in our society in the next generation will be above the zero level but under the threshold below which reproduction is discouraged by the final form of the Lexical Reproductive Freedom Rule (which may be the Expected Value Lexical Reproduction Rule, the Flexible Lexical Rule, or some other formulation). The ideal code permits us to reproduce. However, the code may still be very demanding. From a Rule Consequentialist perspective, it is much easier to justify creating someone above the threshold than below it. The ideal code must permit people to create lives above the threshold. Otherwise, we risk falling out of the optimal population range. By contrast, the creation of lives below the threshold will be strongly discouraged, to ensure as many as possible of the next generation have very worthwhile lives. Such creation will only be permitted if the agent would be severely disadvanged if she were to refrain from reproduction. Those who have internalized the ideal code will not generally feel free to create people below the threshold. Even if they do feel free to create in such circumstances, they may also feel obliged to provide their child with the best possible life. A strict interpretation of the ideal rule regarding reproduction could thus be very demanding.

The challenge is to see if we can reduce those demands in a principled way. We begin by noting that the rule regarding reproduction explicitly refers to the *lexical level*, not the average level in the ideal society. Yet, within the ideal code, the lexical level is context-dependent. We should ask, not what an inhabitant of the ideal society would regard as adequate for her own society, but what she would regard as adequate or acceptable in the context of our own actual society. Her interpretation of the lexical level will be one suited to our context (Sections 3.7.3 and 9.2.3).

This shift in evaluative focus produces plausible results. In particular, it seems likely to ground a plausible degree of reproductive freedom even in the actual world. As we saw in Section 6.4.2, the move to a context-dependent ideal code also has a theoretical motivation. Recall the following two options for dealing with changing circumstances.

The Disaster Avoidance Solution. Reproduction becomes obligatory if the population is too small, and is forbidden if it is too large. Otherwise, the Lexical Reproductive Freedom Rule continues to be applied exactly at it would under full compliance.

The Relativized Solution. We interpret our description of the conditions under which reproduction is permitted to include reference to changing social circumstances.

I argued in Section 6.4.2 that the former is preferable, even under full compliance. This conclusion is strengthened by the recognition that, if the ideal code is to be passed down through generations, then we must take account of how it would operate under partial compliance, as the two alternatives offer very different advice in the actual world.

Begin with the Disaster Avoidance Solution. There is at present no immediate danger of over- or under-population. Most people make their reproductive decisions as if an adequate social framework existed, and so the population remains in the acceptable range. The Disaster Avoidance Solution does not come into play, and we are still covered by the original Lexical Reproductive Rule. So we should not reproduce, as our children would fall below the lexical level (as that level would be defined within the ideal society).

Consider now the Relativized Solution. One feature of my social situation is widespread non-compliance with the ideal code. Suppose I can reasonably expect that any person I might create would have a life above the lexical level as it would be interpreted in the context of a society characterized by this pattern of behaviour. Their life would not be regarded as acceptable in the ideal society, but my social situation is different. The Relativized Solution thus permits reproduction in the actual world, even if life here is below the lexical level as it would be defined by someone who had internalized the ideal code.

The Relativized Solution is thus considerably more intuitively plausible than the Disaster Avoidance Solution under partial compliance. This may affect the different costs of inculcating the two solutions. The Disaster Avoidance Solution may seem unfair in the actual world in a way that the Relativized Solution is not. To teach someone a code of moral rules effectively, one must get them to see how those rules would be applied in different circumstances. A child in the ideal society might object to the Disaster Avoidance Solution as follows. 'If compliance with the ideal code broke down in a particular way [assume this happens to correspond more or less to our actual world], then I would not be allowed to reproduce, simply because other people were failing to follow the code. This is unfair.'[11]

These considerations are relevant to the consequences of inculcating the two competing codes, because our idealization to widespread compliance in the next generation does not rule out the possibility of widespread partial compliance with the ideal code in some future generation, especially if circumstances change so that the demands of compliance increase significantly. The introduction of future generations thus increases the significance of partial compliance effects within Rule Consequentialism as a whole.

There are thus good Rule Consequentialist reasons for introducing an element of relativity into our account of the lexical level when interpreting the rule regarding reproduction. Such relativity is necessary to ensure the continued survival and psychological health of the population over several generations under changing circumstances. Consideration of partial

---

[11] A proponent of the Disaster Avoidance Solution might reply that the alternative, namely the Relativized Solution, would allow this child, once she became an adult, to produce a child whose life is well below what she (in the ideal society) would regard as acceptable. The child might remain unconvinced. She might agree that it would be better not to create such a child in the ideal society, where there is no need to create children who are that badly off. By contrast, in the imagined situation of degradation (our actual world) an additional child brought up by someone who had internalized and still follows the ideal moral code might enhance overall value.

compliance thus reinforces the conclusions of Section 6.4.2. Partial compliance with the ideal code does not directly affect the reproductive freedom defended in Chapter 6.[12]

10.3.1. Three Kinds of Context-Dependence

Given its significance for our discussion of Rule Consequentialism, it is worth pausing to see how this present use of context-dependence relates to our previous discussions. An interpretation of the lexical level might be context-dependent in three distinct dimensions.

1. The Modal Dimension. We ask what someone who had internalized the ideal code and grown up in a society where such internalization was the norm would feel free to do in my situation in the actual world. We might imagine a philosopher in the ideal society, setting out to test his own theory (a kind of idealized version of the ideal code) by asking what someone who had internalized that code would do in a situation such as (our) actual world. (Just as we test our moral theories by pitting them against imaginary scenarios.) We assume both that the ideal code produces a world with moral philosophers, and that they would carry on much as we do. A modal context-dependence thesis says they will interpret flexible moral terms in a way that is suited to the context of the actual world.

2. The Temporal Dimension. How will future generations (who have internalized the ideal code) interpret the flexible moral terms contained in the ideal code we are teaching to the first generation? The temporal context-dependent thesis holds that each generation will interpret those terms in a way that is suited to their own context, with an interpretation of the lexical level that may be significantly higher or lower (and reflect a very different balance of valuable ends) than that applied by the first generation.

---

[12] There is a sense in which some formulations of the ideal rule regarding reproduction require a *greater* sacrifice under full compliance than under partial compliance. This is because, due to the context-dependent interpretation of the ideal code, there is a degree of well-being (x) such that you could legitimately create a child whose life is worth only x under partial compliance, whereas you could not legitimately create such a child under full compliance (Section 6.4.2). We might then object that those unable to create children whose lives are worth more than x must forgo reproduction under full compliance, even though they would have been permitted to reproduce under partial compliance. However, any person able to have a child whose life is worth x under partial compliance could probably have given her child a better life under full compliance. The reason she cannot provide such a life under partial compliance is most likely to be due to the absence of appropriate background conditions, which full compliance would provide. Such a person would thus have been allowed to reproduce under full compliance, even though she would have been deprived of the option of gratuitously creating a worse life than she could have created. As this option is not morally valuable, its removal is not a morally significant deprivation.

3. The Inter-group dimension.   We ask how a person from an affluent nation who has internalized the ideal code will interpret notions such as the zero and lexical levels, when considering the impact of their actions on people in the developing world. For instance, if I tell myself that I should strive to enable people in the developing world to rise above the lexical level, what interpretation of that level is in play? The inter-group context-dependence thesis would hold that such a person will interpret 'lexical' to mean 'worthwhile in their social context, not mine'.

We discussed the temporal and inter-group context-dependence theses in Chapters 5 to 9. In both these cases, connections between the groups can blur the distinction between their social frameworks, this undermining the case for context-dependence. No parallel connections are possible when someone who has internalized the ideal code and lives in a world of full compliance imagines our actual world. Also, contemplating a worse-off group or a decline in well-being for future generations can lead someone who has internalized the ideal code to rethink her own expectations and adopt a more modest interpretation of the lexical level for herself and her society. While contemplating an imaginary world corresponding to our actual world from a world of full compliance might have this effect, it is unlikely to be as forceful as when the group with the lower threshold are real people in the actual world of the person who has internalized the ideal code. The case for context-dependence is thus strongest in the modal case.

Even under full compliance, context-dependence has a significant impact on the ideal code. It supports a liberal approach to intergenerational politics and reduces the demands placed on affluent groups to assist less prosperous unconnected groups (Sections 7.2, 8.1, 9.2.2). It also has a significant impact under partial compliance. Context-dependence renders reproduction permissible and reduces the overall demands of the ideal code considerably, as compared to a non-context-dependent code. It ensures that we are not under an obligation to raise everyone above the lexical level as it would be interpreted within the ideal society.

However, not all aspects of the ideal code are context-dependent. In particular, recall that special obligations do not typically refer to the lexical level at all, nor does the general requirement to do what we can to raise people above the zero level. These obligations are unaffected by the introduction of context-dependence. If partial compliance increases the demands of these obligations, then the present argument has no impact.

The context-dependence argument thus does not provide a general reason to interpret the notion of 'significant sacrifice' in a more lenient way in the actual world than it would be interpreted in a world of full compliance. The crucial difference is that, in the famine relief case, a more lenient interpretation would allow the agent to leave distant others to starve, whereas no one is harmed by the more lenient interpretation in the reproduction case. When an agent is faced with widespread partial compliance, the more stringent famine rule produces significant benefits overall, while the more stringent reproductive rule does not. The solution offered in this section thus cannot be used to save the Rule Consequentialist account of famine relief.

If someone who had internalized the ideal code found herself in a situation where significant numbers of children in her own society were below the zero level, then she would feel an extremely strong sense of obligation to do what she could to help them. In a world of full compliance, such emergencies are comparatively rare, so this obligation does not generally undermine the agent's well-being or autonomy.

The obligations that are unaffected by the context-dependence argument are thus those that are likely to be most demanding under partial compliance. In short, context-dependence ensures that the rule regarding reproductive freedom does not itself prohibit parenthood, but context-dependence alone cannot prevent the agent's reproductive freedom being swamped by other demands.

10.3.2. *Attitudes to Partial Compliance Itself*

We have asked if partial compliance affects the interpretation of the ideal code. We now ask how someone who had internalized the ideal code would think about partial compliance itself. In other circumstances, if she came across an emergency corresponding to our actual situation, someone who had internalized the ideal code would make sacrifices that we would almost certainly regard as extreme. Would it make a difference to them, that the urgent needs in question are the result of partial compliance?

There are three attitudes a moral agent might have to partial compliance.

1. *Partial Compliance is Irrelevant.* What matters is the existence of an emergency where the agent can avert tragedy for individuals, groups, or humanity as a whole. The question of how that emergency arose is irrelevant.

2. *Partial Compliance Reduces Demands.* Many people, including some moral theorists, hold that it is unfair for an agent's moral obligations to increase owing to the moral failings of others. To many people, indeed, this is one of the paradigmatic cases of unfairness. At the extreme, this view holds that an agent's obligations under partial compliance can never be greater than they would have been under full compliance.

3. Partial Compliance Increases Demands.   If the agent herself is responsible for the emergency, then the fact that it results from her own partial compliance rather than some other cause will obviously increase the stringency of moral obligations.

I shall conclude that, to someone who had internalized the ideal code, all three of these responses will be appropriate in different areas of moral life. Obviously, if partial compliance is either irrelevant, or if it increases the demands of the ideal code, then our earlier conclusion that the ideal code is unreasonably demanding under partial compliance is either left unaffected or actually reinforced. Accordingly, we begin with the claim that the demands of the ideal code cannot increase under partial compliance, so that the ideal code will not be nearly as demanding when an emergency results from partial compliance. Unless this argument goes through across the board, we cannot escape significant demands. Unfortunately, it does not, especially when we factor future generations into the equation.

In the philosophical literature, the argument that demands must not rise under partial compliance is most often associated with public goods and public policy. So we now turn to these.

10.4. Public Policy

We intuitively accept a higher level of demands within our community than outside it. By contrast, there are good reasons to think that Rule Consequentialism is *less* demanding when partial compliance relates to public policy within the agent's own community than it is under partial compliance with obligations to those starving in distant countries.

We saw in Section 10.1 that our actual world is a place of partial compliance regarding public policy. How does the ideal code deal with this partial compliance? Presumably, we should support political change and support private organizations that pick up the pieces. As in all cases of partial compliance, the crucial question is how much I am required to pick up the slack if not enough others do their bit.

In Section 10.2.2, I argued that Rule Consequentialism *is* extremely demanding in the (seemingly parallel) case of partial compliance in relation to famine relief in distant countries. To defend the theory in the present case, we must either argue that the ideal code does not demand very high sacrifices, or endorse such sacrifices as it does require. The best defence would do both, defending two claims.

1. Intuitively, it is reasonable to expect more demands in the case of public policy than in relation to famine relief.

2. By contrast, the Rule Consequentialist code is less demanding here than with respect to famine.

Taken together, these two claims suggest that, even though Rule Consequentialism is unduly demanding regarding distant famine, it is not unduly demanding in the case of public policy.

I shall conclude that this defence does not entirely succeed. While Rule Consequentialism is less counterintuitive regarding public policy than elsewhere, its demands are still likely to be excessive.

Cases of partial compliance within the agent's own community often have one of the following two characteristics:

1. They concern a *public good*. This is especially true when partial compliance threatens the ongoing stability or quality of the background social framework within which agents pursue their various projects and goals.
2. They involve *institutional failure*.

These two characteristics are often combined, as the ideal code will often use institutions to provide public goods. When partial compliance involves either of these characteristics, there are good reasons to expect the ideal code to be less demanding than it was in the case of famine relief.

10.4.1. *Public Goods and the Compliance Condition*

Rule Consequentialism faces many problems because its demands can increase under partial compliance. Liam Murphy has recently developed a theory explicitly designed to avoid such problems. Murphy explains his broad conception of beneficence as follows.[13]

Beneficence can be understood in terms of a shared cooperative aim... if we both have a cooperative aim to promote the good... we do not see ourselves as engaged in separate solitary enterprises.... Each of us does not, strictly speaking, aim to promote the good. Each sees himself as *working with others* to promote the good. Thus, the best way to describe the aim of each might be: 'to promote the good together with others.' (Italics in the original.)

---

[13] Murphy, 'The Demands of Beneficence', 285–6. See ibid.; of Mulgan, 'Two Conceptions of Benevolence' (1997); Murphy, 'A Relatively Plausible Principle of Beneficence: Reply to Mulgan'; and Mulgan, *The Demands of Consequentialism*, ch. 4. Murphy defends his theory at greater length in his *Moral Demands in Nonideal Theory*. (My discussion relates primarily to Murphy's earlier presentation. For some doubts about his more recent formulation, see Mulgan, 'Review of Murphy' (2003).)

Such a conception of benevolence is certainly appealing in public good cases. As Murphy notes 'insofar as beneficence is . . . a mutually beneficial project, it is natural to resist taking on the shares of people who could contribute to the project but do not.'[14]

Proceeding from this collective perspective, Murphy suggests the following condition on principles of beneficence.[15]

Compliance Condition   A principle of beneficence should not increase its demands on agents as expected compliance with the principle by other agents decreases.

Murphy aims to develop a principle of benevolence which satisfies the Compliance Condition while avoiding the pitfalls of Rule Consequentialism. He suggests the following principle.

Cooperative Principle of Beneficence.   Each agent is required to act optimally— to perform the action that makes the outcome best—except in situations of partial compliance with this principle. In situations of partial compliance it is permissible to act optimally, but the sacrifice each agent is required to make is limited to the level of sacrifice that would be optimal if the situation were one of full compliance. Of the actions which require no more than this level of sacrifice, an agent is permitted to perform only that action which makes the outcome best. The agent is then required to perform either that action, or some other action which makes the outcome just as good.[16]

It is easy to see that Murphy's principle satisfies the Compliance Condition. His position also has obvious similarities with Rule Consequentialism. To see this, we can split Murphy's theory into two halves:

1. Determining the ideal situation or society.
2. Using the behaviour of someone from that situation or society to determine what actual agents should do in the real world.

Murphy's account of step (1) is analogous to Rule Consequentialism. The ideal situation is an idealized world of full compliance, where everyone acts optimally. The principal difference lies at step (2). Murphy uses the ideal

---

[14] Murphy, 'The Demands of Beneficence', 288. It is important to note that Murphy also defends the cooperative principle in cases where beneficence is not mutually advantageous. (For a fuller discussion of Murphy's defence, see Mulgan, *The Demands of Consequentialism*, 113–17.)

[15] Murphy, 'The Demands of Beneficence', 278.

[16] Ibid. 280. I have reworded Murphy's published formulation, to correct a slight inaccuracy. The version given in the text corresponds to Murphy's own use of the principle. (Murphy himself has confirmed this in correspondence.) In *Moral Demands in Nonideal Theory*, Murphy offers a more complicated account of this principle. See Mulgan, 'Review of Murphy'.

situation, not directly to determine what an agent should do in any given situation, but rather to determine how much sacrifice she should bear. This enables Murphy to avoid objections to Rule Consequentialism based on partial compliance.

The Compliance Condition incorporates a cooperative picture of morality. I have argued at length elsewhere that this picture is not plausible over the whole of morality.[17] However, it may be appropriate for certain moral projects, especially the maintenance of a background framework for goals. The existence of such a framework is a public good, and its maintenance a mutually beneficial collaborative project. While the ideal code is not bound by the Compliance Condition, it may *include* that condition as a constraint on some of its own rules, such as the requirement to maintain that framework. The cost of widely inculcating a rule depends to a significant degree on whether people are disposed to regard it as fair. For a public good such as the background social framework, people may well reject as unfair any rule requiring significantly more from them whenever others free-ride. So the ideal code would not include such a rule.

Even here, we may find the strict Compliance Condition too strong. We might opt instead for a more moderate version. As others fail to do their bit, our responsibility for maintaining the social fabric will increase, but only slowly, and perhaps not beyond a certain threshold. The Rule Consequentialist justification for this condition derives indirectly from people's intuitive sense of unfairness. If a rule requiring too much when others fail to comply will seem too unfair, then it will not be efficient to attempt to inculcate it. Accordingly, Rule Consequentialism will limit its own demands under partial compliance in precisely those cases where we find additional demands most objectionable.

Where extra demands arise due to the failure of others to support appropriate policies governing the background social framework, someone who has internalized the ideal code may well feel the force of Murphy's claim that it is unfair for any principle of beneficence to make extra demands under partial compliance. They may feel, at least, reluctant to go much beyond their 'fair share', as defined by the demands they would face under full compliance. One example might be partial compliance regarding child-rearing practices. Child-rearing is not a pure public good. However, it actually relates to many key public goods, as inadequate policies regarding children undermine the future well-being of the community as a whole, and of all its members. Child-rearing practices are certainly more of a public good for my community than famine relief in distant countries.

---

[17] Mulgan, *The Demands of Consequentialism*, chs. 4 and 8.

It is helpful to ask how someone who has internalized the ideal code might think of a person who fails to make a significant sacrifice to further the cause of disadvantaged children in their own society, where that disadvantage is caused by bad public policy rather than natural disaster. Those in the ideal society will feel sorry for such a person, especially as her demanding situation is caused by the clear moral failings of others. They will also feel that it would be morally praiseworthy if that person did make a significant sacrifice. The crucial question is whether they will feel it is morally blameworthy for a person living under partial compliance not to make a significant sacrifice. In Section 10.2.2, I suggested that the inhabitants of the ideal society operate with a more demanding notion of 'significant sacrifice' then we do. However, it is plausible to think that, in the present case, their notion of an appropriate sacrifice will be tempered by Murphy's argument regarding fairness.

10.4.2. *Institutions and Partial Compliance*

Under full compliance, (almost) everyone will obey the prevailing institutions, which will be at least reasonably just. This situation could result from full compliance with any of the following rules.

1. Always obey whatever institutions are established in one's society.
2. Always (and only) obey perfectly just institutions.
3. Always obey whatever institutions are established in one's society, so long as they are reasonably just.

I first demonstrate why the ideal code will not include rule (1). I then demonstrate the superiority of (3) over (2).

We do not idealize to perfect full compliance. Even in the ideal society some institutions may become unjust, corrupt, or ineffective—especially if they endure for many generations. It will clearly be better if, at least in the most egregious cases, people do not just slavishly obey those institutions. Furthermore, if it were widely known that most people would support existing institutions no matter what, this would encourage the minority of non-compliers to corrupt those institutions. So the ideal code will constrain the obligation to obey institutions, favouring rule (2) or (3) over rule (1).

Now consider rule (2). This rule seems unproblematic. Most institutions in the ideal society will be just, and we clearly want people to comply with those institutions. Actually, this rule is extremely demanding, even under full compliance. The primary demand is epistemic. To follow rule (2), one must determine whether an institution is perfectly just before obeying it. Agents may not be aware of the precise degree of compliance in their own society. They presumably know that most people comply with most of the ideal code, but they may not be confident that compliance is high enough to ensure that their institutions are just. Furthermore, even under full compliance, not all institutions are perfectly just. So full compliance with the ideal code could lead to widespread non-compliance with very good institutions. Therefore, rule (2) is inferior to rule (3).

Those who have internalized the ideal code will thus have a moderate disposition to support and obey existing institutions. They will comply with institutions which are reasonably just, and not worry too much about ascertaining their precise degree of justice. They will thus avoid the disaster of obeying patently corrupt institutions but also leave themselves time to pursue their personal projects. In the actual world, we need only establish that our public institutions are 'reasonably just' before we can justifiably go about our everyday business.

If our basic democratic structures are reasonably just, then someone who had internalized the ideal code would advocate obeying the laws and policies produced by those institutions unless those policies were manifestly unjust. Within that constraint, however, they will feel a strong inclination to campaign for a change of policy, and make donations to charity to alleviate unmet needs. The crucial question is how much they would be prepared to sacrifice overall. We now consider arguments designed to establish that the ideal code does not demand too much under partial compliance with public institutions.

The simplest argument would appeal to a distinction between *dualism* and *monism*.[18] The dualist holds that political morality and individual morality are separate domains. Individuals have an obligation to uphold and obey just (or reasonably just) institutions, but they do not have independent moral obligations individually to pursue the public policy objectives those institutions are designed to pursue. For instance, if the community's obligations to children are placed in the hands of a publicly funded agency, then my obligations are exhausted once I pay my taxes and obey any lawful directives the agency might make. Deficiencies in the agency's performance, even if they result from partial compliance with the obligation to support desirable institutions, cannot place me under any additional obligations.

If dualism were defensible, then partial compliance with the ideal code regarding public policy would clearly generate no additional demands. Unfortunately, whatever we may think of it in general, dualism is especially unappealing for a Consequentialist theory.[19] Within Consequentialism,

---

[18] Murphy, 'Institutions and the Demands of Justice'; and Cohen, 'Where the Action Is: On the Site of Distributive Justice'.

[19] Murphy and Cohen both argue against dualism in general from a non-Consequentialist perspective. (Murphy can afford to embrace monism wholeheartedly, because he has an alternative solution to the threat of extreme demands under partial compliance, as we saw in Section 10.4.1.)

individual obligations, competing public policies, possible institutional structures, and principles of justice, are all derived from a common source: the responsibility of human beings to promote the good, whether individually or collectively. Any distinction between institutional and individual responsibilities must be grounded in purely pragmatic considerations. The ideal code will endorse whatever pattern of responsibilities is most likely to work. The fact that, under full compliance, a public institution would meet a certain need does not automatically imply that, under partial compliance where that institution may not even exist, those who had internalized the ideal code will not feel bound to take up some of the slack themselves. The ideal rules for partial compliance will not be rigidly tied to the particular divisions of labour which work best under full compliance. The foundations of the ideal code are monist, not dualist.

However, although the ideal code will not embrace dualism, it is likely to take several steps in a dualist direction. This tendency is due to the liberal nature of the ideal code. A typical feature of liberalism in general is a strong separation between matters of individual responsibility and matters of public or institutional responsibility. This is seen in the fact that many liberals favour dualism, an especially strong form of this separation. Dualism itself is too rigid to form part of the ideal code. But we might expect to find a more moderate separation. Under full compliance, there are enormous benefits to be gained if individuals do not feel obliged to second-guess institutions, or feel responsible for tasks the institutions are performing more efficiently then any individual could.

No doubt people under full compliance will feel obliged to keep themselves reasonably well-informed about the performance of public institutions. After all, Rule Consequentialism doesn't idealize to perfect full compliance, so some mismanagement is inevitable. (Even under perfect full compliance, mistakes might still occur, causing at least some institutional failure.) However, things will probably go best overall if most people don't hold themselves individually responsible for the direct monitoring of institutions either. The best way to produce this result might be to inculcate a general aversion to taking responsibility for matters which are not in one's own sphere of responsibility under full compliance. This might lead us to expect that those who had internalized the ideal code would be more reluctant to make large sacrifices when local institutions fail than when partial compliance relates to individual moral issues such as famine relief, as the latter already falls under their responsibilities under full compliance.

The argument concludes that, even under partial compliance, the ideal code does not make unreasonable demands in relation to public policy. The fact that such demands are mediated by institutions provides a principled way to limit the impact on the individual agent of the free-riding of others. Proponents of Rule Consequentialism might attempt to extend the argument we are considering to cover famine relief. For instance, they might argue that, under full compliance, our obligations to those who are starving in distant countries would be most effectively met by the creation of an official institution to collect and distribute aid money. In a world of almost full compliance, people might feel disinclined to second-guess that institution, or to make significant sacrifices to redress its shortcomings.

10.4.3. Problems for the Two Arguments

Even if Murphy's argument goes through for public goods, it will not remove all the extra demands associated with partial compliance. This is because those demands relate especially to cases that are not public goods. Similarly, whatever force the institutional argument may have, it is limited to obligations within a single generation within a group. In other words, this argument has force only with respect to public goods.

Three key classes of demands go beyond the scope of both of these arguments.

1. *Obligations to Distant Strangers.*   In this case, those who benefit if I take up the shares of others, and suffer if I do not, are innocent third parties. So the refusal of my potential fellow cooperators is not a case of free-riding, my additional sacrifice does not benefit them, and this is not a public good with respect to the general class of potential cooperators.[20]

The institutional argument also fails for distant strangers. Whatever might be true under full compliance, individuals in the actual world cannot play their part in the officially sanctioned aid agency, as there is no such thing. Those who have internalized the ideal code will feel reluctant to remedy the failings of sub-optimal institutions. However, this reluctance will presumably not extend to a refusal to take *any* remedial action in the absence of an appropriate institution, as such a reluctance could have very bad consequences (even in the ideal society) if, for some reason, the institution disappears. Someone who had internalized the ideal code might reason as follows. 'The appropriate way to deal with problem x is by means of a centralized institution. If such an institution exists, and functions reasonably well, than one is required to play one's part by supporting it. If one finds oneself in a situation when no official agency exists, and where private charity is the way x is dealt with, then one is obliged to make whatever donation

[20] Mulgan, *The Demands of Consequentialism*, 214–16.

to charity is required in the circumstances.' (As we saw in Section 10.2.2, such reasoning could be very demanding in the actual world, if the ideal code were applied to famine relief.)

Rule Consequentialists thus cannot appeal to institutions to defend their theory in the case of famine relief. Indeed, this argument works only in the public good case. To see why, we must distinguish two types of case where those who have internalized the ideal code might opt to establish an institution. In the first case, the collective institutional solution is merely the most efficient means to a common individual end. The ideal code gives each agent the individual project of seeking to alleviate famine and poverty in distant countries, and agents group together to fund an institution, simply because this is more efficient than each trying to meet their obligations separately. In the second type of case, a collective or institutional solution is not merely the most effective way to pursue an independently specified goal, but is also required by the very nature of a collective project shared by different agents. The goal of collaborating in a democratic process would be a prime example. In the first type of case, an agent's goal still remains in its original form in the absence of the desirable institution, so there is no principled reason for the ideal code not to demand that she pursue it. By contrast, partial compliance in the second case can leave the agent effectively unable to meaningfully pursue her goal. (There is an obvious connection here with Murphy's argument that, because morality itself is a collective project, its demands are governed by the Compliance Condition.)

2. The Needs of Future Generations—in our own Group or Elsewhere. From a Rule Consequentialist perspective, the value of maintaining and improving the social framework is largely due to its impact on future generations. This project thus owes most of its moral significance to the fact that, from the perspective of the present generation, it is *not* a public good.

The introduction of future generations clouds the neat dichotomy between individual goods and public goods. Once we picture the background social framework as enduring through generations, it ceases to be a pure public good. While each generation does need to act (collectively) to maintain the social fabric of democratic institutions, their actions in maintaining those institutions for future generations are not reciprocal to the same degree as our collective activity in maintaining them for ourselves. In particular, in cases of partial compliance those who suffer from the inaction of others are not those who free-ride. (This is why attempts to base intergenerational justice on reciprocity fail, as we saw in Section 2.1.2.) Accordingly, insofar as demands under partial compliance do not increase as significantly for public goods as for individual goods, it follows that intergenerational obligations will be more affected by partial compliance than obligations to contemporaries.

The introduction of future generations also impacts on the institutional argument in two ways. The first is that, by broadening our focus to consider the impact of a code on future generations, we greatly increase the undesirability of a code allowing agents to do nothing in the absence of an appropriate institution. Even if the institution exists for the next generation, this is no guarantee that it will not disappear at some future point.

A second impact is on the obligation to provide stable institutions and opportunities. Once future generations are added, this moral project is a curious amalgam. On the one hand, it is not a purely self-regarding (collective) project, as it involves providing benefits to third parties, namely future generations. On the other hand, this project is not purely other-regarding either—in contrast to the moral project of providing famine relief to distant strangers. This is because my own well-being, and in particular my other personal projects, are likely to be entwined with the fate of my descendants, and with the future flourishing of my society more generally, and not with the flourishing of distant strangers among my contemporaries. If someone else in my society fails to play their part in ensuring opportunities and institutions are available to the next generation, then they are partly free-riding on my provision of those opportunities, to the extent that this enhances the value of their own projects by enabling their descendants to flourish.

3. The Survival of Humanity. Future generations are not harmed if they never exist. The survival of humanity is thus not exactly something we seek for the sake of those future generations. However, the survival of humanity is a very significant good for any Consequentialist theory, and the ideal code is chosen to maximize the possibility of that survival. Although this project is interwoven with the individual projects of members of the present generation, the value of the survival of humanity is far greater than its value for present individuals. Once again, the moral significance of this project relies largely on the fact that it is not a public good.

A Murphy-inspired sense of unfairness would thus not be appropriate for any of these three sources of demands. Furthermore, even if it were appropriate, a sense of unfairness would hardly be overwhelming. Given everything that was said in Chapters 5 to 9, the strength of the inclination not to allow humanity or the social framework to disappear, and the strength of the inclination to assist those in dire need, are likely to outweigh any sense of unfairness.

I conclude that, while someone who has internalized the ideal code will feel some reluctance to take on extra burdens due to the non-compliance of others, this reluctance will often be trumped by other, stronger, obligations—notably those involving the survival of the social framework and the basic needs of innocent third parties.

Thus far, we have assumed that the emergency is caused by the partial compliance *of others*. However, the agent herself may be responsible for the emergency. It may result from her own partial compliance. Recall that one of the ways our Rule Consequentialism does not idealize to perfect compliance is that it recognizes the possibility that agents who have internalized the ideal code do not always perfectly obey it. Therefore, the code includes rules for dealing with one's own prior failures of compliance. Here, as elsewhere, Rule Consequentialists typically argue that the ideal code includes many of the standard rules of commonsense morality. Anyone who had internalized that code would feel a much more urgent obligation to assist in an emergency resulting from her own moral failings than she would in an identical emergency resulting from any other cause. This kind of partial compliance thus greatly *increases* the moral demands on the agent.

The agent's responsibility to rectify emergencies she has caused herself, while potentially quite demanding in practice, is unlikely to be controversial. The more interesting question is whether, and to what extent, someone who had internalized the ideal code would feel responsible for past partial compliance by her own group as a whole. Accordingly, we now turn to inter-group ethics.

10.5. Inter-Group Partial Compliance

In both the intra-group and the inter-group cases, the ideal code will include some obligations that make no sense under partial compliance. Suppose full compliance would yield a robust set of international institutions, together with an obligation to contribute to those institutions. Under partial compliance, many of the necessary institutions may be non-existent or ineffectual, so the idea of direct contribution is incoherent. However, each group can contribute in other ways, by lobbying for better institutions or fairer international arrangements, or by direct donations to poorer countries. Furthermore, in some cases the appropriate institutions may already exist, and simply need to be supported (much) more vigorously.

Will someone who has internalized the ideal code feel obliged to make a greater contribution to foreign aid because other groups are not doing their share? This raises two separate questions:

1. What will they feel that their group is obliged to do?
2. What will they feel obliged to do themselves if other members of the group are not living up to the group's obligations?

We begin with the former, and start with an argument that partial compliance requires no additional sacrifices.

I argued in Chapter 9 that, under full compliance, the global ideal code provides an international safety net. This is, in part, a public good from which all groups benefit. Insofar as this is so, Murphy's case for the Compliance Condition has considerable force here, as it does in the case of domestic public goods (Section 10.4.1). This suggests only a modest increase under partial compliance, if any. Furthermore, some obligations to aid disadvantaged groups arise from one particular group's duty to rectify historical injustices from which they have benefited. Duties to provide rectification are stronger than ordinary duties to provide aid, but also less susceptible to increases resulting from the partial compliance of other groups. Each group's level of obligation is primarily a function of its own degree of culpability, and of the extent to which it benefits from past (or ongoing) injustice. A particular group may have no obligation to provide rectification for the unjust actions of other groups.

Unfortunately, the system of international cooperation is not a pure public good, nor are all obligations between groups founded on rectification. We cannot say that the potential beneficiaries of aid are 'free-riding'. The groups who most need aid may not be those whose failure to contribute causes the problem of partial compliance. More directly, individuals within those groups who are in desperate need of assistance have almost certainly had no realistic opportunity to decide whether or not to comply with the ideal global code.

As ever, we must ask how the introduction of an intergenerational perspective affects this picture. In Section 10.4 I argued that the intergenerational maintenance of institutions is clearly less of a public good than the provision of such institutions among my contemporaries. There is some reason to think that this particular argument might have less force in the inter-group case. This is because groups endure across generations in a way that individuals do not. If we are committed to the notion of group autonomy, as well as individual autonomy, then we can speak of some particular groups free-riding when the present generation in that groups fail to play their part in providing stable institutions, or breathable air or a livable climate, for future generations in all communities. While this obviously does not show that the system of international cooperation is a pure public good in the intra-generational case, it does suggest that it is *not* less of a public good in the intergenerational case.

The recognition of group autonomy also suggests a limit on the obligations of well-off groups to other groups. Each group must balance its obligations to other groups against its obligations to its citizens. An ideal code to be taught to ordinary people will require groups to give their domestic obligations priority over inter-group obligations whenever the two conflict (Section 9.2). No group will be required to devote so much to development aid that it is no longer able to meet the basic needs of its citizens, or to provide them with a stable social framework. Many wealthy groups may feel that, as they cannot meet those needs already, the demands of the ideal code will be mild.

Unfortunately, we must distinguish between a group's ability to meet its citizens' needs and its present practices. Many wealthy groups could meet those needs using comparatively little of their GDP, leaving much available for charitable works overseas. (Analogously, wealthy individuals cannot evade their charitable obligations by arguing that they could not provide a worthwhile life for themselves or their children any more cheaply than they currently do.)

The individuals in charge of a particular group might respond that they could not instigate more substantial aid contributions, as this would lead to political instability or economic recession. People will either elect another government, or suffer from excessive rates of taxation. These negative effects of a highly demanding code are relevant to our evaluation of that code. Under Rule Consequentialism these negative effects of a highly demanding code *are* relevant—but only because they enter into our evaluation of the likelihood of successfully internalizing competing codes. If a certain level of sacrifice *is* internalizable, and forms part of the ideal code, then a group's collective refusal to make that sacrifice is a moral failing, not a ground for revising the ideal code. There is thus no guarantee that the ideal global code will not be extremely demanding in circumstances as far from full compliance as the actual world.

I conclude that the global ideal code may be very demanding on wealthy groups living in a world of widespread non-compliance. However, this level of demand is not necessarily objectionable, especially as it often results from empirical connections whose existence, nature, or extent is often underplayed or misrepresented in popular debate, so that any general intuitive aversion to a highly demanding code should be discounted (Section 9.2.4).

If our historical interactions with another group give us a standing obligation to assist them in times of need, then we are obliged to do so even if their need results from failures of compliance by other groups. (Indeed, our historical agreement may be explicitly designed to come into play in just such a circumstance, as with a treaty of mutual aid against aggression.)

The most urgent demands arise when the failure of compliance is from our own group. We return to this in Section 10.5.2. Before doing so, however, we now briefly examine two particular issues of intergenerational inter-group ethics that might be affected by partial compliance from other groups: environmental degradation and population policy.

10.5.1. *Environmental Partial Compliance*

Recall the stark choice pictured earlier. Universal consumption at the current rate will cause an environmental catastrophe. If we unilaterally abandon the use of oil, then that catastrophe will be less severe. Such unilateral abandonment would obviously drastically reduce the quality of life for the next few generations in our own group.

The present generation in our group face two sources of moral demands. The first is from future generations in their own group. The ideal code requires each generation to ensure the continued survival of their community, and the continuance of an adequate social framework. We saw in Sections 7.9 and 8.2.1 that this requirement can be very demanding in extreme circumstances. If the unilateral abandonment of oil-use by our group would enable the present generation to remain above the lexical level, and if it is the only way to ensure that all subsequent generations also live above that level, then those who had internalized the ideal code might feel obliged to collectively opt for unilateral abandonment.[21]

Unfortunately, as we saw in Sections 2.2.4.2 and 9.2, even in a comparatively prosperous group there may be some people whose very survival depends upon the maintenance of the existing standard of living in their society. Taking a stand against some of the worst abuses of current international environmental practice, with a consequent drop in GDP, might leave our group unable to afford medicines necessary for the survival of some of our citizens. (In the real world, it is the clash between these two urgent sources of moral demands, and the need to balance them, that accounts for the moral difficulty surrounding climate change. Section 9.2.7.)

These demands, while certainly severe, would arise whether the need for conservation resulted from natural causes or from partial compliance. To explore the impact of international partial compliance on the demands of the ideal code, we need to alter our tale, to generate a more severe conflict. One very stark possible case involves partial compliance with respect to population policy.

Suppose our nation is large enough crucially to affect the global population. If we continue as we are, then the earth will become overpopulated. However, if we unilaterally adopt a policy of (almost) universal non-reproduction, then the global population will eventually stabilize at a sustainable level. Are we required to make that sacrifice?

---

[21] Indeed, the discussion in Section 8.2.2 suggests that the present generation might feel obliged to opt for unilateral abandonment even if this would leave some generations below the lexical level, so long as life would eventually rise above that level for some future generations.

We must ask what the policy of universal non-reproduction involves. Are we to imagine our own group dying out over the next generation? If so, life will be very unpleasant for the last few elderly inhabitants, as no one will be around to support them. (We could hope for charity from the international community, given the enormous sacrifice our group will have made to ensure their continued survival. However, this might be overly optimistic.) Alternatively, we might combine non-reproduction with increased immigration, especially an influx of refugees from impoverished overpopulated groups. This would enable our group to continue, even though the next generation would be largely genetically unrelated to previous generations.

The policy of abstinence-plus-immigration is almost certainly better for our group in the long run than abstinence alone. However, it still involves a considerable sacrifice. At an individual level, this policy requires individuals to abandon the option of producing and raising children 'of their own'. Given the significance attached to this option within most societies, and to the autonomy involved in deciding for oneself whether or not to embark on this option, this is a very significant sacrifice.

At a collective level, this policy would involve a potentially radical change of our group's values and social structures. The huge influx of people from another country might produce a group in the next generation only marginally connected to our present group. We might view this as the *replacement* of our group by another, rather than as a *continuation* of the same group. There are obvious parallels here with the oft-discussed issue of the relationship between personal identity over time and a person's values (Section 9.3.1). Ultimately, as in the individual case, the question of whether the policy of abstinence-plus-immigration is one of change or of extinction probably has no definitive objective answer. What matters is how the group itself thinks of the change.

In our present tale, the present generation of our group may thus find themselves between a rock and another rock. Both options lead to the disappearance of the group as they know it. Their present population policy will buy them a few more generations of affluent life, all lived under a shadow of impending doom. To make our dilemma more realistic, let us instead place the present generation between a rock and a mere hard place. Suppose our group is not so pivotal. The shift in our population policy would not be sufficient to prevent an otherwise inevitable population crisis. Suppose the global population, given current patterns of behaviour, will eventually stabilize at a sustainable level. However, that level is higher than would be ideally desirable, as the patterns of resource-use and deforestation involved in reaching and maintaining the eventual equilibrium will cause ongoing environmental problems, significantly reducing everyone's quality of life. Unfortunately, the negative effects of this degradation will be disproportionately borne by some of the world's worst-off people. As the present generation of an affluent nation, we must decide how much we should sacrifice to alleviate the burdens caused by the partial compliance of others.

As in the individual case of famine relief, it seems likely that anyone who had internalized the ideal code would feel obliged to make sacrifices here that would strike us as supererogatory. One reason for this is that, given its history, those who had internalized the ideal code would see the actual world as containing overlapping social frameworks, not a set of perfectly isolated ones. Aside from the other implications noted earlier, this also means that they will tend to identify with the global community to a greater extent than we do, and thus regard the loss of their own group identity as less of a sacrifice.

10.5.2. Partial Compliance within a Group

A second reason why partial compliance may lead to high demands is that, in the actual world, our group is unlikely to be completely unconnected to the less fortunate group. So the partial compliance in question may be our own.

A history of interactions has two complementary effects: it gives rise to obligations between the groups and, by interweaving their social frameworks, it undermines the option of using different lexical thresholds in relation to the two groups. Both these effects are relevant in a world of partial compliance. If our group already owes a debt or obligation of rectification to another group, then our present failure to comply with our obligations is more serious than if we were merely failing in an obligation of general benevolence. Our ongoing partial compliance builds up an ever-increasing store of obligations.

In the actual world, one common source of the failure to comply with the dictates of the ideal code, especially at the group to group level, is the failure to recognize the existence or moral significance of both past and present interactions between the two groups. By ignoring their connections, lucky groups proceed as if the two groups were completely separate. This enables them both to believe that their only obligations to the unlucky group are imperfect obligations of general benevolence, and to continue to apply different lexical thresholds when evaluating the two groups.

Partial compliance can also turn general obligations of benevolence into stricter moral obligation. Suppose the two groups were previously unconnected, so that the only present obligations on the lucky group are those of general benevolence. If they fail to comply with those present obligations, however, then this will create a moral debt between two groups, thus perhaps undermining the claim that the two social frameworks are distinct.

Perhaps the worst failure of compliance among real-world lucky groups is a failure to acknowledge their own failures of compliance. In terms of the ideal code, lucky groups fail to recognize that their inter-group behaviour has long been inconsistent with their own most basic moral principles. (In effect, this was the main claim of Chapter 9.)

Strict duties can become more demanding under partial compliance. However, this need not be counterintuitive. From an intuitive point of view, strong duties to provide rectification, or even to redress injustices from which one benefits, do not seem as unreasonable as correspondingly high obligations to meet needs left unmet owing to partial compliance by others.

In the actual world, few groups (if any) meet what someone who had internalized the ideal code would regard as her inter-group obligations. We must now ask how such a person would deal with partial compliance, within her own group, with the group's obligations due to the partial compliance of other groups.

Imagine an individual who has internalized the ideal code, and who lives in a lucky group that refuses to meet its inter-group obligations: not just the extra obligations due to the partial compliance of other groups, but even the obligations it would have under full compliance, that is, those sketched in Chapter 9.

How will such individuals respond? Some answers are obvious. They will campaign for better public policies, perhaps especially highlighting relevant empirical information, if ignorance of the actual connections between the two groups is a primary cause of the lucky group's partial compliance. The crucial question, as ever, is how much they would be prepared to sacrifice.

I argued at the outset that Rule Consequentialism generally makes quite extreme demands when the welfare of distant strangers is at stake (Section 10.2.2). Our present situation is complicated by three other arguments. These pull in opposite directions.

1. One cause of the emergency situation is the partial compliance of other members of the lucky group. Insofar as partial compliance should not increase demands, the individual will be more reluctant to embrace higher demands. Why should she shoulder the responsibilities of others in her group in addition to her own responsibilities of benevolence? She will not feel more responsible simply because others in her group fail to acknowledge any responsibility.

2. On the other hand, as I argued in Chapter 9, in a world of very unequal material resources, the only way for Rule Consequentialism to avoid being very demanding, even under full compliance, is by placing significant weight on group autonomy. The flip-side of this is that agents must

identify themselves with their groups. As each agent takes more responsibility for emergencies resulting from her own failures than she would for emergencies that just happen, she must also take more responsibility for emergencies resulting from failures of her own group. Accordingly, she will make a greater sacrifice than she would if the emergency had just happened.

3. The present behaviour of her group will also impact on the agent's interpretation of the lexical level and lexical thresholds. Suppose she becomes convinced that the interactions between two groups are much more morally significant than most members of her group are inclined to admit. She will thus conclude that it is no longer appropriate to operate with radically different lexical thresholds when judging the two groups. This has two effects: she will set a higher threshold when considering the impact of her actions (or inactions) on the unlucky group, and she will set a lower threshold when considering the impact on members of the lucky group, including herself. Confronted by the vast disparities between the two groups, such a person may well conclude that many of the elements of a typical lucky life are frivolous, and she will then no longer regard it as a great sacrifice to give them up. Here we see another impact of context-dependence. Although a lower threshold can reduce our obligations to others, it also makes us more willing to give things up.

Partial compliance with the ideal global environmental policy threatens the continued existence of a viable ecosystem, and thus the future pursuit of any worthwhile goals by anyone. Partial compliance with ideal principles of international law and the recognition of states creates irresistible incentives for individuals in poor resource-rich nations to seize power, and provides them with the ability to hold that power without any reference to the interests of their citizens. Partial compliance by such individuals, faced with those incentives, produces extreme deprivation across much of the globe. Partial compliance with the optimal rules of international aid leaves most of that deprivation unalleviated.

It is very hard to determine with any precision what an individual who had internalized the ideal code would say under such circumstances of extreme partial compliance. This is especially problematic for small developed nations, and for their citizens. It is easy to say that, under the ideal code (or, indeed, under any plausible moral theory whatsoever), 'we' should at least stop harming others, where harming includes willingly participating in an international economic system which avoidably and unjustly deprives them of the means to meet their own most basic needs. However, small nations may have no option but to remain within the existing financial system, and even actively support it, or risk losing their foothold in the developed world. Their economic survival may depend upon their recognizing governments no one who had internalized the ideal code would ever recognize, as well as encouraging institutions any such person would reject outright. Even more than with other applications of Rule Consequentialism, the distance between the ideal world of full compliance and the actual world threatens to make the ideal global code either extremely demanding, or hopelessly indeterminate.

10.6. Conclusions

Rule Consequentialism makes many demands. Many of these increase significantly under the partial compliance of the real world. While some of these additional demands seem intuitively plausible, others do not. The introduction of future generations increases the significance of partial compliance, especially in the far future, and ensures that the ideal code takes it into account. It also impacts on the specific demands of the ideal code in a number of ways. While it is hard to draw definite conclusions, two clear patterns of relations between the demands of the ideal code and our own intuitions seem to emerge. While the ideal code does not make unreasonable demands when partial compliance concerns activities confined to the agent's own group, the additional demands can seem unreasonably high in relation to the relief of those in need beyond the agent's own group, especially if no previous connection exists between the two groups. (When a history of interaction does exist, we have good reason to distrust our intuitions, and thus we cannot say that the increased demands of partial compliance are 'counterintuitive'.) If we could somehow confine Rule Consequentialism to cases where a history of interaction does exist (either within or beyond a group), then the theory would be intuitively acceptable. The search for a principled way of achieving this is the task of the next chapter.

11

Dividing Morality

Our examination of Rule Consequentialism over the past six chapters has yielded mixed results. In Chapters 5 to 9 we saw that Rule Consequentialism provides an intuitively appealing account of the morality of individual reproduction, and that a political theory built upon that account sheds light on a range of current debates. Unfortunately, Chapter 10 showed that, while the demands of Rule Consequentialism are moderate and plausible in some areas, they are extreme and somewhat implausible in others, and that the comparative stringency of Rule Consequentialism's demands in different areas is often very peculiar.

There are three possible responses. Two are obvious: abandon Rule Consequentialism or bite the bullet—arguing that, whatever its faults and limitations, Rule Consequentialism offers better guidance across the full range of moral issues than any of its competitors. Perhaps the most we can expect from any moral theory is general advice on how we should think about morality, rather than specific injunctions.

The present chapter explores a more complex middle path. When a theory is so well-suited to some moral domains and yet so ill-suited to others, one natural response is to limit the theory's scope. If we could divide morality into different compartments, and somehow confine Rule Consequentialism to one particular compartment, then we might have a plausible theory of an important part of morality, rather than an implausible theory of the whole.

The present chapter mounts such a defence of Rule Consequentialism. I begin by exploring two principled rationales for dividing morality into two distinct realms. I then show that, once morality is thus divided, it turns out that all the moral areas where Rule Consequentialism fails can be grouped together in one realm, leaving the theory untouched in the other realm. Reproduction belongs to this latter realm, along with most other issues concerning our obligations to future generations.

If Rule Consequentialism accounts for only one part of morality, then it must be supplemented by other moral theories before we have a complete account. I explore the possibility of combining Rule Consequentialism with other theories we discarded earlier, especially Scheffler's Hybrid View and Simple Consequentialism. I call the resulting theory 'Combined Consequentialism'.

The particular division used in this chapter draws heavily on the solution to the Demandingness Objection presented in *The Demands of Consequentialism*.[1] However, my principal aim is to defend the general idea of dividing morality into realms, and to show how a Rule Consequentialist account of the morality of reproduction might fit into such a division. A vast array of different combinations of theories are compatible with this general approach. The particular details of the division are secondary. This chapter should thus be of interest to anyone who found the accounts offered in Chapters 5 to 9 promising, but who rejects Rule Consequentialism as a complete moral theory, whether on the basis of Chapter 10 or on other grounds.

11.1. Two Ways to Divide Morality

In *The Demands of Consequentialism*, I offered two different ways to divide morality into realms. The first uses the notion of moral community, while the second relies upon the distinction between needs and goals. For a Consequentialist, morality is about the promotion of the good. There are thus two ways for a Consequentialist to divide morality: using a distinction between goods, or a distinction between ways of promoting the good. The second division is clearly based on the nature of good to be promoted. The first reflects a distinction that runs through the whole Consequentialist tradition, between two competing ways of thinking about the project of promoting the good.

Consequentialism derives much of its initial appeal from its apparent simplicity: it gives me the single moral project of making the world a better place. Complexities multiply as soon as I ask what this project involves. We now turn to a prior question: in what sense does Consequentialism give this project *to me*? In the Consequentialist tradition, two standard answers are interwoven. On the one hand, the Consequentialist project is seen as an individual project given to me as a single moral agent. Alternatively, Consequentialism may be a group project, which is mine only because (and insofar as) I belong to some particular group (which may be the set of all moral agents, or some subset of them). For generality, I refer to these approaches as Individual Consequentialism and Collective Consequentialism respectively. The individual approach is exemplified by Simple Consequentialism, the collective by Rule Consequentialism. If we think both approaches have merit in different circumstances, then we can divide moral choices on the basis of whether they are best analysed in terms of an individual moral project or a collective one.

---

[1] Mulgan, *The Demands of Consequentialism* (2001), pt. IV.

11.1.1. Moral Community

As we saw in Chapter 2, many contemporary moral and political theories assume the possibility of reciprocity and mutual advantage, together with a comparatively equal distribution of power. The parties involved have some degree of both independence and interdependence; they stand apart but can also work together to their mutual benefit. Not all moral situations are of this sort. Our relations with future generations are a classic example. In the absence of time travel, reciprocal interaction with distant generations is impossible. This is why theories *founded* on reciprocity fail to cope with those obligations. Consider also our relations with people starving in distant countries. We are dealing with existent people, whose number, identity, and existence are all fully determinate, in direct contrast to the status of future generations.[2] However, the lack of meaningful reciprocal interaction can be just as striking.

Our Consequentialist approach differs from these pure reciprocity theories in two key ways. The first is that the essence of any Collective *Consequentialism* is to think of the project of promoting the *overall* good as a collective project. While those who are promoting the good are members of a particular community of reciprocal interaction, the good in question may extend beyond the well-being of those individuals. This easily enables a Consequentialist morality of reciprocity to accommodate the interests and concerns of future generations in a way that a morality of pure reciprocity cannot.

The second distinction is that Combined Consequentialism regards the morality of reciprocity as only a part of morality, not the whole of it. Some moral theorists limit the scope of our moral concern to our own actual community. Combined Consequentialism contains no such limits. Some of our strongest obligations concern those who lie beyond the present borders of our moral community. Indeed, one prime motivation for dividing morality in the first place is to construct a coherent account of what those obligations are, and how they can be balanced against obligations within our moral community.[3] Therefore, while Combined Consequentialism does not use Collective Consequentialism beyond the realm of reciprocity, this is explicitly not because it ignores other moral realms.

Suppose we divide morality into a realm of community and a realm of bare humanity, with the former covering relations within a moral community, and

---

[2] I borrow this account of the three types of indeterminacy involved in future generations choices (existence, identity, and number) from Heyd, *Genethics*, 23.

[3] In *The Demands of Consequentialism*, I argue that our obligations to distant strangers are less demanding, taken one at a time, than the obligations we would have to a person in similar need within our own moral community. It does not follow that we have no obligations to distant strangers, nor that the obligations we have do not trump many of the obligations arising within our moral community.

the latter telling its members how to deal with those beyond. The notion of moral community I have in mind here is of a society of comparatively equal moral agents who can interact in mutually advantageous ways in pursuit of their goals. These agents have individual aims (both self-directed and other-directed), as well as shared cooperative aims. In order to participate in such a community, one must possess certain capacities (such as autonomy and rationality), have access to certain resources (such as shelter, clothing, and means of communication), and also meet minimal requirements (such as the absence of starvation or extreme pain).

There are two key points to note.

1. The present division is based on the notion of *moral* community, not actual community. While the notion of moral community is an idealization, the rules designed to cover such a community provide a benchmark for all ongoing interactions in the real world. If moral community is our basic notion, then our interactions with those currently excluded from any actual community should be undertaken with a view to creating a morally respectable community of interaction between us. Persistent relations of unequal interaction are likely to be anathema to any Consequentialist moral community.

2. The division based on moral community does not, in itself, tell us how our moral obligations within and beyond that community are to be balanced. This division certainly does not say that we have no obligations beyond our moral community, nor that those obligations cannot ever trump obligations within our community. A Consequentialist theory built on the present division may include very strong obligations of bare humanity to those beyond our moral community.

The description of starving people as 'potential members of our moral community' thus does not imply that we have no obligations to such people. Rather, it draws attention to the fact that our relations with such a person are crucially different from our relations with those with whom we are able to interact on a basis of (approximate) equality. As a result, some accounts of the basis, nature, and content of morality which work perfectly well for relations of the latter sort may not be well suited to the former.

11.1.2. *Needs and Goals*

A second way for Consequentialists to divide morality is via the impact of my actions on the well-being of others.[4] As ever, I divide the components of

---

[4] A further alternative would be to introduce value elements beyond human well-being, and use these to divide morality. Owing to our focus on human well-being, I put this option to one side.

well-being into two broad categories: needs and goals (Section 3.1). There are two ways to promote the well-being of another agent. The first is to meet her needs, while the second is to assist her in the pursuit of her goals. We can thus distinguish a Realm of Needs and a Realm of Goals, with the former governing our obligations to meet the needs of others, while the latter covers our pursuit of our goals, and any obligations we have in relation to the goals of others. Chapters 3 to 5 focused on these differences, and on their moral significance. The features that distinguish both the Hybrid View and Rule Consequentialism from Simple Consequentialism, especially their commitment to autonomy and moral freedom, are justified by reference to goals. This is because the value of a goal depends upon how it is pursued, whereas the value of a need is not directly affected by the way it is met. Three features of goals are especially significant for moral action: their connections with autonomy, community, and incommensurability. A moral theory emphasizing the significance of these features will offer a more plausible account of the Realm of Goals than one which ignores them. Conversely, theories ignoring these features may be more plausible in the Realm of Needs, where such features are less prominent. We should thus expect the two realms to be governed by different moral principles.

The elements of value theory introduced in this book also reinforce the convergence of the two divisions. In particular, our discussion has often focused on the lexical level, a notion that has close connections both to the distinction between needs and goals, and to ideas of community. Needs come to the fore when we are dealing with someone below the lexical level, while interactions above the lexical level tend to relate to goals. We have also encountered two separate uses of the lexical level. Our foundational value theory may include a basic lexical level below which an agent cannot successfully pursue any worthwhile goals. Below that level, we are exclusively in the Realm of Necessity.

Our Rule Consequentialism also includes a range of context-dependent interpretations of the lexical level, more detailed and ambitious than any foundational lexical level. Each of these interpretations is determined by the social context of the agent, and especially the nature and level of development of her community. This suggests that obligations and permissions derived from context-dependent interpretations of the lexical level belong in both the Realms of Community and Goals. This supports both the claim that goals and community belong together in a single realm, and the claim that Rule Consequentialism offers the appropriate account of that realm.

Combined Consequentialism makes two foundational claims.

1. The two classification schemes generally go together. This is because most interactions between active moral agents relate to their goals rather

than their needs. (This is especially true in the modern developed world, and most especially among its more affluent inhabitants.) Most of our everyday life thus takes place within both the Realm of Goals and the Realm of Community. As Raz puts it, 'all except those who live in circumstances of the most severe deprivation have aspirations, projects and preoccupations which far transcend the satisfaction of the bare biologically determined needs'.[5] On the other hand, if one is dealing with someone who is not an active moral agent, then, by definition, one can only be concerned to meet their needs, as such a person is not in a position to pursue any goals until her basic needs have been met. This explains why deciding whether or not to contribute to famine relief falls within the Realm of Needs and the Realm of Bare Humanity.

2. When the two classification schemes come apart, the division in terms of community takes precedence. Consider a situation where the needs of people in our moral community come under threat. In my view, such cases are best treated as falling under the moral rules governing the legitimate pursuit of goals within a moral community. These will include rules for dealing with disasters within that community, such as rules of mutual aid or cooperation. Our response to a crisis within our own community is often strikingly different from our response to famine or destitution in a foreign land. This is often regarded, especially by Consequentialist moral philosophers, as evidence of morally unacceptable parochialism.[6] Perhaps, on the contrary, it reflects the fact that the crises belong to different moral realms. When a disaster strikes those with whom we interact regularly, we respond in accordance with our code of reciprocity. Our response to distant famine falls instead under the rules governing the realm beyond reciprocity.

We can thus combine our two divisions to yield two realms of moral choice.

The Realm of Necessity.   We, as active members of a moral community, encounter someone who currently lacks the resources or capacities to participate fully in that community. Such a person has many unmet needs and undeveloped capacities. We can add value to his life in many ways. We decide which of his capacities to develop, and which of his needs to meet. One decision we must make is whether to enable the person to participate fully in our moral community. (This unites the realms of bare humanity and needs.)

The Realm of Reciprocity.   We, as active members of a moral community, decide how we will interact in pursuit of our joint and individual goals. (This unites the realms of community and goals.)

---

[5] Raz, *The Morality of Freedom*, 340. See also Griffin, *Well-being*, 67; and Hurka, *Perfectionism*, 150.

[6] See Singer, 'Famine, Affluence and Morality'; and Unger, *Living High and Letting Die*. (For further discussion, see Ch. 1 n. 29 above.)

In *The Demands of Consequentialism*, I argued that our response to the plight of the distant starving belongs to the Realm of Necessity, rather than Reciprocity, while our everyday lives are mostly lived within the Realm of Reciprocity. This division is a key distinguishing feature of a Consequentialist divided moral theory.

The boundaries between the moral realms are fluid. Many (perhaps even most) significant moral dilemmas occur at those boundaries. We may thus wonder whether the division into moral realms does any significant work. I believe that it does. The distinction tracks a significant difference between two ways a situation can invite our moral attention and concern; between two sources of moral reasons; or, perhaps more accurately, two routes from values to reasons. Different moral theories are built upon these different routes. No moral theory based on one route alone can hope to provide a full account of the relationship between values and reasons. Moral dilemmas arise precisely where, and because, different routes intersect. Any attempt to separate the two realms neatly and completely is bound to be an oversimplification. However, such attempts are also a vital preliminary to the construction of an adequate moral theory.

Our project is to take seriously the Demandingness Objection and the two Compulsion Objections, and to explore the implications of this move. These objections highlight the boundary between the two realms. They arise only in a world where both needs and goals are morally significant, where many needs are left unmet and many goals unrealized, and where the only way to pursue goals is to leave the needs of others unmet. In any such world one of the central tasks of moral philosophy is to balance the competing moral reasons generated by needs and goals. This balance is best achieved by combining different moral theories, rather than by seeking to apply a single Consequentialist theory to all the disparate moral realms.

The territorial metaphor of 'realms' is, in many ways, unfortunate, as it suggests two separate, distinct, mutually exclusive spheres. In reality, it is invariably impossible to separate the two realms. Most morally significant decisions involve both reciprocity and necessity. It is more accurate to see the two realms as representing two kinds of reasons, responding to different features of moral life. Even if every actual situation belongs to both realms (because both sets of reasons are ever present) it is still useful to consider their characteristics separately.

Suppose we have divided morality into two realms. The central thesis of *The Demands of Consequentialism* was that these different realms require different approaches to morality. Any adequate moral theory will then have three components: two separate accounts of our obligations and permissions within each realm, and a third component uniting or balancing the two realms. In *The Demands of Consequentialism*, I argued that Rule Consequentialism offers the best account of the Realm of Reciprocity, Simple Consequentialism works best in the Realm of Necessity, and the Hybrid View balances the two realms. I now briefly recap these results.

11.1.3. *The Realm of Reciprocity*

Concepts such as autonomy, community, choice, incommensurability, agency, reciprocity, and freedom are more significant for goals than for needs. Moral theories built upon these ideas are better suited to the Realm of Reciprocity. Conversely, objections to a particular theory based on its inability to accommodate these concepts will have great force in the Realm of Reciprocity, but comparatively little force in the Realm of Necessity. This component of our moral theory will be moulded to the nature and moral significance of goals, and focus on the rational, interpersonal, and social aspects of human nature. This is the natural place for the idioms of Kantian moral theory and of Contractualism. Perhaps more surprisingly, this is also the right realm for Rule Consequentialism.

I argue at length elsewhere that all the prominent objections to Rule Consequentialism are only decisive within the Realm of Necessity.[7] The ideal code of reciprocity is more intuitively plausible than the ideal code of necessity, or than any ideal code designed to fit both moral realms. This applies both to general moral rules, and to particular moral judgements. Within the Realm of Reciprocity, the ideal code is closer to the rules of thumb of commonsense morality. Its particular judgements will thus also be closer to those of commonsense morality.

To take one particular example, Chapter 10 concluded, in effect, that many of Rule Consequentialism's demands are implausible. This was a further strike against Rule Consequentialism as a general moral theory, as our intuitions lead us to expect the exact opposite. However, it may increase the intuitive plausibility of Rule Consequentialism's account of the Realm of Reciprocity. If Rule Consequentialism is less demanding in the Realm of Reciprocity, and commonsense morality is more demanding in that realm, then Rule Consequentialism and common sense will be much closer in the Realm of Reciprocity than in the Realm of Necessity. This significantly enhances the possibility that Rule Consequentialism is plausible in the Realm of Reciprocity and implausible in the Realm of Necessity.

If Rule Consequentialism is plausible only within the Realm of Reciprocity, and if the individual morality of reproduction belongs to that

---

[7] Mulgan, *The Demands of Consequentialism*, 223–7.

realm, then this will reinforce the conclusion of Chapter 6: that Rule Consequentialism provides the best account of individual reproduction. The areas where Rule Consequentialism is plausible would then all fall within the Realm of Reciprocity.

11.1.4. The Realm of Necessity

This part of our moral theory need not pay too much attention to concepts such as autonomy, community, choice, incommensurability, agency, reciprocity, and freedom. It will be moulded to the nature and moral significance of needs, and focus on the physical side of human (and animal) life. It is less likely to include prerogatives or restrictions. This is the natural place for the idioms of utilitarianism, and of Simple Consequentialism more generally.

If the Realm of Necessity were the whole of morality, then Simple Consequentialism would indeed be a contender.[8] Perhaps, in a world without goals, it would be the most appropriate moral theory. However, we do not live in such a world. Indeed, many opponents of Consequentialism object to the theory precisely on the grounds that it proceeds as if we did. There is more to morality than the Realm of Necessity. Our overall moral theory must account for both realms, and balance their competing demands.

Simple Consequentialism leaves no room for any other moral realm. Given the vast amount of unmet need in our world, and the comparative cost of meeting the needs of others rather than pursuing one's own goals, the obligation to meet the needs of others swamps any reasons generated by goals. The Realm of Necessity would overwhelm the Realm of Reciprocity, and the Reason to Promote the Good would be, in effect, the only real moral reason.

Chapter 10 showed that Rule Consequentialism meets the same fate: if it covers both realms, then the demands of necessity will overwhelm the liberties and obligations of reciprocity.

11.1.5. Balancing the Two Moral Realms

This part of our theory balances the two component moral theories. It will balance goals against needs, and explore the common ground between Kantian and Consequentialist moral idioms. Unsurprisingly, this is the natural

---

[8] Mulgan, *The Demands of Consequentialism*, 247–9.

place for Hybrid Moral Theories, such as Scheffler's. However, Scheffler's original theory requires considerable restructuring before it can play this new role.[9]

Within Combined Consequentialism, the role of the Hybrid View is to balance the competing demands of the two realms. The Agent Centred Prerogative doesn't, in itself, tell agents how they should respond to either needs or goals, or to reasons generated within or beyond our moral communities. Rather, it tells us how to balance the competing reasons generated by the two realms.[10]

A key lesson of Chapters 4 to 6, translated into our new vocabulary of realms, is that any plausible account of the Realm of Reciprocity must include constrained prerogatives governing reproduction. The precise content of our reproductive prerogatives, and of the constraints upon them, depend upon the details of our theory of the morality of reciprocity. However, the theory balancing the two moral realms must leave room for those constrained prerogatives, by including a broad prerogative structure of its own. It is here that the Hybrid View comes into its own, enabling the Reason to Promote the Good to be a subordinate component in our moral theory, rather than occupying pride of place.

11.2. A Third Realm?

The introduction of future generations raises several new questions for Combined Consequentialism and for the general project of dividing morality. The most obvious is that our interests in this book appear to require a third realm: a *Realm of Creation* where we decide which people, if any, to bring into existence. We could then think of the Realm of Necessity as occupying a halfway house between the two Realms of Reciprocity and Creation. The Realm of Necessity differs from Creation in that our decision relates to someone who already exists at the moment of choice. The Realm of Necessity differs from Reciprocity in that, at the moment of choice, the object of our decision is not actually a fully participating member of our moral community.

I shall argue that we do not need a separate third realm. Issues of creation can be dealt with using our two realms. The division between those two

[9] In *The Demands of Consequentialism* (pp. 237–47), I argue that the Hybrid View is not suitable for either realm on its own. The Hybrid View seems to straddle the two moral realms, and to be at home in neither. Its rejection of Agent Centred Restrictions is plausible only within the Realm of Necessity, yet its inclusion of Agent Centred Prerogatives is compelling only in the Realm of Reciprocity.

[10] I explore at length several justifications for replacing Scheffler's two reasons with my two realms in Mulgan, *The Demands of Consequentialism*, 250–8.

realms is more fundamental than the distinction between actual and future people. The morality of individual reproduction, and our relations with future members of our own moral community in general, are best thought of as belonging to the Realm of Reciprocity, while our relations with future generations outside our moral community seem much closer to the Realm of Necessity.

One defence of this procedure is that it both provides an intuitively appealing account of the morality of reproduction, and explains that account by deriving it from a theory justified on other grounds. This is preferable to presenting a separate, ad hoc, account of a Realm of Creation, and then having to balance its demands against those of each other realm. The fewer divisions we can make, the greater will be the explanatory power of our theory.

To establish that Combined Consequentialism copes with individual reproductive choices is thus to show how it incorporates them into its two realms. While such choices involve the creation of a new potential moral agent, as well as requiring considerable attention to basic needs, such choices are squarely situated within the boundaries of the potential parent's moral community. They do not extend beyond that community in the way that famine relief decisions do. The creation of new members of a moral community is an activity that takes place within that community.

Furthermore, as we saw in Chapters 4 and 6, the general theoretical justification for reproductive freedom flows from the agent's goals, placing us within the Realm of Reciprocity. Both the addition of prerogatives within the Hybrid View and the inclusion of reproductive freedom rules in the ideal code of Rule Consequentialism are justified by the significance of the connections between goals and autonomy. Autonomy may well be instrumentally valuable for needs, as each agent is especially well-placed and motivated to meet her own needs. However, when we turn to goals, autonomy is intrinsically, and not merely instrumentally, valuable.

Beyond individual reproduction lie the broader obligations of intergenerational justice. Obligations to future generations in my own community straddle the two realms. The lack of reciprocal interaction seems to place them clearly in the Realm of Necessity. On the other hand, the connection between our present projects and the fate of future generations shows that, as we saw in Chapters 7 to 9, any Consequentialist moral code governing reciprocal interaction in the current generation of our moral community must consider the impact of our actions on future generations.

I shall place our obligations regarding future generations in the Realm of Reciprocity. This is implausible if we regard these as obligations *to* those future generations grounded in our reciprocal interactions with them.

However, it is plausible if we regard these as obligations flowing from the code governing reciprocal interactions in the present generation. Rule Consequentialism provides a good example of how such a code extends to future generations, as we saw in Chapters 5 to 9.

The ability to account for both the morality of individual reproduction and our broader obligations to future generations within existing moral realms is due to the Consequentialist account of reciprocity, where the good to be promoted by collective interaction need not be limited to the individual interests or projects of those who interact. This mode of extension is thus not available to non-Consequentialist accounts of the morality of reciprocity, as we saw in Chapter 2.

11.2.1. A Final Boundary

One obvious complication for our division of morality is the boundary between intergenerational and international justice. The best way to construct an account of our obligations regarding future people in our own society is to build it on our account of the morality of individual reproduction. If the latter belongs to the Realm of Reciprocity, then so does the former. So our moral theory will borrow its account of intergenerational justice from Rule Consequentialism, along the lines sketched in Chapters 7 to 9. We saw that, when confined to the future of a single society, this account is fruitful and not incompatible with any intuitions that are decisive—or even reliable. On the other hand, our obligations to present people in other lands fall under the Realm of Necessity. This raises the question of where our obligations to future people in other lands fit into our division of morality.

There are several ways for Combined Consequentialism to deal with obligations to future people in distant lands. The first is to extend the Realm of Reciprocity. If the members of two separate moral communities come together to form a single community of interaction, then this is best seen as analogous to interaction within a moral community.

In previous chapters, we saw that those who had internalized the ideal code would feel a strong inclination to extend their social framework to include anyone who is *either* excluded from *any* social framework *or* operating within a framework offering a lower lexical threshold. Accordingly, the future goal of Rule Consequentialism, even in a world where groups are initially unconnected, is a world where all interactions are brought within a single global social framework offering the highest feasible lexical threshold to everyone. In other words, a universal Realm of

Reciprocity. This inclination would obviously only be strengthened by any historical or present interactions between groups. We might conclude that all our obligations regarding future people are covered by the morality of reciprocity.

Theoretically, it might be possible for two or more separate social frameworks to exist indefinitely in complete isolation. From the perspective of Combined Consequentialism, this is neither practical nor desirable. It is not practical owing to already existing global interactions, and especially the global nature of future environmental problems. Even if it were possible, isolation is not desirable, as a suitable overarching global social framework would make a wider range of goals available to all, thereby promoting the successful pursuit of valuable goals. In both realms, Combined Consequentialism thus aims at a future where all human beings belong to a single moral community, in reality as well as in theory.

Future generations in our own moral community count as members of that community, and our obligations with respect to them fall under the Realm of Reciprocity. Under full compliance, all future people will be members of the moral community that our present community will become. Therefore, ideally, all our obligations to future people fall under the Realm of Reciprocity. The difference between what we owe future people in other lands and what we owe future people in our own is thus far less than the difference between what we owe one another and what we owe to distant present people.

This discussion offers yet another account of why climate change is such a morally difficult problem (Section 9.2.7). The optimistic model, on which our initial discussion of Rule Consequentialism was largely built, pictures a world where the gradual expansion of our moral community is accompanied by increasing prosperity and mutually beneficial interaction. Our obligation to provide opportunities to all people thus expands along with our collective capacity to provide such opportunities. By contrast, the facts of climate change suggest a pessimistic model where our community of interaction, and hence the scope of our Realm of Reciprocity, expands precisely because overall global prosperity is reduced. We thus acquire more urgent obligations (as we saw in Sections 7.9 and 8.2, the pessimistic model generally involves more stringent demands than the optimistic model) just as our collective ability to meet such demands is failing.

Our division of morality thus explains the importance of empirical questions concerning the origins of comparative poverty. Suppose we are rich while distant people are very poor. Until we know how this situation came about, we do not know into which realm our obligations to those people fall. Until we know that, we have only the vaguest idea what those obligations will be, and how they will be affected by partial compliance.[11]

A second alternative is to retain the two realms, and argue that our obligations to distant future people fall under the Realm of Necessity. While a universal Realm of Reciprocity is the ideal goal of Rule Consequentialism, in reality the two sources of moral reasons will persist. In our world of very partial compliance, our actual interactions with very distant present people may be insufficient to ground extensive obligations to them, and our actual connection to their descendants may be even more tenuous. So Combined Consequentialism still has room for obligations based on bare humanity, independent of reciprocal interaction, both with respect to present people and with respect to future people with whom we could but probably will not form a common social framework. Within Combined Consequentialism, these obligations of pure humanity are balanced against the agent's permissions and obligations within the Realm of Reciprocity by the revised Hybrid View.

11.2.2. An Inter-Group Hybrid View

A third alternative for Rule Consequentialism is to redraw our third component: the balance between the two realms, by responding more directly to the role of groups in international ethics.

A purely individual focus can seem inadequate to capture the collective nature of global issues. To accommodate this, we might introduce an inter-group Hybrid View, based on a collective Agent Centred Prerogative granting each group the right to give extra weight to their own interests and goals. As with the original Hybrid View, the justification for this prerogative is founded on the significance of autonomy. It could be derived either directly (from the significance of group autonomy) or indirectly—as the best response to the significance of individual autonomy in a world where people belong to groups. If the prerogative is justified by reference to group autonomy, then only actions which valuably exercise that autonomy will be permitted. (As we saw in Chapter 9, the valuable exercise of group autonomy requires both intra-group policies that respect the autonomy of individuals

[11] If our account of the Realm of Reciprocity were based on actual interactions, rather than the possibility of future interactions, then the boundaries between the realms would be different. Whether certain cases fall under the Realm of Reciprocity depends on the details of our account of the morality of reciprocity. The choice of division and the choice of component theories thus need to be considered together. The claim of this chapter is that the combination of a particular division with a particular Consequentialist account of each realm provides a plausible overall theory.

and further their interests, and external relations policies that do the same for individuals in other groups.)

If we adopt the inter-group Hybrid View, decisions regarding future people in other groups belong to both realms. For instance, our group's obligation to avoid environmental damage is partly a public good issue, partly a rectification of past (and perhaps present) injustices, and partly a matter of charity. The first two sources of obligation belong to the Realm of Reciprocity. These obligations can be quite demanding, but they do not increase markedly under partial compliance. Obligations based on charity do increase in this way. However, they belong to the Realm of Necessity. Insofar as we are in that realm, the ideal code must be balanced against our group prerogative. Recall the abstinence-plus-immigration policy from Chapter 9. We might argue that this policy represents too great a sacrifice, and that our group's Agent Centred Prerogative will permit us to continue with at least some degree of reproduction.

As with an individual prerogative, we must point to the negative impact of the proposed sacrifice on our group's autonomy, goals, and projects. I emphasized earlier the significance for each group of being free (both practically and morally) to choose its own way of life, its own institutions and values, subject to the proviso that it meets the basic needs of its citizens (Section 9.3).

The life of a group spreads over many generations. The ability to reproduce itself across generations is a key component (and, in the long run, a necessary precondition) of group autonomy. Such reproduction is not solely genetic. Indeed, in theory it need not be genetic at all.[12] Group survival requires the transmission of shared and accumulated values, projects, and aspirations. If the ratio of immigration to reproduction is too high, a community might fear that those values and traditions will be lost. Such fear of abstinence-plus-immigration could have unsavoury sources, as when conservative citizens in rural Australia fear an influx of non-white infidels. However, it need not. We might already have broad liberal values, and agree that the projects and traditions which would replace ours are no worse in any objective sense. We are attached to our projects and traditions because they are *ours*, and because of our investment in them, not out of some mistaken belief in their innate superiority.

An individual analogy is instructive here. Suppose a mad utilitarian scientist offers to reprogram my brain so that I become a tireless and single-minded

---

[12] In *The Golden Bough*, James Fraser discusses a nomadic tribe who (allegedly) had no children of their own, but reproduced their culture over many generations by killing adult members of other tribes and adopting their young children. Gibbon also provides a similar account of the military culture of the Janizaries, the elite troups of the Ottoman sultan. (Gibbon, *Decline and Fall of the Roman Empire*, ch. 64. See also, Kinross, *The Ottomans*.)

charity worker. I might reject this offer, on the grounds that it involves annihilating *me* and creating a new person in my body, while still admitting both that this person would be morally better than myself, and that his life would go better overall than my own. (Of course, I might also deny that he *would* be a better or happier person, but that is a separate issue.)[13]

If I have an individual Agent Centred Prerogative at all, then this is clearly an acceptable use of it. If I'm not required to become a tireless charity worker, then I cannot be required to allow myself to be destroyed and replaced by one. A group prerogative is the same. That prerogative reflects our individual interests in living in a group whose guiding values are collectively chosen by, and in harmony with the values and projects of, individual members of that community.

As with any prerogative, the precise boundaries are impossible to specify with any precision, but I hope the foregoing discussion at least brings out some of the considerations relevant to any application of a group Agent Centred Prerogative.

11.2.3. A Test for Combined Consequentialism

To bring all our discussions together, consider a combined case of partial compliance: an individual whose group is failing to live up to its inter-group obligations, in a world where other nations are similarly derelict. I argued in Section 10.5 that Rule Consequentialism cannot accommodate this case. Does Combined Consequentialism fare any better? Can it solve the Demandingness Objection?

The right way to think about this case, within Combined Consequentialism, is as follows. The group's obligation to other nations is an abstraction from each individual's obligation to meet the needs of other individuals in distant countries. These individual obligations belong squarely in the individual Realm of Necessity. The group's Agent Centred Prerogative is derived from the individual prerogatives of its members. That group prerogative ensures that the group as a whole is not required to make an extreme sacrifice. However, the non-compliance of others in her group means that the individual agent cannot discharge her obligations simply by participating in her local community. (As she might have been able to if, for instance, the community levied a special tax to meet its international aid obligations.) So she must meet those obligations by personal charitable works, or by working to change the policies of her community, whichever has the highest expected return. However, she is not required to make sacrifices beyond the

---

[13] See chapter endnote, A, p. 362.

limits set by her individual Agent Centred Prerogative. She need not sacrifice her most cherished goals, even if the result is that her group, as a whole, fails to make an adequate contribution. (This is significant, as, in most actual cases, a single individual cannot ensure that her community as a whole makes a sufficient sacrifice even if she makes an enormous sacrifice herself. For instance, a community's Agent Centred Prerogative may permit it to contribute only 5 per cent of its GDP to development aid. If the current level is 1 per cent, and if others show no inclination to support an increase, then any ordinary citizen will be bankrupted if she attempts single-handedly to reach the required level.)

The intersection between intergenerational and international justice is largely unexplored territory for Consequentialist moral philosophers, as it is for moral and political theorists in general. Our examination of Combined Consequentialism and international relations does not provide anything like a complete account of this vast and uncharted territory. My modest aim has been to show that a moderate Consequentialist approach, founded on a coherent value theory and moulded to the nature of human agents, can shed some light here.

11.3. Rivals within Combined Consequentialism

Our next question is whether there are rivals for the various components of Combined Consequentialism. In particular, does Rule Consequentialism face rivals in the Realm of Reciprocity? Contract theories are explicitly modelled on reciprocity and thus seem to offer a natural account of that realm. Gauthier's contract theory—addressed and found wanting in Section 2.1—was presented as an account of the whole of morality. I focus here on one that is not: T. M. Scanlon's Contractualism. Scanlon's Contractualism is a prominent recent moral theory. It is offered, not as a complete moral theory, but as an account of 'what we owe to each other'. Scanlon is thus offering, more or less, a morality of reciprocity. (We return to Scanlon's own account of the boundaries between realms in endnote D to this chapter.) Scanlon formulates his theory as follows.[14]

an act is wrong if its performance under the circumstances would be disallowed by any system of rules for the general regulation of behaviour which no one could reasonably reject as a basis for informed, unforced general agreement.

---

[14] Scanlon, 'Contractualism and Utilitarianism', 110; Scanlon, *What We Owe to Each Other*, 4. See also Brink 'The Separateness of Persons, Distributive Norms, and Moral Theory'; Nagel, *Equality and Partiality*, ch. 4; and Nagel, 'One-to-One'.

In *The Demands of Consequentialism*, I argued that Rule Consequentialism and Contractualism coincide in the Realm of Reciprocity. The argument proceeds by establishing that the ideal code of rules for that realm, as defined by Rule Consequentialism, is one which no agent can reasonably reject.[15]

The argument proceeds by reductio. I assume that Rule Consequentialism favours one code (C1), but that this code places a greater burden on the worst-off person than some other code (C2) places on anyone. C1 is thus not a code that no one could reasonably reject. I then show that, within the Realm of Reciprocity, C2 must be a code that produces better consequences overall than C1. (The key claim here is that the shift from C1 to C2 extends the scope of the background social framework, the foundation for the successful pursuit of goals. As that framework is a public good, the aggregative cost of any such extension is comparatively low, and is outweighed by the benefits. C2 thus produces better overall results than C1.) Accordingly, Rule Consequentialism actually prefers C2 to C1. The assumption that Rule Consequentialism favours a code that Contractualism rejects thus leads to a contradiction. The two theories coincide.[16]

In the present discussion, the scope of the Realm of Reciprocity has been broadened to include reproduction and future generations. Does this extension undermine the coincidence between Rule Consequentialism and Contractualism?

There are prima facie reasons for thinking that Contractualism cannot extend to future people at all. Contractualism is built on an explicitly person-affecting foundation. It evaluates rules by examining their impact on particular persons. Contractualism thus seems prone to all the usual difficulties facing any person-affecting theory, due to the non-identity problem and the unequal circumstances thesis. In particular, a Contractualist analysis of reproduction seems to face all the same problems as a Kantian account of this area of morality (Section 1.5). For instance, if we are choosing rules to govern the reproduction of future rational agents, then how can potential people accept or reject such principles? Most particularly, like any other Kantian theory, Contractualism owes us an explanation of what is wrong with creating a human child and then deliberately preventing him from becoming a rational agent. Simple Consequentialism also faces different problems with this kind of case, as do many other moral theories. It is a very significant advantage of Combined Consequentialism that it explains clearly why such behaviour is wrong.

Contractualism may thus be inferior to Rule Consequentialism in the Realm of Reciprocity, as it cannot accommodate the whole of that realm.

---

[15] Mulgan, *The Demands of Consequentialism*, 229–33. [16] See chapter endnote B, p. 362.

Suppose, however, that Contractualism can extend to cover future generations. What might it say?

Scanlon himself does not address in any detail the morality of reproduction or our obligations to future generations.[17] Other Contractualists have not tended to explore these issues either.[18] Rather than put words into the mouths of Contractualists, I shall focus on the general structure of Contractualist morality. Most defences of Contractualism focus on demonstrating that it yields familiar Person-Affecting principles. Scanlon himself defends a Contractualist account of promises and of several types of special obligation.[19] If we begin from the supposition that Rule Consequentialism and Contractualism coincide in this realm, then this reinforces the central claim of Section 5.7 that the ideal code will generally have a broadly person-affecting flavour. If Contractualism did deal explicitly with our obligations to future generations, we might expect Contractualism, like Rule Consequentialism, to begin with the morality of individual reproduction, initially treating this as a matter of interaction within the present generation.

My argument that Contractualism coincides with Rule Consequentialism is hardly decisive, even within the Realm of Reciprocity. It remains possible that we may uncover significant divergences, especially in areas where both theories are still tentatively feeling their way. Further exploration of Contractualist accounts of intergenerational justice by philosophers sympathetic to the theory is thus urgently needed. Consequentialists are likely to be too ready to assume that Contractualism mirrors their own preferred version of Consequentialism. Accordingly, I leave a more detailed comparison of the two theories in this area for another day. However, I tentatively conclude that the introduction of future generations does not undermine the claim that Rule Consequentialism and Contractualism coincide in the Realm of Reciprocity.

We turn now to rivals for either the Hybrid View or Simple Consequentialism. We can be briefer here, as it is not clear that our Consequentialist division permits any plausible rivals. Once we admit a realm of bare humanity, the question is not whether to include something analogous to the Reason to Promote the Good, but how to balance that reason against other moral considerations.[20] The Hybrid View then seems

---

[17] However, Scanlon does stress that 'contractualism provides no reason for saying that people who do not now exist but will exist in the future have no moral claims on us.' (*What We Owe to Each Other*, 187).

[18] One recent exception is Kumar, 'Who Can be Wronged?', whose person-affecting Contractualist morality has close affinities with the elements of our Rule Consequentialism developed in Section 5.7.2.

[19] Scanlon's strategy is broadly similar to Hooker's defence of Rule Consequentialism. Scanlon uses Contractualism, not merely to derive principles we already find obvious, but also to construct new intuitively compelling moral principles.   [20] Mulgan, *The Demands of Consequentialism*, ch. 1.

ideally placed to mediate the two realms, as it explicitly balances the Reason to Promote the Good against other moral reasons. Some version of the Hybrid View is thus the only option here.

The introduction of future generations only reinforces these claims. While the Hybrid View cannot itself adequately constrain reproductive freedom, it does provide a plausible framework within which a self-contained account of an agent's reproductive prerogatives could be balanced against the Reason to Promote the Good. Within Combined Consequentialism, that constrained account is provided by Rule Consequentialism.

The main option for non-Consequentialists is thus not to replace the two Consequentialist components of Simple Consequentialism and the Hybrid View, but to deny the need for them altogether. One alternative is to deny the need for any other realms at all. If the Realm of Reciprocity is the whole of morality, so that the Reason to Promote the Good is subsumed within whatever theory accounts for that realm, then it does not matter if non-Consequentialist rivals cannot be found for other realms. Non-consequentialists may simply refuse to play the Consequentialist game at all.

I argue against this strategy in general terms in *The Demands of Consequentialism*. The introduction of future generations exacerbates the limitations of a theory acknowledging only one realm, especially if we replace Rule Consequentialism with an account of the morality of reciprocity that cannot extend to future generations. We must not proceed as if one realm were the whole of morality. If we are to develop an adequate moral theory to cope with everyday life, then we will need accounts of both realms, and of the boundary between the two realms. Mistakes will inevitably arise whenever we treat one realm as if it were the whole of morality. *The Demands of Consequentialism* demonstrates that many of the familiar failings of contemporary moral theories arise from mistakes of this sort.[21] Chapters 1 and 2 provide several striking illustrations in regard to Kantian ethics, Gauthier's Contractarianism, and Rawls's liberal egalitarianism (Sections 1.5, 2.1.3, and 2.2.4 respectively). These are all only able to account for future generations (if at all) by invoking implausible assumptions that, in effect, treat the Realm of Reciprocity as if it were the whole of morality. (Gauthier's optimistic assumption that all basic needs are unproblematically met in both the State of Nature and the Initial Bargaining Position is perhaps the clearest example.)

---

[21] Ibid., chs. 8 and 9.

11.4. Rivals at the Foundations

A more modest way to reject the Consequentialist division is to offer an alternative way to divide morality. Combined Consequentialism thus faces rivals at a more fundamental level. The most controversial aspect of our Consequentialist division of morality is that it places our obligations to distant strangers in a different realm from our obligations to others within our moral community. It may seem that a more inclusive division would be better, one that places all persons in the same realm. In this section I examine one such division, and justify my rejection of it.

In the Kantian moral tradition, a key moral notion is the notion of person (Section 1.5). Some Kantians divide morality into a Realm of Respect and a Realm of Interests.[22] The morality of respect is made up of 'constraints on our behaviour toward others that spring from our recognition of others as mature agents on an equal moral footing with ourselves',[23] while the morality of interests is 'concerned with the effect our action has on the well-being ... or the ... interests of others'.[24] There is an obvious connection with the division based on needs and goals: the realm of respect would cover all our obligations to creatures who have goals.

This Kantian division is the main alternative to our proposed division.[25] Despite its appeal, it faces difficult problems at the boundaries between realms. These are different from the boundary problems facing Combined Consequentialism, but no less severe. In particular, Kantian ethics distinguishes persons from creatures who are not persons. This suggests that all human beings who are not yet persons (or no longer persons, or never will be persons) fall into the latter realm.

It is helpful to distinguish two forms of Kantianism. (We leave aside the vexed question of which, if any, reflects Kant's own view.[26])

Pure Kantianism. The morality of respect exhausts morality. Our only obligation is to respect the personhood of others. Interests never have independent moral weight.

---

[22] These titles are from McMahon, *The Ethics of Killing*, 245, rechristening a distinction introduced by Warren Quinn.

[23] Quinn, 'Abortion: Identity and Loss', 49, quoted in McMahan, *The Ethics of Killing*, 246.

[24] McMahan, *The Ethics of Killing*, 245.   [25] See chapter endnote C, p. 363.

[26] There are many intermediate options. For instance, a 'Personalist Kantian' might hold that, while morality includes both the morality of respect and the morality of interests, the latter applies only to the interests of *persons*. Consideration of interests thus derives from respect for persons. Like the pure version, Personalist Kantianism also completely ignores animals. It is not clear that it fares any better with respect to human beings who are not yet persons, as we still need an explanation of why the fact that a creature *might* become a person gives us a reason to care about its present or future interests. In particular, we need an answer to this question that does not produce an extremely demanding theory, especially if we were to develop the technology to make non-human animals rational. (McMahan, *The Ethics of Killing*, 302–29.)

Moderate Kantianism.   The morality of interests has independent moral weight, so that even the interests of creatures who are not, and will never be, persons count morally.

Like Simple Consequentialism, Pure Kantianism avoids boundary problems altogether, as it recognizes only a single moral realm. However, the price of this monistic purity is that animals, and human beings who are not yet persons, appear to count for nothing, as do all the interests of actual persons except those directly related to their rational agency. Therefore, Pure Kantianism cannot accommodate the morality of reproduction and child-rearing (Section 1.5).[27]

A central theme of this book is that a full account of intergenerational justice must be built on, or at least be consistent with, an account of the morality of individual reproduction and child-rearing. If Pure Kantianism cannot make sense of the latter, then it cannot hope to offer even a coherent account of relations across generations between fully autonomous rational agents.

Moderate Kantianism does allow animal and other non-persons to count but, as with any disjointed moral theory, we must now balance two independent sources of moral demands.

While Combined Consequentialism also offers a bifurcated morality, it has a unified Consequentialist structure. Every component of Combined Consequentialism is traced ultimately to the promotion of value. By contrast, Moderate Kantianism seems to lack a unifying rationale. This makes it prima facie unlikely that moderate Kantianism can offer a coherent account of the balance between these two sources of moral demands.

One key motivation for our original division is to avoid the Demandingness Objection. Any moral theory incorporating a Kantian division must avoid two opposite fates.

1. An Over-Demanding Theory.   Many Kantian theories (often implicitly) place very great demands on every moral agent to meet the needs of all other persons. I illustrate this in *The Demands of Consequentialism* for Kant's own principle of beneficence, and in an endnote for Scanlon's Contractualism.[28]

2. An Under-Respecting Theory.   In practice, many theories based on a Kantian division can avoid the Demandingness Objection only by effectively denying that we have any obligation whatsoever to assist distant strangers or future people (Section 2.1). If the motivation for replacing our original

---

[27] Similarly, we saw in Section 2.1.3 that Contractarians also proceed as if the Realm of Reciprocity were the whole of morality. By relying on the generic notion of preference, they ignore basic needs and gloss over the distinction between needs and goals.   [28] See chapter endnote D, p. 364.

division with a Kantian division is to better respect the personhood of distant strangers, then this is a self-defeating result.

A full discussion of Kantian responses to the Demandingness Objection would take us too far afield. If Contractualism (or some other Kant-inspired theory) can solve the Demandingness Objection, and also accommodate future generations, then it may be superior to any form of Consequentialism. We can thus come full circle. Our search for a Consequentialist account of future generations began with the need to address the Demandingness Objection. Our search for suitable alternatives brings us back to the Demandingness Objection, which poses a challenge for every moral theory, no matter how it divides morality. There is certainly no a priori reason to assume that a Kantian division provides a better balance of the agent's autonomy against the needs of others than Combined Consequentialism. This is enough to show that the Consequentialist division, together with a Rule Consequentialist account of the morality of individual reproduction and of intergenerational justice, is a serious contender worthy of further exploration.

Endnotes

A. In both the individual and the group cases, we could argue, solely on grounds of impartial value, that a single continuous human community is better than a pair of shorter-lived communities. As with individual human lives, duration makes possible a breadth and depth of accomplishment which might be impossible for shorter-lived communities. However, this consideration might be outweighed in a particular case. Perhaps we know that the new group will be *much* healthier, or smarter, or more successful in some other way. (Suppose we consider replacing ourselves with a species of genetically superior creatures, who can only survive in an atmosphere poisonous to us.)

In both the individual and collective cases, we must face the possibility that annihilation-plus-replacement produces a better history of the world than continuation. Under Simple Consequentialism, this generates an obligation to annihilate and replace. The argument in the text suggests that things are not so simple under Combined Consequentialism. An ideal code requiring an individual or group to sacrifice itself might be too demanding to be inculcated successfully. If so, Rule Consequentialism will grant a group the permission to ensure its own continuance.

B. The argument in the text (and the longer version offered in *The Demands of Consequentialism*) assumes a welfarist version of Contractualism: an agent can only reject a code of rules because of its direct impact on her own level of well-being. The equivalence between the two theories is obviously easiest to establish for this simple form of Contractualism.

Unfortunately for this argument, Scanlon rejects welfarist contractualism. He lists several other grounds for rejecting a rule. These consist of independent moral considerations, such as responsibility, fairness, rights, and entitlements. (Scanlon, *What We Owe to Each Other*, ch. 4.)

Rule Consequentialists will reply, of course, that their theory accommodates all of these independent moral considerations. Indeed, previous chapters in this book amount to a defence of this claim. Contractualism could only differentiate itself from Rule Consequentialism by showing how the latter fails to deliver the appropriate balance of independent moral considerations.

Contractualism certainly differs from *Simple* Consequentialism. Two key differences are that the former allows an agent reasonably to reject a rule (R) because either (1) R treats her arbitrarily and is thus *unfair;* or (2) R violates a person-affecting restriction, and thus fails to respect her as an autonomous moral agent. (Some philosophers have questioned whether Contractualism does deliver these advantages over Simple Consequentialism: see Brand-Ballard, 'Contractualism and Deontic Restrictions'; and Kagan, *The Limits of Morality*, 46 n. 37. For defences of Contractualism, see Kumar, 'Defending the Moral Moderate'; and Ridge, 'Saving Scanlon: Contractualism and Agent-Relativity'.)

However, our focus is on Rule Consequentialism. Although it might maximize value to treat someone arbitrarily on some particular isolated occasion, the general inculcation of arbitrary rules would carry considerable costs, as it would undermine people's confidence in the moral code and also contaminate their moral motivations. Similarly, I argued at length in Chs. 5–9 that Rule Consequentialism accommodates a wide range of plausible Agent Centred Restrictions. Scanlon's independent moral considerations are not sufficient to establish a divergence between Contractualism and Rule Consequentialism in the Realm of Reciprocity.

An alternative response for Rule Consequentialists is to reject Scanlon's departure from welfarist Contractualism, on the grounds that the introduction of a list of independent moral considerations which are then fed into the Contractualist apparatus renders Contractualism unacceptably circular. Scanlon himself addresses this criticism in *What We Owe to Each Other*, 194–5, 213–18. For other discussions, see Brand-Ballard, 'Contractualism and Deontic Restrictions'; Hooker, 'Scanlon's Contractualism, the Spare Wheel Objection, and aggregation' (2003); Kamm, 'Owing, Justifying, Rejecting'; Ridge, 'Saving Scanlon: Contractualism and Agent-Relativity'; and Wallace, 'Scanlon's Contractualism'.

C. There are many other ways to divide morality. Two that are prominent in the literature are the following. (1) Dividing morality according to the status of the creatures affected, where creatures are divided according to species, or some other division not based on their actual capacities. (2) A Rawlsian liberal division between individual morality and a theory of political justice that is independent of controversial moral claims. Considerations of scope prevent an adequate discussion of these alternatives. For a Consequentialist, any division based on the notion of species cannot be regarded as foundational, while the Rawlsian liberal division is undermined by its inability to cope with intergenerational or international justice. (For a recent critique, not built on explicitly Consequentialist foundations, of species-based divisions, see McMahan, *The Ethics of Killing*, 302–29.)

The Rawlsian approach has obvious affinities to the dualist position critiqued in Section 10.4. Liberal neutrality is one form of dualism. A key feature of my account of Rule Consequentialism is that, once future generations enter the picture, the ideal code takes a distinctively liberal form. However, future generations also undermine full (Rawlsian) liberal neutrality, as the complexities of intergenerational justice call into question several key components of Rawls's strategy: the decision to put the disabled to one side; the broader decision to bracket off all questions of the scope of political morality; the claim that primary goods are (*a*) the same for all people with all conceptions of the good in all social circumstances, and (*b*) that primary goods can be identified in advance; the claim that controversies regarding science and economics can be resolved within a pre-defined constitutional framework rather than needing to be resolved in advance; and the simple picture of a lexically ordered series of principles of justice. (I have argued at length elsewhere that the introduction of future generations undermines neutrality in the particular case of the ontological and moral status of the dead. Mulgan, 'The Place of the Dead in Liberal Political Philosophy', 1999; Mulgan, 'Neutrality, Rebirth and Inter-generational Justice', 2002.) Rawls proceeds as if political justice dealt only with the Realm of Reciprocity. He thus has no resources to deal with the boundaries between realms.

D. Mulgan, *The Demands of Consequentialism*, 5–6. Scanlon offers Contractualism as an account of 'what we owe to each other' (Scanlon, *What We Owe to Each Other*, 177–87). If 'we' takes a broad scope, then this region of morality seems larger than our Realm of Reciprocity, as it also includes our obligations to anyone lying beyond our current community of interaction, such as famine relief in distant countries. ('What we owe to each other' may be narrower than our Realm of Reciprocity, as well as broader, if the former excludes future people.)

We have already seen that Rule Consequentialism, although it copes well with the Realm of Reciprocity, does not deal appropriately with famine relief (Section 10.2.2). If Contractualism fares any better, then 'what we owe to each other' may be a better way to divide morality.

Several objections to Contractualism emerge from the considerable literature on this topic. It has been argued that Contractualism (1) yields a very demanding principle regarding famine relief; and (2) is even more demanding than Simple Consequentialism, as it gives priority to the worse-off either directly or by its independent moral considerations, in particular fairness; and (3) breaks down entirely in situations of extreme inequality. (For Scanlon's own view, see Scanlon, *What We Owe to Each Other*, 224–5. For two opposing views on the comparative demands of Contractualism and Simple Consequentialism, see Ashford, 'The Demandingness of Scanlon's Contractualism'; and Kumar, 'Defending the Moral Moderate'. Other good discussions include Hooker, 'Scanlon's Contractualism, the Spare Wheel Objection, and aggregation';

Kamm, 'Owing, Justifying, Rejecting'; Kumar, 'Contractualism on Saving the Many'; Ridge, 'Saving Scanlon: Contractualism and Agent-Relativity'; Wallace, 'Scanlon's Contractualism'; Wenar, 'What we owe to distant others'; and Wenar, 'Contractualism and Global Economic Justice'. The argument that Contractualism breaks down altogether when faced with extreme inequality is due to Nagel (Nagel, *Equality and Partiality*; and Nagel, 'One-to-One'.) For similar issues in a Consequentialist context, see Section 3.7.3 above.)

Bibliography

ALEXANDER, L., 'Scheffler on the Independence of Agent-Centred Prerogatives from Agent-Centred Restrictions', *Journal of Philosophy*, 84 (1987), 277–83.

ARHENNIUS, G., 'Mutual Advantage Contractarianism and Future Generations', *Theoria* (1999), 25–35.

—— 'Future Generations: A Challenge for Moral Theory,' doctoral diss., Uppsala University, 2000.

ARROW, K., 'Some Ordinalist-Utilitarian Notes on Rawls's Theory of Justice', *Journal of Philosophy*, 70(1973), 253–4.

ASHFORD, E., 'The Demandingness of Scanlon's Contractualism', *Ethics*, 123 (2003).

BARRO, R., 'Determinants of Democracy', *Journal of Political Economy*, 107/6 (1999), S158–S183.

—— and LEE, J., 'International Comparisons of Educational Attainment', paper presented to World Bank conference, 1993.

BARRY, B., 'Justice Between Generations', in P. M. S. Hacker and J. Raz (eds.), *Law, Morality and Society: Essays in Honour of H. L. A. Hart* (Oxford, Clarendon Press, 1977), 268–84.

—— 'Circumstances of Justice and Future Generations', in R. Sikora and B. Barry (eds.), *Obligations to Future Generations* (Philadelphia: Temple University Press, 1978), 204–48.

—— *Theories of Justice* (Berkeley: University of California Press, 1989).

BEBLAWI, H., 'The Rentier State in the Arab World', in H. Beblawi and G. Luciani (eds.), *The Rentier State* (New York: Croom Helm, 1987), 49–62.

BECKERMAN, W., and PASEK, J., *Justice, Posterity and the Environment* (Oxford: Oxford University Press, 2001).

BEITZ, C., *Political Theory and International Relations*, rev. edn. (Princeton: Princeton University Press, 1999).

BENNETT, J., 'Two Departures from Consequentialism', *Ethics*, 100 (1989), 54–66.

BHAT, P., and RAJAN, S., 'Demographic Transition in Kerala Revisited', *Economic and Political Weekly*, 25 (1990).

BIGELOW, J., et al., 'Parental Autonomy', *Journal of Applied Philosophy*, 5 (1988), 183–96.

BIRDSALL, N., 'Economic Approaches to Population Growth', in H. Chenery and T. Srinivasan (eds.), *The Handbook of Developmental Economics,*: (Amsterdam: North Holland Press, 1988.

BLACKORBY, C., BOSSERT, W., and DONALDSON, D., 'Intertemporal Population Ethics', *Econometrica*, 65(1995), 1303–20.

—— —— —— 'Critical-Level Utilitarianism and the Population-Ethics Dilemma', *Economics and Philosophy*, 13(1997), 197–230.

BONGAARTS, J., 'The Role of Family Planning Programmes in Contemporary Fertility Transition', in G. Jones (ed.), *The Continuing Demographic Transition* (Oxford: Oxford University Press, 1997).

——'Trends in Unwanted Childbearing in the Developing World', *Studies in Family Planning*, 28 (December 1997).

BRAND-BALLARD, J., 'Contractualism and Deontic Restrictions', *Ethics*, 114 (2004), 269–300.

BRANDT, R. B., 'Fairness to Indirect Optimific Theories in Ethics', in his *Morality, Utilitarianism, and Rights* (Cambridge: Cambridge University Press, 1992) 137–57.

——'Some Merits of One Form of Rule-Utilitarianism', in his *Morality Utilitarianism and Rights* (Cambridge: Cambridge University Press, 1992), 111–36.

BRAYBROOKE, D., *Meeting Needs* (Princeton: Princeton University Press, 1987).

BRINK, D., 'The Separateness of Persons, Distributive Norms, and Moral Theory', in R. Frey and C. Morris (eds.), *Value, Welfare and Morality* (Cambridge: Cambridge University Press, 1993), 252–89.

——'Self-love and Altruism', *Social Philosophy and Policy*, 14 (1997), 122–57.

BROCK, G., 'Is Redistribution to Help the Needy Unjust?', *Analysis*, 55 (1995), 50–60.

——'Liberal Nationalism versus Cosmopolitanism: Locating the Disputes', *Public Affairs Quarterly*, 16 (2002), 307–27.

BROOME, J., 'Incommensurable Values', in R. Crisp and B. Hooker (eds.), *Well-being and Morality: Essays in Honour of James Griffin* (Oxford: Oxford University Press, 2002), 21–38.

BURKHART, R., and LEWIS-BECK, M., 'Comparative Democracy and Income Distribution: Shape and Direction of the Causal Arrow', *Journal of Politics*, 59 (1997), 148–64.

CALDWELL, J., BARKAT-E-KHUDA, CALDWELL, B., PIERIES, I., and CALDWELL, P., 'The Bangladesh Fertility Decline', *Population and Development Review*, 25 (1999), 67–84.

CARSON, R., 'A Note on Hooker's Rule-Consequentialism', *Mind*, 100 (1991), 117–21.

CASSEN, R., et al., *Population and Development: Old Debates, New Conclusions* (Washington, DC, Transition Books in Overseas Development Council, 1994).

CHANG, R. (ed.), *Incommensurability, Incomparability, and Practical Reason* (Cambridge, Mass.: Harvard University Press, 1997).

CLELAND, J., PHILLIPS, J., AMIN, S., and KAMAL, G., *The Determinants of Reproductive Change in Bangladesh: Success in a Changing Environment* (Washington, DC: World Bank, 1996).

COCHRANE, S., *Fertility and Education: What do we Really Know?* Baltimore: Johns Hopkins University Press, 1979).

——'Effects of Education and Urbanization on Fertility', in R. Bulatao and R. Lee (eds.), *Determinants of Fertility in Developing Countries*, ii (New York: Academic Press, 1983), 587–625.

COHEN, G., 'Where the Action Is: On the Site of Distributive Justice', *Philosophy and Public Affairs*, 26 (1997), 3–30.

COHEN, J., 'Okin on Justice, Gender, and Family', *Canadian Journal of Philosophy*, 22 (1992).

COHEN, J., 'For a Democratic Society', in S. Freeman (ed.), *The Cambridge Companion to Rawls* (Cambridge: Cambridge University Press, 2003), 86–138.

COLLIER, P., and HOEFFLER, A., 'On Economic Causes of Civil War', *Oxford Economic Papers*, 50 (1998), 563–73.

CONEE, E., 'On Seeking a Rationale', *Philosophy and Phenomenological Research*, 45 (1985), 601–9.

COWEN, T. 'What do we Learn from the Repugnant Conclusion?', *Ethics*, 106 (1996), 754–75.

CRISP, R., 'Utilitarianism and the Life of Virtue', *Philosophical Quarterly*, 42 (1992), 139–60.

—— *Mill: On Utilitarianism* (London: Routledge, 1997).

—— 'Griffin's Pessimism', in R. Crisp and B. Hooker (eds.), *Well-being and Morality: Essays in Honour of James Griffin* (Oxford: Oxford University Press, 2002), 115–28.

CULLITY, G., 'International Aid and the Scope of Kindness', *Ethics*, 105 (1994), 99–127.

—— 'Moral Character and the Iteration Problem', *Utilitas*, 7 (1995), 289–99.

DAHL, R., 'Decision Making in a Democracy: The Supreme Court as National Policymaker', *Journal of Public Law*, 6 (1958), 279–95.

—— *Democracy and its Critics* (New Haven: Yale University Press, 1989).

—— *How Democratic is the American Constitution?* (New Haven: Yale University Press, 2002).

DALLMAYR, F., 'Cosmopolitanism', *Political Theory*, 31 (2003), 421–42.

DANCY, J., 'Non-Consequentialist Reasons', *Philosophical Papers*, 20 (1991), 97–112.

DANIELS, N., 'Democratic Equality: Rawls's Complex Egalitarianism', in S. Freeman (ed.), *The Cambridge Campanion to Rawls* (Cambridge: Cambridge University Press, 2003), 241–76.

DANIELS, N., 'Preface', in N. Daniels, *Reading Rawls: Critical Studies on Rawls's 'A Theory of Justice'* (Stanford, Calif.: Stanford University Press, 1989), pp. xiii–xxx.

DAS GUPTA, M., and BHAT, P. N., 'Intensified Gender Bias in India: A Consequence of Fertility Decline', Working Paper 95.02 (Cambridge, Mass.: Harvard Centre for Population and Development, 1995).

DASGUPTA, P., *An Inquiry into Well-being and Destitution* (Oxford: Oxford University Press, 1993).

—— 'Savings and Fertility: Ethical Issues', *Philosophy and Public Affairs*, 23 (1994), 99–127.

—— *Human Well-being and the Natural Environment* (Oxford: Clarendon Press, 2001).

DENNETT, D., 'Commentary on Sober and Wilson, Unto Others: The Evolution and Psychology of Unselfish Behavior', *Philosophy and Phenomenological Research*, 65 (2002), 692–6.

DRÈZE, J., and SEN, A. K., *Hunger and Public Action* (Oxford: Clarendon Press, 1989).

DWORKIN, R., *Freedom's Law: The Moral Reading of the American Constitution* (Cambridge, Mass.: Harvard University Press, 1996).

EASTERLIN, R., *Population and Economic Change in Developing Countries* (Chicago: University of Chicago Press, 1980).

ELLIOT, R., 'Rawlsian Justice and Non-human Animals', *Journal of Applied Ethics*, 1 (1984), 95–106.

FEHIGE, C., 'A Pareto Principle for Possible People', in C. Fehige and U. Wessels (eds.), *Preferences*, (Berlin: de Gruyter, 1998), 509–43.

FEINBERG, J., 'Harm and Self-Interest', in P. M. S. Hacker and J. Raz (eds.), *Law, Morality and Society: Essays in Honour of H. L. A. Hart*, (Oxford: Clarendon Press, 1977), 284–308.

—— *Harm to Others* (New York: Oxford University Press, 1984).

—— 'Wrongful Life and the Counterfactual Element in Harming', *Social Policy and Philosophy*, 4 (1986), 145–78.

FELDMAN, F., 'On the Extensional Equivalence of Simple and General Utilitarianism', *Noûs*, 8 (1974), 101–16.

—— 'Justice, Desert and the Repugnant Conclusion', *Utilitas*, 7 (1995), 189–206

FOOT, P., 'Morality as a System of Hypothetical Imperatives', *Philosophical Review*, 81 (1972).

—— 'Utilitarianism and the Virtues', *Mind*, 94 (1985), 196–209.

FRASER, J., *The Golden Bough: A Study in Magic and Religion* (London: Macmillan, 1923–7).

GARDINER, S., 'Ethics and Global Climate Change', *Ethics*, 114 (2004), 555–600.

—— 'The Global Warming Tragedy and the Dangerous Illusion of the Kyoto Protocol', *Ethics and International Affairs*, 18 (2004), 23–39.

GAUTHIER, D., *Morals by Agreement* (Oxford: Clarendon Press, 1986).

—— 'Political Contractarianism', *Journal of Political Philosophy*, 5/2, (1997), 132–48.

GIBBARD, A., 'Rule Utilitarianism: A Merely Illusory Alternative?', *Australasian Journal of Philosophy*, 43 (1965), 211–20.

GIBBON, E., *The History of the Decline and Fall of the Roman Empire* (London: Folio Society reprint, 1987–1990).

GILDENHUYS, P., 'The Evolution of Altruism: The Sober/Wilson Model', *Philosophy of Science*, 70 (2003), 27–48.

GOLDMAN, H. S., 'David Lyons on Utilitarian Generalization', *Philosophical Studies*, 26 (1974), 77–95.

GOSSERIES, A., 'What do we Owe the Next Generation(s)?', *Loyola of Los Angeles Law Review*, 35, (2001), 293–354.

GREENHALGH, S., *Situating Fertility: Anthropological and Demographic Inquiry* (Cambridge: Cambridge University Press, 1995).

GRIFFIN, J., *Value Judgement* (Oxford: Oxford University Press, 1996).

—— *Well-being* (Oxford: Oxford University Press, 1986).

—— 'Replies', in R. Crisp and B. Hooker and (eds.), *Well-being and Morality: Essays in Honour of James Griffin*, Oxford University Press, 2000), 281–313.

GRUBB, M., 'Seeking Fair Weather: Ethics and the International Debate on Climate Change', *International Affairs*, 71 (1995), 463–96.

GUTMANN, A., 'Rawls on the Relationship between Liberalism and Democracy', in S. Freeman (ed.), *The Cambridge Companion to Rawls* (Cambridge: Cambridge University Press, 2003), 168–99.

HARRIS, G., 'A Paradoxical Departure from Consequentialism', *Journal of Philosophy*, 86 (1989), 90–102.

—— 'Integrity and Agent Centered Restrictions', *Noûs*, 23 (1989), 437–56.

HASLETT, D. W., 'Values, Obligations, and Saving Lives', in B. Hooker, E. Mason, and D. E. Miller (eds.), *Morality, Rules, and Consequences* (Edinburgh: Edinburgh University Press, 2000), 71–104.

HEATH, J., 'Intergenerational Cooperation and Distributive Justice', *Canadian Journal of Philosophy*, 27 (1997), 361–76.

HESS, P. N., *Population Growth and Socioeconomic Progress in Less Developed Countries* (New York: Praeger, 1988).

HEYD, D., *Genethics: Moral Issues in the Creation of People* (Berkeley and Los Angeles: University of California Press, 1992).

HIRSCHL, R., 'The Political Origins of Judicial Empowerment through Constitutionalization: Lessons from Four Constitutional Revolutions', *Law and Social Inquiry*, 25 (2000), 91–147.

—— *Towards Juristocracy: A Comparative Inquiry Into the Origins and Consequences of the New Constitutionalism*, (Cambridge, Mass.: Harvard University Press, 2002).

HOBBES, T., *Leviathan*, ed. R. Tuck (Cambridge, Mass.: Cambridge University Press, 1988).

HOFFMAN, L. W., and HOFFMAN, M. L., 'The Value of Children to Parents', in J. T. Fawcett (ed.), *Psychological Perspectives on Population* (New York: Basic Books, 1973), 19–76.

HOOKER, B., Rule Consequentialism', *Mind*, 99 (1990), 67–77.

—— 'Rule-Consequentialism and Demandingness: A Reply to Carson', *Mind*, 100 (1991), 270–6.

—— 'Brink, Kagan and Self-Sacrifice', *Utilitas*, 3 (1991), 263–73.

—— (ed.), *Rationality, Rules and Utility: New Essays on the Moral Philosophy of Richard B. Brandt* (Boulder, Colo.: Imprint, 1993).

—— Review of T. Nagel, *Equality and Partiality*, *Philosophical Quarterly*, 43 (1993), 366–72.

—— Review of S. Scheffler, *Human Morality*, *Mind*, 102 (1993), 390–4.

—— 'Rule-Consequentialism, Incoherence, Fairness', *Proceedings of the Aristotelian Society*, 95 (1994), 19–35.

—— 'Is Rule-Consequentialism a Rubber Duck?', *Analysis*, 54 (1994), 92–7.

—— 'Compromising with Convention', *American Philosophical Quarterly*, 31 (1994), 311–17.

—— 'Ross-style Pluaralism versus Rule-Consequentialism', *Mind*, 105 (1996), 531–52.

—— 'Reply to Stratton-Lake', *Mind*, 106 (1997), 759–60.

—— 'Rule-Consequentialism and Obligations toward the Needy', *Pacific Philosophical Quarterly*, 79 (1998), 19–33.

—— 'Sacrificing for the Good of Strangers—Repeatedly' (a critical discussion of Unger, *Living High and Letting Die*), *Philosophy and Phenomenological Research*, 59 (1999), 177–81.

—— *Ideal Code, Real World: A Rule-Consequentialist Theory of Morality* (Oxford: Clarendon Press, 2000).

—— 'Impartiality, Predictability, and Indirect Consequentialism', in R. Crisp and B. Hooker (eds.), *Well-being and Morality: Essays in Honour of James Griffin* (Oxford: Oxford University Press, 2002), 129–42.

—— 'Scanlon's Contractualism, the Spare Wheel Objection, and Aggregation', in M. Matravers (ed.), *Scanlon and Contractualism: Readings and Responses* (Ilford: Frank Cass Publishers, 2003).

—— 'Rule Consequentialism', *The Stanford Encyclopedia of Philosophy (Spring 2004 Edition)*, ed. Edward N. Zalta, <http://plato.stanford.edu.ezproxy.auckland.ac.nz/archives/spr2004/entries/consequentialism-rule/>

—— MASON, E., and MILLER, D. E. (eds.), *Morality, Rules and Consequences* (Edinburgh, Edinburgh University Press, 2000).

HORWICH, P., 'On Calculating the Utility of Acts', *Philosophical Studies*, 25 (1974), 21–31.

HUDSON, J., 'The Diminishing Marginal Value of Happy People', *Philosophical Studies*, 51 (1987), 123–37.

HUDSON, M., 'The Political Culture Approach to Arab Democratization: The Case for Bringing it back in, carefully', in R. Bryner, B. Korany, and P. Noble (eds.), *Political Liberalization and Democratization in the Arab World*, v. i. *Theoretical Perspectives*, (Boulder, Colo.: Lynne Rienner, 1995), 61–76.

HURKA, T., 'Average Utilitarianisms', *Analysis*, 42 (1982), 65–9.

—— 'More Average Utilitarianisms', *Analysis*, 42 (1982), 115–19.

—— 'Value and Population Size', *Ethics*, 93 (1983), 496–507.

—— *Perfectionism* (Oxford: Oxford University Press, 1993).

HURLEY, P., 'Scheffler's Argument for Deontology', *Pacific Philosophical Quarterly*, 74 (1993), 118–34.

—— 'Getting Our Options Clear: A Closer Look at Agent-Centered Options', *Philosophical Studies*, 78 (1995), 163–88.

INGLEHART, R., *Modernization and Postmodernization: Cultural, Economic and Political Change in 43 societies* (Princeton: Princeton University Press, 1997).

JACKSON, F., 'Decision-Theoretic Consequentialism and the Nearest and Dearest Objection', *Ethics*, 101 (1991), 461–82.

JAMIESON, D., 'Sober and Wilson on Psychological Altruism'; *Philosophy and Phenomenological Research*, 65 (2002), 702–10.

JEFFREY, R., *Politics, Women and Well-Being: How Kerala Became a Model* (London: Palgrave Macmillan, 1992).

—— and BASU, A., *Girls' Schooling, Women's Autonomy and Fertility Change in South Asia* (New Delhi: Sage, 1997).

JENSEN, K., 'What is the Difference between (Moderate) Egalitarianism and Prioritarianism', *Economics and Philosophy*, 19 (2003), 89–109.

JOLLY, C., and GRIBBLE, J., 'The Proximate Determinants of Fertility', in K. Foote, K. Hill, and L. Martin (eds.), *Demographic Change in Sub-saharan Africa* (Washington, DC: National Academy Press, 1993).

KAGAN, S., 'Does Consequentialism Demand Too Much?', *Philosophy and Public Affairs*, 13 (1984), 239–54.

—— *The Limits of Morality* (Oxford: Oxford University Press, 1989).

KAMM, F., 'Owing, Justifying, Rejecting: Thomas Scanlon's What We Owe to Each Other', *Mind*, 111 (2002), 323–54.

Kant, I., *Groundwork of the Metaphysics of Morals*, translated by H. J. Paton as *The Moral Law* (London: Hutchinson, 1948).

Kant, I., *Conjectures on the Beginning of Human History*, translated by H. B. Nisbet for the Cambridge University Press edition of *Kant: Political Writings* (Cambridge, 1991).

—— *Idea for a Universal History with a Cosmopolitan Purpose*, translated by H. B. Nisbet for the Cambridge University Press edition of *Kant: Political Writings* (Cambridge, 1991).

—— *Reviews of Herder's Ideas on the Philosophy of the History of Mankind*, translated by H. B. Nisbet for the Cambridge University Press edition of *Kant: Political Writings* (Cambridge, 1991).

—— *Religion within the Boundaries of Mere Reason*, Part One, translated by George di Giovanni, for the *Religion and Rational Theology* volume of the Cambridge University Press edition of the *Works of Immanuel Kant* (Cambridge, 2001).

KAVKA, G., 'The Paradox of Future Individuals', *Philosophy and Public Affairs*, 11 (1982), 93–112.

—— *Hobbesian Moral and Political Philosophy* (Princeton: Princeton University Press, 1986).

KINROSS, P., *The Ottoman Empire* (London: Folio Society, 2003).

KOPP, R., and THATCHER, J., *The Weathervane Guide to Climate Policy* (Washington. DC: Resources for the Future, 2000).

KORSGAARD, C., 'Kant', in R. Cavalier, J. Gouinlock, and J. Sterba, (eds.), *Ethics in the History of Western Philosophy* (New York: St Martin's Press, 1989), 201–43.

—— 'Personal Identity and the Unity of Agency: A Kantian Response to Parfit', *Philosophy and Public Affairs*, 18 (1989), 101–32.

KRISHHAN, T., 'Demographic Transition in Kerala: Facts and Factors', *Economic and Political Weekly*, 11 (1976).

KUMAR, R., 'Defending the Moral Moderate: Contractualism and Commonsense', *Philosophy and Public Affairs*, 28 (2002), 275–309.

—— 'Contractualism on Saving the Many', *Analysis*, 61 (2001), 165–71.

—— 'Who Can be Wronged?', *Philosophy and Public Affairs*, 31 (2003), 99–118.

KYMLICKA, W., *Liberalism, Community and Culture* (Oxford: Oxford University Press, 1989).

—— *Contemporary Political Philosophy* (Oxford: Oxford University Press, 1991).

—— 'Multicultural States and Intercultural Citizens', *Theory and Research in Education*, 1 (2003), 147–69.

—— and STRAEHLE, C., 'Cosmopolitanism, Nation-States, and Minority Nationalism: A Critical Review of Recent Literature', *European Journal of Philosophy*, 7 (1999), 65–88.

LAM, R., and WANTCHEKON, L., 'Dictatorships as a Political Dutch Disease', Working Paper, 19 January 1999, Economic Growth Center, Yale University, Center Discussion Paper 795. http://econpapers.hhs.se/paper/wopyaiegr

LEITE, C., and WEIDMANN, J., 'Does Mother Nature Corrupt? Natural Resources, Corruption and Economic Growth', IMF Working Paper, 1999, WP/99/85.

LEVENBOOK, B., 'Harming Someone after his Death', *Ethics*, 94 (April 1984), 407–19.

LOCKE, D., 'The Parfit Population Problem', *Philosophy*, 62 (1987), 131–57.

LOCKE, J., *Two Treatises of Government*, ed. P. Laslett, (Cambridge: Cambridge University Press, 1988).

LONDREGAN, J., and POOLE, K., 'Does High Income Promote Democracy?', *World Politics*, 49 (1996), 1–30.

LUCAS, G. R., 'African Famine: New Economic and Ethical Perspectives', *Journal of Philosophy*, 87 (1990), 629–41.

LYONS, D., *The Forms and Limits of Utilitarianism* (Oxford: Clarendon Press, 1965).

MCKIBBON, B., *Maybe One: A Personal and Environmental Argument for Single-Child Families* (New York: Simon and Schuster, 1998).

MCMAHAN, J., 'Wrongful Life: Paradoxes in the Morality of Causing People to Exist', in J. Coleman and C. Morris (eds.), *Rational Commitment and Social Justice: Essays for Gregory Kavka* (Cambridge: Cambridge University Press, 1998).

—— *The Ethics of Killing* (Oxford: Oxford University Press, 2001).

MAHDAVY, H., 'The Patterns and Problems of Economic Development in Rentier States: The Case of Iran', in M. Cook (ed.), *Studies in Economic History in the Middle East* (Oxford: Oxford University Press, 1970), 428–67.

MASON, A., 'Egalitarianism and the Levelling Down Objection', *Analysis*, 61 (2001), 246–54.

MILL, J. S., *On Liberty*, 1859.

—— *Considerations on Representative Government*, 1861.

MILLER, D., 'In Defence of Nationality', *Journal of Applied Philosophy*, 10 (1993), 3–16.

—— 'Nationality: Some Replies', *Journal of Applied Philosophy*, 14 (1997), 69–82.

—— *Citizenship and National Identity* (Cambridge: Polity Press, 2000).

—— 'Holding Nations Reponsible', *Ethics*, 114 (2004), 240–68.

MILLER, D. E., 'Hooker's Use and Abuse of Reflective Equilibrium', in B. Hooker, E. Mason, and D. E. Miller (eds.), *Morality, Rules and Consequences* (Edinburgh, Edinburgh University Press, 2000), 156–78.

MOORE, A., 'The Utilitarian Ethics of R. B. Brandt', *Utilitas*, 5 (1993), 301–10.

—— and MULGAN, T., 'Non-Commercial IVF Surrogacy and Harm to the Child', *Otago Bioethics Report*, 5/3 (October 1996), 6–7.

—— —— 'Open Letter: The Ethics of Non-Commercial IVF Surrogacy', *Health Care Analysis*, 5/1 (1997), 85–91.

—— —— 'Surrogacy, Non-existence and Harm', *New Zealand Family Law Journal*, 2/7 (1997), 165–71.

—— —— 'Growing Up in the Original Position', draft manuscript.

MOORE, B., *Social Origins of Dictatorship and Democracy*, (Boston: Beacon Press, 1966).

—— *Social Origins of Dictatorship and Democracy: Lord and Peasant in the Making of the Modern World* (Boston: Beacon Press, 1993).

MULGAN, T., 'Slote's Satisficing Consequentialism', *Ratio*, 6 (1993), 121–34.

—— 'The Unhappy Conclusion and the Life of Virtue', *Philosophical Quarterly*, 43 (1993), 357–9.

—— 'Rule Consequentialism and Famine', *Analysis*, 54 (1994), 187–92.

—— 'One False Virtue of Rule Consequentialism, and One New Vice', *Pacific Philosophical Quarterly*, 77 (1996), 362–73.

—— 'Two Conceptions of Benevolence', *Philosophy and Public Affairs*, 26 (1997), 1–21.

—— 'A Non-proportional Hybrid Moral Theory', *Utilitas*, 9/3 (1997), 291–306.

—— 'Teaching Future Generations', *Teaching Philosophy*, 22 (1999), 259–73.

MULGAN, T., 'The Place of the Dead in Liberal Political Philosophy', *Journal of Political Philosophy*, 7 (1999), 52–70.

—— 'Ruling Out Rule Consequentialism', in B. Hooker, E. Mason, and D. E. Miller (eds.), *Morality, Rules and Consequences* (Edinburgh, Edinburgh University Press, 2000), 212–21.

—— 'Two Moral Counterfactuals', *Philosophical Forum*, 31 (2000), 47–55.

—— review of Unger's *Living High and Letting Die*, *Mind*, 109 (2000), 397–400.

—— 'Dissolving the Mere Addition Paradox', *American Philosophical Quarterly*, 37 (2000), 359–72.

—— *The Demands of Consequentialism*, Oxford University Press, 2001.

—— 'How Satisficers Get Away with Murder', *International Journal of Philosophical Studies*, 9 (2001), 41–6.

—— 'A Minimal Test for Political Theories', *Philosophia*, 28 (2001), 283–96.

—— 'What's Really Wrong with the Limited Quantity View?', *Ratio* (2001), 153–64.

—— 'Neutrality, Rebirth and Inter-generational Justice', *Journal of Applied Philosophy*, 19 (2002), 3–15.

—— 'Reproducing the Contractarian State', *Journal of Political Philosophy*, 10 (2002), 465–77.

—— 'The Reverse Repugnant Conclusion', *Utilitas*, 14 (2002), 360–4.

—— 'Transcending the Infinite Utility Debate', *Australasian Journal of Philosophy*, 80 (2002), 164–77.

—— 'La Démocratie post mortem', *Revue Philosophique de Louvain*, 101/1 (2003), 123–37.

—— 'Obligations to Future Generations', in Paul Demeny and Geoffrey McNicoll (eds.), *Encyclopedia of Population* (Basingstoke: Macmillan, 2003), 439–41.

—— 'When is Non-identity a Problem?', in Heather Dyke (ed.), *Time and Ethics: Essays at the Intersection* (Dordrecht: Kluwer, 2003), 209–18.

—— Review of L. Murphy, *Moral Demands in a Nonideal World*, *Utilitas*, 15/1 (2003), 113–16.

—— 'Critical Notice of Jeff McMahan, *The Ethics of Killing*', *Canadian Journal of Philosophy*, 34 (2004), 443–60.

—— 'Two Parfit Puzzles', in J. Ryberg and R. Tannsjo (eds.), *The Repugnant Conclusion: Essays on Population Ethics* (Dordrecht: Kluwer Academic Publishers, 2004), 23–45.

—— 'Valuing the Future', draft manuscript.

MUNTHE, C., 'The Argument from Transfer', *Bioethics*, 10 (1996), 27–42.

MURPHY, L., 'The Demands of Beneficence', *Philosophy and Public Affairs*, 22 (1993), 267–92.

—— 'A Relatively Plausible Principle of Beneficence: Reply to Mulgan', *Philosophy and Public Affairs*, 26 (1997), 23–9.

—— 'Institutions and the Demands of Justice', *Philosophy and Public Affairs*, 27 (1999), 251–91.

—— *Moral Demands in Nonideal Theory* (New York: Oxford University Press, 2000).

MURTHI, M., GUIO, A., and DRÈZE, J., 'Mortality, Fertility and Gender Bias in India: A District Legal Analysis', *Population and Development Review*, 21 (December 1995), 745–82.

MYERS, R., 'Prerogatives and Restrictions from the Cooperative Point of View', *Ethics*, 105 (1994), 128–52.

NAGEL, T., *The View from Nowhere* (New York: Oxford University Press, 1987).

—— *Equality and Partiality* (New York: Oxford University Press, 1991).

—— 'One-to-One', *London Review of Books*, 4 February 1999.

NASH, T., 'The Bargaining Problem', *Econometrica*, 18 (1950), 155–62.

NELSON, M., 'Utilitarian Eschatology', *American Philosophical Quarterly*, 27 (1991), 339–47.

—— 'Open Government and Just Legislation', in D. Estlund (ed.), *Democracy* (Oxford: Blackwell, 2002), 129–51.

NG, Y.-K., 'What should we do about Future Generations? Impossibility of Parfit's Theory X', *Economics and Philosophy*, 5 (1989), 235–53.

NORTH, D., and WEINGEST, B., 'Constitutions and Commitment: The Evolution of Institutions Governing Public Choice in Seventeenth-Century England', *Journal of Economic History*, 94/4 (1989), 803–32.

NOZICK, R. *Anarchy, State, and Utopia* (New York: Basic Books, 1974).

O'NEILL, O., 'Kantian Ethics', in P. Singer (ed.), *Companion to Ethics* (Oxford: Blackwell, 1991), 175–85.

OKIN, S., *Justice, Gender and the Family* (New York: Basic Books, 1989).

PADEN, R., 'Reciprocity and Intergenerational Justice', *Public Affairs Quarterly*, 10 (1996), 249–266.

—— 'Rawls's Just Saving Principle and the Sense of Justice', *Social Theory and Practice*, 23 (1997), 27–51.

PAGE, E., 'Parental Rights', *Journal of Applied Philosophy*, 1 (1984), 187–204.

PARFIT, D., 'Repugnant Conclusion: A Reply to McMahan', *Ethics*, 92 (1981), 128–33.

—— *Reasons and Persons* (Oxford; Oxford University Press, 1984).

—— 'Overpopulation and the Quality of Life' in P. Singer (ed.), *Applied Ethics* (Oxford: Oxford University Press, 1986), 145–64.

—— 'Equality and Priority', *Ratio*, 10/3 (1997), 202–21.

PEARSON, C., *Economics and the Global Environment* (Cambridge: Cambridge University Press, 2000).

PERRETT, R., 'Libertarianism, Feminism, and Relative Identity', *Journal of Value Inquiry* (1999).

PERSSON, I., 'Equality, Priority and Person-Affecting Value', *Ethical Theory and Moral Practice*, 4 (2001), 23–39.

PETERSEN, T., 'The Claim from Adoption', *Bioethics*, 16 (2002), 353–75.

PETTIT, P., 'Universalisability without Utilitarianism', *Mind*, 96 (1987), 74–82.

—— 'Consequentialism', in P. Singer (ed.), *A Companion to Ethics* (Oxford: Blackwell, 1989), 230–40.

—— 'Decision Theory and Folk Psychology', in M. Bacharach and S. Hurley (eds.), *Essays in the Foundations of Decision Theory* (Oxford: Blackwell, 1989).

—— *The Common Mind: An Essay on Psychology, Society and Politics* (New York: Oxford University Press, 1993).

PLATO, *Symposium*.

POGGE, T., 'Cosmopolitanism and Sovereignty', *Ethics*, 103/1 (1992), 48–75.

POGGE, T., 'Achieving Democracy', *Ethics and International Affairs*, 15 (2001). 3–23.

—— *World Poverty and Human Rights* (Cambridge: Polity Press, 2002).

PORTMORE, D., 'Does the Total Principle Have Any Repugnant Implications?', *Ratio*, 12/1 (1999), 80–98.

PRZEWORSKI, A., and LIMONGI, F., 'Modernization: Theories and Facts', *World Politics*, 49 (1997).

QUINN, W., 'Abortion: Identity and Loss', *Philosophy and Public Affairs*, 13 (1984), 24–54.

RAILTON, P., 'Alienation, Consequentialism and Morality', *Philosophy and Public Affairs*, 13 (1984), 134–71.

RAMACHANDRAN, V., 'Kerala's Development Achievements', in J. Drèze and A. Sen (eds.), *Indian Development: Selected Regional Perspectives* (Delhi: Oxford University Press, 1996).

RAWLS, J.: *A Theory of Justice* (Cambridge, Mass.: Harvard University Press, 1971).

—— 'Justice as Fairness: Political not Metaphysical', *Philosophy and Public Affairs*, 14 (1985), 223–51.

—— 'The Idea of an Overlapping Consensus', *Oxford Journal of Legal Studies*, 7 (1987), 1–27.

—— *Political Liberalism* (New York: Columbia University Press, 1993).

—— *The Law of Peoples* (Cambridge, Mass.: Harvard University Press, 1999).

—— 'Social Unity and Primary Goods', reprinted in his *Collected Papers*, ed. S. Freeman (Cambridge, Mass.: Harvard University Press, 1999), 359–87.

—— 'The Idea of Public Reason Revisited', in his *Collected Papers*, ed. S. Freeman (Cambridge, Mass.: Harvard University Press, 1999), 573–615.

—— *Justice as Fairness: A Restatement* (Cambridge, Mass.: Harvard University Press, 2001).

RAZ, J., *The Morality of Freedom* (Oxford: Oxford University Press, 1986).

—— 'Incommensurability and Agency', in *Engaging Reason: On the Theory of Value and Action* (Oxford: Clarendon Press, 1999).

—— *Engaging Reason: On the Theory of Value and Action* (Oxford: Clarendon Press, 1999).

RIDGE, M., 'Saving Scanlon: Contractualism and Agent-Relativity', *Journal of Political Philosophy*, 9 (2001), 472–81.

—— 'Giving the Dead their Due', *Ethics*, 114 (2003), 38–59.

RILEY, J., *Mill on Liberty* (London: Routledge, 1998).

—— 'Defending Rule Utilitarianism', in in B. Hooker, E. Mason, and D. E. Miller (eds.), *Morality, Rules, and Consequences* (Edinburgh: Edinburgh University Press, 2000), 40–70.

ROBERTS, M., 'Present Duties and Future Persons: When Are Existence-Inducing Acts Wrong?', *Law and Philosophy*, 14 (1995), 297–327.

—— *Child versus Childmaker: Future Persons and Present Duties in Ethics and the Law* (Oxford: Rowman & Littlefield, 1998).

—— 'A New Way of Doing the Best we Can: Person-based Consequentialism and the Equality Problem', *Ethics*, 112 (2002), 315–50.

—— 'Is the Person-Affecting Intuition Paradoxical?', *Theory and Decision*, 55 (2003), 1–44.

ROBERTSON, J., 'Liberty, Identity, and Human Cloning', *Texas Law Review*, 76 (1998), 1406–7.

ROEMER, J., 'The Mismarriage of Bargaining Theory and Distributive Justice', *Ethics*, 97 (1986), 88–110.

ROSS, M., 'The Political Economy of the Resource Curse', *World Politics*, 51 (1999), 297–322.

RYBERG, J., 'Parfit's Repugnant Conclusion', *Philosophical Quarterly*, 46 (1996), 202–13.

—— 'Is the Repugnant Conclusion Repugnant?', *Philosophical Papers*, 25 (1996), 161–77.

—— and TANNSJO, T. (eds.), *The Repugnant Conclusion: Essays on Population Ethics* (Dordrecht: Kluwer Academic Publishers, 2004).

SACHS, J., and WARNER, A., 'Natural Resource Abundance and Economic Growth', Development Discussion Paper 517a, October 1995. www.hiid.harvard.edu/pub/pdfs/517.pdf

———— 'The Big Push, Natural Resource Booms and Growth', *Journal of Development Economics*, 59/1 (1999), 43–76.

SAUVE, K., 'Gauthier, Property Rights, and Future Generations', *Canadian Journal of Philosophy*, 25 (1995), 163–76.

SCANLON, T., 'Contractualism and Utilitarianism', in A. Sen and B. Williams (eds.), *Utilitarianism and Beyond* (Cambridge: Cambridge University Press, 1982), 103–28.

—— *What We Owe to Each Other* (Cambridge, Mass.: Harvard University Press, 1999).

SCHALLER, W., 'A Problem for Brandt's Utilitarianism', *Ratio*, 5 (1992), 74–90.

SCHEFFLER, S., 'Moral Independence and the Original Position', *Philosophical Studies*, 35 (1978), 397–403.

—— *The Rejection of Consequentialism* (Oxford: Clarendon Press, 1982).

—— 'Agent-Centred Restrictions, Rationality and the Virtues', *Mind*, 94 (1985), 409–19.

—— 'Morality's Demands and their Limits', *Journal of Philosophy*, 83 (1986), 531–37.

—— (ed.), *Consequentialism and its Critics* (Oxford: Clarendon Press, 1988).

—— 'Deontology and the Agent: Reply to Bennett', *Ethics*, 100 (1989), 67–76.

—— *Human Morality* (Oxford: Oxford University Press, 1992).

—— 'Naturalism, Psychoanalysis and Moral Motivation', in J. Hopkins (ed.), *Psychoanalysis, Mind and Art* (Oxford: Blackwell, 1992).

—— 'Prerogatives without Restrictions', *Philosophical Perspectives*, 6 (1992), 377–97.

—— 'Families, Nations and Strangers' The Lindley Lecture, University of Kansas, 1994.

—— 'Individual Responsibility in a Global Age', *Social Philosophy and Policy*, 12 (1995), 219–36.

—— 'Précis of Human Morality', *Philosophy and Phenomenological Research*, 55 (1995), 939–940.

—— 'Reply to Three Commentators', *Philosophy and Phenomenological Research*, 55 (1995), 963–56.

—— 'Conceptions of Cosmopolitanism', *Utilitas*, 11 (1999), 255–76.

—— *Boundaries and Allegiances: Problems of Justice and Responsibility in Liberal Thought* (Oxford: Oxford University Press, 2001).

—— 'Rawls and Utilitarianism', in his *Boundaries and Allegiances*, 149–72.

SCHEFFLER, S., 'Relationships and Responsibilities', in his *Boundaries and Allegiances*, 97–110.

SCHNEEWIND, J. B., 'Autonomy, Obligation, and Virtue: An Overview of Kant's Moral Philosophy', in P. Guyer (ed.), *The Cambridge Companion to Kant* (Cambridge/New York: Cambridge University Press, 1992), 309–41.

SCHUELER, G., 'Consequences and Agent-Centered Restrictions', *Metaphilosophy*, 20 (1989), 77–83.

SEN, A., *Poverty and Famine: An Essay on Entitlement and Deprivation* (Oxford: Oxford University Press, 1981).

—— 'Evaluator Relativity and Consequential Evaluation', *Philosophy and Public Affairs*, 12 (1983), 113–32.

—— 'Gender and Cooperative Conflicts', in I. Tinker (ed.), *Persistent Inequalities* (Oxford: Oxford University Press, 1990), 123–49.

—— 'Population: Delusion and Reality', *New York Review of Books*, 22 September 1994, 62–71.

—— *Development as Freedom* (Oxford:Oxford University Press, 1999).

SESARDIC, N., 'Recent Work on Human Altruism and Evolution'; *Ethics*, 106 (1995), 128–57.

SHAPIRO, I., *The Moral Foundations of Politics* (New Haven: Yale University Press, 2003).

SHARABI, H., *Neopatriarchy: A Theory of Distorted Change in Arab Society* (Oxford: Oxford University Press, 1988).

SHIFFRIN, S., 'Wrongful Life, Procreative Responsibility, and the Significance of Harm', *Legal Theory*, 5 (1999), 117–48.

SIDER, T., 'Might Theory X be a Theory of Diminishing Marginal Value?', *Analysis*, 51 (1991), 265–71.

SIDGWICK, H., *The Methods of Ethics*, 7th edn. (Indianapolis: Hackett Publishing Company, 1907).

SIKORA, R., 'Classical Utilitarianism and Parfit's Repugnant Conclusion: A Reply to McMahan', *Ethics*, 92 (1981), 128–33.

SINGER, B., 'An Extension of Rawls's Theory of Justice to Environmental Ethics', *Environmental Ethics*, 10 (1988), 217–32.

SINGER, P., 'Famine, Affluence and Morality', *Philosophy and Public Affairs*, 1 (1972), 229–43.

SKORUPSKI, J., *Ethical Explorations*, (Oxford: Oxford University Press, 1999).

SLOTE, M., 'Satisficing Consequentialism', *Proceedings of the Aristotelian Society*, suppl. vol. 58 (1984), 165–76.

—— *Commonsense Morality and Consequentialism* (London: Routledge and Kegan Paul, 1985).

—— *Beyond Optimizing: A Study of Rational Choice* (London: Harvard University Press, 1991).

—— *From Morality to Virtue* (New York: Oxford University Press, 1992).

SMART, J. J. C., and WILLIAMS, B., *Utilitarianism: For and Against* (Cambridge: Cambridge University Press, 1973).

SMILANSKY, S., 'Is there a moral obligation to have children?', *Journal of Applied Philosophy*, 12 (1995), 1–13.

SOBER, E., and WILSON, D., *Unto Others: The Evolution and Psychology of Unselfish Behaviour* (Cambridge, Mass.: Harvard University Press, 1998).

STEINBOCK, B., 'Wrongful Life', *Hastings Centre Report* (1986), 15.

STRATTON-LAKE, P., 'Can Hooker's Rule-Consequentialist Principle Justify Ross's Prima Facie Duties?', *Mind*, 106 (1997), 751–8.

TAMIR, Y., *Liberal Nationalism* (Princeton: Princeton University Press, 1993).

—— 'Two Concepts of Multiculturalism', *Journal of Philosophy of Education*, 29 (1995), 161–72.

TEMKIN, L., *Inequality* (Oxford: Clarendon Press, 1993).

The Economist Pocket World in Figures, Economist Books, 40 London, (2000).

TILLY, C. (ed.), *The Formation of National States in Western Europe* (Princeton: Princeton University Press, 1975).

UNGER, P., *Living High and Letting Die: Our Illusion of Innocence* (Oxford: Oxford University Press, 1996).

United Nations Development Programme, *Human Development Report 1998* (New York: Oxford University Press, 1998).

—— *Human Development Report 1999* (New York: Oxford University Press, 1999).

—— *Human Development Report 2000* (New York: Oxford University Press, 2000).

VALLENTYNE, P. (ed.), *Contractarianism and Rational Choice: Essays on David Gauthier's Morals by Agreement* (Cambridge: Cambridge University Press, 1991).

—— 'Utilitarianism and Infinite Utility', *Australasian Journal of Philosophy*, 71 (1993), 212–17.

—— and KAGAN, S., 'Infinite Value and Finitely Additive Value Theory', *Journal of Philosophy*, 94 (1997), 5–26.

VANDEVEER, D., 'Of Beasts, Persons and the Original Position', *Monist*, 62 (1979), 368–77.

WAGNER DECEW, J., 'Brandt's new Defense of Rule Utilitarianism', *Philosophical Studies*, 43 (1983), 101–16.

WALDRON, J., *Law and Disagreement* (Oxford: Oxford University Press, 1999).

—— 'What is Cosmopolitanism?', *Journal of Political Philosophy*, 8 (2000), 227–43.

WALLACE, J., 'Scanlon's Contractualism', *Ethics*, 112 (2002), 429–70.

WANTCHEKON, L., 'Why do Resource Dependent Countries have Authoritarian Governments?', Working Paper, Yale University, December 1999, www.yale.edu/leitner/pdf/1999–11.pdf

WEINSTOCK, D., 'Is There a Moral Case for Nationalism?', *Journal of Applied Philosophy*, 13 (1996), 87–100.

WENAR, L., 'Contractualism and Global Economic Justice', *Metaphilosophy*, 32 (2001), 79–94

—— 'What We Owe to Distant Others', *Politics, Philosophy and Economics*, 2 (2003), 283–304.

WILLIAMS, B., 'The Makropolous Case: Reflections on the Tedium of Immortality', in his *Problems of the Self* (Cambridge: Cambridge University Press, 1973), 82–100.

WOLFF, J., *Robert Nozick: Property, Justice, and the Minimal State* (Stanford, Calif.: Stanford University Press, 1991).

WOOD, A. W., *Kant's Ethical Theory* (Cambridge: Cambridge University Press 1999).

WOODWARD, J., 'The Non-Identity Problem', *Ethics*, 96 (July 1986), 804–31.

World Bank, *World Development Report 2000/2001* (New York: Oxford University Press, 2001).

YOUNG, T., 'Overconsumption and Procreation', *Journal of Applied Philosophy*, 18 (2001), 183–92.

Index